The IDG Books Advantage

We at IDG Books Worldwide created *Your Windows 95 Internet Surfboard* to meet your growing need for quick access to the most complete and accurate computer information available. Our books work the way you do: They focus on accomplishing specific tasks — not learning random functions. Our books are not long-winded manuals or dry reference tomes. In each book, expert authors tell you exactly what you can do with your software and how to do it. Easy to follow, step-by-step sections; comprehensive coverage; and convenient access in language and design — it's all here.

The authors of IDG books are uniquely qualified to give you expert advice as well as to provide insightful tips and techniques not found anywhere else. Our authors maintain close contact with end users through feedback from articles, training sessions, e-mail exchanges, user group participation, and consulting work. Because our authors know the realities of daily computer use and are directly tied to the reader, our books have a strategic advantage.

Our authors have the experience to approach a topic in the most efficient manner, and we know that you, the reader, will benefit from a "one-on-one" relationship with the author. Our research shows that readers make computer book purchases because they want expert advice. Because readers want to benefit from the author's experience, the author's voice is always present in an IDG book.

You will find what you need in this book whether you read it from cover to cover, section by section, or simply one topic at a time. As a computer user, you deserve a comprehensive resource of answers. We at IDG Books Worldwide are proud to deliver that resource with *Your Windows 95 Internet Surfboard*.

Karen A. Bluestein
Publisher

Internet: mduffy@idgbooks.com

Your Windows® 95
INTERNET
SURFBOARD

Your Windows® 95
INTERNET
SURFBOARD

by Allen Wyatt

IDG Books Worldwide, Inc.
An International Data Group Company

Foster City, CA ♦ Chicago, IL ♦ Indianapolis, IN ♦ Braintree, MA ♦ Dallas, TX

Your Windows® 95 Internet Surfboard

Published by
IDG Books Worldwide, Inc.
An International Data Group Company
919 E. Hillsdale Blvd.
Suite 400
Foster City, CA 94404

Library of Congress Catalog Card No.: 95-79920

ISBN: 1-56884-721-1

Printed in the United States of America

10 9 8 7 6 5 4 3 2 1

1E/SZ/QZ/ZV

Distributed in the United States by IDG Books Worldwide, Inc.

Distributed by Macmillan Canada for Canada; by Computer and Technical Books for the Caribbean Basin; by Contemporanea de Ediciones for Venezuela; by Distribuidora Cuspide for Argentina; by CITEC for Brazil; by Ediciones ZETA S.C.R. Ltda. for Peru; by Editorial Limusa SA for Mexico; by Transworld Publishers Limited in the United Kingdom and Europe; by Al-Maiman Publishers & Distributors for Saudi Arabia; by Simron Pty. Ltd. for South Africa; by IDG Communications (HK) Ltd. for Hong Kong; by Toppan Company Ltd. for Japan; by Addison Wesley Publishing Company for Korea; by Longman Singapore Publishers Ltd. for Singapore, Malaysia, Thailand, and Indonesia; by Unalis Corporation for Taiwan; by WS Computer Publishing Company, Inc. for the Philippines; by WoodsLane Pty. Ltd. for Australia; by WoodsLane Enterprises Ltd. for New Zealand.

For general information on IDG Books Worldwide's books in the U.S., please call our Consumer Customer Service department at 800-762-2974. For reseller information, including discounts and premium sales, please call our Reseller Customer Service department at 800-434-3422.

For information on where to purchase IDG Books Worldwide's books outside the U.S., contact IDG Books Worldwide at 415-655-3021 or fax 415-655-3295.

For information on translations, contact Marc Jeffrey Mikulich, Director, Foreign & Subsidiary Rights, at IDG Books Worldwide, 415-655-3018 or fax 415-655-3295.

For sales inquiries and special prices for bulk quantities, write to the address above or call IDG Books Worldwide at 415-655-3200.

For information on using IDG Books Worldwide's books in the classroom, or ordering examination copies, contact Jim Kelly at 800-434-2086.

For authorization to photocopy items for corporate, personal, or educational use, please contact Copyright Clearance Center, 222 Rosewood Drive, Danvers, MA 01923, or fax 508-750-4470.

is a trademark under exclusive license to IDG Books Worldwide, Inc., from International Data Group, Inc.

About the Author

Allen Wyatt

Allen Wyatt, an internationally recognized expert in small computer systems, has been working in the computer and publishing industries for over 15 years. He has written more than 35 books explaining many facets of working with computers. He has also written numerous magazine articles. His books have covered topics ranging from programming languages to application software to operating systems. Through the written word, Allen has helped millions of readers learn how to better use computers.

Allen is the president of Discovery Computing Inc., a computer and publishing services company located in Sundance, Wyoming. Besides writing books, he helps further the computer book industry by providing consulting and distribution services. With his wife and three children, he lives on a 390-acre ranch just outside of town, on the edge of the Black Hills. In his spare time, he tends his animals, has fun with his family, and participates in church and community events.

The publisher would like to give special thanks to Patrick J. McGovern, without whom this book would not have been possible.

Welcome to the world of IDG Books Worldwide.

IDG Books Worldwide, Inc., is a subsidiary of International Data Group, the world's largest publisher of computer-related information and the leading global provider of information services on information technology. IDG was founded more than 25 years ago and now employs more than 7,500 people worldwide. IDG publishes more than 235 computer publications in 67 countries (see listing below). More than 70 million people read one or more IDG publications each month.

Launched in 1990, IDG Books Worldwide is today the #1 publisher of best-selling computer books in the United States. We are proud to have received 8 awards from the Computer Press Association in recognition of editorial excellence, and our best-selling ...*For Dummies*® series has more than 19 million copies in print with translations in 28 languages. IDG Books Worldwide, through a recent joint venture with IDG's Hi-Tech Beijing, became the first U.S. publisher to publish a computer book in the People's Republic of China. In record time, IDG Books Worldwide has become the first choice for millions of readers around the world who want to learn how to better manage their businesses.

Our mission is simple: Every one of our books is designed to bring extra value and skill-building instructions to the reader. Our books are written by experts who understand and care about our readers. The knowledge base of our editorial staff comes from years of experience in publishing, education, and journalism — experience which we use to produce books for the '90s. In short, we care about books, so we attract the best people. We devote special attention to details such as audience, interior design, use of icons, and illustrations. And because we use an efficient process of authoring, editing, and desktop publishing our books electronically, we can spend more time ensuring superior content and spend less time on the technicalities of making books.

You can count on our commitment to deliver high-quality books at competitive prices on topics consumers want to read about. At IDG Books Worldwide, we value quality, and we have been delivering quality for more than 25 years. You'll find no better book on a subject than an IDG book.

John J. Kilcullen

John Kilcullen
President and CEO
IDG Books Worldwide, Inc.

Credits

Publisher
Karen A. Bluestein

Acquisitions Manager
Gregory Croy

Acquisitions Editor
Ellen L. Camm

Brand Manager
Melisa M. Duffy

Editorial Director
Andy Cummings

Editorial Assistant
Nate Holdread

Production Director
Beth Jenkins

**Supervisor of
Project Coordination**
Cindy L. Phipps

Supervisor of Page Layout
Kathie S. Schnorr

Pre-Press Coordinator
Steve Peake

Associate Pre-Press Coordinator
Tony Augsburger

Media/Archive Coordinator
Paul Belcastro

Project Editor
Susan Pines

Editors
John C. Edwards
Kerrie Klein

Technical Reviewer
Kate Miller

Project Coordinator
Sherry Gomoll

Production Staff
Gina Scott
Carla. C. Radzikinas
Patricia R. Reynolds
Melissa D. Buddendeck
Leslie Popplewell
Dwight Ramsey
Robert Springer
Theresa Sánchez-Baker
Cameron Booker
Laura Puranen
Anna Rohrer

Indexer
David Heiret

Book Design
Drew Moore
Shelley D. Lea

Cover Design
Kavish & Kavish

Contents at a Glance

Introduction 1

Part I: Getting Started 5

Chapter 1: The Ground Floor 7
Chapter 2: Connection Technology Basics 17
Chapter 3: Selecting an Internet Provider 33
Chapter 4: Installing Your Modem 49
Chapter 5: Configuring Windows 95 for the Internet 71
Chapter 6: Using Dial-Up Networking 87
Chapter 7: Your First Call 101

Part II: Windows 95 Internet Tools 123

Chapter 8: Electronic Mail and Microsoft Exchange 125
Chapter 9: Using Mailing Lists 169
Chapter 10: Using Telnet 185
Chapter 11: Using Ftp 209

Part III: Other Internet Tools 227

Chapter 12: Finding Windows Tools 229
Chapter 13: Using Gopher 241
Chapter 14: Understanding WAIS 265
Chapter 15: Using the World Wide Web 279
Chapter 16: Talking the Night Away 297
Chapter 17: The Microsoft Network 327

Part IV: Appendixes 351

Appendix A: Internet Providers 353
Appendix B: Windows Tools on the Net 395
Appendix C: Glossary 401

Index 409

Reader Response Card .... Back of Book

Table of Contents

Introduction 1

Part I: Getting Started 5

Chapter 1: The Ground Floor 7

What Is the Internet? 7
    History of the Internet 8
    Who runs the Internet? 10
    Who pays for the Internet? 11
The Internet and UNIX 11
Why You Should Connect 12
    Internet resources 13
    Internet information 14
    Internet communication 14
What You Need to Connect 15
Summary 16

Chapter 2: Connection Technology Basics 17

Packet-Switched Networking 17
Understanding TCP/IP 19
TCP/IP and Domain Naming 20
    Understanding DNS 21
    Organizational domains 22
    Geographic domains 23
    How addresses are assigned 25
The IP Address Structure 26
    What TCP/IP workstations require 28
    Understanding DHCP 28
    Understanding WINS 29
    Addressing and the future 30
Connection Protocols 30
Summary 32

Chapter 3: Selecting an Internet Provider 33

What Is an Internet Provider? 33
    Why is a provider important? 34

Where do you find a provider? 34
Acceptable Use Policies 37
Types of Service 37
    Limited access 39
    Full access 39
Types of Connections 39
    Dial-up service 40
    Dedicated service 41
Routers 42
Phone lines 42
Servers 43
What Internet Services Cost 44
Making Your Selection 45
    The dial-up or dedicated decision 45
    The provider decision 45
What You Need from the Provider 46
Summary 47

Chapter 4: Installing Your Modem **49**
Understanding Serial Communications 49
    What do modems do? 50
    Modem speeds 50
    Error correction 52
    Data compression 53
    What type of modem do you need? 53
Installing the Modem 54
    Internal modem 54
    External modem 58
Adding the Modem to Windows 95 59
    Changing modem properties 62
    Setting dialing properties 65
Performing Modem Diagnostics 68
Summary 70

Chapter 5: Configuring Windows 95 for the Internet **71**
Adding the Dial-Up Adapter 72
Installing TCP/IP Protocols 74
Setting the TCP/IP Properties 77
    IP address 78
    Gateway 78
    WINS configuration 79
    Bindings 80
    Advanced 81
    DNS configuration 81
Adding SLIP Support 83
Summary 85

Chapter 6: Using Dial-Up Networking 87

What Dial-Up Networking Does 87
Installing Dial-Up Networking 88
Setting Up Dial-Up Networking 90
  Defining a dial-up connection 91
  Configuring your definition 94
  Dialing-related properties 95
  Server-related properties 96
Renaming and Deleting Definitions 99
Summary 100

Chapter 7: Your First Call 101

Establishing a Dial-Up Networking Connection 101
  Connecting to your provider 104
  Using the terminal window 106
  Special SLIP procedures 109
  You are connected! 110
Using Internet Utilities 113
  The ping command 113
  The tracert command 117
Ending Your Session 118
How You Pay for the Session 119
Setting Up a Shortcut 120
Summary 121

Part II: Windows 95 Internet Tools 123

Chapter 8: Electronic Mail and Microsoft Exchange 125

What Is Electronic Mail? 125
E-Mail Software 126
  Downloading e-mail software 127
  Installing your e-mail software 127
  Configuring your e-mail software 129
  The E-Mail Connection interface 133
Composing a Mail Message 134
  Addressing your e-mail 135
  Selecting a subject 136
  Typing your message 137
  Message attachments 137
Your Internet Connection 138
Reading Your E-Mail 139
  Managing your incoming e-mail 140
  Forwarding a message 140

Replying to a message 141
Printing a message 144
Deleting a message 144
Taking no action 145
Handling mail attachments 145
Parts of a mail message 147
Using Microsoft Exchange 148
Installing Microsoft Exchange 149
Installing the Internet client 154
Configuring for the Internet 157
Microsoft Exchange and the Internet 160
Composing a message 162
Connecting to the mail server 164
Reading your messages 165
Summary 167

Chapter 9: Using Mailing Lists 169

What Are Mailing Lists? 169
Mailing List Administration 170
Automatic management 170
Human management 171
Moderation in all things 171
Finding Mailing Lists 172
Joining a Mailing List 173
Joining a Listserv mailing list 174
Joining a Majordomo mailing list 176
Joining a manual mailing list 177
Participating in a Discussion Group 177
Managing Your Subscription 178
Controlling your Listserv subscription 178
Controlling your Majordomo subscription 179
Controlling your manual subscription 180
Leaving a Mailing List 180
Canceling a Listserv subscription 181
Canceling a Majordomo subscription 181
Canceling a manual subscription 182
Summary 183

Chapter 10: Using Telnet 185

What Is Telnet? 185
Running the Telnet Program 186
The telnet menus 187
Setting telnet preferences 188
Adding telnet to the menu 191
Connecting to a Remote Site 194

Picking a host name 195
Picking a port type 195
Picking a terminal type 196
Making the connection 197
During the connection 198
Using a log file 201
Breaking a connection 202
Finding Telnet Servers 203
Whois 203
Netinfo 206
Summary 208

Chapter 11: Using Ftp **209**

What Is Ftp? 209
Starting the Ftp Client Program 210
Understanding Ftp Commands 211
Connecting to an Ftp Server 213
During the Connection 216
Moving through directories 217
Using index files 220
Transferring files 221
Commands that affect the ftp server 224
Breaking the Connection 225
Finding Ftp Servers 225
Summary 226

Part III: Other Internet Tools **227**

Chapter 12: Finding Windows Tools **229**

Some Tools That Are Available 229
Windows 95–specific programs 231
The cost of tools 232
Using Archie to Find Tools 233
Downloading an Archie client 233
Installing Archie 233
Running WS-Archie 235
Downloading Tools 238
Installing New Tools 238
Summary 240

Chapter 13: Using Gopher **241**

What Is Gopher? 241
What You Need 242

Downloading a Gopher client 242
Installing your Gopher client 243
Connecting to a Gopher Server 246
Understanding the Gopher interface 247
Understanding the Gopher menu 248
Changing your Home Gopher 250
Temporary Gopher servers 252
Searching for Information 254
Saving Information 256
Using Bookmarks 256
Adding a bookmark 257
Retrieving a bookmark 259
Modifying bookmark categories 260
Modifying bookmarks 261
Summary 263

Chapter 14: Understanding WAIS **265**

What Is WAIS? 265
Searching Through WAIS 266
Connecting to a WAIS Client 267
Understanding the WAIS interface 268
Conducting a search 270
Refining your search 271
More on relevance feedback 273
Retrieving Documents 275
The WAIS Command Set 275
Quitting WAIS 277
Summary 278

Chapter 15: Using the World Wide Web **279**

What Is the World Wide Web? 279
What You Need 280
Downloading a Web browser 280
Installing your Web browser 281
Using a Web Browser 284
Understanding Web addressing 285
Understanding viewers 286
Organization of the Web 287
Using hypertext links 287
Finding information on the Web 290
Multimedia on the Internet 293
Speeding Up Your Display 293
Summary 296

Chapter 16: Talking the Night Away 297

Using Usenet 297
    Newsgroup categories 299
    Downloading a newsreader 300
    Installing your newsreader 301
    Your first time on the newsreader 304
    Reading the news 310
    Posting messages 313
Using IRC 314
    Downloading IRC software 315
    Installing your software 316
    Configuring mIRC 317
    Connecting to an IRC server 319
Summary 325

Chapter 17: The Microsoft Network 327

Joining The Microsoft Network 328
    Installing the software 329
    Filling out the sign-up forms 331
    Establishing your account 335
Connecting to The Microsoft Network 338
A Quick Tour around the Block 339
    Navigating through The Microsoft Network 340
    The Microsoft Network forums 342
Accessing the Internet 346
    Internet electronic mail 346
    Usenet newsgroups 347
Disconnecting from The Microsoft Network 348
Summary 350

Part IV: Appendixes 351

Appendix A: Internet Providers 353

Nationwide Providers 353
U.S. and Canadian Providers 354
International Providers 389

Appendix B: Windows Tools on the Net 395

Ftp Sources 395
Web Sources 398

Appendix C: Glossary 401

Index 409

Reader Response Card .... Back of Book

Introduction

It seems that the two hottest computing topics of our day are Windows 95 and the Internet. It only seems natural, then, that one book should address these two topics. Indeed, Windows 95 and the Internet are related to each other — you can use Windows 95 to access the Internet, and you can use the Internet to enrich your use of Windows 95.

This mutual reliance and reinforcement theme was the seed of this book. *Your Windows 95 Internet Surfboard* fills a unique niche in computer books. No other book addresses the Internet so completely for a Windows 95 user. Here you find answers to every question that you may have about connecting your system to the Internet. It is true that Windows 95 contains all the building blocks you need to access the Internet. It is just as true that these building blocks remain hidden unless you have clear, concise, no-nonsense guidance on how to take advantage of them.

Perhaps more than anything else, *Your Windows 95 Internet Surfboard* provides you with a practical guide that you can use to expand the limits of your computer so they encompass the world. You learn about the tools available, how to use them, and how to make your entire system a part of the Internet.

In 17 information-packed chapters, *Your Windows 95 Internet Surfboard* provides the help you need to connect to the Internet. If you have Windows 95, a modem, and an Internet account, you can get connected today. This book tells you how to make the most of each of these three components, so that together they provide the best informational tool that you can find.

In Chapter 1, "The Ground Floor," you learn how the Internet started, why so many Internet tools remain rooted in esoteric UNIX commands, and why you should get connected to the Net. You also learn exactly what you need to get connected — it is much simpler than you may believe.

Chapter 2, "Connection Technology Basics," covers all the computer jargon that you ever need to know to connect to the

Internet. You learn why those obscure terms are important and (in plain English) what they mean to you. Communications technology can be confusing, but by the end of this chapter, you will know your way around TCP/IP and how addressing works on the Internet (yikes!).

The focus of Chapter 3, "Selecting an Internet Provider," is how you can make a wise choice in selecting the all-important Internet provider. Internet providers are responsible for furnishing the Internet connection you need. You learn how they work, why they exist, and what type of account you need from them.

In Chapter 4, "Installing Your Modem," you learn quite a bit about how your modem works and how Windows 95 relates to your modem. You also learn what type of modem is best for connecting to the Internet and how to install it as part of your system. When you complete this chapter, you will know that your modem is correctly installed and functioning as it should be.

Chapter 5, "Configuring Windows 95 for the Internet," gently guides you through setting up the networking part of Windows 95 so that it works with the Internet. Here you start to put those communications basics (learned in Chapter 2) to work in your system. By the end of the chapter, your system will be configured properly for your type of Internet account.

The portion of Windows 95 that allows you to connect with the Internet is known as Dial-Up Networking. In Chapter 6, "Using Dial-Up Networking," you put this powerful tool to work. You learn how to install it, configure it, and create dial-up definitions that match your Internet needs.

In Chapter 7, "Your First Call," you place your first call to the Internet. You learn how easy it is to make your system a part of the vast Internet. You get your first taste of Internet tools and how they work. The chapter rounds out with a discussion of how you pay for your session on the Internet.

Chapter 8, "Electronic Mail and Microsoft Exchange," discusses the most-used feature of the Internet: electronic mail (e-mail). You learn not only what e-mail is but how you can send, receive, and manage e-mail from your desktop. You learn how to use e-mail software that you can get through the Internet as well as how you can configure Microsoft Exchange to access your Internet mail.

Building upon the concept of electronic mail, Chapter 9, "Using Mailing Lists," teaches you how you can access the huge number of mailing lists available on the Internet. These lists aren't used to sell products; they are used to disseminate information in which you may be interested. You can learn about anything from soup to dogs to airplanes to politics in the '90s — all by using your e-mail account.

In Chapter 10, "Using Telnet," you learn how you can connect to distant computers through the Internet and become a terminal to those systems. Windows 95 includes a telnet program that allows you to access many of the millions of hosts attached to the Internet. With the proper account privileges, you can access resources on the remote computers as if you were right there.

Chapter 11, "Using Ftp," covers a very popular use of the Internet. Here you learn how the ftp utility, which is built into Windows 95, can be used to transfer files from around the world to your desktop. You also learn how to find ftp servers that may have the information you need to enhance your productivity.

A wide variety of tools are available on the Internet itself. In Chapter 12, "Finding Windows Tools," you learn how you can find those tools and put them to work for you. You learn not only about Windows tools but about the emergence of tools created specifically for Windows 95.

You can find a great deal of information on the Internet by applying what you learn in Chapter 13, "Using Gopher." This chapter discusses how you can download and install your own Gopher client software so that you can access any Gopher server in the world. You learn how you can download the information directly to your system and how you can access these information deposits again and again.

Chapter 14, "Understanding WAIS," introduces you to a powerful database analysis tool that is available on the Net. Wide-Area Information Server (WAIS) allows you to effectively focus on the information that is most crucial for your needs. You learn how to connect to WAISs around the Internet and how to use relevance feedback to refine your searches.

In Chapter 15, "Using the World Wide Web," you learn about the fastest-growing segment of the Internet. The World Wide Web (Web, for short) does for the Internet what multimedia did for personal computers. You can download and view text and graphics, listen to sounds, or see real-time movies on your system. You can access thousands of Web sites through the Internet, and more become available daily. By the end of this chapter, you will have the necessary skills to grow with this vibrant area of the Internet.

Not everything on the Internet is grim-faced business or boring library information. Chapter 16, "Talking the Night Away," introduces you to some tools guaranteed to add spice to your free time. You learn about Usenet newsgroups and Internet Relay Chat (IRC). These tools allow you to communicate with others on the Net who have the same interests as you do. With IRC, you can communicate with them in real time!

Finally, Chapter 17, "The Microsoft Network," provides a guided tour to the newest service from Microsoft. Through The Microsoft Network (MSN), you can access information, commerce, and areas of interest to you and your family. You can also access the Internet for your e-mail needs and for Usenet newsgroups.

The book wraps up with three appendixes that provide valuable information to enrich your use of the Internet. In Appendix A, "Internet Providers," you learn about the hundreds of providers available around the world. This information, coupled with the information in Chapter 3, helps you make the best choice of a provider.

Appendix B, "Windows Tools on the Net," is a treasure chest of Windows tools that you can find on the Internet. Here you find a road map to uncover many tools you can use to further explore and exploit the Internet.

In Appendix C, "Glossary," you find a concise guide to the terminology that may baffle and befuddle you. Although not a full-fledged computer dictionary, Appendix C defines common terms that you will run across in your Internet travels.

As you read each chapter, you will find important or helpful information highlighted as follows:

♦ **Cool Places.** These sidebars list nifty places on the Internet that you can visit with your new-found skills. I have found these Internet locations to be particularly helpful, very interesting, or just plain fun.

♦ **What Can Go Wrong.** Periodically you may experience troubles as you use Windows 95 to access the Internet. When these situations arise, the information in these sidebars can be invaluable. Here you find information that identifies a potential problem, explains its cause, and tells what you can do to fix it and get back on track.

♦ **Network Etiquette.** The Internet is a community of users, as much as it is a tool you can use. As with most communities, unspoken rules govern proper behavior and acceptance by the community. The hints provided within these sidebars go a long way toward making sure you don't step on any "virtual toes" while online.

♦ **Note.** Sometimes information defies fitting into a category. At other times, information relates to the main text but warrants special attention. In both cases, this Note graphic flags such information, which helps you make the most of your Internet experience.

All in all, *Your Windows 95 Internet Surfboard* provides the best information and guidance you can find about the fast-growing Internet and the easiest way for you to access it — Windows 95. With that in mind, enjoy your reading and enjoy your time on the Internet even more.

If you find this book particularly helpful, I would be interested in knowing about it. Feel free to drop me a note. You can contact me through the Internet at dci@usa.net.

Getting Started

P A R T

1

◆ ◆ ◆ ◆

In This Part

Chapter 1
The Ground Floor

Chapter 2
Connection
Technology Basics

Chapter 3
Selecting an
Internet Provider

Chapter 4
Installing Your
Modem

Chapter 5
Configuring
Windows 95
for the Internet

Chapter 6
Using Dial-Up
Networking

Chapter 7
Your First Call

◆ ◆ ◆ ◆

The Ground Floor

The best place to start anything — especially learning — is at the beginning. To learn about the Internet, you will find it helpful to know some fundamentals. This chapter introduces you to Internet basics, including the following material:

✦ What the Internet is

✦ What UNIX is and how it relates to the Internet

✦ Why you should connect to the Internet

✦ What you need to connect to the Internet

Together, Windows 95 and the Internet create a powerful tool that you can use to increase your productivity and knowledge. By learning the information in this chapter, you lay the ground floor on which you can build further understanding of how to use the Internet from Windows 95. Some readers may know the information presented in this chapter; others may not. In either case, it is essential that you understand it before proceeding.

What Is the Internet?

The Internet has been described as many different things; it seems to be today's hottest topic in many magazines. Perhaps this is because many people are just discovering what the Internet really is — a conduit for information. Virtually any information that you could want can be found on the Internet. Why? Because the Internet is the connection between thousands of computer systems around the world.

Don't worry if you still don't quite understand what the Internet is. Indeed, it is difficult for many people to grasp at first. The Internet is not so much a place as it is a method. For instance, let's say that you want to open a store in your town. You first find a location, order your merchandise, install your fixtures, and finally open your doors to the public. If you are successful, people visit your store, make a purchase, and tell their friends about their experience. This is how a business grows. However, the Internet is different. The Internet is analogous to the roads that bring people to your store. The roads serve as a means for people to visit your store, just as the Internet serves as a means for your computer to communicate with other computers around the world.

History of the Internet

Just as the road system in many communities developed in an incremental and sometimes haphazard way, the Internet has grown piecemeal over the years. Thus, the actual beginnings of the network are hard to determine. It would be similar to asking, "How did the roads in your community begin?" Most people would be hard pressed to indicate a place or date when they actually began. The road system just grew over time.

By most accounts, the Internet has its roots in the mid 1960s. Researchers were beginning to experiment with connecting computers over vast distances, using ordinary telephone lines. Each research facility had its own local networks that were used in the laboratories or on campus, but there was no way to connect distant facilities to each other. The first experiments involved using specialized equipment to allow similar networks to communicate. Thus, an IBM-based network in one town could communicate over a special phone line with an IBM-based network in another town.

In 1969, the U.S. Department of Defense funded a project for widespread networks. The Advanced Research Projects Agency (ARPA) handled the undertaking and developed a network called ARPANet. This network did not rely on centralized control, as many networks to that point had. Instead, the agency defined the connections or routes between existing networks, allowing each connected network to control its own access, security, and operations. For instance, consider several different computing facilities spread out across the country — a military installation in Georgia, a university in Illinois, a research facility in Colorado, another military facility in California, and another university in Oregon. Using ARPANet, the layout of such a widespread network might look similar to what is shown in Figure 1-1.

Remember that each of the computing facilities at the different locations is actually a network in its own right; each has its own rules and culture. ARPANet simply provided a way for the different facilities to communicate with each other. All of a sudden, scientists, researchers, and military personnel were able to communicate through their computers over vast distances. When another computer system wanted to join the network, all it had to do was establish a connection between its facility and the nearest system already connected to the network. For instance, if a military installation in Texas wanted to join, it established a link between its location and the Colorado facility, as shown in Figure 1-2.

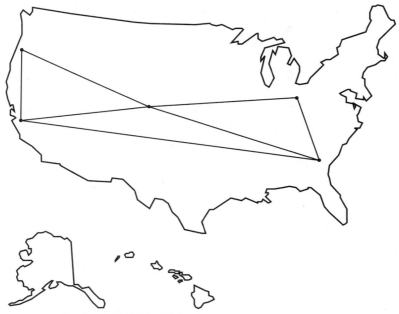

Figure 1-1: A simplified network layout.

One interesting sidelight of ARPANet's development was that researchers were attempting to develop a computer network that would be reliable, even under enemy attack. They were particularly concerned about what would happen to the network in a nuclear attack. The organization of ARPANet, using distributed control and processing, was ideal in meeting such a challenge. Even if one or more of the network sites were destroyed, all between-site connections would not be destroyed. Take another look at the network diagram shown in Figure 1-2. Notice that, in general, no point is particularly vulnerable on the network. For instance, if the California facility were lost, the Oregon one could use a different route to communicate with the remaining facilities.

Because connecting to the ARPANet was so easy, and the new communication channels fostered research so well, the network grew quickly. Soon, a series of *protocols* (rules) was developed that allowed fundamentally different systems to communicate with each other. Thus, the network became independent of the systems connected to itself. This caused more rapid growth.

In the early 1980s, ARPANet joined MILNet (a primarily military network), NSFNet (the National Science Foundation Network), and a few other smaller networks to create the Internet. By this point, thousands of facilities were connected to the network.

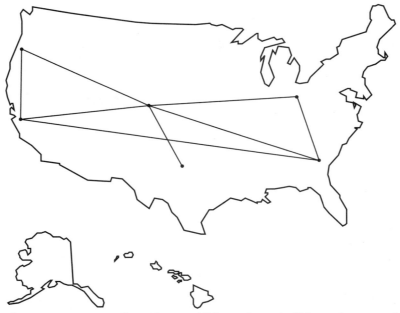

Figure 1-2: ARPANet allowed easy additions of new facilities to the network.

The name *Internet* was derived from what it was designed to do — interconnect networks. You have already learned that these networks can be anywhere in the world. The Internet (or the Net, for short) provides the conduit between the networks that allows information to be freely and easily communicated. Since the inception of the Internet, its growth has been phenomenal. In recent years, the growth has been exponential, with millions of new sites added yearly. Some calculate that, at this growth rate, everyone on the planet should be connected to the Net by the turn of the century.

Who runs the Internet?

The Internet is not really run by anyone — at least, not in the traditional sense. In companies, organizations, and families, everyone is used to having someone in charge. You may belong to an online service such as CompuServe or America Online. In these cases, someone is in charge of the service. With the Internet, no company runs it and no institution sets rules. The closest thing to a regulating body is perhaps the Internet Society, or ISOC. ISOC is a voluntary group of Internet users whose aim is to promote growth of information exchange using the same technology as that used in the Internet.

The ISOC is led by the Internet Architecture Board, or IAB. This board is responsible for technically managing the Net, and its primary task is to standardize the technology used in the Internet. The IAB sets standards as necessary, and everyone on the Net has an opportunity to contribute to the process. Contributions to the IAB are typically handled through another branch of the ISOC — the Internet Engineering Task Force, or IETF. This group, again made up of volunteers, solves technical problems facing the Internet. After input from all interested parties, the group can issue their decisions as suggestions, or they can submit them to the IAB for formal standardization.

Who pays for the Internet?

Just as the management of the Internet is egalitarian, so is the payment for the network. In general, everyone pays for his or her piece of the Net. Earlier in this chapter, in discussing ARPANet, I point out that if someone wanted to join, all the person had to do was to create a link between his or her location and the nearest network node. The Internet functions in much the same manner — if you want to join, you pay for the cable to connect you to the nearest Internet point. This payment is typically collected by the telephone company. In addition, if you connect through someone else's facility, you probably pay this facility a fee for using its equipment.

This brings up *Internet providers,* which are essential to joining the Internet. I assume you want to connect to the Internet. You may think that all you need to do is to run a cable between your system and one at the local university. (You may be able to do this if your uncle is on the board of trustees.) Typically, you can't do this because the university maintains its Internet connections for the use of faculty, staff, and students. Instead, the university will direct you to a commercial Internet provider, a company in the business of providing access to the Internet. This company sets up the computer equipment and establishes the communications links necessary to connect you to the Net.

You can then establish a connection with the provider, either through a *dial-up arrangement* (you call the provider on your modem) or through a dedicated line between your system and the provider. Again, you pay for the connection, along with a fee for using the provider's equipment. You learn more about Internet providers and costs in Chapter 3.

The Internet and UNIX

UNIX is an operating system used on a wide array of computer systems throughout the world, particularly in the research and educational arenas. Many people are under the mistaken impression that to use the Internet, they must learn UNIX. This is less true today than it once was, and it is becoming less critical each day.

Because UNIX was the operating system used at many of the original sites connecting to the ARPANet and later to the Internet, many commands used to communicate across the Net are UNIX-based. If you are not familiar with UNIX, the commands can appear confusing and cryptic. Remember that there is no common method of using the Internet. Instead, each system connected to the Internet still operates under its own rules and uses its own operating system. Thus, you may use your system to access a remote system that is using a different operating system, such as UNIX. (Your system is often referred to as a *local system,* and the computer to which you are connecting — even through the Internet — is called a *remote system.*)

When accessing such a system, it helps to know a few UNIX commands. However, don't despair. A handful of commands takes you quite far, and many commands you may otherwise need are quickly being updated in more familiar ways. For instance, one common command on the Net, which has its roots in UNIX, is the *telnet* command. (This command is covered in Chapter 10.) While originally a UNIX utility that relied on users entering lines of commands, in Windows 95 telnet has been replaced with a program that uses the familiar Windows interface.

Throughout this book you see different commands based on UNIX systems. I fully explain these commands when introduced so that you can use them right away. Take your time to learn these commands; they will help make your Internet experience richer and more productive.

Why You Should Connect

You have probably heard from many people that you must connect to the Internet. For those who are in the computer industry or who use a computer often, the pressure to connect can be amazing. Exactly why you should connect can be directly related to why and how you use your computer.

If you are from an educational background, you know that the computer can be a powerful educational tool. Connecting to the Internet opens a door to virtually unlimited educational possibilities. In the blink of an eye, you can communicate with educators or students around the world. You can receive information on the latest teaching techniques or on new information about your teaching subjects. You can use the Internet to tap into the best research libraries in the world. Many university libraries have at least their card catalogs on the Net, and some are starting to give access to private collections.

If you do a great deal of research, you probably have some computer-based tools already. By searching the Internet you gain access to huge databases that contain large amounts of information. Along with that information is the ability to search, sift, and analyze the data in new and exciting ways. Before spending large amounts of time, you can also see if anyone else connected to the Net has previously done work in your research area. Findings or results may be available online and only a moment away.

If you use your computer for recreation, thousands of shareware game programs appear on the Net. There are repositories of games around the world, some in foreign languages. You can even use the Internet to increase your enjoyment of recreational topics that are not traditionally computer oriented. For instance, hundreds of special interest groups cover topics such as music, musical groups, television shows, and board games. You can get information from these sources quickly and easily.

If you use your computer for business, the Internet is appealing more to business every day. Not only are there business opportunities, but you can use the Internet to trade stocks, determine business-related information, and perform market research. If you need computing resources beyond what you have available, you can use the Internet to access resources from personal computers to supercomputers. Many businesses use the Net to perform complex modeling and forecasting on remote computers with capabilities far beyond what they have available locally.

If you are civic-minded and actively involved in a cause, you can use the Internet as a communications and organizational tool. You easily can find people of like mind and interest, and communicate freely with them. Sharing ideas and information across the Net is the next best thing to holding meetings in your living room. When you are ready, you can reach out and let members of Congress or other elected representatives know your feelings — all via the Internet.

Chances are, you use your computer for a wide variety of purposes. You do research on one day, conduct business on the next, and relax with a game or two on the weekend. Thus, you can use the Internet in all your computing activities. In general, you connect to the Internet for three main reasons:

✦ resources

✦ information

✦ communication

Internet resources

You know that computers and networks from around the world connect to the Internet. The resources represented by these systems are astounding. If you establish an account at a remote site, you can use its facilities to accomplish tasks that you may not be able to otherwise do. To give a simplistic example, consider that you are doing work for an advertising company. You have developed a four-color brochure using desktop publishing software, and you must output it to a high-end color printer. You don't have such a printer at your local office, but you have located a system in Chicago that can do it for you at an agreeable price. If you contact the company that runs that system, you can probably send your work to the company via the Internet and have its printer perform the output for you.

Internet resources are important to companies and individuals involved in research and development. Massive computing power is not cheap, but it is often required for complex calculations or operations. For instance, you may be developing a new product and you must simulate how the product would react under stress. Modeling such a situation on your own computer system could take weeks but may take only an hour or two on a supercomputer. Several regional supercomputer centers are attached to the Internet, and you can set up accounts with them. You schedule your work, transfer your information, and receive your results — all via the Internet. In such a situation, the justification of connecting to the Net is apparent.

Internet information

The information on the Internet is astounding. You could spend your life trying to sort through it all and never complete the task. New information is placed online every day. Analysts predict that someday you will be able to find anything that has ever been published provided on the Net. While that day may indeed come, this represents only a fraction of the information available. Much of the information on the Net is unpublished, and much is raw data. Tools are available to help you sift through the mountains of data and extract the information you need. You learn about many of these tools within this book, from the perspective of a Windows 95 user.

As an example, you may need to find information on the 1995 legislative agenda for Wyoming. Believe it or not, you can find the agenda on the Internet. What if you need to find information about whale migration between 1980 and 1989? This information is also on the Net. Notice that these examples consider data that are not readily available in your local library. While you may be able to find such information in a well-stocked library, it is not always available when you need it. You may not find the legislative agenda for Wyoming in libraries outside the state, and locally it is only available after it has been printed, shipped, received, cataloged, and filed. Using the Internet, the information is always at your fingertips.

Internet communication

Communication through the Internet is fast and cheap. When you think about all the costs associated with traditional communication, it doesn't take much to justify an Internet connection. For instance, the cheapest form of traditional communication is via U.S. mail. For 32 cents you can send a letter anywhere within the United States (up to one ounce). This is roughly equivalent to five sheets of paper and the envelope. Sending the same letter via the Internet can cost a couple of pennies, and it is delivered to the recipient within minutes, if not seconds. You also do not need to worry about the letter ending up in some postal employee's basement for a couple of years!

The vast majority of Internet communication occurs through electronic mail, or *e-mail*. This form of communication is built directly into Windows 95, and in Chapter 8, you learn how it works. You can include video, sound, or programs as part of your e-mail messages — none of which are easily (or cheaply) sent through more traditional communications methods.

What You Need to Connect

You don't need a whole lot to connect to the Internet. Because you are reading this book, I assume that you are fairly comfortable with the PC environment. At the least, you probably have a PC system and are using Windows 95. To use the Internet from your vantage point, all you need are the following items:

✦ A computer

✦ Windows 95

✦ A modem

✦ An Internet account

That's it! The list of what you need is similar to what is required to connect to a regular online service such as CompuServe or Prodigy. As a reader of this book, you may already have at least three of the necessary items, and in some instances, you may not need the modem. For instance, you may work in a company that uses a *local area network* (LAN). If you do, the company may have already connected the network to the Internet. If this is the case, you can get detailed information about accessing the Internet from your network administrator.

If you are a solitary user or you are on a network that is not connected to the Net, you learn in later chapters how to set up an Internet account and how to use your modem. In Chapter 3, you learn what it takes to set up an Internet account. In Chapter 4, you learn how to use your modem with Windows 95.

Summary

The Internet is a powerful tool that you can use to be more productive and to enrich your use of computers. When combined with the power and flexibility of Windows 95, you not only have a powerful tool, but you have one that is easier to use than ever before.

In this chapter you discover the basics about the Internet. These basics give you a firm basis on which you can build further learning. Here you learn the following items:

✦ The Internet is a structure and means by which diverse computers can communicate with each other.

✦ The Internet has its roots in the research, educational, and military communities of the 1960s and 1970s. It has grown to encompass a wide variety of networks from a wide array of disciplines.

✦ Many programs used to access the Internet have roots in the UNIX operating system. Learning UNIX commands, while not absolutely necessary, is beneficial when working on the Internet.

✦ The three main reasons to connect to the Internet are resources, information, and communication. As you learn to use the Internet, each of these reasons will become obvious at some point.

✦ Connecting to the Internet is rather simple, once you meet a few criteria. If you are already using Windows 95, all you need is a modem and an Internet account. In some environments, such as a company where you already have Internet access, you may not need the modem. The Internet account is established either through your network administrator or through an Internet provider.

In the next chapter, you learn more basics — this time related to the technology on which the Internet is based.

✦   ✦   ✦

Connection Technology Basics

The Internet is a network at heart, and networks operate on a series of rules, technologies, and standards. It is impossible to fully grasp the Internet without understanding the technology on which it operates. The purpose of this chapter is to familiarize you with the concepts inherent to networking on the Internet. These concepts affect how you use the Internet as well as what you can get from it. Here you learn the following items:

+ How a packet-switched network functions

+ What TCP/IP is and why it is important

+ How domain naming works in a TCP/IP environment

+ How Internet addresses work

+ What an IP address is and why you need one

+ What connection protocols are available for dial-up access to the Internet

This chapter contains quite a bit of information to digest; some of it may be daunting. However, I try to approach a somewhat deep subject in a manner that makes it understandable. By the time you finish this chapter, you will have a good understanding of the Internet's building blocks. These blocks will aid you in building a solid comprehension of not only how you interact with the Internet, but how you can use Windows 95 to do the interacting.

Packet-Switched Networking

In the broadest sense, the Internet relies on a technology known as *packet-switched networking*. You remember from Chapter 1 that the seeds for the Internet were planted in the mid-1960s. This was the time when researchers came up with the idea for packet-switched networks. Using this paradigm, data that must travel across a network is broken up into small, independent units of information called *packets*. These packets consist of three primary parts:

- ✦ **Header.** This portion of the packet contains information about the intended recipient of the packet, along with an indication of the sequence in which the packet belongs.

- ✦ **Body.** This portion contains the main information being conveyed. This can either be an entire message (if the message is short) or a part of a larger message.

- ✦ **Trailer.** The trailer simply indicates when the end of the packet has been reached.

As information is broken down into packets, it is transmitted over the network. Each station that encounters a packet examines the header to determine if the packet is intended for that station. If not, the packet is passed on in a direction closer to the ultimate destination. Eventually, the packets arrive at the intended destination and are reassembled in the order originally intended. One interesting item about packet-switched networks is that packets in a message do not have to travel to the destination along the same route. Indeed, many different routes can be taken, as shown in Figure 2-1.

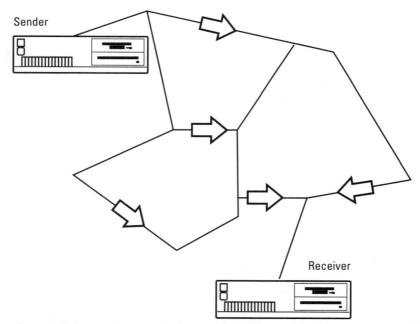

Figure 2-1: In a packet-switched network, all information does not have to follow the same route.

Why use packets? The answer is simple: congestion. If information were not broken down into packets, the overall information transferred across a network would be quite sporadic. Imagine that the packets transferred across a network are cars on a highway. If you have ever watched the cars on a busy highway, it seems they are everywhere, all moving to different destinations. In reality, however, many cars are going to the same general destination.

For instance, some cars may be heading to Detroit whereas others are going to Houston or Denver. What if every passenger going to Denver from St. Louis crammed into one big vehicle for the trip? The vehicle would be so big that it would occupy the entire highway for miles. No other vehicles would be able to get on the road, and all traffic feeding onto the highway from side streets would be blocked.

The same is true with networks. Some messages would be so big that they would effectively stop all other communication on the network for a time. The use of packets relieves congestion and helps smooth the information transfer.

That brings us to the advantages of packet-switched networking. Sending packets along differing routes provides three major advantages. First, it allows for more even use of the network. If you try to cram all the message packets along a given route when other routes are available, you are not using resources wisely. The second advantage is that alternate routes mean it is harder to break down the entire network. In Chapter 1, you learn that one of the design considerations for the Internet was that it must keep functioning even if a portion of the Net were disabled or destroyed. Packet switching allows this action to occur smoothly.

The final major advantage is that error correction is easier when dealing with packets. If, at the receiving end, a packet error is detected, only that packet, not the entire message, must be re-sent. This saves both time and network resources.

Understanding TCP/IP

The transfer of information over networks is done according to a *protocol,* or a set of rules. The collection of rules used in the Internet — and indeed in many other types of networks — is called *TCP/IP.* This is an acronym for transmission control protocol/Internet protocol. It refers to a collection of standards that defines how communication between computers takes place, even if the computers are different from one another and separated by large distances.

In the late 1960s when ARPANet was taking shape, a network protocol named *network control protocol* (NCP) was used. Designers quickly discovered that this protocol was not dynamic or robust enough to support the type of network that ARPANet would become. For one thing, NCP was intended for use in a homogenous environment, meaning that all computers on the network were running the same operating system.

Designers decided up front that such a restriction could not be placed on a wide-spread network, so TCP/IP was developed in the early 1970s. Its biggest strength was its ability to use a heterogeneous network environment, meaning that it could be implemented on a wide variety of hardware and operating systems.

In some operating systems, TCP/IP is built in. For example, UNIX uses TCP/IP. When you connect two UNIX systems with a network wire, TCP/IP handles communications chores. This is not the case with other operating systems, including Windows 95. If you want to use TCP/IP with Windows 95 (which you will), you need to install the proper network drivers and configure them properly for your system. This is covered in depth in Chapter 5.

TCP/IP and Domain Naming

Within any networking protocol, a way must exist to identify individual systems, or *nodes,* on the network. TCP/IP is no exception. It includes an addressing scheme that pervades everything you do with the Internet. If you fail to understand how addressing works, you severely limit what you can do on the Internet.

If you think about it, the idea of addresses is not that confusing. You probably use addresses every day. The first place this occurs is with physical addresses. When you address a letter, you provide enough information for the postal service (or other delivery company) to uniquely identify who should receive the letter. You typically give a name, street address, city, state, and ZIP code. Without all the elements of the address, you have the potential for confusion about the recipient. For example, consider the following hypothetical address:

> John Davis
>
> Carpenter Widget Co.
>
> 1234 Burgess Ave.
>
> Anytown, CA 98765

If you look at the address backward, you see how it identifies a unique recipient. The ZIP code is shorthand for the local post office that will deliver the mail; it can be thought of as a combination of the city and state for the recipient. The next level is the street address, in this case 1234 Burgess Ave., which gets the mail closer to the intended recipient. The next level is the company name. This gets the letter to the company's front desk or mailroom. Finally, the recipient's name — John Davis — identifies the person within the company who should receive the mail.

Another way you use addresses is with phone numbers. It may seem odd to think of phone numbers as addresses, but they really are. Consider the following phone number:

> 307-555-1212

This phone number has three parts, and each part is generally recognized by everyone in the United States. The first three numbers represent the area code. This identifies which region of the country the phone number refers to. (The region may be a state or a portion of a state.) The next three numbers (555) identify the exchange to which the phone belongs. Exchanges can be thought of as neighborhoods; the larger the city, the more neighborhoods and exchanges it has. The final four numbers identify a telephone within the exchange. Thus, every ten-digit phone number uniquely identifies an individual phone in the United States.

Both physical addresses and phone numbers are used every day by millions of people. Network addresses, as used within a TCP/IP system such as the Internet, follow the same concepts. Take a look at the following hypothetical address for the Internet:

jdavis@cwc.com

This address is divided into two parts. The first — the part before the @ sign — is referred to as the *user ID*. It identifies a person within a network system. The portion of the address to the right of the @ sign is referred to as the *domain* or *host;* it identifies the organization or computer network to which the user ID belongs. (You learn more about domains shortly.) When you combine the user ID and the domain name, you get a unique address that identifies any individual on the Net.

Where are addresses used? In any network activity that involves transferring information from one location to another. You most often use addresses in e-mail, but they are used in other network activities as well.

Understanding DNS

You have learned a bit about domain naming as used in the Internet. The proper term for this type of naming structure is *domain naming system,* or DNS for short. Domain names can be rather short, or they can be long. Longer domain names simply mean that more organizational levels are necessary to uniquely identify a host system. Again, this is analogous to physical addresses. Depending on the recipient of your letter, you may only need a three-line address. Other recipients may need a four- or five-line address to properly address the letter.

As an example, examine the following hypothetical address:

kwilson@mis.farsite.uwm.edu

If written out as a physical address, it may be something like this:

K. Wilson

MIS Department

Farsite Campus

University of Wyoming at Moskee

Each period within the domain name identifies another level of the overall organization through which the message must pass to arrive at the ultimate destination. The order of levels in a domain always proceeds from the most specific to most general when viewed from left to right. Thus, in the example address, the most specific level is *mis,* and the most general is *edu.*

No common way exists to decode the meaning of different levels within a name. The nomenclature used in the address is defined by the person setting up the address. It is not unusual to have different domain levels in a name represent different levels within an organization. For instance, one domain level may refer to an overall organization, while the name to the left of it refers to a department or building. The level to the left of that may represent a specific network within the department or building, and still another level may identify a workgroup within the network. The complexity of a domain address is limited only by the structure and imagination of the individuals assigning the names.

Organizational domains

You may have noticed that at the end of all the Internet addresses discussed so far is a three-letter domain level such as *com* or *edu.* These are referred to as *organizational domains.* An organizational domain is an indication of the organization that owns the address, and it always appears at the end of the domain name. Within the United States, you find seven different organizational domains, as shown in Table 2-1.

Table 2-1 Organizational Domains Used within the United States	
Organizational Domain	*Purpose*
com	For-profit commercial entities
edu	Educational facilities
gov	Nonmilitary government organizations
int	International (NATO) institutions
mil	Military installations
net	Network resources
org	Nonprofit groups

The purpose of the organizational domain is to provide another level of distinction for a full domain address. Thus, you could have two addresses that were exactly the same except for the organizational domain, and the messages would be routed to completely different places.

Geographic domains

Some domain names don't include organizational domains, but instead rely on *geographic domains.* This is particularly true with domain names outside the United States. Geographic domains indicate the country in which the name originates. In almost all instances, the geographic domains are based on the two-letter country codes specified in ISO 3166, which is a document of the International Standards Organization. Although scores of geographic domains exist, Table 2-2 shows some common geographic domains in use as of this writing.

Table 2-2
Common Internet Geographic Domains

Geographic Domain	Country
AR	Argentina
AU	Australia
AT	Austria
BR	Brazil
CA	Canada
CO	Colombia
CR	Costa Rica
CU	Cuba
DK	Denmark
EG	Egypt
FI	Finland
FR	France
DE	Germany
GR	Greece
GL	Greenland
HK	Hong Kong
IS	Iceland
IN	India
IE	Ireland
IL	Israel
IT	Italy

(continued)

Table 2-2 *(continued)*	
Geographic Domain	**Country**
JM	Jamaica
JP	Japan
MX	Mexico
NL	Netherlands
NZ	New Zealand
NI	Nicaragua
NO	Norway
PK	Pakistan
PA	Panama
PE	Peru
PH	Philippines
PL	Poland
PT	Portugal
PR	Puerto Rico
RU	Russian Federation
SA	Saudi Arabia
SG	Singapore
ZA	South Africa
ES	Spain
SE	Sweden
CH	Switzerland
TH	Thailand
TR	Turkey
GB	United Kingdom
US	United States
VN	Vietnam

Note that geographic domains change as country names change or as new countries connect to the Internet. Although the United States has a geographic domain (US), this is seldom used on domestic domain names. If you don't see a geographic domain at the end of a name, you can assume that the address originates within the United States.

How addresses are assigned

Domain names are chosen by the organization requesting the name and then registered with the *InterNIC*. The InterNIC is the shortened name for the Internet Network Information Center, which is a service provided by three different companies. The information that is compiled, maintained, and distributed by the InterNIC splits into three categories, as follows:

✦ **Registration services.** These services relate to registering domain names (addresses) so that they are not used by others. InterNIC registration services are provided by Network Solutions, Inc.

✦ **Directory and database services.** These services include information about different databases and resources on the network, as well as a white pages and yellow pages directory of Internet addresses. AT&T provides InterNIC directory and database services.

✦ **Information services.** These services include training and newsletters regarding how to use the Internet more effectively. The information disseminated by this part of the InterNIC is directed toward technical people responsible for organizations and networks connected to the Internet. InterNIC information services are provided by General Atomics/CERFNet.

The part of the InterNIC responsible for domain names is Registration Services. To register your domain name, you must follow these steps:

1. Contact your Internet provider and indicate that you want to register your domain name.

2. Determine from the Internet provider who will provide the DNS server functions for your domain name. (A DNS server is a computer that provides the translation services between a DNS address and an IP address.) You will need an IP address for both the primary and secondary DNS servers related to your organization. (IP addresses are discussed in the next section.)

3. Together with your Internet provider, fill out the registration forms required by the InterNIC Registration Services. These forms are available online, and your provider will know where to get the latest copies.

4. Submit the forms to Registration Services.

After submitting the forms, it takes approximately two weeks for the name to be registered (assuming there are no conflicts or problems). The time it takes also depends on the workload of Registration Services. With the recent popularity of the Internet, the Registration Services workload is fairly heavy; thus, a two-week delay is common.

If you are connecting to the Internet from your home computer, don't worry about getting a domain name for yourself. You generally only need a domain name if you are establishing a full-time connection to the Internet. Otherwise, you connect through dial-up access to an Internet provider, as discussed in Chapter 3, and you use the provider's domain address as part of your own.

The IP Address Structure

You have probably been around computers long enough to know that although humans think in terms of images, objects, letters, and numbers, computers understand only the latter — numbers. Thus, even though you enter a DNS address, such as jdavis@cwc.com, as the recipient of a message, your computer must translate the address to an *IP address.*

An IP address is a unique 32-bit address that defines a single location on the network. For human usage, IP addresses are written as a series of four numbers separated by periods. For instance, the following is a hypothetical example of an IP address:

> 152.8.207.21

This notation for an IP address is sometimes called a *dotted-decimal notation,* or *dotted-quad notation.* Each of the four numbers in this IP address — 152, 8, 207, and 21 — is called an *octet* and represents one byte of the full 32-bit address.

No octet can have a value above 255. This means that the lowest possible IP address is 0.0.0.0 and the highest is 255.255.255.255; however, this is misleading, because some IP addresses are used for overhead purposes by the network itself. An IP address refers to a host on the Net, meaning an individual computer system responsible for distributing mail or messages. Thus, no two hosts on the network can have the same IP address.

IP addresses are assigned to networks divided into three classifications: A, B, and C. The breakdown of IP addresses among different classes may sound a bit confusing, but it is simply a way of allocating addresses among the different networks that access the Internet.

Class A addresses are provided for very large networks. Only 126 Class A addresses are possible in the world, and each Class A network can have in excess of 16 million computers in its individual networks. The first octet of an IP address is between 1 and 126 for Class A networks, and all remaining octets identify members of that network.

In a Class B network, there can be up to approximately 65,000 workstations on the network. In IP addresses, the first octet is a number between 128 and 191, and the second octet further denotes the network address. Thus, there can be approximately 16,000 Class B networks in the world. The last two octets of the IP address denote individual workstations.

Class C networks have an IP address in which the first octet is between 192 and 223; the second and third octets further define the network, and the final octet identifies the workstation on the network. Several million Class C networks are possible, with each having about 250 workstations.

Table 2-3 shows a summary of IP network classifications.

Table 2-3 IP Address Classifications					
Type	**First Octet Values Workstations per Net**	**Net ID Octets**	**Workstation ID**	**Octets**	**Nets in Class**
Class A	1–126	1	2–4	126	16,777,214
Class B	128–191	1–2	3–4	16,384	65,534
Class C	192–223	1–3	4	2,097,151	254

When you provide an address for an Internet operation (such as sending e-mail), you can use either the domain name method or the IP address method. Most people use the former because it is easier to read and understand. The process of converting human-readable addresses (such as jdavis@cwc.com) to machine-readable addresses (such as 152.8.207.21) is called *resolution*. During the resolution process, the domain name is translated automatically into an IP address by a computer called a *DNS server*. (DNS is an acronym for *domain naming system*, which was discussed earlier in this chapter.)

Because name resolution occurs behind the scenes, you generally won't need to be concerned with it. There may be times, however, when you need the full IP address for a host. For example, if you supply a domain name that the DNS server cannot resolve for some reason, you are notified that your action cannot be completed. In such a case, you can use the IP address instead of the domain name. This simply means that you would use an address of jdavis@152.8.207.21 instead of jdavis@cwc.com.

WHAT CAN GO WRONG

Bad addresses

If you find a domain name that you cannot use for some reason, you should try the operation again using the IP address (assuming you have it). If the operation is then successful, you should contact the person in charge of your DNS server and let him or her know about the problem. (This will be either someone in your company, if you have a DNS server on site, or someone at your Internet provider.) This individual can then modify the server so that you can use the regular domain name in the future.

What TCP/IP workstations require

In order for a computer to function properly within a TCP/IP environment (such as the Internet), several addresses must be identified for every computer connected to the network. For most casual Internet users, these addresses are assigned automatically by your Internet provider. The necessary addresses include the following:

✦ An IP address for the workstation

✦ A subnet mask for the network

✦ A default gateway address

The IP address is unique and identifies the workstation within the grand scheme of TCP/IP. You learn the purpose and implications of the IP address in the preceding section. The second component, the *subnet mask,* allows the workstation to identify the network of which it is a part. You can think of a subnet as a workgroup within a larger domain or network, or as all of the computers physically connected to a particular network. In reality, the subnet mask is used to mask out the parts of the IP address that are not necessary for the type of network you belong to. For example, if your IP address is for a Class C network (the most common type), then the first three octets of the address are of no importance; only the last octet defines the computers in your network. Thus, a subnet mask of 255.255.255.0 can be used to "wipe out" the first three octets in an IP address.

The third component required for successfully living in a TCP/IP environment is the *default gateway address.* This is an IP address of the system to which your workstation should route data packets not destined for computers on the local network. The default gateway address is used in conjunction with the subnet mask. The subnet mask identifies which portions of the IP address are contained within the local network and is used to route local network mail. The default gateway address identifies the address for packets filtered out by the subnet mask. The system at the default gateway address can then route the packets toward their ultimate destination.

It may sound complex to say that a TCP/IP workstation requires three address components to function properly. Windows 95 provides no exceptions to these requirements, however. To connect your Windows 95 system to a TCP/IP network (such as the Internet), you must determine the three addresses necessary to enable proper communication with the network. In Chapter 3, you learn what additional information you must obtain from your Internet provider. Then, in Chapter 5, you learn where to use these addresses in your system.

Understanding DHCP

DHCP is an acronym for dynamic host configuration protocol. This is a set of rules developed by Internet members (including Microsoft) that allows IP addresses, subnet masks, and default gateway addresses to be assigned to workstations as needed. Traditionally, the three address components necessary for a TCP/IP workstation are statically assigned to workstations and must be entered into the network drivers by someone sitting at the workstation. This can create a headache in an environment where a network may have 250 workstations spread across several buildings. Either the network administrator must go to each system and set it up manually, or the user (who may be less technically savvy) must perform the setup from written instructions.

The administrative problem becomes more acute if the network has 5,000 workstations. This is often the case with Internet providers who must provide proper addressing information for many of the systems that connect to the Internet through their facilities. To say the least, administering such a large number of IP addresses could quickly become very difficult.

The DHCP protocol effectively removes the requirement that individual workstations must have static IP addresses. Instead, a network can designate a DHCP server that automatically manages the assignment of IP addresses and routing information to network nodes as they sign in. The server then manages the IP address table, making sure that only one address is assigned to each active workstation. The IP address is leased to the workstation, meaning that it is provided for only a limited time. As the end of the lease period approaches, the workstation must obtain either an extension on the IP address lease or a new IP address. From a user's perspective, these negotiation and assignment procedures are transparent, and it is much easier than managing IP addresses by hand. From the perspective of the Management Information Services (MIS) Department, the potential for error in IP address assignments is greatly reduced, if not eliminated.

Windows 95 supports DHCP. This means that if you are connected to a network that has a DHCP server (such as a Windows NT network or many networks maintained by Internet providers), then you can indicate where the DHCP server is located, and Windows 95 takes care of communicating with the server and determining the IP address and routing information to use. After an IP address is assigned, the WINS protocol (discussed in the next section) is used.

The existence of a DHCP server also implies the existence of a DHCP client (servers and clients work together in a server/client environment). You already know that Windows 95 supports DHCP; it does so as a DHCP client, not as a server. You cannot use your Windows 95 system as a DHCP server, because the software used to function as such a server is not built into the operating system.

Understanding WINS

Windows 95 also supports a protocol called *WINS*, an acronym for Windows Internet name service. WINS manages the mapping of information between the symbolic names assigned to systems and resources in a Windows network, and the IP addresses dynamically assigned to those same systems and resources by a DHCP server.

Effectively, it is the responsibility of WINS to handle routing of information to a workstation after the IP address has been assigned. WINS is designed to work with DHCP and cannot function without a DHCP server in place.

Although WINS may sound like one more level of complexity, its purpose is to save you from dealing with otherwise complex issues. Because Windows 95 supports WINS, many addressing tasks that you would need to handle personally (and manually) are handled automatically by the operating system. Because you definitely will run into discussions or descriptions of this technology, it is important to possess background information so that you are not completely lost.

Addressing and the future

When the IP addressing specifications were drafted in the early 1970s, many criticized the use of a 32-bit address as wasteful. They could not envision a scenario in which all 32 bits would be used. Obviously, those critics never foresaw the conditions that exist today. One InterNIC staffer recently commented, "It seems everyone in North America wants an Internet address." At this rate, it won't be long before the 32-bit IP address is inadequate to meet the demand.

At some time in the near future, probably by the end of the century, the Internet Architecture Board will need to adopt a new or expanded addressing standard. (In some parts of the Internet community, the term *IPng* has been coined to refer to the next generation of IP addressing.) The biggest problem is with the allotment of IP addresses currently in use. As more people crowd onto the Internet (You are still getting on the bandwagon, aren't you?), the smallest IP address that can be allocated represents a Class C network. Thus, if you get an IP address for yourself, you automatically tie up approximately 256 IP addresses — you either get none or 256. The problem is also evident for larger networks. For example, if a network of 350 computers requests a single IP address, it automatically gets a Class B address that allows it in excess of 60,000 workstations. The unused IP addresses between 350 and 60,000+ are wasted: a casualty of the allocation schemes used.

When the IAB finally addresses the issue (which it is scrambling to do now), the address field will most likely be doubled to 64 bits, but time will tell. When a change is made, some allowance must be made for backward compatibility — it is unreasonable and unrealistic to assume that every network in the world will immediately replace its routers to accommodate the larger address fields.

Connection Protocols

So far in this chapter, you have learned about TCP/IP networking — the heart of the Internet. This is all fine and good, but you may be wondering what this has to do with you and Windows 95. It is really quite simple. If you are going to use Windows 95 to connect to the Internet, you must understand TCP/IP, because it has a bearing on how you make your connection.

Once you understand the underlying principles of a connection, the next task is to look at the protocols used to establish a dial-up connection to the Internet. This is done through one of two protocols: SLIP or PPP.

SLIP is an acronym for serial line Internet protocol, and it is used to define how TCP/IP transactions occur over a dial-up connection. SLIP was developed in the early 1980s as a method of allowing UNIX systems to communicate with other UNIX systems over modems. (Remember that TCP/IP is native to UNIX systems.) Versions of SLIP were introduced for UNIX systems as early as 1984. Several products on the market implement SLIP for Windows systems. Perhaps one of the most popular is WinSock, a program that not only includes the SLIP protocol implementation, but also has a built-in dialer for connecting with your Internet provider.

The problem with SLIP is that it was never accepted as an Internet standard. This means that the protocol is widely viewed as a nonstandard solution, and support for the protocol is giving way to PPP instead. *PPP* is an acronym for point-to-point protocol. PPP is used to accomplish the same purposes as SLIP, but it does so in a much more robust manner. A PPP connection includes error detection and correction, as well as packet authentication. (Packet authentication refers to making sure that the data packets received are really from the sender — it is a security feature.) These features combine to make a more secure connection over ordinary phone lines. In addition, PPP is a recognized Internet standard protocol, so it is receiving the widest share of development efforts today.

Windows 95 comes with support for both SLIP and PPP, so you don't need add-on products such as WinSock. The PPP drivers are installed automatically when you install TCP/IP support; the SLIP drivers are not. This automatic installation of one protocol over the other is done for the reasons already cited. If you instead want to revert to the older SLIP protocol (for example, if your Internet provider does not support PPP), you can load the support from the Windows 95 installation disks or CD-ROM. Information on how to do this appears in Chapter 5.

Summary

It seems that computer programmers are very good at using new jargon whose only purpose is to confuse the public. Nowhere is this as evident as in networking and data communications. In this chapter, you learn quite a bit about the technology on which the Internet is based. Here you receive a crash course in several different areas. You specifically learn the following items:

✦ The Internet is a packet-switched network in which information is divided into separate packets that can be routed on various paths to reach a common destination.

✦ The networking protocols used within the Internet are collectively known as TCP/IP. These protocols define how information is transferred over the Net as well as how individual systems can access the network.

✦ Internet addresses consist of a user ID and a domain name. The user ID defines which individual at an address is to receive the information, and the domain name identifies an individual computer system on the Internet.

✦ Domain names uniquely identify network hosts. A domain name typically includes either an organizational or geographic domain that indicates the origin of the name.

✦ IP addresses are the numeric equivalent of domain names. IP addresses uniquely identify host systems. Historically, the conversion from a domain name to an IP address is handled by DNS servers.

✦ A variety of defined protocols is used to manage IP addresses within a network. DHCP and WINS are two such protocols supported by Windows 95.

✦ When establishing a dial-up Internet connection, a connection protocol is necessary. Both SLIP and PPP are supported by Windows 95, although PPP is recommended because it is newer and more robust.

If you don't fully understand all these topics, you may want to read through the chapter again. You need a firm grasp of these concepts to understand the steps presented in the next few chapters.

In the next chapter, you learn how to select an Internet provider, which is necessary for successfully connecting to the Internet.

✦   ✦   ✦

CHAPTER 3

Selecting an Internet Provider

Unless you are connected to a network that has access to the Internet, selecting an Internet provider is one of the steps you must go through to connect to the Net. This chapter focuses on this important step and how you can make the proper decision. Here you learn the following items:

✦ What, exactly, an Internet provider is

✦ Why an Internet provider is important

✦ Where you can find providers

✦ Types of Internet service available through providers

✦ What various services cost and how you pay

✦ How you can decide which service you should get

✦ What information you need from a provider

When you have finished working through this chapter, you will have all the external information and services you need to connect to the Internet. Then you can sit in front of your computer and work through setting up Windows 95 for accessing the Net.

What Is an Internet Provider?

In Chapter 1, you learn the basic definition of an Internet provider — a system that provides Internet access to everyday people like you and me. Although this definition is true, it sounds as if all providers are the same, when in fact they can be quite different. Different providers have different services, provide different degrees of access, and charge different rates. In many respects, the provider you select is just as important as the computer you select or the operating system you choose — particularly if you will be using the Internet quite a bit.

To provide you with Internet access, a provider goes through a great deal of work. This work can be divided into three categories:

✦ **Equipment.** A great deal of specialized equipment is necessary for allowing hundreds of users to connect to the Internet. The provider takes care of purchasing the com-puters, routers, multiplexers, and phone equipment necessary to maintain the link with the Internet. This mitigates an expense you would otherwise need to bear.

✦ **Communications.** Not only does providing Internet access deal with computer equipment, it is intimately related to phone service as well. The provider handles setting up and maintaining the communication lines between its facilities and the Internet, and in some cases, provides communication all the way from you to the Internet.

✦ **Billing.** Because you are not the only customer for the provider, it must have some way to equitably bill you and all of its other customers. This involves metering time on its systems and making sure that billings, collections, and security are handled properly.

Why is a provider important?

In some ways, you can view an Internet provider as a consolidator. It purchases a service available only in bulk (access to the Internet) and then repackages and sells it in small quantities to hundreds or thousands of people like you, as illustrated in Figure 3-1. Without such a company, you would need to purchase the bulk amount and pay for service you could never use.

Providers also give expert advice. Most providers maintain a help desk for those times when you are having problems (some are available 24 hours a day, seven days a week). If you can't get connected, they can help. If you have problems maintaining your connection, they can help. If you are thinking of upgrading your service, again they can help. If you didn't use a provider, you would need to develop the expertise in-house, on your own.

The bottom line is cost. Connecting directly to the Internet (bypassing a service provider) is expensive. Just the access charges can run in excess of $100,000 per year — and this doesn't count the equipment, personnel, and expertise involved with such a connection. The provider helps you by putting an otherwise expensive commodity within your reach.

Where do you find a provider?

Internet providers are springing up all over the place and so are their ads. If you look in the back of *PC Magazine* or a similar periodical, you can often find advertisements placed by Internet providers. These outfits are the exception, however; although they provide a legitimate service, they don't represent the wide array of choices you may have.

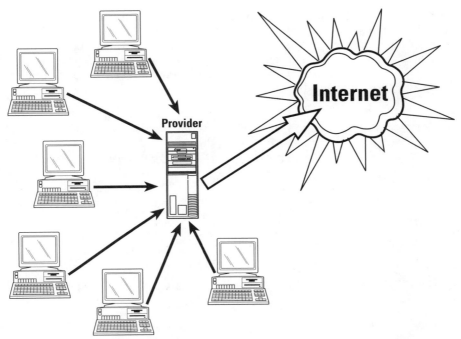

Figure 3-1: Internet providers consolidate many people's usage of the Internet.

To find a provider, the best place to start is with your friends. Ask them if they are connected, and if so, which provider they use. Then contact your local computer store to see if its personnel know of Internet providers with local access for your community. Finally, if you or a friend has access to an Internet account, you can get a list of services off the Net. You do this by using the World Wide Web (covered in Chapter 15). Simply use your Web browser to connect to the server at the following address:

http://www.celestin.com/pocia

The list at this address is known as the POCIA Directory. POCIA is an acronym for providers of commercial Internet access. You can browse through information that shows service areas, fees, and contact points for providers.

With resources like the POCIA Directory, I think it's odd that you need access to the Internet to find out how to get access to the Internet. For many people, this may be no problem, because they can ask friends to connect to the directory for them. With others, it can be a problem, because they may not know anyone with Internet access. If you fall into this latter category, consult Appendix A as a starting point. It provides a concise listing of the POCIA Directory, which should allow you to locate and contact a provider directly.

Even in this age of information, computers, and communication, many areas of the country are not serviced by an Internet provider — at least not at a local level. This isn't a problem if you live in an urban area, but it can be vexing if you live in a remote, rural area. Some Internet providers offer toll-free service for nationwide access. This is helpful for the more remote areas and for people who are on the road a great deal. Table 3-1 lists companies that offer toll-free Internet access.

Table 3-1 Internet Providers Offering Toll-Free Access	
Company	*Phone Number*
Allied Access Inc.	618-684-2255
American Information Systems, Inc.	708-413-8400
Association for Computing Machinery	817-776-6876
CICNet, Inc.	313-998-6103
Colorado SuperNet, Inc.	303-296-8202
DataBank, Inc.	913-842-6699
Global Connect, Inc.	804-229-4484
Internet Express	719-592-1240
Mnematics, Inc.	914-359-4546
Msen, Inc.	313-998-4562
NeoSoft, Inc.	713-684-5969
New Mexico Technet, Inc.	505-345-6555
Pacific Rim Network, Inc.	360-650-0442
Rocky Mountain Internet	800-900-7644
Synergy Communications, Inc.	800-345-9669
WLN	800-342-5956

Remember that toll-free access does not necessarily mean that it is free. Most Internet providers with toll-free lines add a surcharge for access in this manner. For example, my provider adds a flat $6 per hour fee for using its toll-free access.

Acceptable Use Policies

Many Internet providers maintain an *acceptable use policy,* or AUP. These policies provide a framework that the provider uses to govern the types of communication that it can handle through its facilities. An AUP is often rooted in history, philosophy, or bureaucracy rather than practicality. For example, in the early days of the Internet, nearly all providers were either educational institutions or government agencies. The educational institutions may have received funding from a government agency, such as the National Science Foundation (NSF), and a stipulation of the funding was that the Internet connection could only be used for noncommercial traffic. Thus, if a business wanted to establish an Internet connection, it could not do so through the school.

Let me give you a personal example. I live in a small rural town in northeastern Wyoming. The nearest college is about 30 miles to the east, and it has an Internet connection. I thought it would benefit our community to tap into the excess capacity of the college's Internet link and perhaps get people in our community online. When I approached the college about this, I was informed that it could not help us, because carrying commercial traffic through its Internet link would violate its acceptable use policy. Instead, I was left with the option of contacting the nearest commercial provider, which was 250 miles to the south.

You can typically determine whether the provider or organization has an AUP by asking the person who is in charge of the system. Policies can differ in breadth and detail; as an example, see the sidebar on the next page for the acceptable use policy for NorthWestNet, a commercial Internet provider.

Although an AUP may seem stifling and capricious at times, its purpose is to make sure that the resources remain available for their intended use and to ensure that government-subsidized links are not used to compete with commercial Internet providers. When you contact an Internet provider, you may want to have a copy of its AUP (if it uses one) faxed or mailed to you so you can review it completely.

Types of Service

As previously mentioned, not all providers offer the same types of service. Depending on the provider you select, your access to the resources of the Net may be limited. For some people, this may be acceptable, but you must be aware that lower prices from some providers may mean more limited Internet access.

When you contact Internet providers, make sure that you question them about what services are provided with your account. You want maximum access to the Internet, because this allows the best flow of information. The following sections discuss the types of service that you may find from your providers.

NorthWestNet acceptable use policy

NorthWestNet is a regional data communications network serving a consortium of universities and research groups in the northwestern United States. Its goals are summarized in the Articles of Incorporation for the Northwest Academic Computing Consortium, Inc. All use of NorthWestNet facilities must be consistent with the goals and purposes of NorthWestNet. The intent of this statement is to describe certain uses that are consistent with the purposes of NorthWestNet, not to exhaustively enumerate all such possible uses.

Acceptable uses of NorthWestNet facilities include:

✦ Use for scientific research or instruction at member and associate member institutions through the provision of high-speed data communications;

✦ Use as a vehicle for scholarly communications;

✦ Use as a means for NorthWestNet members to access remote computing resources for scientific research or instruction. Notable examples of such resources are the NSF supercomputing facilities;

✦ Use necessary to support other acceptable uses. For example, administrative communications that are part of the support infrastructure needed for research and instruction are acceptable. Similarly, communication directly between nonmember institutions in support of research or instruction at member institutions is acceptable;

✦ Use required by agreements with NSF, the primary funding agency for NorthWestNet;

✦ Use by member institutions as a laboratory for research and experimentation in computer communications, where such use does not interfere with production usage. However, any experimental use requiring modification to router software or protocol layers below ISO Layer 4 requires prior review by the Technical Committee.

In general, commercial and general administrative use is prohibited. Use for scientific research or instruction at nonmember institutions and at for-profit institutions may be consistent with the purposes of NorthWestNet and will be reviewed on a case-by-case basis.

Use of NorthWestNet for any illegal purpose or to achieve unauthorized access to systems, software, or data is prohibited.

NorthWestNet is a production communications network on which many researchers depend. Uses that significantly interfere with the ability of other users to make effective use of the network are not acceptable.

Limited access

A limited-access account does not offer the full range of Internet services and resources. These accounts typically only allow e-mail service and possibly Usenet access, but they are less expensive than a full-access account. (Usenet is a network on the Internet that allows you to participate in specialized newsgroups. Usenet is very similar to traditional electronic BBS systems. You learn more about Usenet in Chapter 17.)

The drawback to a limited-access account is that you cannot electronically visit other computer systems, nor can you take advantage of some of the most exciting, new Net advances such as the World Wide Web. You also cannot transfer files to your system unless they are attached to a mail message. So, why would you want a limited-access account? Only if you were absolutely certain that you only need e-mail access and you want to save some money. Otherwise, do not limit yourself. You should acquire a full-access account.

Full access

A full-access account is necessary if you want to take advantage of the full scope of Internet services and resources. With this type of account, you can get e-mail, access other computers, transfer files, use the World Wide Web, and otherwise fully participate in the Internet community. Another advantage of a full-access account is that if you have the proper security clearances at a remote computer attached to the Internet (usually granted when you establish an account at the remote site), you can take advantage of that system's resources through the Internet.

Full-access accounts are the types most sought after and the types most often offered by Internet providers. However, you should not assume that paying more for your account with a particular provider automatically guarantees more access to the Net. On the contrary, prices among providers can vary quite a bit, and you should compare services before you start comparing prices.

Types of Connections

Along with the level of service that you receive from a provider, you also need to understand the types of connections offered. In general, you can establish two types of connections through a provider: dial-up and dedicated. These are discussed fully in the following sections.

Dial-up service

For most individual or small business users, a *dial-up* Internet account makes the most sense. Dial-up service simply means that you are using a modem to connect with the Internet provider's computers, and in turn connecting with the Internet. What you see when you establish a connection with the provider's computer depends on how it has implemented its dial-up service. Many providers offer different classes of dial-up service, and you must specify the one you want to use.

Some providers offer an interface that looks like those offered by BBS services. These are menu-driven, and you can select different features and services from the screen. For example, Internet Express is a provider that I have frequently used, and it has a BBS screen that looks like the one shown in Figure 3-2.

To use such an interface, you can use your favorite modem terminal software. After you are connected, you make menu choices.

Other providers offer a *shell account.* This means that you are connected to its computers as if you were a remote terminal. You see nothing but a command prompt, where you can enter operating system commands to take advantage of the Internet connection. These commands are typically UNIX-based, and you can type on your keyboard as if you were sitting at a computer in the provider's office.

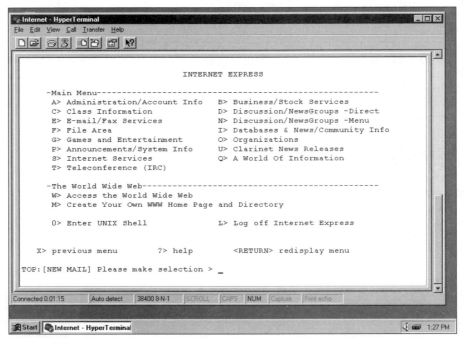

Figure 3-2: Some providers allow you to use a menu-driven interface to access Internet services.

Assuming that you are familiar with the command language, a shell account offers great latitude in what you can do on the Internet. You can use a wide variety of commands and features. You are only limited by the power of the computer to which you are connected (the computer at the provider's site) and the connection between the provider and the Internet itself.

Still another type of dial-up service is SLIP or PPP service. These were addressed to some extent at the end of Chapter 2. Either type of service allows you to exercise a full range of TCP/IP options over the phone link. In practical terms, it means that you are not functioning as a remote terminal to the provider's computer system — you are actually connected to the Internet *through* its computer system. The distinction is in where the software you use resides. If you are using a shell account, you are using software residing on the provider's computer. If you are using a SLIP or PPP account, you are using software on your system.

Another item to remember about SLIP or PPP accounts is that your software is responsible for the appearance of what you see on the screen. Thus, you are not tied to the interface the provider may use in its menu system. Instead, you can select the software you are most comfortable with and use it. You can also use more than one software package at a time. For example, once you have a PPP account and have established a successful connection, you can use a Web browser in one window, conduct a telnet session in another window, and read your e-mail in a third window — the PPP connection takes care of sorting out the tasks for you. (Individual Internet tools are discussed in other chapters of this book.)

How should you pick a service? The answer depends on your comfort level with computers. Many people are quite happy with their menu interfaces or their shell accounts. If you are using Windows 95 (you are using it, right?), then go for the gusto and secure a PPP account. This allows you to connect directly to the Internet. PPP accounts may cost a couple of dollars more per month, but they allow you to control the tools you use instead of relying on the tools that the provider may have installed on its systems.

Dedicated service

The major distinction between a dial-up account and a *dedicated* account is when you can access the Internet. You already know that a dial-up account allows you to dial in and use the Internet as you need to. If you find yourself dialing in quite a bit, or if you have many people in your office who each dial in quite a bit, then you may need to look into dedicated service. This involves establishing your own Internet gateway and paying to have a direct, full-time link with the network. Your computers, in effect, become a full-time part of the Net.

To establish a dedicated service account, you still need to work with an Internet provider. This type of service is where the providers really start to differ, however.

Some providers can provide only low-volume dedicated accounts, and others may charge exorbitant fees for setting up dedicated accounts. After you decide exactly what you need, you must do some serious comparison shopping to find the deal that is right for you.

Some people have characterized dedicated service accounts as "the Holy Grail" of the Internet. Why would you want such an account? Primarily because you can have instant and full access at any time, and everyone else in the world can have instant access to you. The drawback, however, is the cost and complexity of maintaining the link between you and the provider. For this type of account, you need several things:

✦ A router

✦ A dedicated phone line

✦ A series of servers

None of these items are necessary with a dial-up account, and the costs associated with them must be carefully weighed against the expected benefits. The next few sections address each of these requirements.

Routers

A *router* is a computer device that inspects data packets that it encounters to determine where they should be sent. (Routers are integral to the information presented in Chapter 2.) In laypersons' terms, a router acts as a traffic cop to determine what information gets sent where. It is essential that you have a router to direct information between your network and the Internet.

Depending on the Internet provider you use, a router may be leased to you, or the provider may give you direction on which one to purchase. Some services require that you use its routers to guarantee compatibility with its equipment. Routers can cost from several hundred to several thousand dollars, depending on the complexity of your network and the capabilities of the router itself. If you lease a router, expect to pay several hundred dollars a year in lease fees in addition to the other fees you may pay.

Phone lines

This component of dedicated service refers to the actual communications channel between your business and your Internet provider. In most instances (unless your Internet provider is next door to your office), procuring a communications channel involves working with your local phone company. If you and your Internet provider are not located in the same city, it may involve working with several different phone companies. Some providers may help you set up the phone link, whereas others will not. In the latter case, you need to arrange for the link, and once the wire is installed at the provider's office, you can then deal with them again.

Dedicated phone links come in several varieties, each distinguished by the capacity of the channel. In general, there are three types of dedicated links:

✦ **56-kilobit channel.** This is a common small-capacity, dedicated channel. When you talk with a phone representative about leased lines, this is typically where he or she begins. A 56-kilobit channel can handle up to 56 kilobits of information per second, twice the throughput of the fastest asynchronous modems on the market today.

✦ **T1 channel.** This type of connection is equivalent to 24 56-kilobit channels, operating at a bandwidth of 1.544 megabits per second. T1 service refers to the type of wiring used in the connection, not the data rate and composition, however. That is referred to by the nomenclature DS1. A T1 line is often referred to as a point-to-point connection, because you bypass the normal phone company switches entirely. To implement such a point-to-point connection, you need special phone company equipment at your facility. The two points are typically at your office and at the phone company switch, where your signal is compressed onto normal phone company lines and ends up at the phone company switch serving your Internet provider. There, the signal splits off of the normal phone company lines and is routed directly to the provider's facilities.

✦ **T3 channel.** The fastest connection you can get is a T3 channel, which operates at 45 megabits per second. At this bandwidth (referred to as DS3), the link has 28 times the capacity of the T1 line and 672 times the capacity of the 56-kilobit line. (You must be doing some serious Internet work to use a T3 channel.) T3 lines are also point-to-point and typically use fiber-optic wires as the connection media.

The phone line component of a dedicated link has the potential of being the most expensive part of your Internet connection. The costs vary, depending on the capacity of the link and the distance between you and your provider. If you are within the same exchange, 56-kilobit links can cost up to $600 per month, whereas T3 channels can easily run well above $10,000 per month.

Internet providers use these same types of dedicated links to connect to the Internet. The weakest providers use 56-kilobit lines, whereas the strongest use direct T3 connections to access the Internet backbone. You can judge the capacity of your provider by asking what type of lines it uses to connect to the Internet. If you are considering using a T1 or T3 channel, you should talk to only the largest national Internet providers. Many of the smaller regional providers rely only on 56-kilobit or T1 links, and your needs would easily strip them of their capacity.

Servers

If you decide to establish a dedicated link to the Internet, you need to add servers to your network. (You may already have servers in place in your network, so this may not be an issue.) These servers handle routing functions such as IP address assignment and DNS resolution. IP addresses are best managed through a DHCP server, as described in Chapter 2. DNS name-handling resolution depends on the size of your network. If you are responsible for a large network, then your provider may want you to field your own DNS server. If you have a small- to medium-size network, then you can use the DNS server at the Internet provider's facilities.

Adding appropriate servers to your network may mean adding computers or functions to existing servers. They will also add to the workload of your network administrator, or additional personnel responsible for maintaining the new servers will be needed.

What Internet Services Cost

You have seen some cost figures in this chapter. These costs, however, only get you connected to the Internet provider. You still must pay the provider a fee for access to the Internet. The fee depends, in large part, on the type of access you are making through its equipment, as well as the burden you are placing on its corporate structure.

For example, the cheapest type of Internet connection you can make is a limited-service connection over dial-up lines. If you can find these from a provider, you can often get them for only a couple of dollars per month.

The next cheapest route (and the route of choice for most individual and small-business users) is a SLIP or PPP connection over dial-up lines. This offers full Internet access at a low cost. Some providers charge by the hour ($1.50 – $2.00 per hour), while others charge a flat monthly fee ($20 – $30 per month). Still others use a combination of the two pricing schemes (such as $12 per month and $2 per hour for any usage over two hours per day). Because pricing schemes vary considerably, you should match the pricing method to the amount of access that you need. You can then pick the scheme that is most cost effective for your situation.

When you rely on dedicated Internet access, charges often exceed $100 per month. The exact charges depend on the bandwidth (line capacity) that you expect the Internet provider to service.

The payment terms required by different vendors can vary greatly. If you are an individual, most providers require a credit card number. Your usage charges are billed directly to the credit card at semimonthly or monthly intervals. If you are a business user, most providers bill you and provide an itemized statement of your access. These invoices are either due upon receipt or within 30 days. If you need different terms from your provider, you must make this clear up front.

Making Your Selection

The whole point of this chapter leads to two basic decisions that you must make regarding the Internet: what type of service you need and who will provide that service to you. The logical first decision covers the type of service you require, dial-up or dedicated. After this decision is made, you can then make your selection of Internet providers.

The dial-up or dedicated decision

If you are an individual user or a small business with limited funds, making this decision is easy. You should choose a dial-up PPP account and access the Internet only when you need it. If you are not in this position and your Internet needs are a bit more demanding, then you must do a cost analysis to determine which type of account is right for you.

For example, if you can get local dial-up service in your area for $3 per hour and dedicated service would cost $700 per month, then you can determine your break-even usage — just under eight hours per day, based on a 30-day month. Achieving this amount of usage is not that hard if you have 15 to 20 employees accessing the Internet. To determine your break-even point per employee, divide your work hours per day by the number of employees.

Don't forget to consider the added advantages of a full-time connection. The first advantage is instant access. With a full-time connection, your e-mail is received and delivered right away, not every couple of hours when you may dial in to the provider. Also, with full-time access, the number of people using the Internet at your facility is bound to increase, therefore decreasing your per-person access fee.

The provider decision

Once you know the type of service you expect from your provider, you can select the provider. Earlier in this chapter, you learn where you can locate the different Internet providers. Take a look at those resources, and then start calling around. For each provider you contact, you should ask questions that satisfy the following key points:

✦ **Services.** Does the provider meet your service needs? Does it provide full Internet access? Does it have a high-capacity link to the Internet? (If it has a low-capacity link, then your response times may be low during peak hours.) Are any advanced computing services available?

✦ **Access.** If you are using dial-up service, does the provider have enough dial-up ports so you won't get a busy signal? Are the provider's acceptable use policies too restrictive for your intended Net use? How secure is the provider's system?

✦ **Cost.** What does the provider charge for the services required? Are there any hidden or up-front charges? What are the payment terms? Is detailed access reporting available?

✦ **Support.** Is user support provided at no additional charge? How knowledgeable are the customer support personnel? Can the provider help you with telecommunications consulting, if necessary?

✦ **Stability.** The more stable your provider, the better service you generally receive. Find out how long the provider has been in business.

In addition, if your company is a bit larger and you have offices in more than one area, you may want to determine the following:

✦ Can the provider support you across the nation or around the world?

✦ If you roll all your locations into a single account, can the provider do better on the pricing?

✦ Does the provider have toll-free access for times when your personnel are on the road? (If you are establishing a dedicated Internet link, this becomes less of an issue, because your mobile workers can call in through your in-house computer system.)

What You Need from the Provider

If you are establishing a dedicated Internet link, you must work closely with your Internet provider to make sure that your account is satisfactory. If you are using Windows 95 and you are establishing a PPP dial-up account, then your provider must answer some specific questions:

✦ What access phone number should I dial with my computer?

✦ What is my user ID?

✦ What is my password?

✦ What is my e-mail address?

✦ What is the IP address of the DNS server used by the provider?

✦ What default gateway IP address should I use?

✦ Does the provider use a DHCP server? (If the answer to this question is yes, you can skip the next two questions.)

✦ What TCP/IP address is assigned to my system?

✦ What IP subnet mask should I use?

Once you find the answers to these questions, make sure that you write them down. You need the answers later as you configure Windows 95 for the Internet. This is discussed in Chapter 5.

Summary

No one gets on the Net without a provider; it's a sad fact of life. Selecting an Internet provider can be frustrating, but it is essential in getting the most from your Net experience. The frustrating part is when you consider the sheer number of providers and the fact that each provides different services at different costs according to different terms. You should plan to spend some time making this important decision.

In this chapter, you learn quite a bit about Internet providers. Specifically, you learn the following items:

✦ An Internet provider supplies a connection between you and the Internet. You cannot get on the Internet without using a provider.

✦ Internet providers function as consolidators — they bundle communications from a number of smaller customers and place them onto the Internet.

✦ You can find Internet providers in a number of places, but the best place to look is on the Internet itself. Several online lists give information on providers.

✦ Internet providers can supply you with either dial-up or dedicated Internet service. For individuals and small businesses, dial-up service is typically more than adequate.

✦ You pay your Internet provider based on the services you select and the connection you make. Different providers charge different amounts, and payment options differ among providers.

✦ Once you understand your service and connection options, making decisions on which options you select is difficult only if you have above-average access needs or if you are responsible for a number of people who access the Internet. In these cases, you must do a cost analysis to determine the level of service that is best for you.

✦ To use Windows 95 to access the Internet, your Internet provider must answer very specific questions. The answers to these questions are used when configuring your Windows 95 system.

Now that you are armed with a provider and the information from the provider, you are ready to start working with Windows 95 directly. In the next chapter, you start by configuring your modem to work with Windows 95.

Installing Your Modem

To connect to the Internet, a connection must be made between your machine and the Internet provider. If you have obtained a dial-up account (as discussed in Chapter 3), then the connection is established using a modem and your phone line. This chapter discusses, in depth, serial communications and how you install your modem under Windows 95. Here you learn the following items:

+ What serial communications are and how they work

+ How modems function and what features determine the capabilities of a modem

+ How to pick the modem that works best for connecting to the Internet

+ How to install your modem

+ How to add your modem to Windows 95

+ How to make sure your modem is working properly with Windows 95

Understanding Serial Communications

Serial communications are analogous to communicating through a modem. The information transfers to the modem and over the phone line in a serial fashion — one bit at a time. Contrast this with how information is transmitted within your computer, where it zips around in parallel. Information moves 16, 32, or 64 bits at a time. Even when communicating with a device hooked to a parallel port, information moves eight bits at a time.

Although parallel modems exist, most modems rely on serial communications. Because serial data can be sent on a single wire, this data is well suited to communicating over phone lines. Parallel data, on the other hand, requires a single wire for each data bit being transmitted. For eight data bits to be transmitted over a parallel connection, eight data wires are needed (along with some additional wires to manage the connection).

What do modems do?

Modems facilitate data communications over ordinary phone lines. The phone system was designed and established long before computers arrived on the scene, so modem technology is built around an analog representation of sound. These five-dollar words simply mean that when you talk into a telephone, your voice is converted into electrical impulses that directly reflect the frequency of your voice and the amplitude (volume) at which you are speaking. At the other end of the phone line, the impulses are converted back into audible speech through a speaker.

Computers, on the other hand, do not use analog data representations. Instead, they use data stored in digital format. This means that information is stored as a series of binary digits, each representing one of two conditions: on or off. Because digital information is so "black and white," it is easy to transmit, duplicate, and convert into many other formats. (That is one reason why computers are such wonderfully productive tools.)

Do you see the problem? Computers manipulate data in one format (digital), and the phone system transmits data in a different format (analog). To use the phone system to communicate data, a conversion from digital to analog format is necessary. Then, at the other end of the connection, a conversion back into digital format is required before the data can be used by the remote computer. This conversion process is what your modem does, and it does it at a very fast rate using quite sophisticated circuitry. That is where the term *modem* comes from; it is a contraction of words describing the data conversion process — modulate and demodulate.

The modulation and demodulation process is controlled by computer chips in the modem. The chip that does the processing is the universal asynchronous receiver/ transmitter, referred to as a *UART* (pronounced *you-art*).

Not all modems are created equal, however. They differ in their capabilities. In general, three areas define a modem's capabilities: speed, error correction, and data compression. I discuss each area in the following sections.

Modem speeds

The primary measure of a modem's capability is the speed at which it transmits or receives data. The faster the modem, the faster it sends information over the phone lines. A fast modem is only profitable if a correspondingly fast modem is at the other end of the phone line. A data connection is limited by the highest speed of the slower modem in the link.

Modem speeds are expressed as bits per second (bps). This indicates the number of binary digits (bits) that the modem produces during a given period of time (each second). A few years ago, the fastest modems were capable of 2400 bps; now you find them moving data at 28,800 bps, or 12 times faster. The amazing thing is that today's top-of-the-line modems cost no more (and are sometimes cheaper) than their slower ancestors!

In the world of data communications, high modem speeds are accomplished by building the modem to conform to published standards or protocols. These protocols are developed by the International Telecommunications Union — Telecommunications sector (ITU-T), which has international responsibility for developing and maintaining standards for telegraphic and telephone equipment (including modems and fax machines). Thus, V.34 is a specific standard developed by the committee and adhered to by the data communications industry.

The standards developed by the ITU-T are known as *modulation standards*. This means that the standards cover more than just modem speed — they cover how the speed is to be attained. The standards are very technical and intended for engineering audiences. Table 4-1 shows some standards that the ITU-T developed for modulation standards.

Table 4-1 Modulation Standards Developed by the ITU-T	
Standard	**Data Rate, bps**
V.21	300
V.22	1200
V.22 bis	2400
V.23	1200
V.32	9600
V.32 bis	14,400
V.34	28,800

Notice the term *bis* after some ITU-T standard designations. This identifies which version of the particular standard is being referenced. The term *bis* is French for *second;* thus, V.22 bis is the second version of the V.22 standard. Also, as you look at Table 4-1, remember that the ITU-T standards represent more than just modem speed. Thus you see several standards that have the same data rates. The standards differ, however, in how the data rates are achieved.

The other item that affects the speed at which the modem communicates information is the UART it uses. Older UARTs, such as those used in early PCs, cannot handle the demanding requirements of high-speed data communications. The newer UARTs, such as the 16550A, are designed to be very efficient under high-speed conditions. The problem, however, is that once you have the UART, you must also have the software that engages the high-end capabilities of the UART. (That is, you must be able to kick it into overdrive.)

Fortunately, Windows 95 supports the use of the high-speed 16550A UART. The only thing you must do is make sure you purchase a modem that includes this chip. If you purchase a 28,800-bps modem, or even one that performs at 14,400 bps, chances are good that it includes a 16550A. If you purchase a slower-speed modem, the inclusion of such a chip is questionable.

Error correction

When you are communicating with a distant computer, you want error-free communication. In the early days of data communications, software handled error detection and correction. While it is still possible to find data communications software that incorporates error correction, it is much more efficient to implement these features into your hardware — in the modem.

The first hardware-based error detection and correction algorithms were introduced in the modems produced by Microcom, Inc. These protocols were known by the names MNP-2, MNP-3, and MNP-4. Each protocol was designed for modems operating at different speeds, and they became so popular that they were incorporated into many different types of modems (not just those from Microcom).

WHAT CAN
GO WRONG

External modem blues

You just got a brand new external modem that boasts 28,800 bps, and you plug it into your system. You transfer a few files and notice that the modem is no faster than your older one, or you notice that the modem port locks up. What the heck is going on?

Chances are good that you have an unseen bottleneck inside your computer. When you use an external modem, the serial port into which you plug the modem must match or exceed the capabilities of the modem itself. If it doesn't, then while you may have a new modem that is analogous to a steam shovel, you are putting information into the steam shovel using a teaspoon. The only solution is either to use an internal modem (which bypasses your internal serial ports) or to upgrade your serial port. New serial ports are relatively inexpensive, and you can find them at your local computer store or from a mail-order business. Before you purchase, however, make sure the new serial card also includes a 16550A UART.

A competing error-correction protocol was introduced by Hayes Microcomputer Products for use in its modems. This protocol, referred to as *link-access protocol — modem* (LAP-M), is incompatible with MNP-2–4 because it relies on a different algorithm. The protocol was originally developed by the CCITT (the predecessor to the ITU-T) but was not widely used in the United States outside of the Hayes product line.

In 1989, the ITU-T recognized the popularity of the MNP-2–4 protocols by introducing an error-correction standard that encompassed not only its own LAP-M, but also MNP-2–4. This became known as the V.42 standard and is used in many modems today. If a modem uses V.42, then it first attempts to negotiate a connection with the remote modem that uses LAP-M. If a connection cannot be established (for instance, if the remote modem does not support LAP-M), then the modem tries to use MNP-2–4. If the remote modem does not have this capability, then the connection is established without error detection and correction.

Data compression
Many modems can compress data on the fly as well as perform error detection and correction. Data compression means that the modem analyzes the data being transmitted and removes redundant or predictable data using complex algorithms. At the other end of the connection, the information is decompressed, or restored to its original condition. Data compression is desirable in a modem because it can increase the effective throughput of a modem dramatically. Depending on the composition of the data being transmitted, compression ratios of nearly 2:1 can be achieved. This means that you can get the effective transmission speed of a 57-kbps modem from a 28,800-bps modem.

As with error detection and correction, there are several competing standards for data compression; unlike error detection and correction, there is no all-encompassing ITU-T standard in this area. The two competing protocols are again from Hayes Microcomputer Products (for use in its V-class modems) and from Microcom, Inc. The Hayes protocol is proprietary, but the Microcom protocol (MNP-5) is used in many different modems.

In 1989, the CCITT delivered an expanded version of the V.42 standard (called V.42 bis) that included data compression. This standard does not include either the Hayes protocol or MNP-5. It does, however, include the same error control capabilities inherent in the V.42 standard. V.42 bis relies on a data compression algorithm (Lempel-Ziv) that is similar to that used in popular data compression software such as PKZip.

What type of modem do you need?
To access the Internet, you need no particular modem. The entire market of modems is open to you (and that includes many modems). Selecting the best modem for your system can be tricky, and many features distinguish modems from each other. Often these features (such as internal versus external modem) appeal to your personal

preferences but have little to do with the performance of the modem. First focus on the performance-related issues. Once these are satisfied, the other features are icing on the cake.

You want the fastest modem you can afford. Most Internet providers have installed dial-up modems that are capable of 28,800-bps speeds. If you use a slower modem on these links, you mark time and allow your access charges to build. To understand this concept, a small explanation is in order.

In a PC, information is stored in bytes. Each byte contains eight data bits and is used to represent a single character, such as a number or letter. Groups of characters are used to form sentences, paragraphs, and entire documents. Bytes also store instructions that the computer executes as programs. Because bytes contain eight bits each, you might assume that a 9600-bps modem could transfer 1200 bytes of data ($9{,}600 \div 8$) every second. You would be wrong. In asynchronous communication, which is used in most PC-related communications links, framing bits are added to each character. These bits indicate the start and stop of transmitted data, thereby giving the receiving modem time to catch up with the data being transferred. These framing bits, often called start and stop bits, add two bits to each character. Thus, it takes ten bits to represent a single character.

This 10-bit rule means that a 9600-bps modem transfers roughly 960 characters every second. This is equivalent to 14–15 lines of straight text every second. While this may sound fast, remember that straight text is rarely transferred. If you are using your Internet connection to transfer a multimedia file (one that contains sound, graphics, or video), you easily have files that are several megabytes long. At 9600 bps, a 2MB file takes just under 37 minutes to transfer. If you pay your Internet provider $2.00 per hour, you spend $1.20 to transfer the file.

Now, if you use a 28,800-bps modem, you transfer information at 2,880 characters per second. You therefore download the same 2MB file in just over 12 minutes, racking up charges of only 40 cents. If you cut your online time in half by stepping up to a faster modem, you easily amortize the cost of the new equipment in a short time. (V.34 modems capable of 28,800-bps transfers are currently available for under $200.)

Installing the Modem

Once you have purchased your modem, the next step is to physically install it in your system. The steps you follow to do this vary, depending on whether you have an internal or external modem.

Internal modem

Adding an internal modem is a relatively painless task, depending on your affinity with computer systems. If you have never had the cover off your computer, and you don't feel comfortable with a screwdriver, you are wise to ask someone else to install your internal modem. If, on the other hand, you don't fit into this category, you can safely install the card yourself. (And don't be surprised if you are called by your friends to install their modems some day.) It is impossible to provide detailed steps for you, simply because all computer systems are not the same. It is possible, however, to provide general steps that should be readily adaptable to your situation. To install your internal modem, follow these steps:

1. Remove the modem from the packaging and give it the once over. You are examining the modem to become familiar with how it is laid out.

2. Look for any dip switches or jumpers on the modem. If you find any, you may need to change them. If you don't find any, consider yourself lucky, and proceed to Step 16. If you do find some, this means you need to set the COM port, I/O address, and IRQ used by the modem. Steps 3 through 15 are designed to help you figure out the values you should use with your system.

3. Start Windows 95 and right-click on the My Computer icon on your desktop. This displays a Context menu for the object.

4. From the Context menu, select Properties. This displays the System Properties dialog box.

5. Click on the Device Manager tab. The System Properties dialog box now appears similar to what is shown in Figure 4-1.

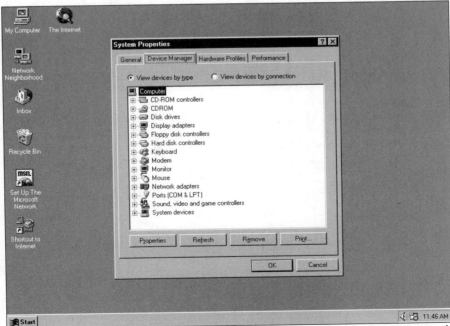

Figure 4-1: The System Properties dialog box, after clicking on the Device Manager tab.

6. About two-thirds of the way down the device list, you should find an item entitled Ports (COM & LPT). Click on the plus sign to the left of this item. The device list expands to show the ports in your system; two or three ports probably will be listed.

7. Double-click on the COM1 port entry. This displays the Communications Port Properties dialog box.

8. Click on the Resources tab. The Communications Port Properties dialog box now appears similar to what is shown in Figure 4-2.

9. On a piece of paper, note the settings shown in the Resource settings area of the dialog box. You should note both the Input/Output Range and the Interrupt Request. Also indicate in your note the COM port that this applies to (shown in the title bar for the dialog box).

10. Close the Communications Port Properties dialog box.

11. Repeat Steps 7 through 10 for each of the other COM ports in your system. For instance, if the Device Manager shows a second or third COM port, repeat the steps for each of those ports.

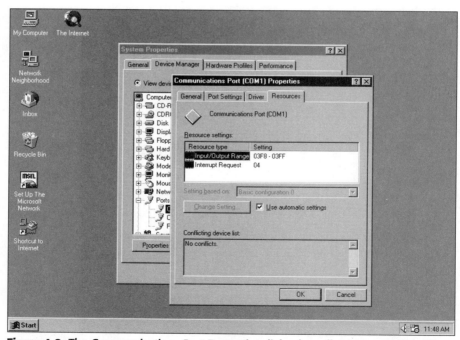

Figure 4-2: The Communications Port Properties dialog box allows you to determine the current system settings.

12. Take a look at the note you made in Step 9. This note indicates the resources in use on your system. You must now select a different COM port to use for your new modem. Select a COM port that is not currently defined within your system from the possibilities of COM1 through COM4.

13. Open the manual that came with your modem and find the section on configuration. This should include diagrams and charts that indicate the functions of the dip switches and jumpers.

14. In the manual, find the proper settings for the COM port you have decided on. These will be shown in a table somewhere; the table should indicate the proper jumper or dip switch settings.

15. Change the jumpers or dip switches on the modem to match those required for the COM port you want to use. Make sure you set the input/output range and IRQ settings to match those suggested for the COM port you have selected.

16. Shut down Windows 95 and turn off your computer. Unplug the computer from the wall outlet and disconnect all cables from the back of the unit.

17. Remove the screws that secure the computer's cover. Typically, there are from three to six screws around the perimeter of the computer case.

18. Remove the computer cover, making sure that you don't snag and break or disconnect any wires in the process.

19. Inside your computer, locate an empty expansion slot. You can identify an expansion slot because other computer cards are probably plugged into the other slots in your system.

20. Remove the cover plate for the expansion slot from the computer case at the back of the computer. There should be a single screw holding the cover plate.

21. Carefully insert the modem card into an expansion slot. Use firm, even pressure to fully seat the card within the expansion slot.

22. Use the screw removed in Step 20 to secure the modem card to the computer case. You should be able to easily access the modem connections from the rear of your computer system.

23. Replace the cover, securing it with the screws that you removed in Step 17.

24. Reconnect the cables and power cord that you removed in Step 16. Also, plug in a phone cord from your new modem's line or wall connector to the nearest phone jack.

25. Start up your computer system, and use the Device Manager (see Steps 3 through 5) to ensure that the new COM port used by the modem is recognized by your system.

If all has gone well, you have successfully installed your internal modem. (And to think it only took 25 steps!) Your next step involves letting Windows 95 know that you have a new modem on board. This is covered in a later section.

WHAT CAN GO WRONG

Dueling COM ports

If, when you later attempt to use your modem, you find that you either see garbage on the screen or your mouse won't work, then you obviously have a problem. The problem is caused by the way most PC systems use IRQs for COM ports. Although you can install up to four COM ports in your system (COM1 through COM4), there are some inherent conflicts between different ports.

Even though all the COM ports use different input/output ranges, they don't use different IRQs. On many PC systems, COM1 and COM3 use the same IRQ, while COM2 and COM4 use the same IRQ. The secret to peaceful cohabitation is to make sure that you don't want to use the devices on COM1 and COM3 (or those on COM2 and COM4) at the same time. For instance, if you have your mouse on COM1 and your modem on COM3, you cannot use them at the same time. When the modem on COM3 generates an interrupt on its IRQ, the mouse driver may think it was the mouse on COM1 that did the interrupting and vice versa. To say the least, confusion reigns.

To solve the problem, make sure that the devices you will be using at the same time are not using the same IRQ. For instance, if your mouse is on COM1, install your modem on COM2 or on COM4.

Note

An entire book section could be written on picking a COM port and an IRQ number. If, after following these instructions, you cannot get your modem to work, you may need more detailed instructions. I suggest investing in a book geared toward upgrading or repairing your computer system. These books are very helpful when it comes to resolving resource conflicts. As an alternative, you may want to contact a computer technician to install the modem for you.

External modem

Compared to adding an internal modem, adding an external one is a breeze. Virtually anyone can add an external modem. All you need to do is follow these steps:

1. Remove the modem from the packaging and look it over. Typically, you see the modem, a power adapter, and a phone cable. The package may also include a modem cable to connect the modem to the PC. If it does not, you need to get such a cable from your local computer store. Make sure that you let them know it is to connect a modem; that identifies the type of cable you require.

2. Position the modem close to your computer. Most external modems are made to be placed either on top of the computer (if the computer is a floor model) or beside the computer (if it is a desk model).

3. Plug the modem cable into the back of your computer. The cable should plug into either a 25-pin serial connector or a 9-pin serial connector. (If you have one type of cable and another type of serial port, you may need to use an adapter that is available at your local computer store.)

4. Plug the other end of the modem cable into the back of your modem. There should be only one place on the modem where the cable fits properly.

5. Plug a phone cord from your new modem's line or wall connector into the nearest phone jack.

6. Plug the power adapter into the modem and into a wall receptacle. Turn on the modem's power switch to verify its operation.

That's it! You have installed your external modem, and you are ready to let Windows 95 know that you have done so. This process is covered in detail in the following section.

Adding the Modem to Windows 95

Now that you have physically added the modem to your system, you need to let Windows 95 know what you have done. Depending on your system, this may involve adding device drivers that are compatible with the operating system.

Windows 95 makes it easy to add a modem to your system. In fact, it is much easier to do in Windows 95 than in previous versions of Windows. If you have a new computer system that features plug-and-play compatibility and your new modem is also plug-and-play compatible (and internal), plug in the modem and skip most of the rest of this chapter — Windows 95 recognizes the modem and sets it up for you automatically.

Most people don't have such a dream system, however. If you're in that category, you need to go through a series of steps to let Windows 95 know you have added the modem. This is easy to do, however. Follow these steps:

1. Choose Settings from the Start menu. This displays the Settings menu.

2. From the Settings menu, choose the Control Panel option. This displays the Control Panel.

3. Double-click on the Modems icon. This displays the Modems Properties dialog box, as shown in Figure 4-3.

4. If your modem name already appears in the list of modems installed on your computer, then you don't need to do anything further. Only complete the remaining steps if your modem is not listed.

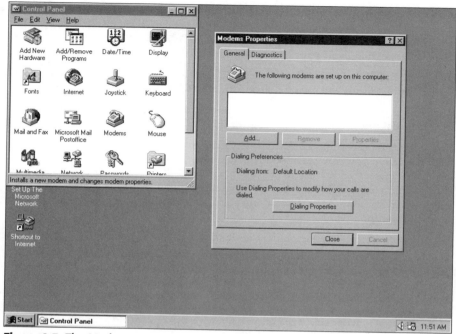

Figure 4-3: The Modems Properties dialog box is where you inform Windows 95 what modems are attached to your system.

5. To add your new modem, click on the <u>A</u>dd button. You see the Install New Modem dialog box, as shown in Figure 4-4. This is the first dialog box in a Wizard that Windows 95 uses expressly for setting up modems.

6. Click on the Next button. This instructs the Wizard to start searching for your new modem. This process may take a while, but when it is complete, you see the Verify Modem dialog box, similar to what is shown in Figure 4-5. Remember, the name of the modem shown in the dialog box will differ, depending on what you have installed.

7. If the modem shown in the Verify Modem dialog box is not the modem that you have installed (for some strange reason), click on the <u>C</u>hange button and select your modem from the list offered.

If a modem has never been installed on your system, you may see a dialog box asking you information about where you are located, what your area code is, and whether you need to dial a number for an outside line. You only see this dialog box once — when you have never installed a modem. The values you supply in this dialog box are dialing properties; they are discussed more fully in the "Setting dialing properties" section later in this chapter.

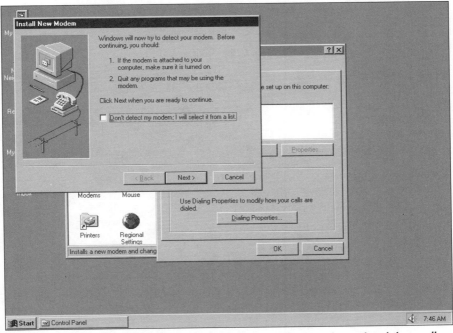

Figure 4-4: The Install New Modem dialog box is the first step in a Wizard that walks you through adding your modem.

WHAT CAN
GO WRONG

Little lost modem

Most of the time, if the modem installation Wizard can communicate with your modem, it determines what type of modem you have. If the Wizard cannot determine the modem type, it means one of several things. First, you may have a modem that is so new, it is one that Windows 95 can't pin down. In such an instance, you need to either use a compatible modem definition in Windows 95 or get a configuration disk from the manufacturer. (Some modems are compatible with other modems. If this is the case for your modem, you should be able to find such information in the modem documentation.)

If you can determine that your modem is, indeed, in the modem list that Windows 95 can recognize, then there is some problem with your modem installation, because Windows 95 cannot communicate with the modem. Check the simple things first. For instance, if the modem is external, is it turned on and is the proper cable used to connect the modem to the proper ports? If the modem is internal, you may need to again work through the installation steps presented earlier in this chapter.

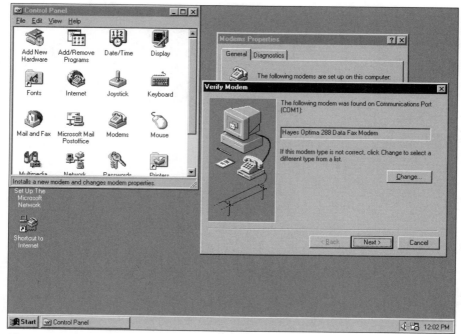

Figure 4-5: The Verify Modem dialog box indicates the type of modem detected by Windows 95.

8. Click on the Next button, and you see the final dialog box for the installation Wizard. (See Figure 4-6.) This dialog box informs you that Windows has finished installing the modem.

9. Click on the Finish button to end the Wizard. You are returned to the Modems Properties dialog box, as shown in Figure 4-3. The only difference is that your new modem is now listed in the modems installed in Windows 95.

Changing modem properties

In Windows 95, objects have *properties* that define how they are to be treated and how they relate to the system. Modems are no exception; they also have properties. In most cases, you never have to change the properties of your modem once it is installed. When would you think about changing them? Typically only if you want to change the default operational settings for the modem. To change modem properties, you follow these steps:

1. Choose Settings from the Start menu. This displays the Settings menu.

2. From the Settings menu, choose the Control Panel option. This displays the Control Panel.

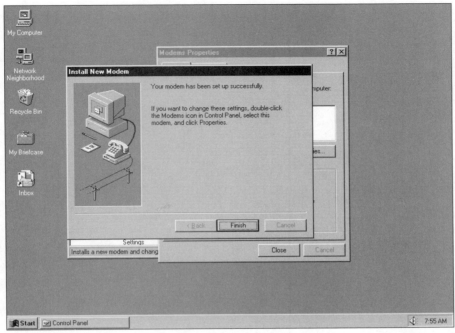

Figure 4-6: The final dialog box in the installation Wizard states that you have successfully installed your modem.

3. Double-click on the Modems icon. This displays the Modems Properties dialog box, as shown in Figure 4-3.

4. From the list of installed modems, select the modem whose properties you want to change.

5. Click on the Properties button. This displays the Properties dialog box for the specific modem. An example of such a dialog box is shown in Figure 4-7.

The Properties dialog box shown for an individual modem is tailored to that modem. While some properties are applicable to a variety of modems, other properties are unique. The properties you can set using the tabs within this dialog box include the following items:

✦ **Port.** This setting indicates the system port to which the modem is connected. If you are using an internal modem, the information for this item must match the port for which the modem is configured. If you have an external modem, then this setting should match the port to which your modem cable is connected.

✦ **Speaker volume.** Most modems have a speaker that allows you to hear the progress of a call. This setting allows you to set the speaker's volume.

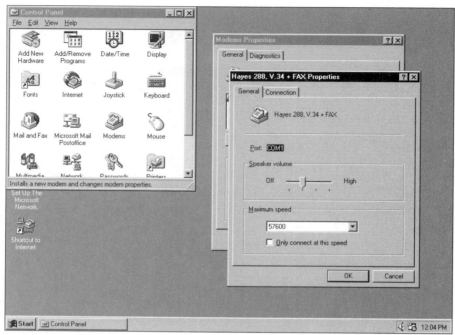

Figure 4-7: Windows 95 allows you to modify properties assigned to an individual modem.

✦ **Maximum speed.** This setting is determined when you first install your modem, and it specifies the fastest speed that information can be passed to your modem. Change this parameter to a lower value if you want to limit the speed at which the modem operates; change it to a higher value only if you are sure your port and modem can handle that speed.

✦ **Data parameters.** The three settings (data bits, parity, and stop bits) refer to the framing bits used in asynchronous modems. (The purpose of these bits was defined earlier in this chapter.) The setting you make here is the default; you can still change these parameters for the type of system with which you are connecting.

✦ **Call preferences.** These settings control items such as whether the modem should wait for a dial tone before dialing, how long the modem should let the phone ring (at the other end) before giving up, and how long a connection can stay open with no activity.

✦ **Error control.** These settings allow you to specify whether the modem should use its built-in error control and data compression features as described earlier in the chapter.

✦ **Flow control.** This determines how communication between your computer and the modem is regulated. Flow control is sometimes necessary to stop the transmission for a short time until the information that was already sent can be fully processed.

In addition, you may be able to set other miscellaneous properties that are unique to your modem. Again, if Windows 95 recognized your modem correctly when it installed it, you should be able to operate the modem successfully without changing the parameters. Change them only if you want your modem to function in a nonstandard manner.

Setting dialing properties

Dialing properties affect all modems in your system; these are the attributes by which Windows 95 dials a modem from a particular location. You need to set up your dialing properties for all the places where you may be using this copy of Windows 95. If you are using a desktop system, you probably only need to set the properties for the single location where you have the machine installed. If you are on the road with a mobile computer, then you should set up dialing properties for each location from which you may use your modem. For example, using the modem from your office may require you to dial 9 before dialing the number, and when on the road you may want to dial using a credit card. Setting dialing properties means that you configure Windows 95 for all the places from which you may place a modem call.

To change the dialing properties, follow these steps:

1. Choose Settings from the Start menu. This displays the Settings menu.

2. From the Settings menu, choose the Control Panel option. This displays the Control Panel.

3. Double-click on the Modems icon. This displays the Modems Properties dialog box, as shown in Figure 4-3.

4. At the bottom of the dialog box, click on the Dialing Properties button. You see the Dialing Properties dialog box, as shown in Figure 4-8.

Notice that at the top of the dialog box, you define where you are located, and at the bottom, you indicate how to make a call from that location. If you don't move your computer around, you simply make the changes for the Default Location. If you want to define additional dialing locations, click on the New button, provide a location name, and then make your changes.

There are only a few items that you need to set up for each dialing location. The first is the area code that applies to the location as well as the country in which the location is situated. At the bottom of the dialog box, you specify how your modem calls should be made from that location. The first option allows you to indicate any special numbers that must be dialed to get an outside line (for both local and long distance calls). This is handy if you are in an office or a hotel where you must first dial a number to secure a line.

The second option, Dial using Calling Card, allows you to use a company (or personal) credit card for the calls. There is quite a bit to using this property, so I discuss it in a moment.

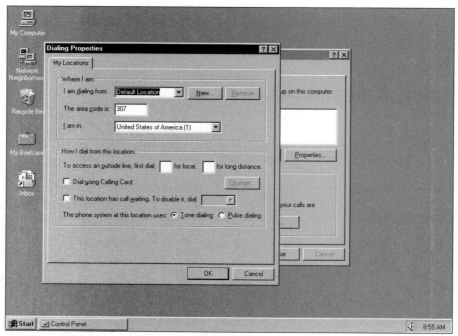

Figure 4-8: The Dialing Properties dialog box allows you to define how Windows 95 should dial the phone in different locations.

The third option allows you to specify how Windows 95 should handle the call-waiting feature on your phone. Many people get call waiting, especially for use at home, where they may only have a single line. The problem with call waiting, however, is that it can play havoc with a modem connection. The click you hear, indicating that another call is coming in, disconnects a modem. Different phone systems have various codes that you use to disable call waiting. If you select this property and enter the code (which you get from your phone book or the phone company), then Windows 95 disables call waiting whenever it places a modem call.

The final option in this dialog box allows you to indicate what type of signaling your phone understands. Most phones in the United States use tone dialing, but some lines do not. You cannot tell which setup you have by looking at your telephone. The easiest way is to listen to your phone as you dial a call. If you hear a series of different-pitch tones, then you have tone dialing. If you hear a series of clicks, then you have pulse dialing. While you can use pulse dialing on a tone-dial line (even if it is slower), the reverse is not true. If you attempt to use tone dialing when your phone line is set up for pulse dialing, then you will not be able to complete the call.

Now, back to the issue of calling cards. Windows 95, unlike previous versions of the operating system, allows you to specify calling cards with which calls can be made. This is a great boon to travelers or those who make modem calls regularly while on the road. You can configure Windows 95 to dial any sequence of numbers necessary (including credit card numbers) in order to establish a modem connection.

To specify calling card information, enable the Dial using Calling Card property. Immediately, you see the Change Calling Card dialog box, as shown in Figure 4-9. At the top of the dialog box, you should select the calling card that you want to use. Windows 95 comes with 22 different calling cards defined, and you can add more if you desire by clicking on the New button.

Once you have selected the calling card that you want to use, you enter your calling card number in the appropriate field. When you are satisfied with the settings, click on the OK button, and your information is changed.

Remember that a calling card allows anyone to charge phone calls to you, and there is a good chance that you will have to pay for these calls. If you use a mobile computer and other people may later use the same computer, delete your calling card information before passing on the computer.

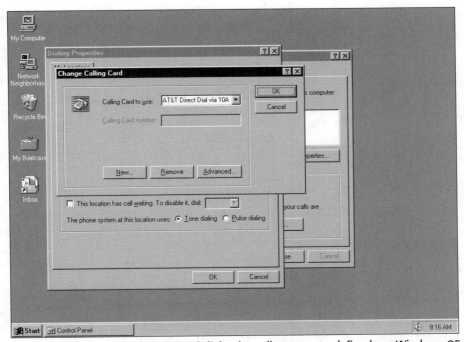

Figure 4-9: The Change Calling Card dialog box allows you to define how Windows 95 uses your calling card.

Performing Modem Diagnostics

The final step in installing your modem is to make sure it is functioning properly. Use the built-in diagnostics that Windows 95 provides for modems. These diagnostics are nothing exciting, but they do a good job of making sure that Windows 95 can at least communicate with the modem. To use the diagnostics, follow these steps:

1. Choose Settings from the Start menu. This displays the Settings menu.

2. From the Settings menu, choose the Control Panel option. This displays the Control Panel.

3. Double-click on the Modems icon. This displays the Modems Properties dialog box, as shown in Figure 4-3.

4. Click on the Diagnostics tab. The Modems Properties dialog box now appears similar to what is shown in Figure 4-10.

The number of ports shown in the dialog box may be different on your system, as is the indication of what is connected to each port. To test your modem, click on the port associated with the modem you want to test. Thus, in Figure 4-10, you would make sure that COM1 is highlighted. Next, click on the More Info button. This causes Windows 95 to attempt to communicate with the modem. (If you have an external

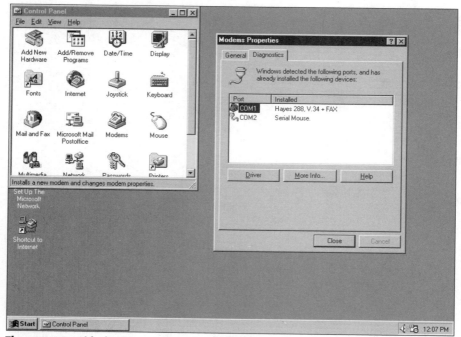

Figure 4-10: With the Diagnostics tab selected, you are ready to test your modem connection.

modem, you should see the modem lights start flashing.) After a short time, you should see a new dialog box, which indicates the results of the testing. Figure 4-11 shows an example of such a dialog box.

If your dialog box does not show information about the identity of the modem or a list of commands and responses at the bottom of the dialog box, then Windows 95 could not communicate with the modem. If this is the case, you must determine the problem with your modem. Try the following steps to correct the problem:

1. If you are using an external modem, make sure it is turned on.

2. Sometimes the cable used for external modems may come loose. Check the cable to make sure that it is securely fastened to both the computer and the modem.

3. If you have an external modem, make sure that the cable you are using to connect it to the computer is a modem cable. With most modems, you cannot use a standard serial cable; you must use a modem cable. Check the cable, replacing it if necessary.

4. If you are using an internal modem, use the Device Manager (described earlier in this chapter) to make sure that there are no conflicts between the modem configuration and the settings on other devices in your system. Check port designations, input/output ranges, and IRQ assignments.

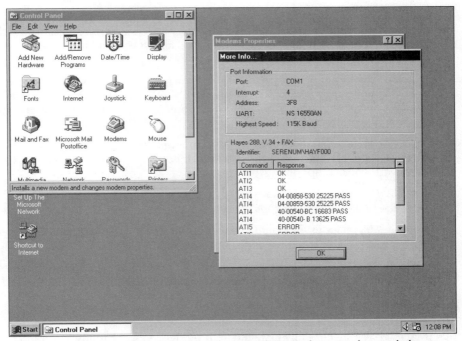

Figure 4-11: The More Info dialog box displays what Windows 95 detected about your modem.

After attempting to correct the problem, restart Windows 95 and try the diagnostics again. If the modem still does not work, you may have a defective modem. The only way to tell is to take your system to a technician or to use a modem that you know works on another system. You may also want to use any diagnostics software provided with the modem, or refer to the modem documentation for assistance.

Summary

Data communication is a wonderful computing area. At times, it can seem quite bewildering, with all of the specialized terms and conflicting standards that you can run into. Nevertheless, more people are making the leap and connecting their computers to other systems via phone lines.

This chapter provides the information you need to understand, select, install, and configure a modem with Windows 95. You learn the following items:

✦ Serial communication is a specific type of data communication over a serial connection. This term describes virtually all communications using a modem.

✦ Modems work by changing the internal digital signals used by your computer into analog signals that can be transmitted over the public phone system. At the other end of the connection, a modem again converts the analog signal back into digital information.

✦ Modem capabilities are most often defined by speed, error correction, and data compression. Most high-speed modems available today include impressive features in all these areas.

✦ When choosing a modem, you should get the fastest one you can while making sure it supports the widest variety of established data communications standards. The faster your modem, the lower your access charges are when connecting to the Internet.

✦ Installing an internal modem is easy if the modem is plug-and-play compatible. If it is not, there are specific steps you must follow to configure the modem to work with your computer system.

✦ Installing an external modem typically involves getting the proper cable and connecting the modem to your computer using the cable.

✦ Windows 95 includes a modem installation Wizard that can automatically detect the type of modem you have and set up your system to use it.

✦ You can use the diagnostic capabilities of Windows 95 to test the communications channel between your computer and modem. If the channel is working, you are ready to go; if not, you must resolve the problem and make sure the modem works properly.

Now that you have successfully installed your modem, you are ready to set up Windows 95 so that it works properly with the Internet. In Chapter 5, you do just that.

✦   ✦   ✦

CHAPTER 5

Configuring Windows 95 for the Internet

You have installed your modem and made account arrangements with an Internet provider. You are ready to access the Internet, right? Wrong. You must accomplish a few more items before you connect for the first time. The biggest remaining item is to configure Windows 95 so that it can communicate with the Internet.

You have learned that the Internet is a huge network of computer networks, all communicating with each other using a protocol called TCP/IP. In this chapter, you discover how to set up your system to talk the same language as the Internet. Here you learn the following items:

+ What a dial-up adapter is and why you need to add it to your system

+ How to install the TCP/IP protocols

+ How to configure TCP/IP by setting the protocol properties

+ How to add SLIP support to Windows 95

The information in this chapter is applicable if you are connecting to the Internet through a PPP or SLIP account. If you are using some other type of account, or if you are connecting only through The Microsoft Network, then you can safely skip this chapter. However, as has been mentioned earlier, you achieve the best Internet performance when you establish a PPP or SLIP account and configure your system to work directly with the Internet.

Adding the Dial-Up Adapter

Before you can connect to any network, you must have certain things in your system. These items work together to provide the connectivity you require. In Windows 95, three items are necessary:

✦ A network adapter

✦ A network protocol

✦ A network client

The *network adapter* is typically a physical network interface card that you install in your system. (This item is discussed more in just a moment.) A *network protocol* is necessary because it forms the instructions that Windows 95 follows when communicating over the network. The protocol you need to install is discussed in the next section. Finally, *network clients* are programs that make resources on your system available to other workstations on the network. For instance, network clients allow you to share your disk drives or printers with other people in your workgroup.

Even if you are not physically connected to a network, you connect to a network when you connect to the Internet. To connect, you need to meet all the criteria described here for normal network connections. Does this mean that you need to purchase and install a network adapter in your system? No, not necessarily. If you want to communicate with other computers in a local area network, then you need such an adapter. To connect to the Internet through a modem, however, you use a logical network adapter instead of a physical one; you use a *dial-up adapter.*

Windows 95 includes configuration information for many different network adapters. Most of these are geared toward working with adapter cards that you physically plug into your system. One unique addition to Windows 95, however, is the ability to use a dial-up adapter. This adapter does not represent a physical device but instead represents a logical network connection made through a modem — a dial-up link. To install the dial-up adapter, follow these steps:

1. Choose Settings from the Start menu. This displays the Settings menu.

2. From the Settings menu, choose the Control Panel option. This displays the Control Panel.

3. Double-click on the Network icon. This displays the Network dialog box, as shown in Figure 5-1. You should note that you may have entirely different network components installed on your system, or you may have none at all. If one of the network components listed is Dial-Up Adapter, then you can skip the rest of these steps; you already have the proper component installed.

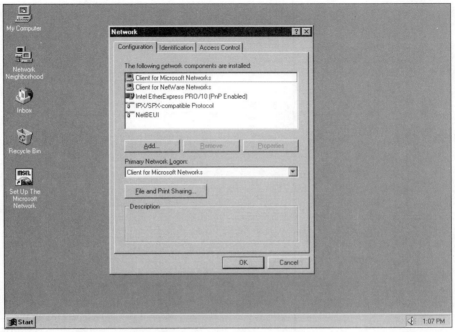

Figure 5-1: The Network dialog box is where you configure Windows 95 to work with various network setups.

4. Click on the Add button. This displays a dialog box where you can select what type of network component you are installing.

5. Since you are installing the dial-up adapter, click on the Adapter option. This makes the Add button accessible.

6. Click on the Add button, and you see the Select Network adapters dialog box, as shown in Figure 5-2.

7. Scroll through the Manufacturers list until you see the Microsoft option displayed. Select Microsoft as the manufacturer you want by clicking on the option. The choices in the Network Adapters list should change.

8. In the Network Adapters list, select Dial-Up Adapter (this may be the only option in the list).

9. Click on the OK button.

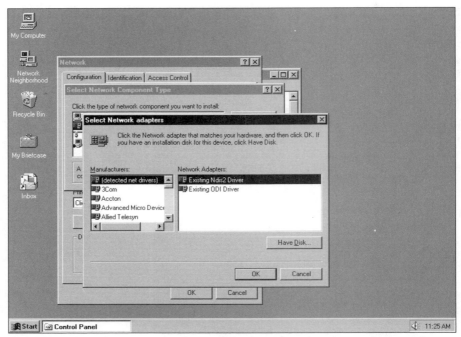

Figure 5-2: The Select Network adapter dialog box is used to choose the type of adapter you want to add to your system.

At this point, you have successfully installed the dial-up adapter, and it should show up in the network components list of the Network dialog box (see Figure 5-1). If it does not show up, then repeat the steps for installing the adapter.

Assuming that your dial-up adapter is installed (it is listed in the network components list), you are ready to proceed with adding the TCP/IP protocol. Don't close the Network dialog box; you start from this point in the next section.

Installing TCP/IP Protocols

Installing the dial-up adapter is only half of the story; you also need to tell Windows 95 how you want to communicate with other computers through the adapter. You do this by installing a network protocol that is used by the network to which you are connecting. With the Internet, that protocol is TCP/IP. (Refer to Chapter 2 for further discussion of the TCP/IP protocol.)

To install the TCP/IP protocol on your system, you need to start from the Network dialog box. (This should be visible from installing the dial-up adapter.) At the Network dialog box, follow these steps:

1. Click on the Add button. This again displays the dialog box where you can select what type of network component you are installing. (See Figure 5-3.)

2. Since you are installing TCP/IP, which is a network protocol, click on the Protocol option. This makes the Add button accessible.

3. Click on the Add button, and you see the Select Network Protocol dialog box, as shown in Figure 5-4.

4. In the Manufacturers list at the left side of the dialog box, click on the Microsoft selection. The choices in the Network Protocols list should change, showing four options.

5. In the Network Protocols list, click on the TCP/IP option.

6. Click on the OK button.

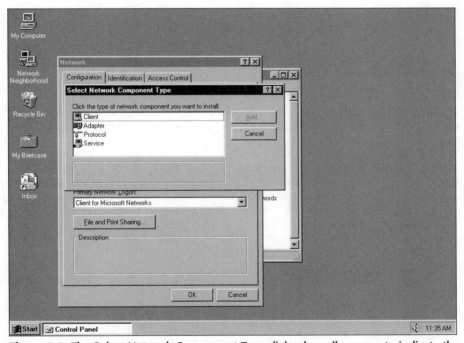

Figure 5-3: The Select Network Component Type dialog box allows you to indicate the category of network component that you want to add to your system.

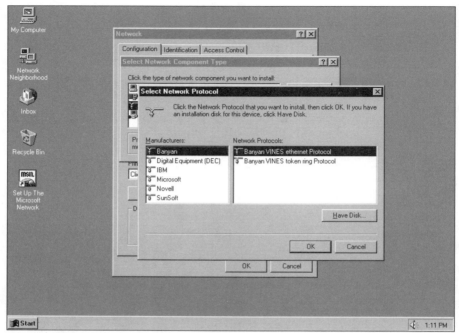

Figure 5-4: The Select Network Protocol dialog box is used to specify the type of language you want to use in your network connections.

At this point, Windows 95 adds the TCP/IP protocol. When you return to the Network dialog box, you should be able to scroll through the list of network components and see TCP/IP listed in the protocols section. Notice that you see a component entry for TCP/IP that uses the following notation:

TCP/IP —> Dial-Up Adapter

This simply means that TCP/IP has been installed, and it will be used through the dial-up adapter. This relationship between the protocol and the adapter is referred to as a *binding.* If you have other network adapters installed in your system, Windows 95 may also have bound TCP/IP to them. Unless you need that particular binding, you can delete it. Do this by selecting the protocol binding to be deleted (from the network component list) and then clicking on the Remove button. The binding is immediately removed, and the component list is updated.

When you are through adjusting any bindings, you should click on the OK button. You are informed that for your changes to be implemented, Windows 95 must be re-started. Go ahead and restart the system; when that is complete, you have installed all the components you need for your Internet connection to work properly.

Setting the TCP/IP Properties

Once you have added the dial-up adapter and the TCP/IP protocols, you still need to perform a couple of configuration changes to your system. These involve changing the TCP/IP properties. These properties define how your system should appear in relation to other systems on the Internet. You can change the properties by following these steps:

1. Choose Settings from the Start menu. This displays the Settings menu.
2. From the Settings menu, choose the Control Panel option. This displays the Control Panel.
3. Double-click on the Network icon. This displays the Network dialog box, as shown in Figure 5-1.
4. In the network components list, select the TCP/IP protocol that is bound to the dial-up adapter. This makes the Properties button accessible.
5. Click on the Properties button. This displays the TCP/IP Properties dialog box, as shown in Figure 5-5.

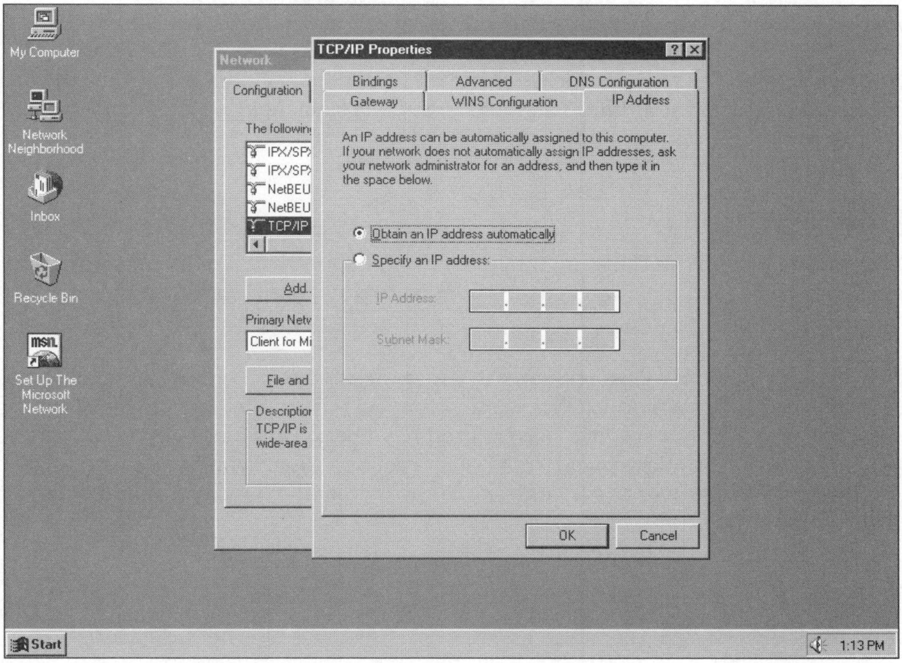

Figure 5-5: The TCP/IP Properties dialog box is where you specify what parameters should be used in connecting to a TCP/IP network.

Notice that there are six different tabs in the TCP/IP Properties dialog box. The options on each of these tabs define how your system interacts with the Internet. Remember in Chapter 3, where you need to ask your provider some specific questions (nine of them, to be exact)? Here is where you need the answers to several of those questions. Dig out your answers, and then work your way through the following sections to make sure you have your TCP/IP setup properly configured.

IP address

The IP Address tab is the one first selected when you open the TCP/IP Properties dialog box; it appears as shown in Figure 5-5. Here, you need to enter some of the addresses that you received from your Internet provider.

Notice that there are two main options in the dialog box. The first is Obtain an IP address from a DHCP server. You may remember from Chapter 2 that a DHCP server is used to dynamically assign IP addresses. Some Internet providers use DHCP servers, and some do not. If yours does, then you should make sure that this first option is selected. This causes Windows 95 to query the server, when the connection is first made, to determine what IP address to use.

If your provider does not use a DHCP server, it should have provided you with both an IP address for your system and a subnet mask. In this case, you should click on the Specify an IP address option, which makes the address boxes available. In the IP Address field, enter the IP address assigned to you by the provider. Enter the address carefully, one octet at a time. Then, in the Subnet Mask field, you can enter the mask specified by the provider.

Gateway

When you click on the Gateway tab, the TCP/IP Properties dialog box changes as shown in Figure 5-6. This tab is used to indicate the default routing gateways for your Internet provider.

Notice that the cursor (insertion point, for readers who are purists) is blinking in the New gateway field. Windows 95 is waiting for you to provide an IP address for a gateway. The address you use here should have been provided by your Internet provider. Enter the address carefully, one octet at a time. When you finish, click on the Add button. This moves the IP address to the Installed gateways list and clears the New gateway field.

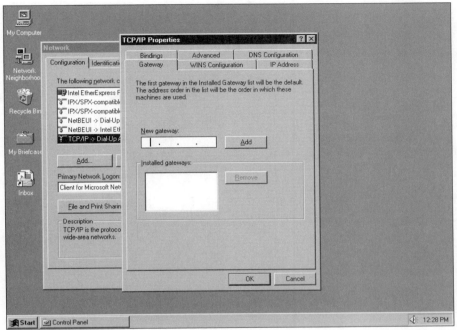

Figure 5-6: The Gateway tab in the TCP/IP Properties dialog box is used to specify the default mail gateway for your provider.

For most readers, you only need to supply a single gateway address. Some larger providers may have multiple gateway addresses that you could continue adding to the gateway list. If your provider gave you more than one gateway address, add each of them by entering the address and clicking on the Add button.

WINS configuration

You learn how WINS works in Chapter 2. Windows 95 supports WINS as a method of converting IP addresses to symbolic Microsoft network names. To configure your TCP/IP setup for WINS, click on the WINS Configuration tab. The TCP/IP Properties dialog box now appears as shown in Figure 5-7.

Support for WINS varies from one Internet provider to another. If the provider is running a Windows NT server, then it probably supports WINS. If it is running other types of servers (such as those based on UNIX), then it probably does not support WINS. If in doubt, check with your provider directly.

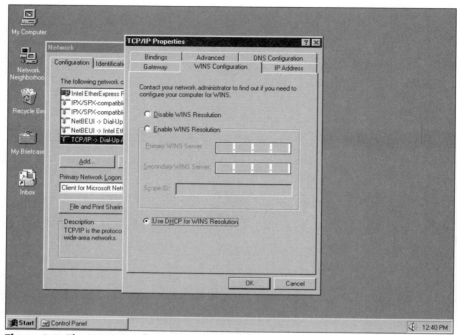

Figure 5-7: The WINS Configuration tab in the TCP/IP Properties dialog box is where you specify how Windows 95 should handle WINS.

Three main choices appear in the WINS Configuration tab. The first choice, Disable WINS Resolution, does just that — it turns off Windows 95 support for WINS entirely. You should turn this option off only if you are sure that your provider supports neither DHCP nor WINS.

The second choice, Enable WINS Resolution, forces WINS resolution at a specific location. You should choose this option only if your provider indicates the IP address of a WINS server. When you choose this option, you are able to enter the IP addresses for a primary and secondary server.

Finally, in most instances where DHCP is supported by the provider, you choose the third option, Use DHCP for WINS Resolution. This leaves it up to the DHCP negotiation to figure out if there is a WINS server, and if so, where it is located.

Bindings

You should remember from earlier in this chapter that bindings are relationships established between various protocols and other network components. When you click on the Bindings tab, you have an opportunity to change the components that use the TCP/IP protocol. With this tab selected, the TCP/IP Properties dialog box appears as shown in Figure 5-8.

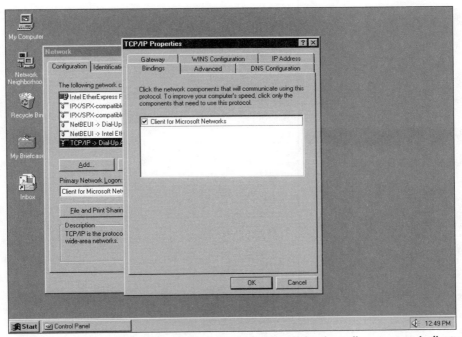

Figure 5-8: The Bindings tab in the TCP/IP Properties dialog box allows you to indicate which network components will use the TCP/IP protocol.

The number of components shown in the bindings list varies among machines. In most instances, you won't need to make any changes here. If you need to make changes at some time, these changes are relative to your local area network rather than to the Internet. At such a point, your network administrator is the one to specify which changes should be made.

Advanced

For a TCP/IP system, nothing really appears in the Advanced tab. When you select it, you have a single option — to set TCP/IP as the default protocol. You do not need to do this unless TCP/IP is also used as the protocol in your local area network. Again, check with your network administrator before you make any changes on the Advanced tab.

DNS configuration

The final configuration area is related to DNS — the domain naming system. You learn about this in Chapter 2. If you click on the DNS Configuration tab, the TCP/IP Properties dialog box appears as shown in Figure 5-9.

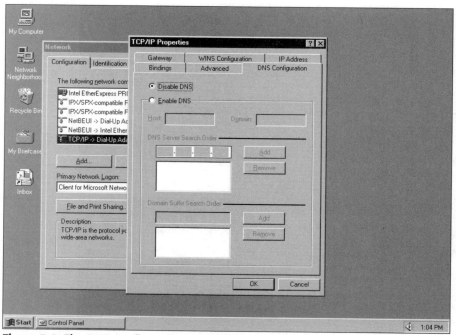

Figure 5-9: The DNS Configuration tab in the TCP/IP Properties dialog box provides a way for you to specify how Windows 95 should handle DNS name resolution.

Two options appear on this tab. The first option, Disable DNS, is the default setting. If you connect to an Internet provider with DNS disabled, you cannot use domain names to access Internet resources. For instance, you won't be able to use domain names with utilities like ftp or telnet. Instead, you would need to supply IP addresses for those utilities.

Because remembering and using IP addresses is a bother, it is best to choose the Enable DNS option. This allows you to then access the other options on the tab that control how the DNS server is located. To use DNS, you need to make only two settings. First, you need to supply your host and domain name. This is done, naturally, in the Host and Domain fields. For the host name, supply the first part of your e-mail address — the part to the left of the @ sign. For the domain name, use the part of your e-mail address that is to the right of the @ sign.

Next, you must supply the IP address of the DNS server you will use. This address should have been supplied to you by your Internet provider. In the DNS Server Search Order field, carefully enter the four octets of the DNS server's IP address. When you finish, click on the Add button to add the address to the list of DNS servers. If, for some reason, your provider gave you additional IP addresses for DNS servers, you can continue to enter them in the server list.

Adding SLIP Support

In Chapter 2, you learn about connection protocols such as SLIP and PPP. The former is an older technology but is still used on many systems. Even though more Internet providers are offering both SLIP and PPP support, you may want to use SLIP instead of PPP. Windows 95 provides support for both protocols, although only PPP support is installed automatically.

To add SLIP support, follow these steps:

1. Choose Settings from the Start menu. This displays the Settings menu.
2. From the Settings menu, choose the Control Panel option. This displays the Control Panel.
3. Double-click on the Add/Remove Programs icon. This displays the Add/Remove Programs Properties dialog box.
4. Select the Windows Setup tab. The Add/Remove Programs Properties dialog box changes, as shown in Figure 5-10.

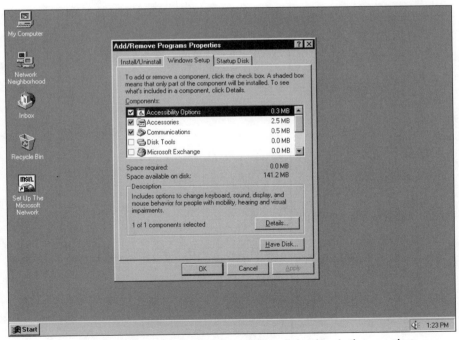

Figure 5-10: The Add/Remove Programs Properties dialog box is the way that you typically add and remove either applications or portions of Windows 95.

5. Click on the <u>H</u>ave Disk button at the bottom of the dialog box. This displays the Install From Disk dialog box.

6. Insert your Windows 95 CD-ROM, and in the Install From Disk dialog box, enter the path **E:\admin\apptools\dscript**. (If necessary, you should replace the E drive designator with the drive designator for your CD-ROM drive.)

7. Click on the OK button. You should now see the Have Disk dialog box, as shown in Figure 5-11.

8. The one component shown in the component list is the SLIP support for Dial-Up Networking. Select this component by clicking on the check box at the left of the component name.

9. Click on the <u>I</u>nstall button. The SLIP support is installed, and you are returned to the Add/Remove Programs Properties dialog box.

10. Click on OK or Cancel to close the dialog box.

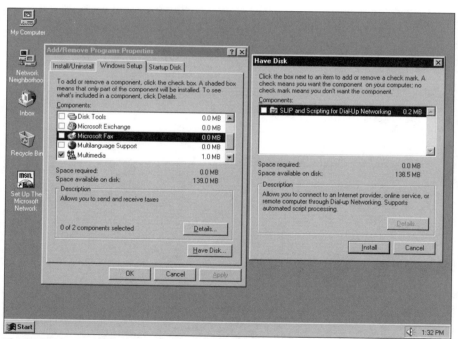

Figure 5-11: Installing the SLIP support in Windows 95 is fairly straightforward.

Summary

For your individual system to get along with the rest of the world (as embodied in the Internet), a bit of configuration work is necessary. In particular, you need to install the proper network components to make your system work with the Net. This chapter walks you through the process that is necessary to do this. Here you learn the following items:

✦ If you are going to use a dial-up Internet account with either SLIP or PPP, you must install the dial-up adapter. This is a logical network adapter that allows you to use the proper protocols through the modem link that you establish with your Internet provider.

✦ TCP/IP is the lingua franca of the Internet. It is used for all communication between your system, the provider's system, and every other system on the Net. You can install TCP/IP by adding it as a network protocol in the Network portion of the Control Panel.

✦ Before the TCP/IP protocols that you installed can take effect, you must modify the properties for the protocol to reflect the parameters necessary for your provider. You need to change the settings related to DHCP, default gateways, and DNS servers. This information is covered in Chapter 2 and should be available from your Internet provider.

✦ Windows 95 can support SLIP, but it is not installed automatically when you install or configure Dial-Up Networking. Detailed instructions are provided for SLIP support on your system.

You have now configured your system to operate in the network environment of the Internet. You need only to complete one more step before you can make your first connection. In the next chapter, you learn how to define and configure Dial-Up Networking for your Internet provider.

✦   ✦   ✦

CHAPTER 6

Using Dial-Up Networking

Y ou already know that you are establishing a connection to the Internet through a remote system managed by your Internet provider. In previous versions of Windows, and in Windows NT, network communication through a modem link was handled by a feature called *Remote Access Service,* or RAS. In Windows 95, RAS has been replaced with *Dial-Up Networking.* While it provides many of the same features as RAS, the name of the service is much more descriptive.

This chapter introduces you to Dial-Up Networking. Here you learn how to use this tool to establish a communications link with your Internet provider. Specifically, you learn the following items:

- ✦ What Dial-Up Networking is and why it is used for Internet connections
- ✦ How to install Dial-Up Networking on your system
- ✦ How to set up Dial-Up Networking so that it works with your Internet provider
- ✦ How to rename and delete connection definitions

What Dial-Up Networking Does

Dial-Up Networking is a program that has two facets: It can function either as a server or a client. When functioning as a server, Dial-Up Networking allows remote users to dial into your computer and access it just as if they were connecting from another computer on the network. As a client, the roles reverse. In this case, Dial-Up Networking allows you to establish a communications link with a remote computer, and then you function as if you were connected to the system through a regular network.

Even though Dial-Up Networking can function as a server, that is not how you use the program when connecting to the Internet. Instead, you function as a client. Because the server portion of Dial-Up Networking is not germane to accessing the Internet, it is not covered in this book.

Using Dial-Up Networking, you can connect to a variety of other systems. The only requirement is that the system you connect to must be capable of supporting one of the connection protocols supported by Windows 95. The Dial-Up Networking client provided with Windows 95 allows you to connect to a server using any of the following connection protocols:

✦ Point-to-point protocol (PPP)

✦ Serial line Internet protocol (SLIP)

✦ Windows NT RAS

✦ Windows for Workgroups RAS

✦ Novell Netware Connect

Dial-Up Networking is not general-purpose communications software; it was never intended as such. Dial-Up Networking's purpose is to establish a network link over a modem line.

For establishing a dial-up Internet connection, you use Dial-Up Networking with either the PPP or SLIP protocols. Microsoft and many others recommend that you use PPP whenever possible, because it is the official new-and-improved method of running TCP/IP over a modem link.

Installing Dial-Up Networking

Unless you did a custom installation when you first installed Windows 95, Dial-Up Networking is not automatically installed by the Setup program. This means that if you did a typical or portable setup, you need your Windows 95 disks or CD-ROM at this point. To install Dial-Up Networking, follow these steps:

1. Choose Settings from the Start menu. This displays the Settings menu.

2. From the Settings menu, choose the Control Panel option. This displays the Control Panel.

3. Double-click on the Add/Remove Programs icon. This displays the Add/Remove Programs Properties dialog box.

4. Click on the Windows Setup tab. The Add/Remove Programs Properties dialog box now appears, as shown in Figure 6-1.

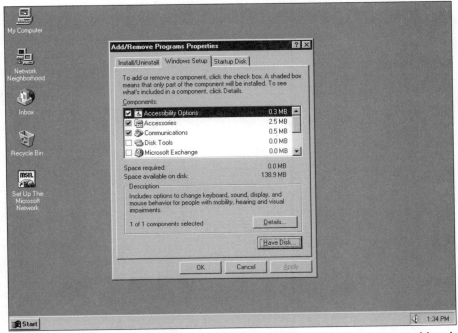

Figure 6-1: The Add/Remove Programs Properties dialog box is the way you add and remove portions of Windows 95.

5. At the top of the dialog box, click on the Communications component.

6. Click on the Details button at the bottom of the dialog box. You now see the Communications dialog box, as shown in Figure 6-2.

7. If a check mark appears next to the first component in the Communications dialog box (Dial-Up Networking), then Dial-Up Networking is installed on your system. If this is the case, click on the Cancel button in the Communications dialog box and then on the Cancel button in the Add/Remove Programs Properties dialog box.

8. If Dial-Up Networking has not been installed on your system, select the Dial-Up Networking check box in the Communications dialog box.

9. Click on OK in the Communications dialog box and then on OK in the Add/Remove Programs Properties dialog box. The proper files are copied from the Windows 95 CD-ROM or disks, and Dial-Up Networking is added to your system.

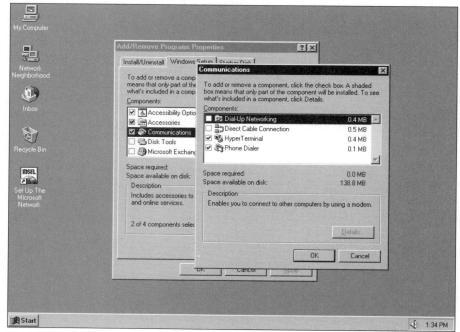

Figure 6-2: The details for the Communications portion of Windows 95 list four components.

Setting Up Dial-Up Networking

You will use Dial-Up Networking as a client process to connect to your Internet provider. To do this, you need to perform the following tasks:

✦ Start Dial-Up Networking for the first time.

✦ Create a connection definition.

✦ Configure your new connection definition.

Once these tasks are done properly, you are one phone call away from connecting to the Internet.

You can start Dial-Up Networking in two ways. The first is to double-click on the My Computer icon on your desktop. This displays objects defined within your system; one of those items is Dial-Up Networking. Double-click on the Dial-Up Networking icon, and the Dial-Up Networking window appears. You can also start Dial-Up Networking by selecting Programs from the Start menu, choosing Accessories, and finally selecting Dial-Up Networking.

Regardless of which way you start Dial-Up Networking, the program appears as another window on your desktop, similar to the Printers folder. Figure 6-3 shows what the Dial-Up Networking window looks like when you first open it.

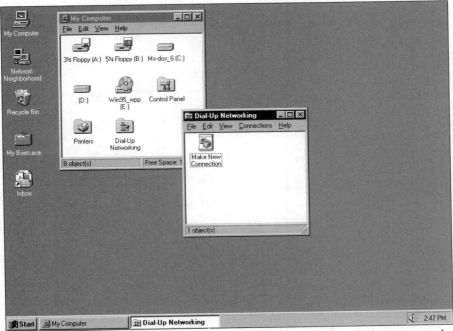

Figure 6-3: The Dial-Up Networking program looks like any other window on your desktop.

Notice that the Dial-Up Networking window contains an icon entitled Make New Connection, and nothing else. As you have learned, you use Dial-Up Networking by defining connections and then initiating a communication session according to those definitions.

Defining a dial-up connection

If you look back at Figure 6-3, you notice that the Dial-Up Networking window initially contains only an icon entitled Make New Connection. This icon runs a Wizard that guides you through creating a connection definition. Follow these steps to define a connection for your Internet provider:

1. Double-click on the Make New Connection icon in the Dial-Up Networking window. This starts the connection definition Wizard and displays the Make New Connection dialog box, as shown in Figure 6-4.

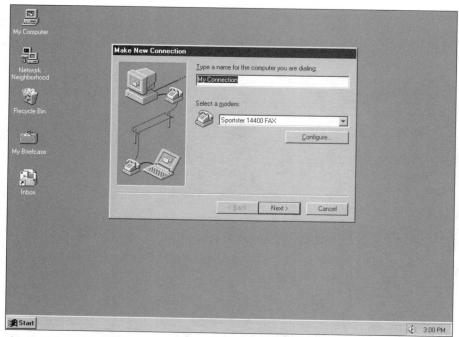

Figure 6-4: The Make New Connection dialog box is the start of the Wizard used for defining Dial-Up Networking connections.

2. In the field at the top of the dialog box, enter the name you want to use for this connection. The default value of My Connection should be changed to something descriptive, such as Internet. If you are going to have more than one Internet dial-up account, you may want something even more descriptive, such as the name of the Internet provider.

3. In the Select a modem field, choose the name of the modem you will use for this connection. You probably have only a single modem defined, and it is already the default in the field. If not, select the modem you defined in Chapter 4.

4. Click on the Next button. You see a dialog box asking you for phone number information about this connection. (See Figure 6-5.)

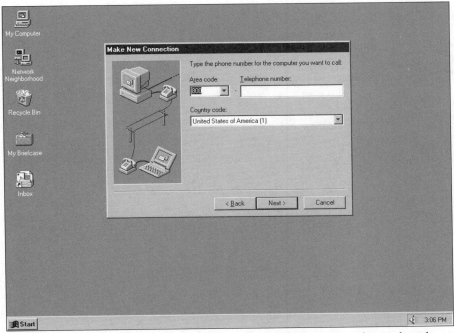

Figure 6-5: Part of a connection definition is providing information about what phone number to dial.

5. In the appropriate dialog box fields, enter the area code and phone number for your Internet provider. You should have received this information when you set up your account, as indicated in Chapter 3.

6. Click on the Next button, and you see the final dialog box for the Wizard, as shown in Figure 6-6.

7. Even though the name of your definition is highlighted in what appears to be a field at the top of the dialog box, you cannot edit it. The name is only shown here to remind you of the definition you are creating. To complete the definition, click on the Finish button. The definition is saved and appears in the Dial-Up Networking window.

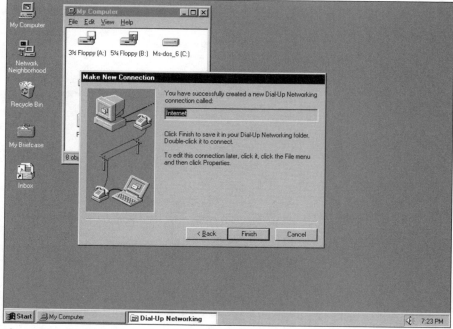

Figure 6-6: As the final step in creating a connection definition, you have an opportunity to review the name under which the connection is saved.

Configuring your definition

Once you have defined a connection, you can easily configure it for exactly what you need for your Internet provider. The easiest way to do this is to open the Dial-Up Networking window and right-click on the definition you want to configure (the definition for your Internet provider). This displays a context menu for the definition. You should choose the Properties option from the menu. At this point, a dialog box appears, as shown in Figure 6-7, that allows you to modify properties.

The information in this dialog box should look familiar; you provided it when you created the connection definition. However, two buttons at the bottom of the dialog box are unique to this dialog box. The Configure button allows you to change the modem properties, and the Server Type button allows you to change the parameters by which a connection is established with the server.

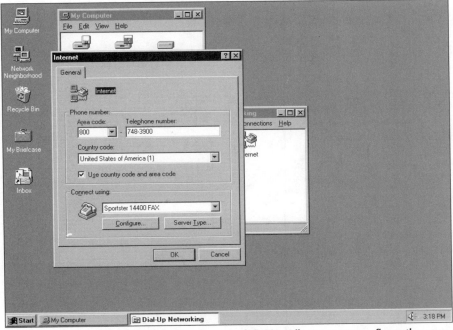

Figure 6-7: The properties dialog box for your definition allows you to configure the connection.

Dialing-related properties

Click on the Configure button. This displays a dialog box that looks similar to the Properties dialog box for the modem (you remember — you used it in Chapter 4). However, there are differences, both overt and subtle. The subtle difference is that any changes you make here don't get applied to the modem *except when the modem is used for this connection.* In other words, the default modem properties are not changed. The overt difference is that now an Options tab appears in the Properties dialog box. If you click on the Options tab, the dialog box appears similar to what is shown in Figure 6-8.

The Options tab is primarily used to specify what should happen before or after the connection is made. Notice that the top part of the dialog box is an area entitled Connection control. Two options appear in this area, both of which control the display of a terminal window.

Why would you want to use a terminal window? Simple. Some Internet providers require you to manually log in to their systems before the connection protocol is enabled. For instance, I use a provider called Internet Express, and it requires you to provide a user ID and a password, and then to press a letter that indicates what protocol or interface you want to use. Thus, using a terminal window after dialing is necessary so that I can follow the steps required by my provider. To enable such a window at the appropriate time, I enable the option entitled Bring up terminal window after dialing.

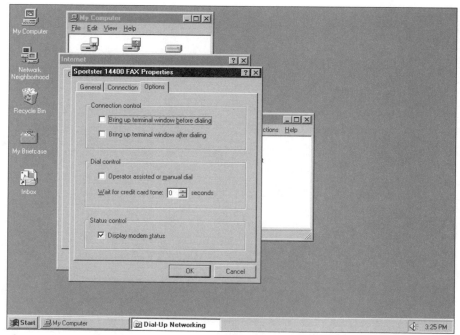

Figure 6-8: The Options tab in the modem Properties dialog box allows you to modify what happens either before or after the connection is made.

Because most providers require you to log in to their systems, you might reasonably ask when you wouldn't need to set this option. If you are connecting to a server that sends you directly into a PPP or SLIP environment, you wouldn't need to use the terminal. For instance, some Internet providers have separate access phone numbers for their different connection protocols. You might dial one number for a menu interface, a different one for PPP, and a third for SLIP. In such a situation, logging on can be handled automatically by the protocol you use. In other words, you only need to use the terminal window if your provider requires human interaction before initiating your connection protocol.

When you finish changing the modem properties, click on the OK button, and you return to the dialog box for your connection definition (as shown in Figure 6-7).

Server-related properties

To change the connection properties related to the server you are contacting, click on the Server Type button in the properties dialog box for your connection definition. This displays the Server Types dialog box, as shown in Figure 6-9. This dialog box allows you to modify both the protocol used by Windows 95 and what happens during the connection sequence.

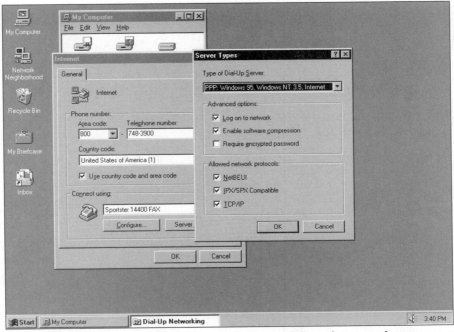

Figure 6-9: The Server Types dialog box is where you define what type of server you are connecting with using Dial-Up Networking.

At the top of the dialog box is a pull-down list that is used to define the connection protocol that will be used by the server to which you are connecting. The default value is PPP, but you can change it to any of the following items:

✦ CSLIP: Unix Connection with IP Header Compression

✦ Netware Connect

✦ PPP

✦ SLIP: Unix Connection

✦ Windows for Workgroups and Windows NT 3.1

WHAT CAN GO WRONG

My SLIP isn't showing

If you want to use SLIP and it is not showing up in the pull-down list of server types, don't panic. When you install Dial-Up Networking, only PPP support is included automatically by Windows 95. To enable SLIP support, you must install it separately. This process is covered in Chapter 5. Finish setting your other parameters, close the properties dialog boxes, install SLIP support, and then try to change the properties again.

Select the connection protocol that is required by your Internet provider. Changing your protocol also modifies the other options available in the Server Types dialog box. This is because different protocols support different capabilities. By definition, PPP supports all six of the options shown in the dialog box. Other options provide only subsets of these options.

If you installed SLIP support, you should notice two SLIP choices. One is regular SLIP (noncompressed), and the other is CSLIP (compressed SLIP). You should pick the version of SLIP that is appropriate for your provider. This may entail a phone call to your provider, as different providers have implemented different versions of SLIP.

After you have selected a connection protocol, the only other options that you may need to change are in the Advanced options area. These options are discussed here:

✦ **Log on to network.** This option is initially checked, because Windows 95 assumes you are connecting with a server that supports this capability. If your provider does not, disable the option.

✦ **Enable software compression.** (This option is available only under PPP.) Some systems support PPP with the software compression option, but not all do. If you find that your provider does not, turn this option off.

✦ **Require encrypted password.** (This option is available only under PPP.) A few systems have a PPP option that supports encrypted passwords. If your provider does this for security purposes and you have selected Log on to network, then select this option.

When you are done defining the options for the server with which you are connecting, click on the OK button. This returns you to the properties dialog box for your connection definition. Because you are done configuring your connection, you can click on OK here as well.

Renaming and Deleting Definitions

Once you define a connection, it is stored in the Dial-Up Networking window. You can see the definition when you look at the window, which is similar to how you view printer definitions in the Printers folder. Figure 6-10 shows an example of how your Dial-Up Networking window may appear after you define and configure your connection.

There may be times, after creating a definition, that you want to rename it. For instance, when you first create a definition, you may misspell the name you have used, or you may later decide to use a more descriptive name. In some ways, renaming a definition is similar to renaming other objects in Windows 95. At first, you may be tempted to right-click on the definition — after all, the context menu for many other objects has a choice for renaming the object. This is not so with connection definitions; the context menu does not allow you to rename the object.

To rename a definition, you must first select the icon by clicking on it. Then, pull down the File menu in the Dial-Up Networking window. This menu has a Rename option, which, when selected, allows you to change the name associated with the definition icon.

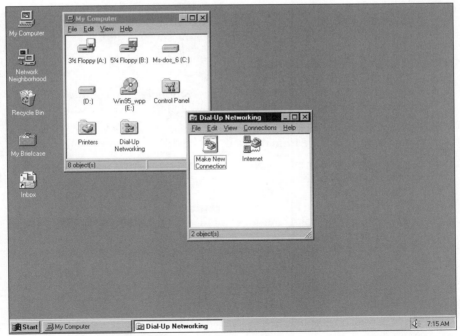

Figure 6-10: The Dial-Up Networking window shows connection definitions in the same way that the Printers folder shows printer definitions.

At some point, you may also decide that you want to delete a definition. For instance, you may have created a definition in error, or you no longer have an account with a particular Internet provider. In these instances, you should delete the definition so that it no longer confuses your Dial-Up Networking window and no longer occupies disk space. The easiest way to delete a definition is to select the definition icon (click on it) and then press Delete. Instead of pressing Delete, you can also choose the Delete option from the File menu in the Dial-Up Networking window.

Summary

If you plan on full access to the Internet through a SLIP or PPP account, you need to understand how Windows 95 uses Dial-Up Networking. This powerful system feature allows you to define network connections through a modem link and then configure them to your specific needs. This chapter introduces you to Dial-Up Networking and provides specific information on the following items:

✦ Dial-Up Networking is used to establish a communication channel with a remote server. It can support several different communications protocols, including SLIP and PPP, which are used in dial-up Internet accounts.

✦ Windows 95 does not automatically install Dial-Up Networking. Instead, you must either make it part of a custom installation, or you must install it later. It is not difficult to install, but you need to follow specific steps.

✦ When using Dial-Up Networking as a client (which is how you connect with the Internet), you must define a connection and then set properties for the connection.

✦ How you set the properties for your connection depends on the type of connection you are establishing and the needs of your Internet provider.

✦ You can rename a definition, after it is created, by selecting the definition icon and choosing Rename from the Dial-Up Networking window's File menu.

✦ The easiest way to delete a connection definition is to select the definition's icon and then press Delete.

Now that you know how Dial-Up Networking functions, you are ready to put it to work. In the next chapter, you make your first call to your provider and hopefully have your first excursion on the Internet.

✦   ✦   ✦

Your First Call

Placing your first call to connect to the Internet can be fun and exciting. It is similar to opening a door for the first time and finding a whole world of opportunity on the other side. It can also be frustrating if you have not done all the work necessary to get ready for the call. You may have succumbed to the temptation to skip directly to this chapter, bypassing the first six. Don't do it! Those chapters contain important information that you need to understand to connect to the Internet successfully. If you have not already done so, go back and make sure that you have read the chapters and performed all the homework necessary to proceed.

Are you done? Good. You are now ready to open the door and venture into the exciting world of the Internet. In this chapter, you learn what to expect on that first call. Here, you put the knowledge of the first six chapters to work to accomplish the following items:

✦ Establishing a dial-up networking connection

✦ Logging in

✦ Using some Internet utilities

✦ Logging out

In addition, you learn how to pay for your phone call (because very few Internet connections are free) and how to create a shortcut for connecting to the Internet.

Establishing a Dial-Up Networking Connection

Once you have set up a connection definition for your Internet provider, making the connection is relatively easy. (Defining a connection is covered in Chapter 6.) To make your first call, open the Dial-Up Networking window; it should appear similar to Figure 7-1.

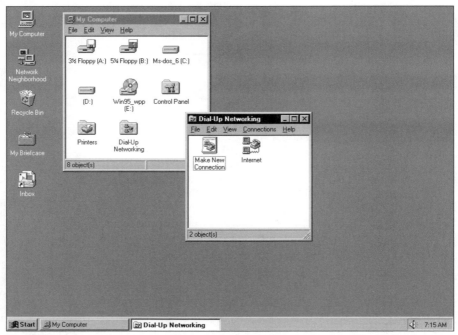

Figure 7-1: The Dial-Up Networking window, showing your connection definition to your Internet provider.

You can initiate the connection in two ways. First, you can double-click on the defini-tion icon. Second, you can select the icon and choose Connect from the Connections menu in the Dial-Up Networking window. Either way, the result is the same. Soon you see the Connect To dialog box, as shown in Figure 7-2. (The information in the dialog box reflects how you set up your connection definition.)

The information at the bottom of this dialog box indicates where you are calling to and where you are calling from. This information should be familiar to you by now; you set it up when you went through the configuration process in the last couple of chapters. You can, if you want, click on the Dial Properties dialog box to change how the call is dialed. (You probably won't need to change these properties on this first call, but you may want to change a credit card number or a dialing prefix on a future call.)

At the top of the dialog box are fields for your user name and password. The impor-tance of these two fields varies based on how you connect with your Internet pro-vider. The key issue is whether you will use the terminal window during your connec-tion process. In Chapter 6, you learn that some Internet providers require human interaction prior to initiating a PPP or SLIP connection. If your provider has this requirement, you need to use a terminal window after dialing the provider.

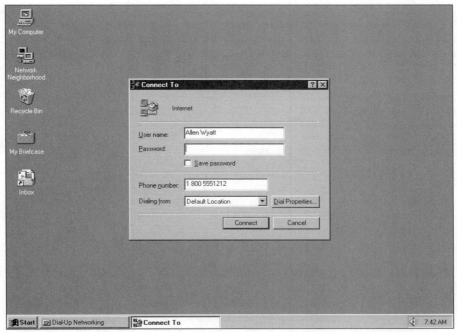

Figure 7-2: The Connect To dialog box is the final step before your modem is dialed.

The purpose of using the terminal window is to log in to your provider — pure and simple. The purpose of the Connect To dialog box, which is on your screen, is to specify a user ID and password that are used to log in. The bottom line is that if you are using a terminal window to log in, the information in this dialog box has no meaning; it is not used. If you fall into this category, you don't need to make changes in the dialog box.

If, on the other hand, you don't use a terminal window during your log-in procedure, you must specify your user ID and password in this dialog box. This information should have been given to you by your Internet provider when you set up your account. Note that these values are not necessarily the same as the values you use when you log in to Windows 95 (if you are using a local area network). Replace your name in the User Name field with the user ID for your provider. In the Password field, type the password you obtained. (As you type the password, asterisks appear in the field instead of the actual characters. This is so someone looking over your shoulder cannot see your password.)

Notice the Save password check box below the Password field. If you check this box, Dial-Up Networking remembers the password, and you won't have to enter it on subsequent dial-up sessions. There is a down side to this, however. If you have an Internet provider for which the login is automated and this information is really used (remember, it isn't if you use the terminal window), then anyone can use your machine, make a couple of clicks, and get right onto the Internet with full privileges under your name. If you don't care for this idea, don't enable this option. That way, you must input your password every time you connect to the Internet.

Connecting to your provider

When you are ready to proceed and you have provided any necessary information in the Connect To dialog box, click on the Connect button. Windows 95 immediately tries to make a connection to your provider based on the information in your modem setup and Dial-Up Networking configuration. While a connection is being attempted, you see a status box, as shown in Figure 7-3.

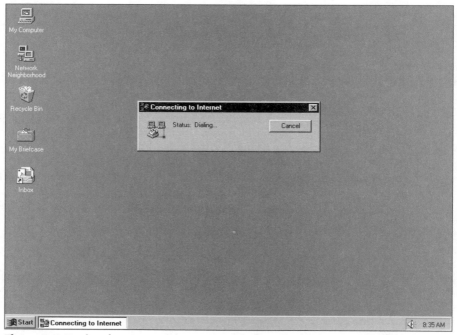

Figure 7-3: During the connection process, Windows 95 keeps you informed about what is going on.

During the first part of the connection process, the modem is dialed and the communications link is negotiated. If you set up your modem correctly and provided the proper phone number and dialing parameters, little can go wrong at this stage. With some modems, you may even be able to hear what is happening during the phone call.

After a modem connection is established, what happens next depends on whether you have specified the use of a terminal window. If you see a terminal window appear on your screen, then you should skip to the next section. If you did not specify a terminal window when you configured your Dial-Up Networking definition, then Windows 95 attempts to directly log you in to the remove server. During this phase, you see the status box change, as shown in Figure 7-4.

Once your identity has been confirmed and the security system at the remote server is satisfied, you are connected to the Internet. At this point, you can skip ahead to the section "You are connected!" for additional information about what you can do.

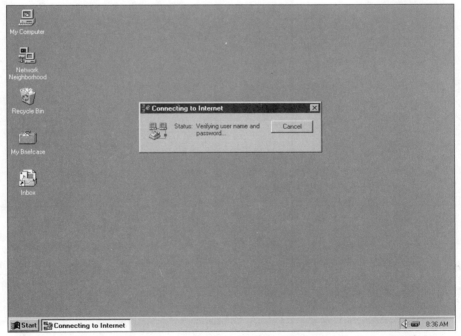

Figure 7-4: After establishing a modem connection, Windows 95 attempts to log you in to the remote server.

My login is stuck

If everything seems to be going great in the connection process but you can't get past the logging-in message box, your Internet provider probably does not support an automatic login. To correct this, follow these steps:

1. Open the Dial-Up Networking window.

2. Right-click on the connection definition for your Internet provider.

3. From the context menu, select the Properties option.

4. Click on the Server Type button.

5. Disable the Log on to network option.

6. Click on OK.

7. Click on the Configure button.

8. Select the Options tab.

9. Enable the Bring up terminal window after dialing option.

10. Click on OK.

11. Click on OK again.

You can now try your connection again, and you should not have the same problem.

Using the terminal window

If a terminal window appears during login, exactly what you see and what you do in the window depend, for the most part, on your Internet provider. Different providers have different procedures for logging in. As an example, however, this section explains what happens when I log in to Internet Express, a provider based in northern Colorado. You should be able to adapt the procedures discussed here to your own provider.

When the terminal window is displayed, my screen shown in Figure 7-5 appears. Notice that the terminal window almost looks like an MS-DOS window, and I can see information that the provider has sent over the communications link.

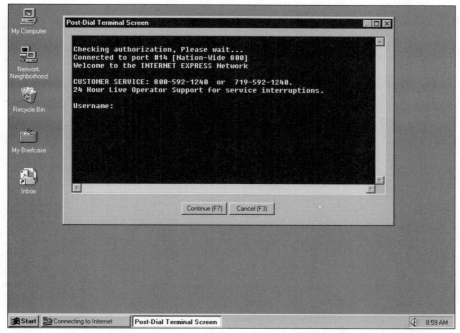

Figure 7-5: After establishing a modem connection, Windows 95 displays a terminal window so you can interact with the computer at the provider's site.

In many ways, the terminal window is like a traditional communications software package. There may not be all the bells and whistles normally associated with communications software, but I can see what the remote computer is sending me, and I can type responses.

At this point, my provider's computer has displayed a welcoming message and is asking me to identify myself. Here is where I enter my user ID (in my case, the ID is dci). After typing it and pressing Enter, I am asked for my password, which I dutifully enter. (Sorry, I *won't* tell you my password.) Internet Express then displays one last message that instructs me to press *c* to continue, as shown in Figure 7-6.

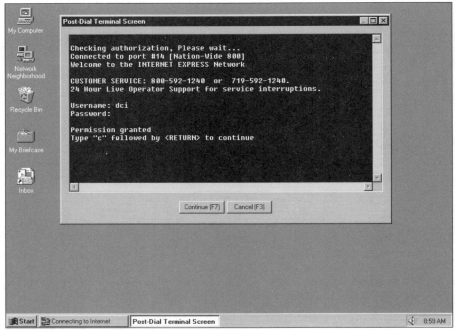

Figure 7-6: The login process at many providers only requires answers to a couple of questions.

At this point, I actually have three options because of the way my account is set up with Internet Express. I can enter any of the following:

✦ **c.** If I enter the letter *c*, I am shown a menu-based interface that is similar to what you see in many BBS systems. This is the standard, text-based way to access the Internet through my provider.

✦ **p.** If I enter the letter *p*, I am indicating that I want to establish my connection using PPP.

✦ **slip.** If I enter the word *slip*, I am indicating that I want to establish my connection using SLIP.

Because I configured my Dial-Up Networking definition to use PPP, the logical choice is to press *p* and Enter. When I do this, miscellaneous wording appears in the terminal window. This is nothing to worry about; the server at Internet Express is simply attempting to establish the PPP connection. All I need to do at this point is to click on the Continue button at the bottom of the terminal window. The terminal window then closes, and a status box appears, as shown in Figure 7-4. This status box informs me that my user name and password are being verified. In reality, they are not — these were already verified manually using the terminal window. Actually, Windows 95 is attempting to negotiate a successful PPP connection.

Special SLIP procedures

In the preceding section, you learn how you can use the terminal window to connect to your Internet provider. If you are connecting through a SLIP account, you should follow all procedures in that section. However, when you indicate in the terminal window that you want to connect through SLIP (for example, if I had entered the word *slip* instead of pressing the letter *p*), then what happens next is a bit different from what happens with PPP.

You already know that you need an IP address to connect to the Internet. When you are using PPP, this address is supplied to Windows 95, and your system is automatically updated. If you are using SLIP, however, you must provide the address. When you indicate in the terminal window that you are using SLIP, you should see a message indicating what your IP address will be. For example, when I enter the word *slip* on Internet Express, my terminal window appears as shown in Figure 7-7.

When you see this address, write it down. (If you do not, you cannot connect to the Internet.) You may be shown two addresses, as indicated in Figure 7-7. In most cases, yours is the second address shown, but you should always write down the one indicated as your address. After you write it down, click on the Continue button at the bottom of the terminal window. You then see a dialog box that allows you to enter your newly assigned IP address, as shown in Figure 7-8.

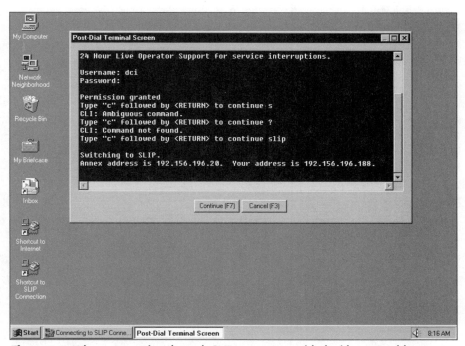

Figure 7-7: When connecting through SLIP, you are provided with an IP address.

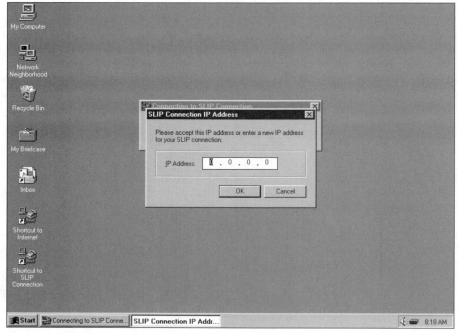

Figure 7-8: If you are using SLIP, you must manually enter your IP address whenever you connect.

Carefully enter all four octets of the IP address you wrote down. When you finish, you can click on the OK button to complete the connection process.

Most Internet providers will gladly switch your account from SLIP to PPP free of charge, or if you already have access to a SLIP account, you may automatically have a PPP account if you use a different log-in process. Perhaps the biggest initial advantage in switching to PPP is that you won't have to write down that pesky IP address every time you log in to the Internet.

You are connected!

Once you have logged in to the Internet provider, you are informed by Windows 95 that the connection is complete. Again, you see a status box to this effect, as illustrated in Figure 7-9.

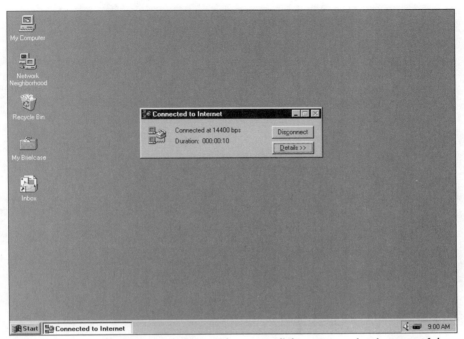

Figure 7-9: Windows 95 lets you know when your dial-up connection is successful.

That's it! There is no big fanfare, welcome screen, or fireworks. Even though you see no other changes on your screen, you are connected to the Internet. Be sure that you don't confuse what a communications program (such as HyperTerminal or Procomm Plus) does with what Dial-Up Networking does. With a communications program, things appear within a defined area of your screen. For example, you may work within a terminal window where you interact directly with the remote system.

In reality, this is the key to the difference — communications software lets you interact with a remote system, whereas Dial-Up Networking simply connects you to a remote network. In this case, you are connected to the Internet. In effect, you have become part of the Net. You can perform many of the same operations across the Net that you would on your own local network. In the next section, you start to see how you can use special tools to take advantage of the Net.

For now, take a look back at the status box shown in Figure 7-9. The information in the box lets you know that you are connected (and at what speed) as well as how long you have been connected. Two buttons appear on the right side of the status box, and you can probably figure out what the Disconnect button does. If you click on the Details button, you see additional information about your dial-up connection, as shown in Figure 7-10.

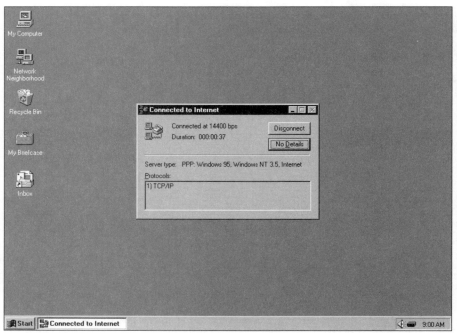

Figure 7-10: The Dial-Up Networking status box can provide additional information about your connection.

The information shown in the expanded status box varies based on how you configured your networking. If you want to show the smaller status box, you can click on the No Details button to again hide the details.

At this point, the status box serves no real purpose, except to clutter the screen. You can't get rid of the status box (at least not as long as the connection is active), nor would you necessarily want to. You can, however, minimize the box so that it appears only on the taskbar instead of in the middle of the screen. This is done in the same manner as with any other window; you click on the minimize control in the upper-right corner of the box. When the status box is minimized, the name used for the task on the taskbar is the same as the name of the Dial-Up Networking connection definition. At this point, you have the entire screen available to do other work.

Unexplained disconnections

There may be times when you are connected to the Internet and things seem to be going fine. All of a sudden, you see a message indicating that the connection between you and the Internet provider has been broken. What could be happening?

If you've ruled out the dog chewing through the phone cord, perhaps someone else in your house (if you are calling from home) is picking up a phone extension. This can play havoc with the connection, often causing disconnection. More likely, however, the culprit is call waiting. There are millions of homes and small businesses that have call waiting; it can be a very handy feature. It is not handy, however, on a phone line being used for data communications. The signal that you have another call coming in (that distinctive click) disconnects a modem — right away.

The solution is to disable call waiting. You can have Windows 95 automatically disable call waiting if you set up the modem correctly. For more information, refer to Chapter 4.

Using Internet Utilities

A wide range of utility programs will help you work on the Internet. Some programs are based on a command line, and others are full-fledged Windows programs. The command-line tools are reminiscent of UNIX tools. Tools placed in the Windows environment should be familiar to you right away.

In this chapter, it is impossible to cover all the tools that you will use on the Internet. Some tools are so complex and powerful that it takes a full chapter to explain them. These larger tools are explained in later chapters of this book. Here, however, I spend some time reviewing a couple of tools to get you started. The next two sections examine the *ping* and *tracert* commands, which you can use anytime that you are connected to the Net.

The ping command

Perhaps the simplest command that you can first use on the Internet is the ping command. This command is considered a TCP/IP utility and is used on virtually every UNIX system in the world. Windows 95 includes its own version of the ping command.

The ping command received its name from the way sonar is used on submarines. In a submarine environment, sailors operate in the dark — without windows, they can't see where they are going. Instead, they rely on sonar, which allows them to "see" what is around them based on reflected sound waves. If you saw the movie *Hunt for Red October,* you know that a sonar crew can "ping" an enemy to verify its presence. This means that the crew sends out a sound, at a specific amplitude and frequency, and then measures the response to the sound.

On the Internet, you are also often operating in the dark (no pun intended). There are no windows that allow you to see who is out on the Net. The ping command sends an IP packet requesting a response from a remote site. If the remote site responds, you know that the system is active.

To use the ping command, open an MS-DOS window. You do this by selecting Programs from the Start menu and then choosing MS-DOS Prompt. Once the window is open and you are at the command line, enter the following command:

```
ping -n 1 nic.funet.fi
```

After you press Enter, you should receive a response shortly. The response I received is shown in Figure 7-11.

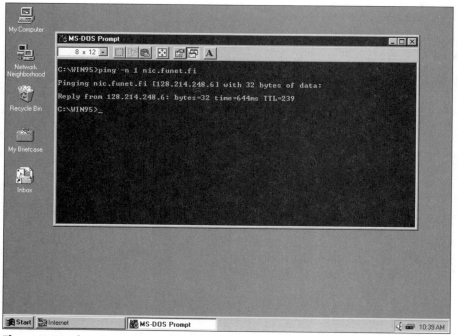

Figure 7-11: The ping command lets you know how long it took a message to reach a remote host and return.

You may remember from the discussion of Internet addresses in Chapter 2 that a DNS name can end with either an organizational domain or a geographic domain; the one in the figure ends with the latter. If you look back at the information in Chapter 2, you can determine that you just pinged a system in Finland — and it only took a few milliseconds (644 in my case) for your message to travel there and be processed, and for a response to travel back. (Isn't technology wonderful?)

You can use a wide array of different switches with the ping command. In the example just provided, you used the -n switch. This indicated that ping should try to check the host address only once. If you don't include this switch, ping sends four messages and expects four responses. Table 7-1 shows the different switches available for the ping command.

Using the ping command on a dial-up link is different from using it on a native UNIX system that is connected directly to the Internet. It shocked me the first time I used ping on Windows 95 and received response times in excess of 600 milliseconds (ms) — I had been used to response times of less than 300 ms. The difference lies with the weakest link in the chain — my modem. Operating at only 14,400 bps, my modem adds quite a bit of delay to an otherwise fast process.

WHAT CAN
GO WRONG

Bad addresses

If your response to the ping command was not similar to that shown in Figure 7-11, and you instead received a message indicating that you provided a bad host name, then you have a problem. If you checked your typing, you entered the host address (nic.funet.fi) correctly, and you still got the message, then the problem lies with your DNS server.

Recall from Chapter 2 that a DNS server resolves Internet names and turns them into IP addresses that the network can understand. If you received a *bad host* message on a perfectly good (and common) address, then either your DNS server is not available or you have not configured your TCP/IP properties with the proper DNS server address. Refer back to Chapter 5 for the proper procedures.

Table 7-1
Command-Line Switches for the Ping Command

Switch	Meaning
-a	Shows network addresses in IP address format instead of as host names.
-f	Causes echo packets to remain unfragmented by intermediate gateways.
-i *x*	Specifies the time-to-live field of the ping packet. You indicate (by *x*) how many intermediate gateways the message can travel through before it stops trying to reach the destination.
-j *hosts*	Specifies the route that you want the packet to include, where *hosts* is a series of host names. Ping can use additional hosts in the route, if necessary.
-k *hosts*	Same as the -j switch, except no additional hosts can be used.
-l *x*	Indicates the length of the ping echo packet sent, in *x* bytes. This can be any value up to 8,192.
-n *x*	Specifies how many pings to make, where *x* is an integer value.
-r *x*	Indicates that you want up to *x* legs of the route (going and coming) recorded.
-s *x*	Indicates the time stamp to be used for each leg of the route when you use the -r switch.
-t	Pinging is done continuously, until you press Ctrl+C.
-w *x*	Indicates the timeout interval (in *x* milliseconds). The default is 1000, or 1 second.

COOL PLACES

Ping places

You could use millions of host names with the ping command, but you can use the ping command with the following addresses to see how long it takes to contact each:

Host Name	Where It Is Located
whitehouse.gov	Washington, DC
nbc.com	New York, NY (NBC News)
luxor.cc.wakato.ac.nz	Hamilton, New Zealand (University of Waikato)
aristo.tau.ac.il	Tel Aviv, Israel (Tel Aviv University)

The tracert command

This command is related closely to the ping command, except it can be used to tell you how your packet got there and back. The command name (tracert) is a shortened version of its purpose — trace route. When you used the ping command, you reached out and touched a host system in Finland. What if you want to know how you had reached that host? To figure this out, type the following command in an MS-DOS window:

```
tracert nic.funet.fi
```

Each leg of the journey from your computer to the host in Finland is documented on the screen for you. When I did this from my system, I saw the information shown in Figure 7-12.

Notice that this route had 18 steps between Wyoming and Finland. The message traveled across various networks and through gateways in places like Denver, Chicago, Cleveland, Hartford, New York, Washington, and Stockholm. Remember, however, that this is my route, through my provider. Your messages will probably take a different route entirely.

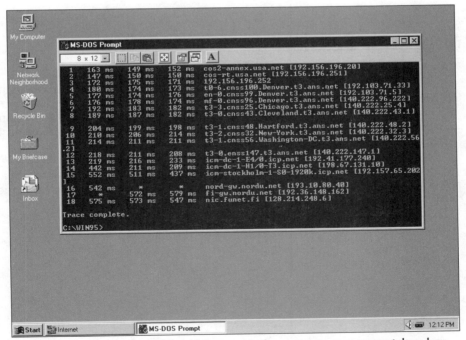

Figure 7-12: The tracert command lets you see the route your messages take when reaching a remote host.

There are command-line switches that you can use with the tracert command, although there are fewer than with the ping command. Table 7-2 shows the various switches that you can use.

<table>
<tr><td colspan="2" align="center">Table 7-2
Command-Line Switches for the Tracert Command</td></tr>
<tr><th>Switch</th><th>Meaning</th></tr>
<tr><td>-d</td><td>Shows network addresses in IP address format instead of as host names.</td></tr>
<tr><td>-h x</td><td>Indicates that tracert should only go through up to x gateways searching for the target.</td></tr>
<tr><td>-j hosts</td><td>Specifies the route that you want the packet to include, where hosts is a series of host names. Ping can use additional hosts in the route, if necessary.</td></tr>
<tr><td>-w x</td><td>Indicates the timeout interval (in x milliseconds). The default is 1000, or 1 second.</td></tr>
</table>

Ending Your Session

Disconnecting from your Internet provider is easy. When you are ready to break your connection, display the status box maintained by Dial-Up Networking. Earlier in this chapter you minimized this status box, so it should be visible on the taskbar. (Remember that it is shown with the same task name as the name you provided your connection definition.) Click on the task button, and the status box is maximized and again accessible, as shown in Figure 7-13.

To terminate your session, click on the Disconnect button. The modem link terminates immediately. Remember that you won't be able to use any other Internet tools until you later establish a connection to your Internet provider.

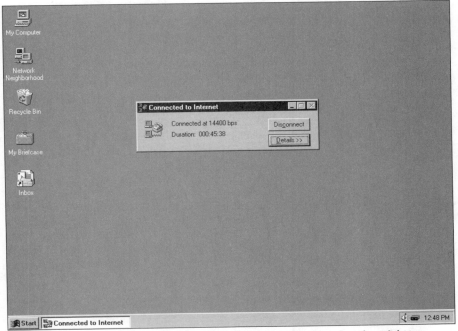

Figure 7-13: You can disconnect your Internet connection by using the Dial-Up Networking status box.

How You Pay for the Session

Now that you have finished your first session on the Internet, you may wonder how you pay for the time you spent there. In reality, there are two charges that you may accrue every time you connect to the Internet. The first charge has to do with your Internet provider, and the second is related to your phone company.

In Chapter 3, you learn that different providers levy their charges in different ways. Some charge a flat rate, whereas others charge based on the time that you are connected. If your service plan falls into the first category, then you pay a flat monthly bill, regardless of how many times you connect. If your service plan falls into the second category, you are charged based on how long you are connected to the Internet.

Take a look back at Figure 7-13. The status box indicates that I was connected to my Internet provider for 45 minutes and 38 seconds. Because I pay based on how long I am connected, this time becomes the basis of my charge. It is important to remember that you are charged for every minute that you are *connected* — not just for when you are using Internet tools or accessing remote systems on the Net. For this call, if I am charged at a rate of $3.00 per hour, I have racked up charges totaling $2.28.

The other thing you need to pay for is the phone call to the provider. In many areas of the country, Internet access is only a local phone call away. If this is the case where you live, then nothing appears on your phone bill about the session (unless, of course, you have metered local service, where you are charged for each local call).

Many people in the United States don't have local Internet access yet. These folks must pay any long distance charges associated with calling the Internet. These charges appear on your monthly phone bill in addition to anything the Internet provider may charge you. Depending on your long distance carrier, interstate calls are typically billed at an average of 13–27 cents per minute. (During some hours with some carriers, you can get rates as low as 10 cents a minute.) If you are calling an Internet provider within your state, then intrastate long distance calls can be even more expensive.

To overcome the hassle of two bills associated with your Internet account, some providers offer toll-free service, where you dial a toll-free number to connect with their servers. If you have such a service, you almost always pay a surcharge for it. With my provider, the surcharge amounts to $6.00 per hour, or 10 cents a minute. At the times of day that I access the Internet, this surcharge is definitely cheaper than paying long distance fees.

Setting Up a Shortcut

Now that you have successfully connected to the Internet for the first time, you probably want to do it over and over again. To make the process of connecting just a bit easier, you may want to place a shortcut on your desktop that connects you to your Internet provider. To create such a shortcut, follow these steps:

1. Open the Dial-Up Networking window.

2. Right-click on the definition icon for the connection to your Internet provider. This displays a context menu for the object.

3. Choose the Create Shortcut option from the context menu.

4. You see a message box indicating that the shortcut cannot be created in the Dial-Up Networking window, but asking if you want the shortcut to be placed on the desktop. Click on the Yes button.

Windows 95 creates a shortcut to your connection definition and places it on the desktop. Now, instead of opening the Dial-Up Networking window every time you want to connect to the Internet, double-click on the icon for the shortcut you just created.

Summary

Well, you finally made it. You joined what seems like everyone else in the world on the Internet. You opened the door and stepped through into a previously unknown world — a world that holds new challenges and opportunities. In this chapter, you take your first steps on the Internet. Here, you learn how to make, use, and break a connection. In particular, you learn the following items:

✦ You can establish a dial-up connection with your Internet provider by using the Dial-Up Networking definition created in the preceding chapter.

✦ How you log in to your provider's system depends on the capabilities of that system. You may be able to log in automatically, or you may need to do it manually using a terminal window.

✦ The ping utility is diagnostic, and it is used to determine if a remote host is actively on the network.

✦ The tracert command is similar to the ping command, except that it is used to determine the route taken to reach a remote host. Routes differ based on many variables, including who your provider is, the traffic loads, and the time of day.

✦ Logging off of a remote server is easy. All you need to do is click on the Disconnect button in the Dial-Up Networking status box.

✦ You pay for your time on the Internet based on the pricing policies of your provider. In addition, you may pay tolls to your phone company based on the type of call you make to connect with your provider.

✦ Windows 95 allows you to create shortcuts so that you can quickly access common functions. It is a good idea to create a shortcut for a working connection to the Internet.

In the next chapter, you learn about the most common use of the Internet — electronic mail. You also learn how you can use Microsoft Exchange to manage your mail.

✦   ✦   ✦

Windows 95 Internet Tools

P A R T

◆ ◆ ◆ ◆

In This Part

Chapter 8
Electronic Mail and
Microsoft Exchange

Chapter 9
Using Mailing Lists

Chapter 10
Using Telnet

Chapter 11
Using Ftp

◆ ◆ ◆ ◆

Electronic Mail and Microsoft Exchange

Perhaps the most common use of the Internet is for sending and receiving electronic mail. Millions of electronic mail messages transfer over the Internet daily. This chapter covers the following items:

+ What electronic mail is

+ What type of software is needed to access electronic mail

+ How you can compose messages for other people

+ How to address your e-mail

+ How you can attach computer files to your messages

+ How e-mail is transferred between your system and the mail server

+ How to read your e-mail and act upon it

+ How to interpret the parts of an e-mail message

What Is Electronic Mail?

Electronic mail (or e-mail, for short) is nothing more than communication sent between parties through electronic means rather than physical means. The concept behind e-mail is simple. You (the sender) have a message that you want to transmit across a network to one or more recipients. Special software, generically called e-mail software, allows the efficient management of both the messages you send and those you receive. E-mail software is discussed fully starting in the next section.

Even though e-mail is a common use of the Internet, you don't need to use the Internet to use e-mail. Many companies and organizations use e-mail every day without ever using the Internet. Instead, they use local area networks to connect their computers and then transmit e-mail messages over these networks. In this environment, the only people who can send and receive messages are those connected to the local area network. When the network becomes connected to the Internet, then everyone else connected to the Internet is available as either a sender or recipient of electronic mail.

E-Mail Software

A variety of programs allow you to send and receive electronic mail. One such program, Microsoft Exchange, is included with Windows 95. This program allows you to exchange messages with others on your local area network. It does not, however, allow you to exchange messages with other people on the Internet. This is because Internet e-mail messages are constructed a bit differently than the messages composed by Microsoft Exchange. Thus, special filters must be added to Microsoft Exchange so that it can both understand and compose Internet e-mail messages. These filters are called *clients,* and the Internet e-mail client is available in the Microsoft Plus! Companion for Windows 95 (the Plus! pack). This is an add-on to Windows 95 and should be available from your local retailer for a nominal fee (well under $50). Later in this chapter, you learn how to use Microsoft Exchange, along with the Plus! pack, to manage your Internet e-mail.

Microsoft Exchange is not the only e-mail software available, however. You can download e-mail software directly from the Internet, or you can purchase commercial e-mail software. The cheapest way to get e-mail capability is to use some downloaded software. You can transfer e-mail software to your system using the ftp command, which is described in Chapter 11. Once downloaded to your system, you can install the e-mail software and begin to use it right away.

The following is a list of the most popular e-mail software packages that you can find on the Internet, along with the ftp site where they are located:

Name	Ftp Site	Directory
E-Mail Connection	emc.connectsoft.com	pub/emc25
Eudora	ftp.qualcomm.com	windows/eudora/1.4
Ladybird	tpts1.seed.net.tw	UPLOAD/jenwen
Pegasus Mail	risc.ua.edu	pub/network/pegasus

Although these e-mail programs perform the same basic functions, each handles the functions in its own way. For instance, one program may use a particular command sequence to send e-mail, while another program uses a completely different command. It doesn't matter which e-mail program you use; you simply download one, and then install it on your system. The examples used in the first part of this chapter focus on using the E-Mail Connection software; you may want to use a different program.

Downloading e-mail software

To download the E-Mail Connection software, use the ftp command, as covered in Chapter 11. Without going into much detail here (and ruining the anticipation for Chapter 11), you use the ftp command to download the software by following these steps:

1. Connect to your Internet provider using what you learned in Chapter 7.

2. Open an MS-DOS window on your system.

3. Change to the folder in which you want to download the software. Typically this is a folder such as *mail;* you can create any folder you want on your system.

4. At the command prompt, enter the following command:

```
ftp emc.connectsoft.com
```

5. When prompted for a user ID, type **anonymous.**

6. When prompted for a password, enter your e-mail address (as discussed in Chapter 2).

You now should be connected to the remote server, and you should see the ftp prompt on your screen. You can then enter the following commands at the ftp prompt:

```
cd pub/emc25
binary
get emcsetup.exe
```

The file you are transferring is over 1.3MB in size, so it takes a while to transfer it to your system. When the transfer is complete, you can break your Internet connection, because installing the software does not require that the connection be active.

Installing your e-mail software

Once you have transferred the software to your system, you are ready to install it on your machine. You do this by running the program that you just transferred. You can do this either from the command prompt, or you can use Windows 95 to browse to the appropriate folder and run the emcsetup.exe program. Either way, you soon see a dialog box (shown in Figure 8-1) indicating that you are about to set up the E-Mail Connection software.

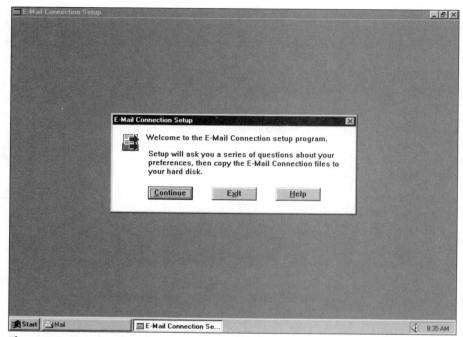

Figure 8-1: Running the emcsetup program starts the process of installing the software on your system.

Click on the Continue button, and you are asked for the name of the directory (folder) in which you want the software installed. This should be a folder other than the one in which you downloaded the software. The setup program suggests that you use C:\EMCINT as the folder; if this is OK, click on the Continue button. If you want to use a different folder, enter its name in the dialog box, and then click on Continue. Shortly you see the dialog box that is shown in Figure 8-2.

Here you are asked for the name of a program group to which E-Mail Connection should be added. This is a holdover from earlier versions of Windows; Windows 95 does not use program groups. Instead, what you enter at this dialog box is used as a directory for placing a shortcut to the program. If the default name (ConnectSoft) is OK, click on the Continue button. If you want to use a different name, then enter it in the dialog box, and click on Continue.

At this point, the setup program copies the files from the huge file you downloaded to the folder that you specified on your hard drive. This process should take only a few moments, and then you are notified (through a dialog box) that the setup process is complete. Clicking on the Continue button ends the setup program, and you should see the ConnectSoft window on your screen, as shown in Figure 8-3.

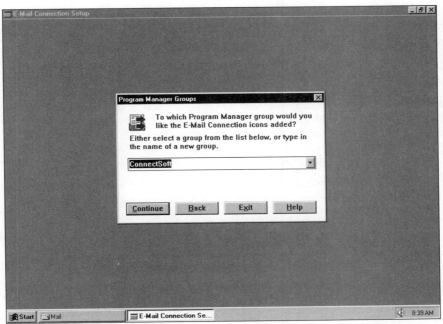

Figure 8-2: During the installation, you are asked for the name of the program group to which you want E-Mail Connection added.

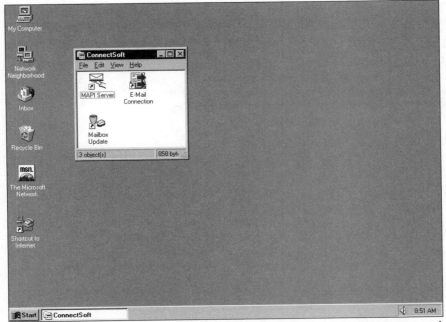

Figure 8-3: After installation, shortcuts to the E-Mail Connection program are contained in the ConnectSoft window.

With E-Mail Connection installed on your system, you can delete the file that you downloaded through the Internet (emcsetup.exe). You no longer need the file, and deleting it frees up a great deal of space on your system.

Configuring your e-mail software

The first time you use your E-Mail Connection Software, you must configure it for your system. You don't need to be connected to the Internet when you do the configuration, but you do need several pieces of information:

- ✦ Your mail server address
- ✦ Your SMTP relay name, if any (*SMTP* is an acronym for simple mail transfer protocol, which is used by many e-mail systems that access the Internet.)
- ✦ Your user ID
- ✦ Your password
- ✦ Your return e-mail address

You should know some of this information (such as your user ID and password). For the other information, you must contact your Internet provider personnel; they should be able to supply this information. You can explain that you are setting up your e-mail software and need the answers to a few questions. Write down their answers, since you will need them later in the configuration process.

The first time that you run E-Mail Connection, you see a license agreement appear on the screen, as shown in Figure 8-4. Once you have read and agree with the information in the license, click on the I agree, continue button.

E-Mail Connection then takes a moment to set up the programs and settings it needs to operate properly. This entire process takes only a couple of seconds, and you see status messages on the screen that keep you informed of what is happening. Then you see the New User Information dialog box, as shown in Figure 8-5.

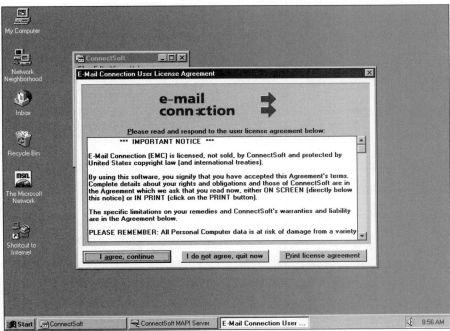

Figure 8-4: The first thing you see when starting E-Mail Connection is the license agreement.

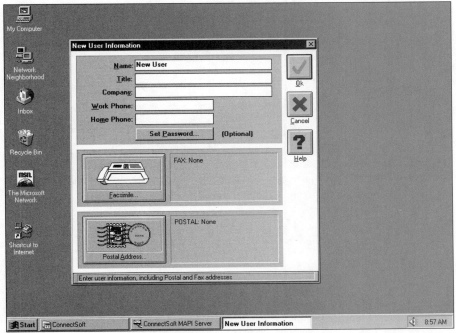

Figure 8-5: The New User Information dialog box is used to specify information about yourself.

Here you enter the information about yourself that you want to be used in composing your e-mail messages. If you click on the Facsimile button, you can enter your fax number. Likewise, clicking on the Postal Address button allows you to specify your U.S. mail address. When you finish entering the information about yourself, click on the Ok button. After the information is saved, you see the E-Mail Connection program screen, along with the Internet Mail Setup dialog box, as shown in Figure 8-6.

This is where you enter the information that you gathered at the beginning of this section. Enter the information in each of the supplied fields, and make sure that the connection type is set to SLIP/PPP in the lower left corner of the dialog box. You don't necessarily need to use any of the other buttons on the dialog box (such as Schedule, More, or View Log) at this time. When you are done entering information, click on the Ok button. Your information is saved, and you are finished configuring E-Mail Connection.

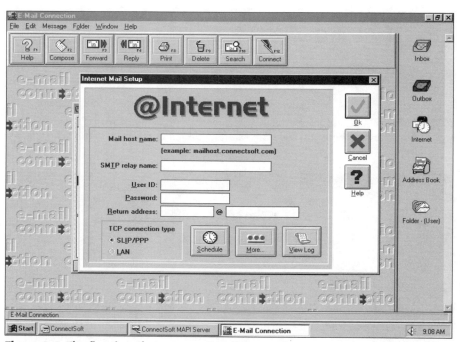

Figure 8-6: The first time that you use E-Mail Connection, you must specify information that helps the program find your e-mail on the Internet.

The E-Mail Connection interface

Once your software is configured, the program screen should appear as shown in Figure 8-7. This window contains several components that you must understand to effectively use the program.

At the top of the program window are two features that should be familiar to you if you have used Windows software. The menu bar contains six choices, and each contains commands that you can use at any time:

✦ **File.** Commands referring to program configuration, printing, and exiting the program

✦ **Edit.** Commands related to cutting, copying, pasting, and spell-checking text within a message

✦ **Message.** Commands used for creating, copying, moving, deleting, forwarding, and replying to messages

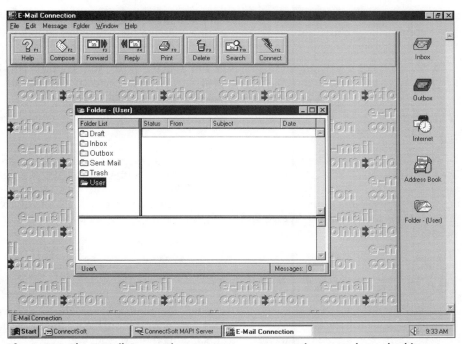

Figure 8-7: The E-Mail Connection program screen contains several standard items you use to manage your e-mail.

✦ **Folder.** Commands for managing different folders in which your messages are saved

✦ **Window.** Commands for organizing and selecting different windows within E-Mail Connection

✦ **Help.** The help system available for the program

Below the menu is a toolbar that contains the eight most common commands. These commands are a subset of the commands that you access through the menu system. Each icon on the toolbar also shows which function key (F1, F2, F3, and so on) you can use to initiate the command.

At the right side of the program window are five icons that represent different parts of the program:

✦ **Inbox.** Clicking on this icon displays the contents of the inbox. The inbox is a folder that contains messages recently received through e-mail.

✦ **Outbox.** Clicking on this icon displays the contents of the outbox. Again, this is a folder that contains messages that you have composed but have not yet sent.

✦ **Internet.** This icon is used to control the configuration of and connection to your Internet e-mail server. You set up this information when you configured E-Mail Connection.

✦ **Address Book.** Clicking here allows you to manage your address book. This is a list of commonly used e-mail addresses that you define. Effective use of the address book can save you a great deal of typing and misrouted mail.

✦ **Folder – (User).** This icon displays the contents of the User folder, which stores your messages.

As you click on different icons at the right of the screen, the window in the middle of the screen changes. You can also select folders from the folder list to see the contents of different e-mail folders. When you first install E-Mail Connection, six folders are created, but you can create additional folders as desired. The folders allow you to manage the e-mail that you receive and send; they are only organizational tools or storage locations you can use.

Composing a Mail Message

With the E-Mail Connection software downloaded, installed, and configured, you are ready to begin using the software for your e-mail needs. To compose e-mail, you do not have to be connected to the Internet. This means that you can compose your e-mail messages without running up a bill with your Internet provider. You only need to connect to the Internet when you are ready to send your mail.

To compose a message, click on the toolbar's Compose icon, or press F2. A message template appears on the screen, as shown in Figure 8-8. Also notice that a Draft icon appears at the bottom right side of the screen.

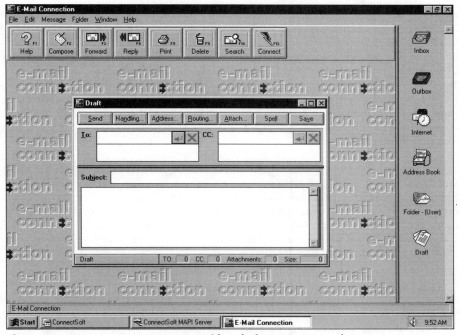

Figure 8-8: You compose a message with a draft message template.

To create a message, you define a recipient (through proper addressing), indicate the subject of the message, and type the message itself. Each of these tasks is discussed in the following sections.

Addressing your e-mail

In Chapter 2, you learn all about Internet addresses. Everyone who uses the Internet has an e-mail address that can be used to send and receive mail. At the top of the draft e-mail template on your screen is a section called To:. Here you indicate who should receive your e-mail. For instance, if you want to send an e-mail message to me, you enter my address (dci@usa.net) in the To: field and then click on the left-pointing arrow at the right side of the field. You can also specify multiple recipients for the e-mail. Keep entering addresses, clicking on the left-pointing arrow between each address.

E-Mail Connection also allows you to specify who should receive copies of the message. A message original and a copy contain no differences; these designations are provided solely for human needs. You would use the To: field to indicate the primary recipients of the message. The CC: field is used to indicate others that may be interested in the message as well, but who are not primary recipients. For example, you may compose a message to seven colleagues working on a project with you; these are the primary recipients, and their addresses are entered in the To: field. You may also want your boss to receive a copy of the same message, just so he or she knows the status of the project; this message is a copy, and your boss's address is entered in the CC: field.

If the person to whom you are sending the e-mail has been added to your address book, you can click on the Address button at the top of the message template. This displays your address book and allows you to select addresses from it to add to the To: and CC: fields.

When you are addressing your e-mail message, it is good to know where the recipient will be receiving the e-mail. If the recipient has access to the Internet, there is no problem — you simply use his (or her) Internet e-mail address. If the recipient uses an online service that has e-mail capability with the Internet, then you must know how to convert his address on that system into an Internet address that you can readily use. Use the following guidelines to convert addresses for three popular online systems that can receive Internet e-mail:

Online System	*Address Conversions*
CompuServe	Start with the recipient's CompuServe address. Change the comma in the address to a period, and then add @compuserve.com at the end. Thus, my address would be 72561.2207@compuserve.com.
America Online	Start with the recipient's AOL user name, and then add @aol.com at the end. Thus, an address could be stewart@aol.com.
Prodigy	Start with the recipient's Prodigy user ID, and then add @prodigy.com at the end. Thus, an address could be wilson12@prodigy.com.

Selecting a subject

The second part of your message is the Subject field. Here you enter the subject of your message. The subject appears in the mail list of the e-mail software that is used by the recipient and should concisely reflect the message content. It is a good idea to make the subject interesting enough to grab the recipient's attention, because it is the first clue of your message that the person sees. Type a few words, a phrase, or a complete sentence in the Subject field.

Typing your message

You type your message in the large area at the bottom of the message template. This is the body of the message, and you can compose it in any way you choose. Simply click anywhere within the message field, and start typing. Press Enter at the end of a paragraph or when you want to add extra blank lines in the message.

Message attachments

Most e-mail messages are plain text, but you are not limited to only text. You can attach computer files to your messages, and these files are sent through the Internet as attachments. The recipient then can save the attachment to a hard disk, for use in any way. To attach a file to your message, click on the Attach button at the top of the message template. You then see the dialog box that is shown in Figure 8-9.

This dialog box should look familiar; it is similar to file-selection dialog boxes used by many Windows programs. Select the file that you want to attach to the message. When you select the file and click on the Ok button, you again see the message template, but it has changed. Now the bottom right corner of the dialog box shows the attachments that you have made to the message, as shown in Figure 8-10.

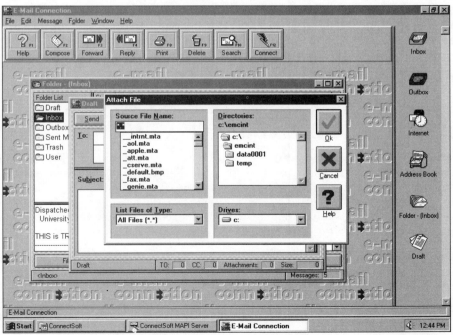

Figure 8-9: E-Mail Connection allows you to specify the file to attach to an e-mail message.

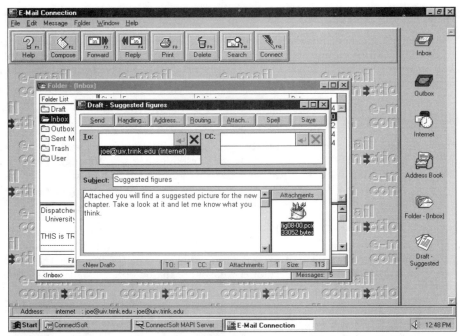

Figure 8-10: Once you have attached a file to a message, it is indicated in the message template.

From this point, you can continue to compose your message.

Your Internet Connection

When you finish composing your message, you are ready to send it. Click on the Send button at the top of the draft message template. This does not send the message; it simply saves it in the Outbox folder. The message remains here until you actually transmit it to your mail server on the Internet. Since the message remains in the Outbox folder until you transmit it, you can recall, edit, or delete the message at any time prior to transmittal.

When you are ready to transmit your message, you must establish your connection with the Internet. Once you connect to your provider, you can start the E-Mail Connection program, if it is not already started. To transmit the contents of the Outbox folder (your outgoing mail), click on the Connect icon on the toolbar, or press F12. The program establishes a connection with your mail server, and the following happens:

   1. The contents of your Outbox folder are transmitted to the mail server.

WHAT CAN GO WRONG

My mail wasn't sent

If your e-mail did not get sent, chances are it was because E-Mail Connection could not establish a link with your mail server. This could be due to several reasons. First and most likely, you entered the mail server address incorrectly when you were configuring the program. Click on the Internet icon at the right side of the program window, and then click on the Configure button. Check the mail server address with the one you received from your Internet provider.

Another cause that the mail did not get sent is that your mail server, for whatever reason, is not available. Most mail servers are available 24 hours a day, but sometimes problems occur that "take down" a mail server. If you suspect this is the problem, a quick call to your Internet provider can verify the fact. In such an occurrence, you have no choice but to try your connection again later.

2. The contents of your Outbox folder move to the Sent Mail folder.

3. The mail server is queried to see if there is any mail for you.

4. If there is mail, it is downloaded to your system and stored in your Inbox folder.

Once you complete these steps, you can disconnect from the Internet. Remember that E-Mail Connection allows you to read, compose, and manage your mail without an active connection.

Reading Your E-Mail

Once you have connected to your mail server on the Internet and retrieved your mail, it is stored in the Inbox folder. To view your messages, click on the Inbox folder in the middle of your screen. This opens the Inbox and displays the list of e-mail messages, as shown in Figure 8-11.

At the right side of the dialog box is the list of messages that you received. Here you can select your messages and view the contents of each message at the bottom of the dialog box. In the message box, you can scroll through the text of the message as desired. You can also resize the Inbox folder window so that you can see more of your message, and you can modify the borders within the window so that they represent the proportions you desire.

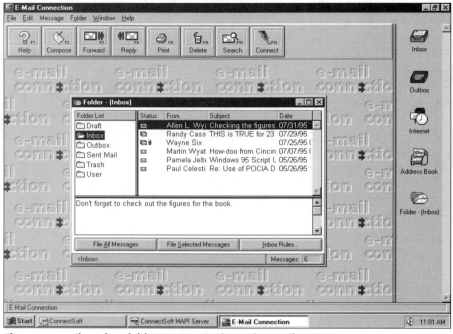

Figure 8-11: The Inbox folder stores your incoming mail.

Managing your incoming e-mail

If you use e-mail quite a bit, you can quickly become overwhelmed with messages. Part of effectively working with e-mail is learning how to manage the daily flow of messages. As you are working with each e-mail message, you can take five actions:

✦ Forward the message

✦ Reply to the message

✦ Print the message

✦ Delete the message

✦ Take no action

I discuss these actions in the following sections.

Forwarding a message

Forwarding a message means that you send an e-mail message you have received to another person. You take this action when someone else should receive the message instead of or in addition to you. Click on the toolbar's Forward icon or press F3. You see the dialog box shown in Figure 8-12.

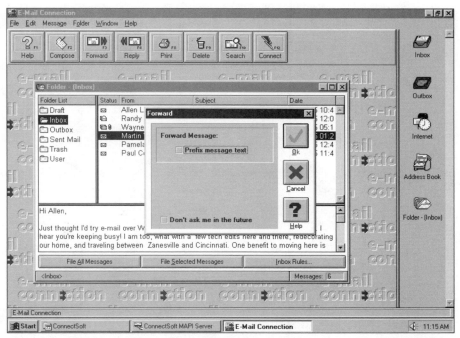

Figure 8-12: When you forward a message, you can add prefix marks to the original message.

Here you are asked if you want modify the original message so the new recipient can more easily tell it was forwarded. If you select the option, a prefix mark (>) is added to the beginning of each line of the original message. Whether you add the marks is up to you; there is no right or wrong method. When you make your choice, click on the Ok button. A message template appears, as shown in Figure 8-13.

This template is similar to the message template used when you compose a message, as discussed earlier in the chapter. The only difference is that the Subject field and the message body are filled in. At a minimum, all you need to do is supply an address for the new recipient and click on the Send button. Optionally, you can also change the Subject field or the contents of the message prior to sending.

Replying to a message

Replying to a message is similar to forwarding a message, except the recipient of the message is already known — it is the person who originally sent you the message. To reply to a message using E-Mail Connection, click on the Reply icon on the toolbar, or press F4. You then see the dialog box that is shown in Figure 8-14.

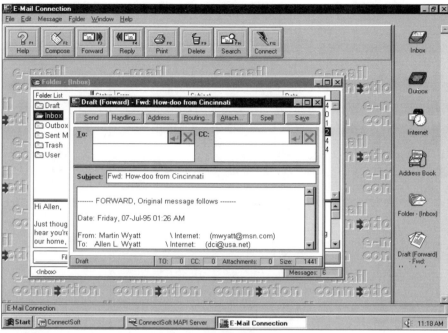

Figure 8-13: A message template is used when forwarding e-mail.

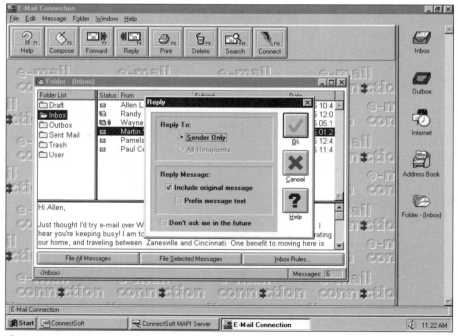

Figure 8-14: You can reply to a message in several ways.

Here you are asked exactly how you want the reply to be handled. At the top of the dialog box, you can specify who should receive the reply. If the message was sent only to you, then you can only reply to the sender. If you were one of several recipients of the message, then you can allow all other recipients to see your response.

At the bottom of the dialog box, you can indicate what should be included in the reply. Most people include the text of the original message as part of the reply to jog the original sender's memory. If you choose to do this, then you can also prefix each line of the message with a prefix character, as discussed in the previous section.

Once you are satisfied with the reply settings, click on the Ok button. A message template appears, as shown in Figure 8-15.

Notice that the only difference between this template and the message template used for forwarding a message is that the To: field already notes a recipient. You can, of course, add additional recipients. With the cursor in the message field, add your reply comments. When you finish with the message, click on the Send button, and the message is marked as ready to send.

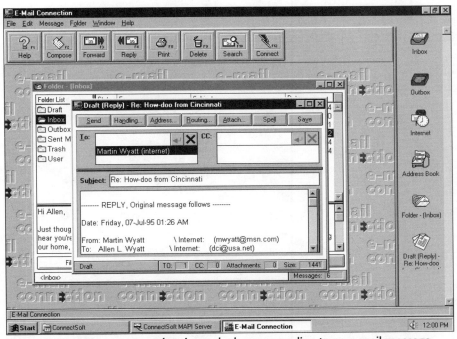

Figure 8-15: A message template is used when responding to an e-mail message.

Printing a message

You may want to print a hard copy of an e-mail message. This is easy with E-Mail Connection. Click on the toolbar's Print icon or press F8. The message is automatically sent to the default printer specified for your system. When the message is sent to the printer, it gets reformatted to fit a normal letter-size page.

Deleting a message

Some messages may require no action on your part. These are the type that you generally read and then discard, the same as with hard copy memos that you receive in your office. To delete a message, click on the toolbar's Delete icon or press F9. You then see a dialog box asking you to confirm your action, as shown in Figure 8-16.

As you can tell from this dialog box, you can delete a message in two ways. First, you can simply move the message from the current folder to the Trash folder. (This is the default method of deleting.) The Trash folder is similar in purpose to the Recycle Bin in Windows 95. It is a halfway stop before final deletion. By default, the message remains in the Trash folder until you permanently delete it from your system. The other deletion choice is Delete from database. This choice deletes the message entirely. After you chose your deletion option, click on the Ok button.

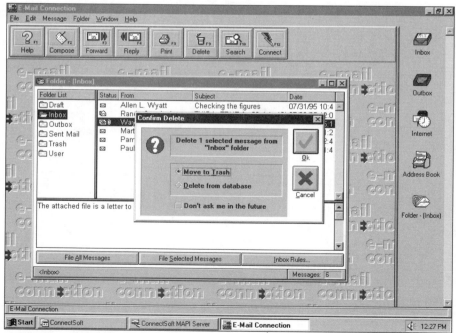

Figure 8-16: Before deleting a message, you are asked to confirm your actions.

Taking no action

No rule says that you have to do anything with your e-mail messages. You can allow them to accumulate in your Inbox folder. Many times I do this until I decide how to handle the messages. To take no action, simply leave the message in the Inbox; it will be there the next time you use the program.

Handling mail attachments

Earlier in this chapter, you learn how you could attach files to your e-mail messages. These files can be virtually anything you can think of, but they are typically word processing or spreadsheet documents. When you receive a message that has an attachment, it is represented in the folder window with a paper clip next to the Message icon. For instance, Figure 8-17 shows an e-mail message that has an attachment.

To save the file attached to the message, select the message that has the attachment you want to save. Then choose Attachments from the Message menu. You get the Message Attachments dialog box, as shown in Figure 8-18.

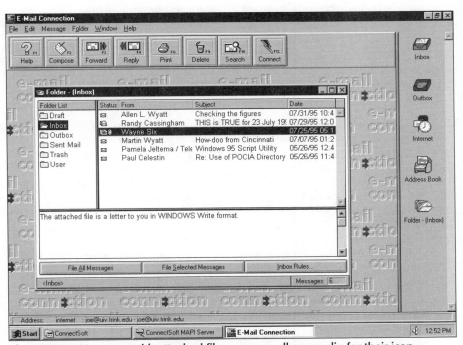

Figure 8-17: Messages with attached files use a small paper clip for their icon.

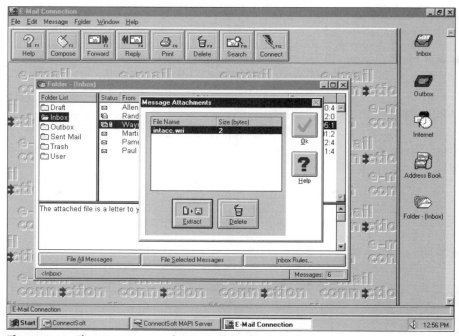

Figure 8-18: The Message Attachments dialog box indicates the files that are attached to a mail message.

This dialog box indicates the files attached to the message. Because a message can have more than one file attached to it, select the file that you want to save. When you click on the Extract button, you see a new dialog box, as shown in Figure 8-19.

You then indicate where you want the extracted file to be saved. You can also change the name of the extracted file. At the bottom of the dialog box, you can even indicate what you want to have done in addition to saving the extracted file. You can do either of the following:

✦ **Delete the file attachment.** If you click on the Delete file from message after extracting check box, the file is saved to disk and then removed from the original message.

✦ **Run the extracted file.** If you click on the Launch file after extracting check box, then the file is not only saved to disk, but Windows attempts to run the file. Choose this selection only if you are certain that the file is an executable program or if the file type is associated with an application that can use it. For instance, if Excel is installed on your system, then you could execute a file with an XLS extension, because those files are associated with the Excel application.

When you are satisfied with your selections, click on the Ok button, and the file is extracted.

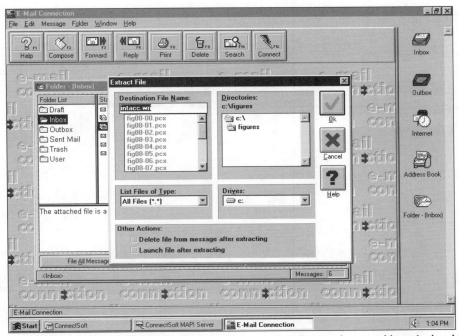

Figure 8-19: Before a file can be extracted, you must indicate where and how it should be saved.

Parts of a mail message

For an e-mail message to successfully travel through the Internet, it must be composed in the proper manner. Much of the complexity of an e-mail message is hidden by the e-mail software that you use. One mark of a good e-mail program is that it makes sending a message appear to be very easy.

An e-mail message consists primarily of two parts: the header and the message body. In addition, there can be message attachments, as described earlier in the chapter. You know about all these parts except for the message header. This portion of the message indicates the routing information for transmission of the message. At a minimum, the header contains the sender's address as well as that of the intended recipient. In reality, the header can contain quite a bit more information, such as the subject of the message (which you see in the mail list for a folder) and intermediate routing information.

If you are interested in seeing a message header, select the Header command from the Message menu. This displays the Message Header dialog box, as shown in Figure 8-20.

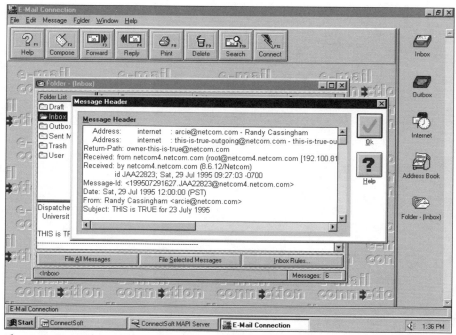

Figure 8-20: Each transmitted e-mail message includes a header that contains administrative information about that message.

The information in the header is created automatically by the e-mail software used to compose the message. On some messages, the lines in the header appear in a different order or additional information is included. The exact information or its order is not particularly important. What is important is that you realize that the first several lines of any received message are used for housekeeping; you can safely ignore this information unless you find it of interest. (This is why software such as E-Mail Connection does not show the header unless requested.)

Using Microsoft Exchange

Microsoft Exchange is the "communications center" provided with Windows 95. You use the program primarily for e-mail and for sending faxes. Microsoft Exchange is designed to act as an e-mail program for small local area networks. When you set up the program, you designate a place on the network that serves as the *post office* — a centralized database of messages that is used by Microsoft Exchange on every computer in the network.

As provided with Windows 95, Microsoft Exchange works only with other Exchange programs or with older versions of Microsoft Mail. The way Microsoft Exchange is written, however, allows mail clients to be added to the program. These clients provide the filters and coding that are necessary to access different mail systems such as the Internet. The client software that allows Microsoft Exchange to access Internet e-mail is part of the Microsoft Plus! Companion for Windows 95 (the Plus! pack), which is an add-on for Windows 95. Thus, to use Microsoft Exchange for Internet e-mail, you not only need Windows 95, but you also need the Plus! pack.

The purpose of this chapter is not to provide a detailed description of how you can use Microsoft Exchange. Instead, you learn the basics of installing the software and using it, along with the Plus! pack, to retrieve your e-mail from the Internet.

Installing Microsoft Exchange

You may have Microsoft Exchange installed on your system; this program is one of the installation options when you first installed Windows 95. Even if it is not installed, an Inbox icon should appear on your desktop. This icon, when double-clicked, starts either Microsoft Exchange or the installation program for Microsoft Exchange.

When you double-click on the Inbox icon, if you see the Microsoft Exchange inbox, then you know that you have Microsoft Exchange installed. If this is the case, skip to the next section; the balance of this section describes the process that you follow to install Microsoft Exchange. If you did not see the Microsoft Exchange inbox, then you should see the dialog box that is shown in Figure 8-21.

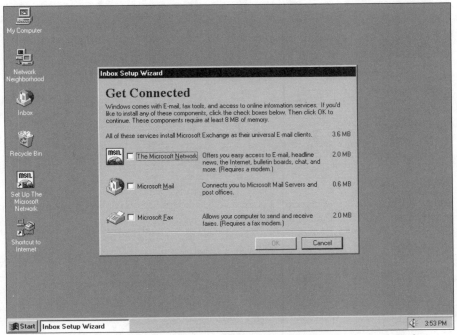

Figure 8-21: Windows 95 lets you know that it is about to install Microsoft Exchange.

This dialog box allows you to install any of the three major communications programs included with Windows 95. The one that you are interested in at this time is the mail portion of Microsoft Exchange, so click on the Microsoft <u>M</u>ail check box. When you click on the OK button, the proper files transfer to your hard disk. At this point, you may be prompted to insert your setup disks or the CD-ROM that you used to install Windows 95.

When the files have been transferred to your hard drive, Windows runs the Inbox Setup Wizard so that you can indicate how Microsoft Exchange should work. The first dialog box for the Inbox Setup Wizard is shown in Figure 8-22.

If you are not an experienced Microsoft Exchange user, accept the default setting of <u>N</u>o, and then click on the Next button. Shortly, you see the dialog box shown in Figure 8-23.

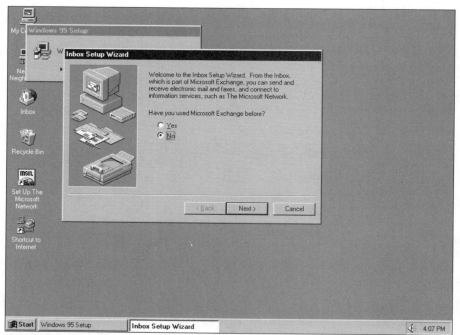

Figure 8-22: Once the Microsoft Exchange software has been installed, you need to configure it using the Inbox Setup Wizard.

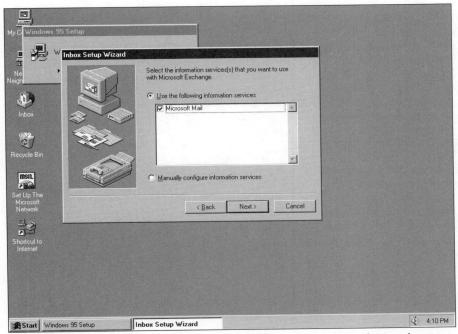

Figure 8-23: The first configuration step is to indicate which information services you will be using with Microsoft Exchange.

If you are going to use Microsoft Exchange on your local area network (LAN), then make sure that the Microsoft Mail option is selected. If you will not be using it on a LAN, then clear the check box. In the next section, you learn how to configure Microsoft Exchange to work with the Internet. When you have made your selection, click on the Next button. If you have indicated that you are using Microsoft Mail, you are prompted for the network path to your post office, as shown in Figure 8-24.

A post office is a centralized database that is used by Microsoft Exchange for storing and managing e-mail messages. If you aren't sure of your e-mail post office's location, check with your system administrator. You should have only one post office on any LAN; having more than one causes errors in delivering mail over the network. You can also click on the Browse button to check where your post office is located.

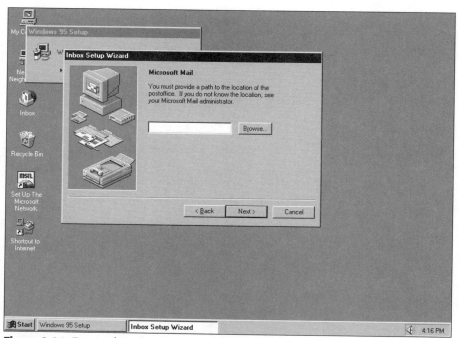

Figure 8-24: To use the Microsoft Mail portion of Exchange, you must indicate where your post office is located.

When you are satisfied with the path you have entered, click on the Next button. The Inbox Setup Wizard then accesses the post office and determines the names of the people registered there. You are presented with the dialog box that is shown in Figure 8-25.

Everyone on your network should have his or her own e-mail account set up at the post office. Setting up an account is done by the mail administrator, who is typically your network administrator. Click on the name for your e-mail account, and then click on the Next button. You are asked for the e-mail account password, as shown in Figure 8-26.

Enter the password assigned to you by the mail administrator. If you have forgotten the password, check with your administrator. When you have entered the password, click on the Next button, and the Inbox Setup Wizard finishes configuring Microsoft Exchange. You are now ready to begin using the program for regular e-mail.

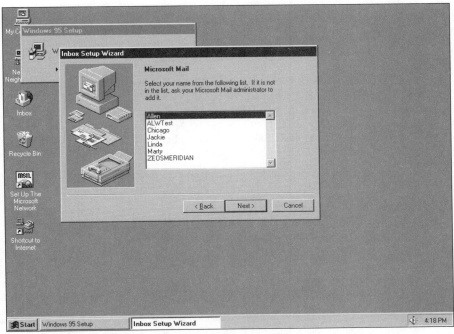

Figure 8-25: You must indicate the name used for your mail account.

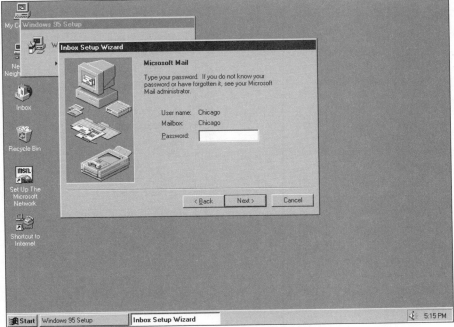

Figure 8-26: Every e-mail account is associated with a password.

Installing the Internet client

The Microsoft Plus! Companion for Windows 95 is a product that provides a collection of add-ons for the Windows 95 operating system. These add-ons provide a wide range of capabilities that can enhance the use of your computer. One of the tools provided with the Plus! pack is the mail client, which allows you to access an Internet e-mail server with Microsoft Exchange. To install this portion of the Plus! pack, follow these steps:

1. Insert the Plus! CD in your CD-ROM drive. The CD is configured to automatically run, and you soon see the screen shown in Figure 8-27.

2. Click on the icon to the right of the first option, Install Plus! This starts the setup program on the CD-ROM, and shortly you see the welcome screen.

3. Click on the Continue button. You are asked to verify your name and organization. These should be the same as those that you entered when you installed Windows 95, so click on the OK button to continue.

4. You are asked to confirm your user information by clicking OK. Do so, and you see the dialog box shown in Figure 8-28.

Figure 8-27: The Plus! CD runs automatically when you insert it in your system.

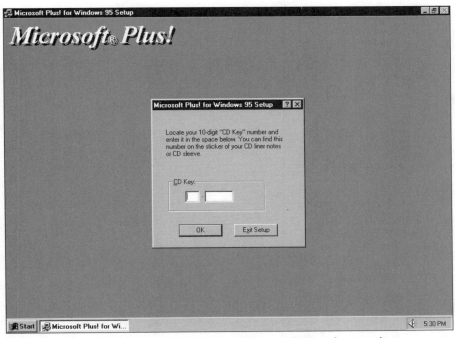

Figure 8-28: To use the Plus! CD, you must have a 10-digit CD key number.

5. Enter the 10-digit CD key number for your CD, which is attached to your CD. When you finish, click on OK.

6. The setup program shows you your product ID for the Plus! pack and asks you to write it down. In practice, there is little reason to do this, because you can always find the number while you are online. Click on the OK button to continue. Shortly, you see the dialog box shown in Figure 8-29.

7. Here you are asked to indicate where you want the Plus! files to be installed. For most users, the default location is fine, but you can change the location if you want to. Click on OK when you are ready to proceed, and you are asked if you want a typical or a custom installation.

8. Click on the Typical button if you want to install the normal portions of Plus!; click on Custom if you want complete control over the installation. I prefer clicking on Custom. Shortly, you see the dialog box shown in Figure 8-30.

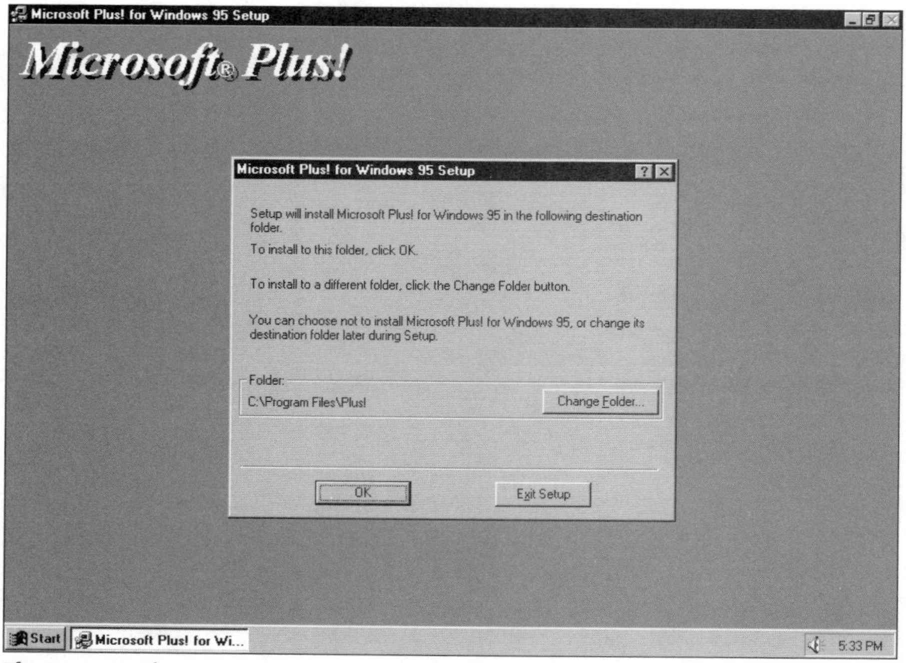

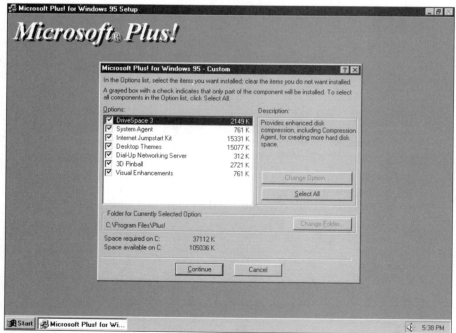

Figure 8-29: The setup program must know where to install the Plus! programs.

Figure 8-30: You can install all or part of the Plus! pack.

9. Click on the check boxes of those options that you do not want to install. For the purposes of this chapter, you must at least install the Internet Jumpstart Kit. When you are satisfied with your selections, click on the Continue button.

10. Depending on which Plus! options you are installing, you may be asked configuration questions for the specific options. Answer them as appropriate for your needs.

At this point, the necessary files of Plus! are copied to your hard drive. Copying the files may take a while, depending on the speed of your system. When copying is completed, your system files are updated and the setup program ends. The Internet Jumpstart Kit starts automatically, as discussed in the next section.

Configuring for the Internet

After you have installed the Plus! pack, you are ready to configure your system for the Internet. This configuration process starts automatically when you first install Plus!, or you can choose to run the Internet Jumpstart Kit at any time. (To do this, double-click on the Internet icon that appears on your desktop.) The first dialog box that you see in the Internet Setup Wizard is shown in Figure 8-31.

Figure 8-31: To use Microsoft Exchange to access your Internet e-mail, you must run the setup procedure.

Click on the Next button to proceed. You are asked how you want to connect to the Internet. For most readers, the answer is the default — Connect using my phone line. Click on the Next button to continue, and you are asked how you want to connect to the Internet, as shown in Figure 8-32.

You have two choices on how you can connect to the Internet: through The Microsoft Network or through a provider. If you have successfully completed the first seven chapters of this book, then you are using an Internet provider. (The Microsoft Network is covered in Chapter 17.) Click on the second dialog box option (I already have an account with a different service provider), and then click on the Next button. You then see the dialog box that is shown in Figure 8-33.

This dialog box is waiting for you to enter the name of your provider. Fortunately, you already set up your provider in Chapter 6. Click on the arrow to the right of the field, and choose the name that you set up for your provider. In my case, I simply chose the word *Internet*, which was the name that I gave to the dial-up account for my provider. When you have completed this step, click on the Next button.

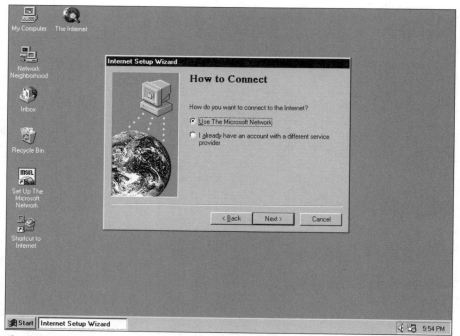

Figure 8-32: You can connect to the Internet through a provider or through The Microsoft Network.

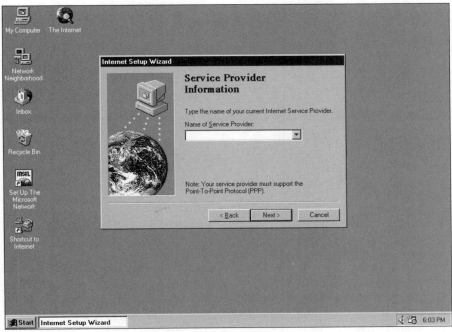

Figure 8-33: You must supply the name of your Internet provider.

Because you have already set up your Internet provider in Windows 95, you can breeze through the next couple of screens. In the first screen, you see the phone number used to connect to your provider. Because this is taken directly from your earlier configuration, accept it by clicking on the Next button. You are then asked for your user name and password. If you must manually sign on to your Internet provider (as discussed in Chapters 6 and 7), then leave the fields blank. Otherwise, if you are logged in automatically, the information should already be correct. Either way, click on the Next button.

The next screen asks you how you want your IP address assigned. Again, this is taken from the configuration information that you provided when you set up Windows 95 for using the Internet. Click on the Next button to continue. You are next asked for a DNS server address; here again, you can accept your earlier configuration information by clicking on the Next button. Finally you see the dialog box shown in Figure 8-34.

Click on the Use Internet Mail option to enable Microsoft Exchange to work with your Internet mail server. You can then supply your e-mail address (such as dci@usa.net) and the address for your e-mail server. (E-mail server addresses were discussed earlier in this chapter; they can be obtained from your Internet provider.) When you have filled in both values, click on the Next button. Your configuration information is saved, and you see a dialog box indicating that the setup is finished.

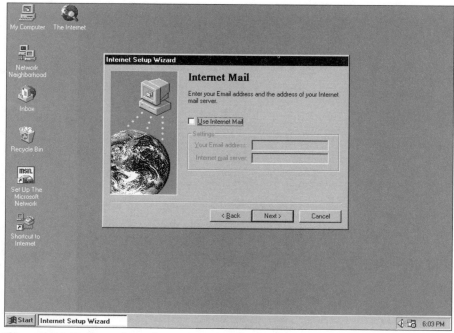

Figure 8-34: Here you have the option of setting up for Internet e-mail.

Microsoft Exchange and the Internet

As you may have noticed, you need to follow quite a few installation and configuration steps to make Microsoft Exchange work with the Internet. It may be some consolation, however, that you only have to perform the steps once. When you are done with them, you are ready to use Microsoft Exchange with the Internet. The next time you run Microsoft Exchange (by double-clicking on the Inbox icon), you are asked which configuration profile you want to use with the program, as shown in Figure 8-35.

The default, Internet Mail Settings, is perfectly acceptable. After all, that is why you went through all those configuration steps. Click on the OK button to accept the default profile, and you see the Inbox window, as shown in Figure 8-36.

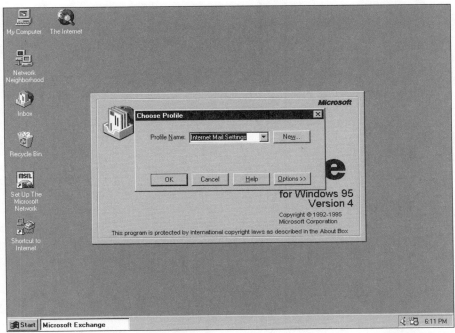

Figure 8-35: When you start Microsoft Exchange, you must select the configuration profile you wish to use.

If you worked through the first part of this chapter, this window may look familiar. In many ways, it is similar to the windows used with the E-Mail Connection software. Most e-mail programs perform the same basic functions, and many use similar interfaces. This means that many of the skills that you learned working with E-Mail Connection transfer easily to working with Microsoft Exchange.

At the top of the Inbox window is a command menu, and below that is a toolbar. You can select commands from either the menu or the toolbar. Many of the commands that are available through the menus are also accessible through the toolbar. The common e-mail operations that you may want to perform are described in the following sections.

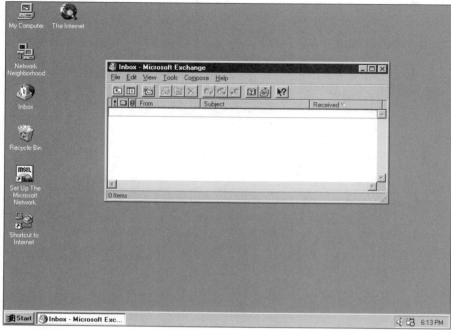

Figure 8-36: The Microsoft Exchange Inbox window.

Composing a message

To compose a message using Microsoft Exchange, you follow steps similar to the ones that you followed to accomplish the task under E-Mail Connection. Click on the New Message tool on the toolbar. This is the third one from the left, the one with the envelope on it. Shortly, you see the new message template, as shown in Figure 8-37.

In the template, fill out the To, Cc, and Subject fields. These fields serve the same purpose as those described earlier in the chapter. Addressing is also handled as described earlier. Once you supply this information, you can enter the message in the bottom portion of the template.

To attach a file to your message, click on the Insert File tool on the toolbar; the tool looks like a paper clip. This displays the Insert File dialog box, as shown in Figure 8-38. This is a standard file selection dialog box with one exception — there are a few extra controls at the bottom of the dialog box.

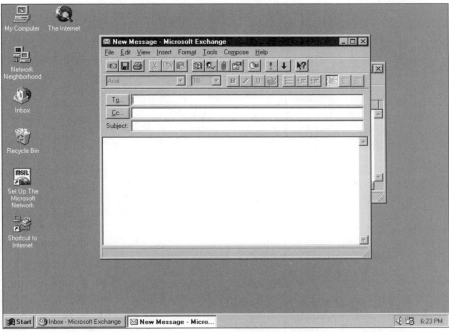

Figure 8-37: In Microsoft Exchange, you use a template to create a message.

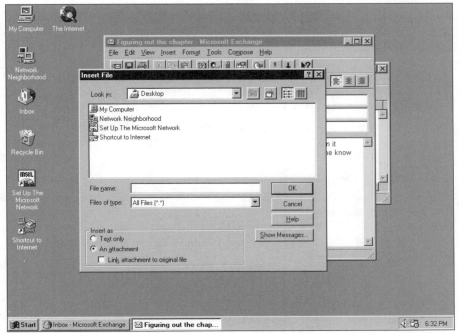

Figure 8-38: You can attach files to e-mail messages by selecting them from a dialog box.

WHAT CAN GO WRONG

Why can't I see other folders?

Microsoft Exchange uses the concept of folders, as does E-Mail Connection. These folders organize your e-mail into different categories. When you first start Microsoft Exchange, you see only the contents of your Inbox folder. If you want to see the contents of your other folders, you must display the folder tree. This is done by choosing the Folders option from the View menu. You can then choose different folders from the folder tree displayed in the Microsoft Exchange window.

Select the file that you want to attach, and then indicate the type of attachment it should be in the Insert as area of the dialog box. You can insert the file either as text or as an attachment. For most binary files (word processing documents, pictures, or spreadsheets), you should attach the file. If the file contains only a short amount of text, you may want to add it to the document as text. Doing so, however, may not be as handy for the recipient, who may find it easier to work with the binary file. When you have made your selection, click on the OK button.

When you finish addressing your message, entering the text of the message, and attaching any files, click on the toolbar's Send icon. This is the first one at the left, the one with the "speeding envelope" on it. This moves the message to the Outbox folder, pending your connection with the mail server.

Connecting to the mail server

To connect with your mail server, choose Deliver Now from the Tools menu. The actions taken by Microsoft Exchange then depend on whether you have an active connection to the Internet.

✦ If an active connection exists, Microsoft Exchange connects to the mail server. The mail in your Outbox folder is sent to the server, and any mail destined for you is sent to Microsoft Exchange.

✦ If no active connection exists, Microsoft Exchange dials the Internet for you and connects you to the mail server. The mail in your Outbox folder is sent to the server, and any mail destined for you is sent to Microsoft Exchange. When this two-way transfer is complete, the Internet connection is severed.

Microsoft Exchange does not close the connection if one is already open, because you could be using other tools on your system to access other Internet features. If you do not have an active connection, the program assumes that you want to connect, transfer your mail, and disconnect as quickly as possible. This reduces your online charges.

Reading your messages

Once you retrieve your mail, it appears in your Inbox folder as shown in Figure 8-39. This is similar to the way messages appeared in E-Mail Connection. Each line in the window lists a message, showing the sender, the subject, the day and time that the message was received, and whether the message has attachments.

To read a message, double-click on that message. A message window appears, and you can scroll through the message. As you can see in Figure 8-40, the toolbar at the top of the message window allows you to perform common actions on the message. The eight tools, starting at the left side, allow you to do the following:

✦ Print the message

✦ File the message in a folder

✦ Delete the message

✦ Reply to the sender

✦ Reply to the sender and all other recipients

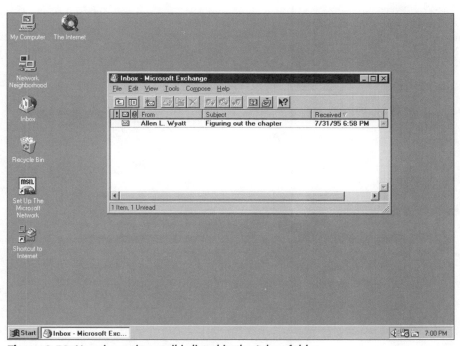

Figure 8-39: Your incoming mail is listed in the Inbox folder.

✦ Forward the message

✦ Move to the previous message

✦ Move to the next message

Figure 8-40: You can read and perform common actions on a message in the message window.

Summary

E-mail is the most common use of the Internet. Through the Internet you have access to millions of people around the world. If you know a person's address, then you can use special e-mail software to send your messages. In this chapter, you learn the following about e-mail:

✦ Many different software packages allow you to access and manage Internet e-mail. Many such programs are available directly through the Internet, or you can use Microsoft Exchange, which is provided with Windows 95.

✦ If you use Microsoft Exchange for your Internet e-mail, you also need the Microsoft Plus! Companion for Windows 95. This software, available at an additional cost, provides the client software that is necessary for Microsoft Exchange to interact with an Internet mail server.

✦ Regardless of the software that you use, you compose a message in similar ways. At a minimum, you must know the address of the recipient and a subject for the message — in addition to the body of the message itself.

✦ The e-mail address is the most important part of the message. Without the proper address, your mail cannot be delivered properly. The basics of addressing are discussed in Chapter 2.

✦ Most e-mail programs allow you to attach files to your e-mail messages. Attachments are transmitted with the message, and the recipient can save the attachment as a file on his or her computer. This capability is great for sending word processing documents, graphics files, and spreadsheets through the Internet.

✦ To send and receive e-mail, your software connects with a mail server on the Internet. This e-mail server is generally provided and maintained by your Internet provider. You need the address of the mail server to correctly configure your e-mail software.

✦ When you receive e-mail, you can read it on your computer and perform a number of actions on the message. For instance, you can delete it, print it, respond to it, forward it to someone else, or file it.

✦ An e-mail message consists of three basic parts: a header, a body, and attachments. The header and body are mandatory; the attachments are optional. The header contains administrative information that is necessary to properly deliver the body of the message.

In the next chapter, you learn one of the best uses for e-mail — mailing lists.

✦   ✦   ✦

Using Mailing Lists

Now that you know how you use your e-mail account, you may be interested in knowing how you can start using it to exchange information with other people on the Net. In this chapter, you learn all about mailing lists and what they can do for you. Here you learn about the following items:

✦ What a mailing list is

✦ How mailing lists are administered

✦ What a moderated mailing list is

✦ How to find mailing lists that you can join

✦ How to subscribe to a mailing list

✦ How to participate in a mailing list

✦ How to manage your mailing list subscription

✦ How to cancel a mailing list subscription

What Are Mailing Lists?

At the most fundamental level, the Internet's purpose is to share information. Whether the user is a researcher sharing information with a colleague across the country or a student finding information to complete a term paper, the same basis is there — the fast, efficient, and reliable transmission of information.

One vehicle for sharing information over the Internet is a *mailing list*. A mailing list is an electronic version of subscribing to a periodical. When you subscribe to a newspaper, newsletter, or magazine, you receive your periodical on a regular basis (that's why it's called a periodical). When you join an Internet mailing list, you receive information on a periodic basis that is related to the topic of the mailing list. The frequency of your receipts can vary: With some mailing lists, it may be weekly or monthly; with others, it may be every hour or two.

The mail that you receive as a result of joining a mailing list is the outpouring of a *discussion group.* Technically, a discussion group consists of people discussing a related topic. The information generated by the group is disseminated among other members of the group, with the intent that all will be interested. The mailing list is comprised of the addresses of the people who belong to the discussion group. When you add your address to the mailing list, you become part of the discussion group. When you remove your address from the list, you leave the discussion group.

Mailing List Administration

With millions of people connected to the Internet and thousands of discussion groups available, you may conclude that managing a mailing list can be a real headache. Two ways to manage mailing lists on the Net exist — by machine or by a human being.

Most mailing lists available through the Internet are managed automatically by computer programs, but many are handled individually. In addition, a mailing list can be moderated or unmoderated. The following sections discuss each of these management approaches.

Automatic management

Two primary programs are used for administering mailing lists accessible through the Internet. The first program is called *Listserv,* and the second is *Majordomo.* Listserv is a computer program used to administer mailing lists that originate on Bitnet. Bitnet is one of the older networks of the Internet; in fact, Bitnet predates the Internet itself. Majordomo is a program that is similar in purpose to Listserv — it automates the administration of Internet mailing lists.

A mailing list administration program maintains the names and addresses of the members of a discussion group; in effect, it manages the mailing list. The purpose of a program such as Listserv or Majordomo is twofold:

✦ **Membership maintenance.** The program allows names to be added or deleted from the mailing list. The program does this task by automatically processing requests from individual subscribers.

✦ **Mail routing.** As mail is sent, the program routes the messages to the other members of the group. In this way, the program acts as an information distribution point, using the mailing list as a guide.

To accomplish these two tasks, Listserv and Majordomo use a series of commands. You embed these commands in an e-mail message and send the message to the server's e-mail address. The server detects, parses, and acts upon these commands. Later in this chapter, you learn many of the commands that you can use with Listserv and Majordomo.

Human management

Not all mailing lists are managed by a computer program. Many lists are maintained by dedicated people who take care of the mundane management chores themselves. These individuals examine the mail you send, acting upon your requests (for example, to be added to the mailing list) and forwarding mail as necessary.

If a mailing list is managed by a computer program, a single e-mail address is used for the server. If it is administered manually, generally two e-mail addresses are available. One, used for the administrator, is reserved for administrative tasks. For example, you would use this address to send requests to be added to the mailing list or to have your name deleted. The other address is a relay address, meaning that if you send your mail to this address, it is automatically relayed to all people on the mailing list.

Moderation in all things

Regardless of the mechanics of managing a mailing list (automatic or human), the content of the discussion group can be *moderated* or *unmoderated*. A moderated mailing list means that a human being looks at the message before it is relayed to all mailing list subscribers; an unmoderated list is one in which the broadcast is automatic, without any intervention.

If a list is moderated, the moderator generally acts as a filter. He or she stops irrelevant messages (messages sent to the mailing group by mistake), harmful or objectionable messages (those that contain improper content), and duplicate messages (those usually posted in error more than once).

Netiquette

The correct address

Keep in mind the purpose of the two e-mail addresses associated with a manually administered discussion group. If you send your administrative requests to the relay address, then everyone on the mailing list (which could be thousands of people) knows that you want to join — and they also know that you don't have the slightest idea what you are doing. You will probably get a couple of hundred responses, providing everything from a helpful reminder of what you did wrong to a severe bashing for using the wrong address.

Some people object to the idea of a moderated discussion group, but it can be much more enriching than an unmoderated list. (Many of those same objectors seem to have no problem with the fact that their daily newspaper is effectively a moderated vehicle for transmitting information.) They view moderation as a form of censorship to be avoided. The reality, however, is that if a discussion group is too strictly moderated, it tends to fade away over time; subscribers leave the group, and new ones don't take their place.

Most mailing lists available through the Net are unmoderated. This fact is not because of any high-minded ideals (such as freedom of the press or airwaves), but simply because most mailing list administrators do not have the time to filter all postings that come through a discussion group. Although some may view the uncensored nature of these groups as enticing, getting a fair amount of "junk mail" is not unusual when you belong to such a group. For example, you may get the duplicate messages, subscription requests (broadcast by mistake), or irrelevant mail that a moderator would have stopped.

Finding Mailing Lists

The Internet provides access to thousands of mailings lists to which you can subscribe. Unfortunately, no single place exists in which you can look to find mailing lists. A few places are available where you can start your search, however.

The first thing you can do is subscribe to a mailing list that has the avowed purpose of informing subscribers about new mailing lists on the Net. The subscription address for this mailing list is interest-groups-request@nisc.sri.com. (This is an unmoderated Listserv mailing list; you can use the subscription commands that are covered later in this chapter to join.) The only problem with this route of finding mailing lists is that it only informs you about new mailing lists — those starting now or in the future.

To find the addresses of existing mailing lists, you can refer to several online sources. Indexes to mailing lists are available. You can access these indexes either through anonymous ftp (as discussed in Chapter 11) or through the World Wide Web (as covered in Chapter 15).

The best list of existing mailing lists is maintained at the Massachusetts Institute of Technology, and you can access it by using ftp to connect to the server at rtfm.mit.edu. Once connected, switch to the pub/usenet/news.answers/mail/mailing-lists directory. You will find 14 files (part01 through part14), which contain a huge list of public mailing lists.

The following are good Web locations to search for mailing list indexes:

http://www.neosoft.com/internet/paml

http://alpha.acast.nova.edu/listserv.html

COOL PLACES

Try this!

Thousands of mailing lists are available on the Net, but you may find the following interesting:

Subscription Address	Content
free-join@vix.com	Fathers' Rights & Equality Exchange (FREE)
gps-request@tws4.si.com	Discussion of Global Positioning System (GPS) technology
listserv@kli.org	Klingon language discussion group. Subject in body of message should be tlhingan-hol.
majordomo@global.org	Review of daily Texas Lotto drawing winners. Subject in body of message should be lotto-texas.
ultralight-flight-request@ms.uky.edu	Discussion of flying ultralight aircraft. Subject line should be subscribe, with no body to message.

Joining a Mailing List

Because mailing lists involve subscriptions, you may rightly assume that mailing lists include not only a group of recipients but also a way to add your name to the list and later remove it. Subscribing to a mailing list — regardless of the type of mailing list — is relatively simple. In most examples, all you need to do is send a single e-mail message, and you are added to the list.

When putting together your e-mail message, the wording you use (how you compose the message) depends on how the mailing list is administered. You can generally tell which type of program administers a mailing list by the e-mail address that you use to subscribe to the mailing list. The following will help you determine which type of system is responsible for a mailing list:

If the Address Contains This Word	It Is Administered By
listserv	Listserv
mailserv	Listserv
majordomo	Majordomo
request	A human being
subscribe	A human being

In addition, if the mailing list address does not have a domain name (such as edu, com, gov, or net), then the list is probably administered by Listserv. If the e-mail address does not contain any of these telltale signs, then the list is probably administered by a human being. In the following sections, you learn what is required to join each type of mailing list that you may run across on the Internet.

Joining a Listserv mailing list

The Listserv program automates the process of managing a mailing list. This program is typically found only on systems connected to Bitnet, although these systems are accessible through the Internet. When you send an e-mail message to a server, the server attempts to figure out exactly what it should do with the message. For this reason, the message that you send needs to follow a rather structured format. If it does not, then your desired action will not take place.

You may recall from Chapter 8 that an e-mail message generally consists of a subject, an address, a "copies to" field, and a body. When sending a message to a Listserv, you should not supply a subject, and you do not need to send copies to anyone else. The body of the message is where you enter the command that is interpreted by the Listserv program. This command has three parts, and you must format it as follows:

```
subscribe topic name
```

The *subscribe* key word is mandatory; your message must start with this word. The *topic* portion of the message is the subject of the mailing list. This subject is typically shown in every mailing list index you find. Finally, the *name* element is your full name. Thus, if I want to subscribe to a mailing list on copyediting (such as the one at listserv@cornell.edu), then my message would appear as follows:

```
subscribe copyediting-l Allen Wyatt
```

The topic, *copyediting-l*, was determined by finding the mailing list in an index of mailing lists.

Notice that your Listserv command line does not include information about your e-mail address. Listserv picks up your address from the e-mail message that it receives. Remember that various e-mail software programs add header information to an e-mail message; you have probably noticed the header in the messages you receive. This header indicates who sent the message, by address. Listserv gets the address from this header and thereby determines where to send the subscription.

Proper syntax

You must format your Listserv messages correctly. If you do not — even if you simply misspell a word — your message generates an error and returns to you.

If you get returned mail when trying to subscribe to a mailing list, don't worry. Check your spelling to make sure that it is correct, and make sure that the expected command elements are in the proper sequence. Make sure that the command is the only thing in your message, and try to send it again.

Before sending your subscription request, take a look at where the message is being sent. If you find an address for the mailing list and it does not contain any domain information, then you can assume that the address supplied is an original Bitnet address. For example, the address for subscribing to a mailing list about British and Irish history is the following:

> listserv@ucsbvm

It is easy to tell that this mailing list is administered by Listserv; the word *listserv* is the only user ID, and no domain is shown in the address. If you try to use this address in your e-mail, it will not be handled properly by the Internet. Instead, the message will return to you, indicating that the address could not be located.

To convert a Bitnet address to one that you can use on the Internet, try adding the suffix .bitnet to the address. For example, the mailing list address would become the following:

> listserv@ucsbvm.bitnet

It is possible, however, that the DNS server used by your Internet provider may balk at this address. Not all DNS servers do, but some may. In this case, you must route the message through a Bitnet gateway. Any of the following does fine:

> ✦ vm1.nodak.edu
>
> ✦ cunyvm.cuny.edu
>
> ✦ cornell.cit.cornell
>
> ✦ mitvma.mit.edu

To use these gateways, you must completely reformat the e-mail address using either a bang path or a modified Internet address. A bang path uses the following format:

> gateway!domain!user

All you need to do is provide these three parts, separated by the exclamation sign. (The exclamation sign is referred to as a *bang,* thus the name *bang path.*) For example, if you want to subscribe to the British and Irish history mailing list through a gateway, you use the following e-mail address:

cunyvm.cuny.edu!ucsbvm.bitnet!listserv

The other form, a modified Internet address, uses the following format:

server%user@gateway

Again, simply provide the three parts that are separated by the symbols indicated in the preceding example. Thus, the mailing list subscription address becomes the following:

ucsbvm%listserv@cunyvm.cuny.edu

It doesn't matter which naming convention you follow; any of the three provided here gets your message to Listserv on Bitnet.

Joining a Majordomo mailing list

Subscribing to a Majordomo mailing list is simple. All you need to do is send an e-mail message that contains a single command. Simply use the command *subscribe* followed by the topic to which you want to subscribe. For example, if I want to subscribe to the mailing list for those with an interest in telecommuting, I send an e-mail message to remote-work-request@unify.com. The message has no subject, and it contains the following line:

```
subscribe remote-work
```

The Majordomo server examines my message, pulls my e-mail address from the message header, and adds me to the mailing list.

WHAT CAN GO WRONG

Choke!

It seems that everyone likes to be unique (or cute) with his or her e-mail. Most e-mail packages have an option for adding the signature block automatically to your outgoing messages. If your e-mail package does this, Majordomo may try to parse and act upon the contents of your signature. To prevent this, always use the command "end" as the final command (on a line by itself) in your messages to Majordomo. The server then ignores everything in the message after this command.

Netiquette

> ## So how are the spouse and kids?
>
> Sending long, rambling requests to mailing list administrators is not polite. They may need to process several dozen or a hundred requests a day, and they probably don't have time to wade through a long, flowery message. Short, sweet, and to the point is usually a good rule of thumb.

Joining a manual mailing list

If the mailing list that you want to join is administered by a human being, the messages that you send do not need to be as formal or structured. In fact, the messages can seem almost free-form in nature. To subscribe, you simply send a request to the administrator. You can use any subject you want (the word *subscription* is generally good), and you can compose your message body in any manner you want. The following format is more than acceptable as the body of a subscription request:

```
Please add me to the subscription list for your Dungeons &
        Dragons discussion group.
My address is:  Allen Wyatt awyatt@whitehouse.gov

Thanks
```

Typically, after your request has been processed, the administrator acknowledges it. You should allow a day or two for acknowledgment, however. Human administrators, in spite of their best intentions, are not as fast as computerized administrators (which may take only a minute or two). If you do not receive an acknowledgment within a couple of days and you do not start receiving discussion group e-mail, check the address and send the message again.

Participating in a Discussion Group

After you subscribe to a mailing list, you should start receiving e-mail periodically. The amount of e-mail that you receive depends on how active the discussion group is and on the subject of the mailing list. For example, if the mailing list is simply for an Internet newsletter or magazine, you only get your e-mail every week or month. However, if the discussion group is an unmoderated mailing list in which everyone can respond, you may get mail every few hours. It is not unusual for an active discussion group to generate several dozen messages a day.

As you participate in your discussion group, you perform two main tasks: reading your e-mail and responding to the e-mail. Reading your e-mail is straightforward; you read it as discussed in Chapter 8. Responding is another matter, however.

Netiquette

> ## Oops!
>
> Don't forget that in an unmoderated mailing list, the messages you send out arrive in the mailbox of every user who subscribes to that mailing list. Consequently, you may not want to say anything personal, harsh, sexist, or otherwise offensive. The best guideline is to only send messages that you don't mind being made completely public.

You can take several approaches when participating in a discussion group. First, you can *lurk*. This means that you read messages but don't respond. Many Internet users are lurkers, either for lack of time, lack of interest, or self-consciousness. No rules exist that say you must respond to discussion group e-mail. No one will pull your subscription for "inactivity," and you will never be questioned as long as you stay quiet.

The other approach is to actively participate, meaning that you respond to the e-mail you receive. When you do this, you are actually responding to a large group of people; everyone who is a member of the mailing list receives a copy of your message. Make sure that you don't fire from the hip. Take your time to think through your response before sending off the first thing that comes into your head.

Managing Your Subscription

There may be times when you need to do more than start or stop your subscription to a mailing list. For example, you may need to suspend your subscription while you are away from your e-mail account for a week or so. Most types of mailing lists allow you to perform some sort of managerial tasks related to your subscription; otherwise, you could amass huge amounts of e-mail while you are away for a few days.

As with other mailing list related topics, how you control your subscription depends on how the mailing list is administered. The next few sections describe the steps to take for different types of mailing lists.

Controlling your Listserv subscription

The Listserv program has been around long enough that it has quite a few commands you can use to manage your subscription. These commands allow you to perform a number of actions besides starting and stopping your subscription, as you see in Table 9-1.

Table 9-1
Common Listserv Subscription Management Commands

Command	Meaning
get *filename filetype*	Receive a file (see index command)
index	Receive a list of files at this Listserv
info *topic*	Get information about a particular help file
lists	Get a description of available topics (can also use the modifiers detail, short, or global to affect information returned)
query *topic*	See a list of your distribution options for a particular mailing list
register *yourname*	Specify your name as you want the Listserv to use it
review *topic options*	Review a particular topic
set *topic options*	Set distribution options, such as suspending your subscription
stats *topic options*	Review statistics for a particular topic

Many of these commands require you to use the mailing list subject in place of the topic parameter. This is the same subject that you use when you first subscribe to the list. Additionally, some commands, such as *review*, *set*, and *stats*, rely on the specification of options. These options vary from server to server as well as from topic to topic.

Because the Listserv commands change from time to time and may vary from server to server, you can get a complete list of the commands supported by a particular Listserv by sending a single-word command message to the server. In the body of the message, use this command:

```
help
```

You receive a reply shortly thereafter that includes the requested list of commands and how to use them in your e-mail messages.

Controlling your Majordomo subscription

The commands offered by Majordomo are similar in purpose to those used with a Listserv, but subtle differences make the two command structures incompatible. Table 9-2 lists the various commands you can use with a mailing list administered by Majordomo.

Table 9-2
Common Majordomo Subscription Management Commands

Command	Meaning
end	Mark the last line of a command message (useful if your e-mail adds signature lines)
get *topic filename*	Receive a file (see index command)
index *topic*	Receive a list of files on the topic
info *topic*	Get information about a particular topic
lists	Get a description of available topics at the server
which	Receive a list of which topics you subscribe to at the server
who *topic*	Receive a list of who subscribes to a particular topic

Majordomo commands can vary from server to server, so it is a good idea to query your server regarding the commands it understands. You can get a complete list of the commands supported by a particular Majordomo by sending a single-word command message to the server. In the body of the message, use this command:

```
help
```

You receive a reply shortly thereafter that includes the requested list of commands and how to use them in your e-mail messages.

Controlling your manual subscription

When dealing with a human mailing list administrator, no special commands exist that you can use to control your subscription. Instead, if you have a problem or need to change your status, you send a message to the administrator indicating what you want to do. You receive a reply indicating what has been done with your subscription, or you may receive a request for clarification. Either way, because you are dealing with a human, management is not always as simple as a command message or two.

Leaving a Mailing List

When you are no longer interested in receiving the e-mail of a particular discussion group, you can cancel your subscription. Canceling a subscription is part of managing your mailing list memberships. Exactly how you cancel a subscription varies, again, by how the mailing list is administered. The following sections cover the steps that you take when the end has come.

Netiquette

| **The number you have dialed...** |
| You should remember to cancel your mailing list subscriptions if you stop using the Internet, abandon or change your e-mail address, or go on sabbatical. This courtesy cuts down on network clutter and reduces the amount of work done by a network administrator. |

Canceling a Listserv subscription

You can cancel a Listserv subscription by sending an e-mail message to the administration address for the mailing list. All aspects of the message should be the same except for the command line in the body of the message. Here you use the following format:

```
signoff topic name
```

Again, substitute the mailing list subject for *topic* and your full name for *name*. For example, if I want to cancel my copyediting mailing list subscription, I use the following command line:

```
signoff copyediting-l Allen Wyatt
```

When Listserv receives your message (assuming no other problems occur with the message), your name is immediately removed from the mailing list, and you stop receiving mail from the server.

Canceling a Majordomo subscription

You can cancel a Majordomo subscription by sending an e-mail message to the same e-mail address that you use to subscribe to the mailing list. All aspects of the message should be the same as your subscription request except for the command line in the body of the message. Here you use the following format:

```
unsubscribe topic
```

Substitute the mailing list subject for *topic*. For example, if I want to cancel my telecommuting mailing list subscription, I use the following command line:

```
unsubscribe remote-work
```

When the server receives the message, my name is immediately removed from the mailing list.

Canceling a manual subscription

As with placing a subscription, you don't need to formally word the request to remove your name from a manually administered mailing list. Simply compose a simple e-mail message, such as the following:

```
Please cancel my subscription to your Dungeons & Dragons
        discussion group.
My address is:  Allen Wyatt awyatt@whitehouse.gov

Thanks
```

This message is similar to the subscription message, but it is short and to the point. You can include a short explanation as to why you are dropping your subscription (administrators are sometimes curious), but stay away from long diatribes. Few administrators have time to read and respond to long-winded explanations of how your feelings were hurt or how your dog is sick and needs your attention. Again, the rule is short, sweet, and to the point.

Summary

A mailing list is a collection of individuals who want to participate in a discussion group about a particular topic. Thousands of mailing lists are available on the Internet, and you can join any or all of them. When you join a mailing list, messages from the discussion group are sent directly to your e-mail box, and you respond at will. Participation in a good mailing list takes time, but it can be rewarding and enriching.

This chapter discusses the ins and outs of mailing lists. Here you learn a broad range of skills that relate to this integral part of the Internet. Specifically, you learn the following items:

✦ Mailing lists can be administered by a computer program or by a human being. If administered by a program, several types of programs are used on the Internet, including Listserv, Majordomo, SmartList, and ListProc.

✦ Mailing lists can be moderated or unmoderated. A moderated mailing list simply means that the messages broadcast to the group are filtered by a human being, whereas an unmoderated mailing list has no human intervention.

✦ Indexes of mailing lists are available on the Net. Several excellent ones are available either through anonymous ftp or through the World Wide Web.

✦ You subscribe to a mailing list by sending a request to the administrator. If a program administers the list, then the message contains a command to add you to the mailing list. If it is administered by a human, a somewhat more verbose request is required.

✦ Mailing lists do not require a particular level of participation. You can choose to respond as you desire, or you can simply not respond at all.

✦ If your mailing list is administered by a program, commands that allow you to control your subscription are typically available. The commands vary from program to program and server to server, so it is a good idea to get a list of the available commands.

✦ You cancel a subscription in the same way that you start it — by sending an e-mail message to the administrator. The composition of the message depends on how your mailing list is administered.

In the next chapter, you learn how you can use the telnet program to visit distant places on the Internet.

✦   ✦   ✦

Using Telnet

One of the programs provided with Windows 95 is called *telnet*. You won't find it on any menu, but telnet is on your system nevertheless. (The program name is typically shown in lowercase letters to reflect its UNIX heritage.) This chapter covers the telnet program and shows how you can use it to access services on the Internet. Here you learn the following items:

- ✦ What telnet is
- ✦ How to run the telnet program
- ✦ How to connect to a remote system
- ✦ How to use log files
- ✦ How to find telnet servers

After you complete this chapter, you will understand the ins and outs of telnet, and you will be able to use it to enrich your experience on the Internet.

What Is Telnet?

When you use communications software and your modem to dial a computer BBS or online service, you connect to the BBS or service as if you were a terminal on that system. The communications software acts as an intermediary between your system and the remote system, handling routine communication chores for you.

The telnet program serves the same purpose as the communications software — it allows you to connect to other computer systems as if you were a terminal for that system. Through the program, you are able to connect your system to any other host on the Internet, provided you have the correct security privileges to access that system. Most computer systems on the Internet require user IDs and passwords to gain access, but some systems can be freely accessed. (Later in this chapter, you learn about a few of these systems.)

Once connected through telnet, all intermediary computers between you and the remote system become inconsequential. As far as the remote system is concerned, you are another user at another terminal connected to the computer. While you are connected, everything you type is sent to the remote computer, and everything sent to you by the remote computer is displayed on your system. Thus, telnet allows you to conduct real-time, two-way communication with the remote host.

Running the Telnet Program

Telnet started as a utility program in the UNIX environment. Most view it primarily as a TCP/IP program, meaning that telnet is one of the core programs you can expect to find in any system that implements TCP/IP. Normally the program operates at the command line, much like the ping or tracert commands that you use in Chapter 7. In Windows 95, however, the telnet command has been converted into a full-fledged Windows program.

To use the telnet program, you must be connected to your Internet provider. Don't worry about connecting yet, however. Later in this chapter, you learn how to use the program to connect to remote hosts. You can actually start telnet without connecting to the Internet first. To start the program, simply enter the following at the command prompt:

```
telnet
```

That's it. Shortly thereafter you see the telnet window, as shown in Figure 10-1. Notice that telnet uses the same interface as many other Windows programs, even though you start it from the command line.

Figure 10-1: The telnet program uses an interface like many other Windows programs.

The telnet menus

At the top of the telnet window is a menu bar with four choices. The Connect menu is used to control the connection with the remote system. It includes the following choices:

✦ **Remote System.** This option is used to specify the remote system with which you want to establish a connection.

✦ **Disconnect.** After you use the Remote System command to establish a connection, you can use this command to break the connection.

✦ **Exit.** This option is used to exit the program. (You can also exit by clicking on the Close button in the upper-right corner of the telnet window.)

Additionally, the <u>C</u>onnect menu maintains a list of the telnet sites that you most recently visited. These sites are listed at the bottom of the <u>C</u>onnect menu.

The next menu is the <u>E</u>dit menu. This menu serves much the same purpose as similar menus in other Windows programs. The menu choices are as follows:

✦ <u>C</u>opy. This command is the same as pressing Ctrl+C; it copies the selected text onto the Clipboard.

✦ <u>P</u>aste. This command is the same as pressing Ctrl+V; it copies the contents of the Clipboard to the location of the cursor.

✦ Select <u>A</u>ll. This command selects all text on the screen. It provides a fast way to select everything before you use the <u>C</u>opy command.

You use the <u>T</u>erminal menu to change the attributes of your telnet window or telnet session. Just as with the other telnet menus, this menu offers three choices:

✦ <u>P</u>references. This option allows you to change the attributes of the telnet window. The available attributes are discussed in the following section.

✦ Start <u>L</u>ogging. When this option is selected, you can choose a file into which you want to record your telnet session. Log files are discussed later in this chapter.

✦ <u>S</u>top Logging. This option stops the recording and closes a log file. The effects of this command are discussed later in the chapter.

The final menu, <u>H</u>elp, provides assistance for running telnet. After you learn the basics of the program, I doubt that you will ever need the help system.

Setting telnet preferences

Many Windows programs allow you to configure how the program should operate and how it should appear on the screen. Telnet is no different; it allows you to set configuration preferences that affect the operation of the program. To do this, select the <u>P</u>references option from the <u>T</u>erminal menu. You then see the Terminal Preferences dialog box, as shown in Figure 10-2.

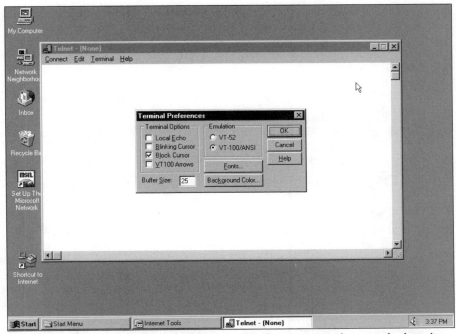

Figure 10-2: The telnet program allows you to indicate your preferences for how it operates and looks.

The Emulation section is perhaps the most important section of this dialog box. Here you indicate how you want telnet to behave in relation to the remote system. Remember that each system you connect to using telnet assumes that you are nothing but a terminal for that system. This assumption means that your system, through the telnet program, must behave like a dedicated terminal. Two types of terminals exist that telnet can emulate — a VT-52 and a VT-100/ANSI. The setting you make here, in the Terminal Preferences dialog box, instructs telnet how to react to the terminal control codes that the remote system sends. For example, the code to clear the screen may be different for one type of terminal than for another. Setting the proper terminal emulation ensures that the telnet program behaves as it should.

To the left of the Emulation section is the Terminal Options section. Here you specify how you want some aspects of the telnet terminal to appear. This section lists these four options:

✦ **Local Echo.** Some remote systems do not echo your characters as you type them. If, as you are typing, you cannot see the characters that you are entering, you should select this option. If you see two of each character that you type, turn this option off.

✦ **Blinking Cursor.** This option allows you to toggle (on or off) whether the cursor blinks. Sometimes a blinking cursor helps you locate it on the screen; other times it is distracting. Set the option according to your personal preferences.

✦ **Block Cursor.** Normally the telnet terminal includes a block cursor, about the width of the letter *C*. If you prefer, you can turn the block cursor off, in which case the cursor appears as an underline of the same width.

✦ **VT100 Arrows.** This option indicates what character sequence telnet should transmit when you press the arrow keys. With most systems, leaving this option unselected works fine; pressing the arrow keys results in "application mode" character sequences being sent. If you know that the system to which you are connected can actually use the cursor control keys to control the cursor, then select the option.

Just below the Terminal Options section is a setting identified as Buffer Size. This setting indicates how large a buffer you want telnet to set aside for received information. The value represents lines of text; thus, the default of 25 tells telnet to retain the previous 25 lines of received text, or about a full screen. You can specify a higher value, up to 399 lines, by changing the setting. During a terminal session, you can then scroll through the lines received by using the scrollbar at the right side of the telnet window.

It is a good idea to choose a buffer size larger than 25 lines. Often, while you are connected to a remote system, you receive more than 25 lines of information in a single burst. If you have your buffer set to 25 lines, you have no way to see the information that has scrolled off your screen. Set the Buffer Size to a value of 50 or 100.

You can also set the font used by the telnet program. To do this, you click on the Fonts button. You then see the Font dialog box, as shown in Figure 10-3. This dialog box may look familiar, because it is very similar to other font-selection dialog boxes in Windows 95.

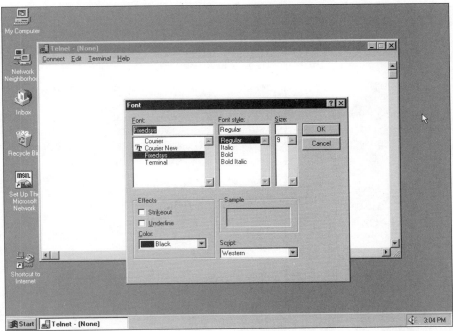

Figure 10-3: The Font dialog box allows you to pick the font you want used in telnet.

This dialog box also allows you to specify the color of the font (in the Color pull-down list) and the effects to be applied to the font (Strikeout or Underline). After you make your font selection, click on the OK button, and the change is made.

If you click on the Background Color button, you can select the color used for the background of the telnet window. White is the default; you should pick a color that contrasts well with the text color you selected.

Adding telnet to the menu

Rather than opening an MS-DOS window every time you want to run telnet, you may want to add the program to your Windows 95 menu system. For example, you can add a selection in your Start menu that contains access to all of your Internet tools, including telnet. You can create the selection in the Start menu in a number of ways, including the following:

1. Exit the telnet program, if you have not already done so.

2. Right-click on the Start button. This displays the Start Menu folder in a window.

3. In the window, select New from the File menu, and then choose Folder. A new folder appears in the Start Menu folder window.

4. Change the name of the folder to something descriptive, such as Internet Tools.

Now, whenever you click on the Start button, you see a menu choice entitled Internet Tools. If you select the option, you find it is empty; this makes sense because you just created the option. To put your first selection into the menu (the telnet program), simply follow these steps:

1. Double-click on the new Internet Tools folder that you just created. The contents of the folder (nothing is in it) are displayed in a window.

2. Select New from the File menu, and then choose Shortcut. The Create Shortcut Wizard appears, as shown in Figure 10-4.

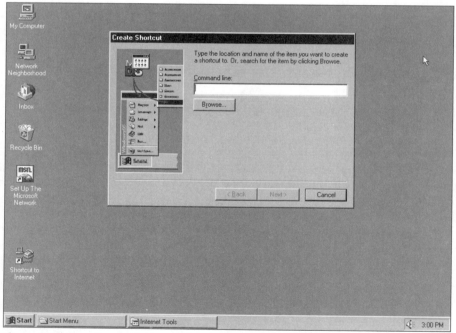

Figure 10-4: The Create Shortcut Wizard allows you to make your own shortcuts.

3. In the Command line field, enter the name of the command that you want to run — telnet.

4. Click on the Next button. The Wizard now appears as shown in Figure 10-5.

5. The Create Shortcut Wizard asks you for the name that you want to use for this shortcut. The default name, Telnet, is derived from the telnet program itself. If this default is OK, click on the Finish button. Otherwise, change the name, and then click on the Finish button.

The window for the Internet Tools folder appears, as shown in Figure 10-6. The folder now contains a single shortcut to the telnet program. When you double-click on the shortcut, the telnet program starts. Better yet, the telnet command now appears as an option in your menu system; you simply select Internet Tools from the Start menu, and then choose Telnet to run the program.

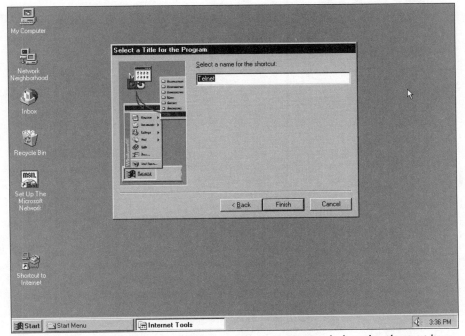

Figure 10-5: The name you specify for your shortcut appears below the shortcut icon, once the shortcut has been created.

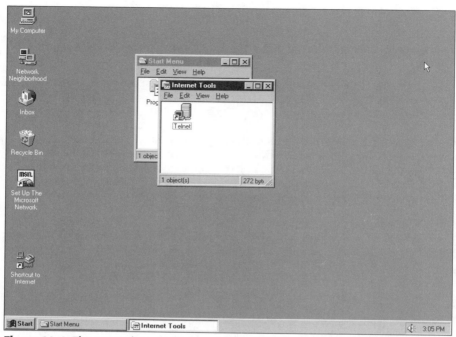

Figure 10-6: The new telnet shortcut appears within the Internet Tools folder.

Connecting to a Remote Site

To use telnet to connect to a remote site, you must first establish a connection with your Internet provider. After you make the connection, start the telnet program as previously described. The telnet window appears, as shown in Figure 10-1. You are now ready to use telnet to make a connection. You can connect to any system on the Internet, provided that you have the authorization to use that host. Some systems allow free access, whereas others require you to have an account set up on them. To set up an account, you should contact the system administrator for the remote site. You can usually do this using e-mail.

To make a telnet connection, select the Remote System option from the Connect menu. This option displays a dialog box, shown in Figure 10-7.

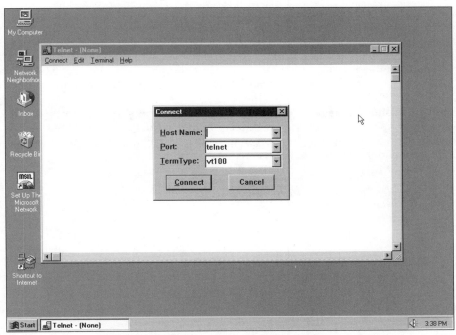

Figure 10-7: The Connect dialog box is used to initiate a telnet connection.

In the Connect dialog box, three fields appear. These fields are used during the connection process to specify the type of connection that you want to establish. The following three sections describe the purpose of each field.

Picking a host name

In the first field in the Connect dialog box, you enter the address of the system to which you want to connect. Addressing is discussed in Chapter 2. You may remember from the chapter that two types of addresses are used on the Internet: DNS and IP. The address you enter in the Host Name field can be either a DNS address (such as abc@xyz.net) or an IP address (such as 215.142.32.5); telnet understands both types.

Picking a port type

In the second field, you specify the type of port to use at the remote system. A port is nothing more than a connection to a computer. For example, on your system, you probably have two or three ports. These ports go by names such as serial port, parallel port, or mouse port. Remote systems on the Internet also have ports, al-though there may be dozens or hundreds of ports on the same system. These ports are used exclusively for communications.

A computer port is analogous to a marine port. To conduct any business with a ship (such as loading or unloading cargo), the ship must be docked in port. The same is true with computer ports; to conduct any business with a remote computer, you must be connected to a port. The port is the point through which information flows. When you connect to a remote computer, you do so through a port. When you later break the connection, the port is then available for other systems to use.

Ports have different names. Some systems assign numbers to their ports, whereas others use specific names, such as main or telnet. In the Port field of the Connect dialog box, you can specify the port that the telnet program uses while it is negotiating a connection. When you first use telnet, five port names are defined in the pull-down list for this field:

- ✦ telnet
- ✦ daytime
- ✦ echo
- ✦ qotd
- ✦ chargen

Of these port names, telnet is the default. The names represent common port names recognized by a variety of computer systems. In most instances, you can accept the default. Some systems may expect you to use a different port name or number; in such a case, you can either pick it from the list (if the port is available) or enter the specific port information. Some systems may also use different ports for different programs. It is not uncommon to have different services running on the same computer but accessed through different ports. In these instances, knowing the port number is important so that you can access the information you want.

Picking a terminal type

Earlier in this chapter, you learn about terminal types. In the telnet Preferences dialog box, you indicate the type of terminal that you want telnet to emulate. Although that setting controls the online behavior of telnet, the TermType field in the Connect dialog box indicates the terminal type that telnet uses to negotiate a connection with the remote system. Five choices are available in the pull-down list for this field:

- ✦ vt100
- ✦ ansi
- ✦ DEC-VT100
- ✦ VT100
- ✦ ANSI

Although some of these choices may seem the same, remember that many remote systems on the Internet make a distinction between uppercase and lowercase letters. Thus, vt100 and VT100 are not the same choices (at least not to some computer systems). The default setting for this field is the first option, vt100. In most cases, this terminal type is fine. You can enter a different terminal type if one is necessary for the system to which you are connecting.

It is important to understand the purpose of the TermType field. You should not confuse it with the terminal emulation setting in the telnet Preferences dialog box. Although both settings deal with terminals, the two are not related. Setting the TermType field does not modify the terminal emulation setting or vice versa.

Making the connection

As an example of how telnet works, assume that you want to connect to the LawNet legal network. The address for this connection is lawnet.law.columbia.edu. If you enter this address into the Host Name field of the Connect dialog box and then click on the Connect button, telnet tries to connect with the remote system. You do not see any screen activity while this is occurring. Shortly, however, you see a login prompt on your screen, as shown in Figure 10-8.

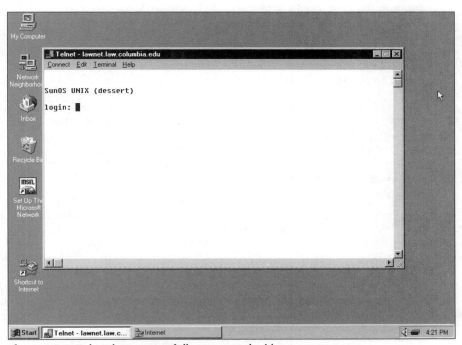

Figure 10-8: Telnet has successfully connected with a remote system.

Hey! What I type looks funny

After you connect to a remote site, if you cannot see what you are typing, then the remote system probably is not echoing your characters to you. Most systems provide the echo; an echo allows you to know that what you typed was received. If you cannot see what you type, then you can turn on local echoing to overcome the problem:

1. Choose Preferences from the Terminal menu. This displays the Terminal Preferences dialog box.

2. Make sure that the Local Echo option (at the left of the dialog box) is selected.

3. Click on the OK button.

If, instead of no characters, you can see two of each character that you type, follow these same steps, but make sure that the Local Echo option is not selected.

LawNet is a free-access system; the only thing that you need to know is the login ID. Type **lawnet,** and then press Enter. This login connects you to the system, and you quickly see quite a bit of other information pass by on the screen. Eventually, you are asked for additional information, as shown in Figure 10-9.

This prompt is common for most Internet systems. The LawNet computers want to know what type of terminal you are using. The default is VT100, which is one of the terminal emulations supported by Windows 95 telnet. To accept this option, press Enter. If you are using the VT-52 emulation instead, then choose VT52 and press Enter.

Finally, you are connected to LawNet, and you see the main LawNet menu, as shown in Figure 10-10. This menu is unique to LawNet; other systems have different menus or different command sequences.

During the connection

Exactly what you do after you connect to a remote system depends on the system to which you connect. Most free-access telnet sites contain some type of menu or help system so that you are not stranded. You should try different commands and menu choices to explore the information available to you.

Remember that, while you are connected, you are nothing but a terminal to the remote system. Thus, you interact with the remote system directly; what you see is up to that system. As far as telnet is concerned, the only thing that you can do while connected is type at the keyboard or capture your session in a log file (as described in the next section).

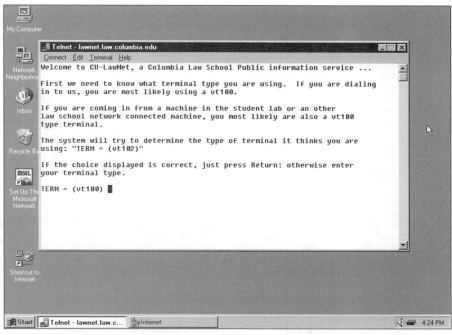

Figure 10-9: The first information screen from the LawNet system.

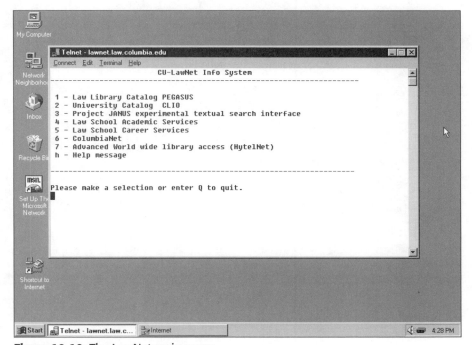

Figure 10-10: The LawNet main menu.

Telnet places

You can connect to literally thousands of places with telnet. The following addresses, however, may be fun to try:

Host Name	Port	Service
culine.colorado.edu	859	Basketball (NBA) information
culine.colorado.edu	860	Hockey (NHL) information
culine.colorado.edu	862	Baseball (MBA) information
culine.colorado.edu	863	Football (NFL) information

My screen contains gibberish

If, after you connect to a remote system, you find that your telnet window is filled with many meaningless characters, your terminal emulation may be set incorrectly. Earlier in this chapter, you learn that remote systems may send control characters to your system; these characters control the way information is displayed on the terminal. If the terminal type you specified in telnet preferences does not match the terminal type used by the remote system, then you may see gibberish on the screen.

To correct the problem, change the terminal type in telnet (if necessary) to match the terminal type used by the remote system. The process for doing this is covered earlier in this chapter. If this still doesn't work, and you are connected to a UNIX system, then follow these steps to change the terminal type that the UNIX system expects you to use:

1. At the UNIX shell prompt (usually a $), type **set.** This displays information about the terminal settings used by the remote system.

2. Verify that the environment variable TERM is set to VT100.

3. If the TERM variable is not set to VT100, enter the following two command lines at the UNIX prompt:

```
set TERM=vt100
export TERM
```

For most UNIX versions, this process resets the terminal type to VT100, and telnet behaves as normal. If you still have problems, contact the administrator of the remote system to see how you can specify a different terminal type.

Using a log file

If you have used a regular communications program, you may know what a *log file* is. Log files contain the contents of a communications session. You typically use log files to create a record of your session for later use. For example, you may be connected to a system with which you are having problems. By creating a log file, you can save a record of what occurred and later analyze it without racking up online charges with your Internet provider.

To create a log file, select Start Logging from the Terminal menu. When you select this option, you see the dialog box shown in Figure 10-11.

In the Open log file dialog box, you specify the name of the file that you want to create. Specify a drive and folder where the file should be stored, and then indicate a name for the log file (in the File name field). All log files have a filename extension of log, unless you indicate a different extension. For example, if you enter a filename of MyLog, then the file created is MyLog.log. If you enter a filename of MyLog.txt instead, then the default extension is not used and your file has the txt extension you specified.

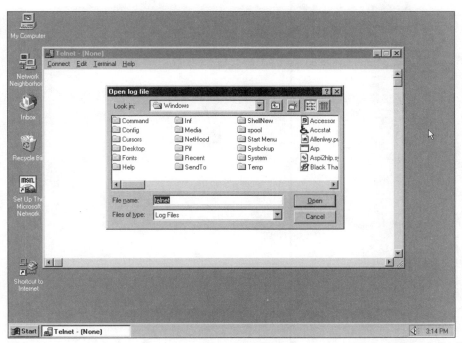

Figure 10-11: When you create a log file, telnet allows you to specify the name of the file.

After you open a log file, everything that appears in the telnet window is saved to the log file. The created log file is a regular ASCII text file, which includes the contents of your session. To close the log file, either quit the telnet program or choose Stop Logging from the Terminal menu. You can then examine or change the contents of the log file using a text editor (such as the Notepad accessory) or a word processing program.

Breaking a connection

After you finish communicating with a remote location, you can end your session in one of three ways. The most genteel method is to inform the remote system that you are finished. Different systems use different commands for this task. For example, one system may have a menu choice to end the session, whereas another may use a command such as quit or exit. When you end a session in this manner, the remote system breaks the connection, and telnet informs you that the connection has been lost (as shown in Figure 10-12).

Figure 10-12: When the telnet connection is broken by the remote system, you are informed of the event.

Another way to end your session is to choose the Disconnect option from the Connect menu. After you choose this option, the connection breaks, the telnet screen clears, and you are ready to make another connection. When you break a connection in this manner, no dialog box appears to indicate what happened, and you are not asked to confirm your action.

The final method of ending your session is to simply exit the telnet program. When you do this, the connection is not only lost but the telnet window is removed from your desktop.

Finding Telnet Servers

Many times, finding telnet servers just happens. You may run across a server address in a magazine or book, or on another online service. After you become aware that telnet is available, the addresses start to pop out as you go about your normal affairs.

Internet resources are available, however, that help you locate addresses. Many of these addresses offer telnet service, and some have specialized telnet servers that you can access. It is interesting that the services that allow you to find Internet addresses also use the telnet interface.

Two primary services are available. The first is called a *whois* server, and the second is the *netinfo* service. These services are described in the following sections.

Whois

Several different whois servers are located around the Internet. These servers are used to locate addresses for the different systems connected to the Net. Perhaps the best whois server is the one maintained by InterNIC. (This group is described in Chapter 2.) You can connect to this server by following these steps:

1. Open a telnet window.

2. Choose Remote System from the Connect menu. This option displays the Connect dialog box.

3. Use whois.internic.net for the Host Name.

4. Click on the Connect button. Shortly thereafter you see the first screen, as shown in Figure 10-13.

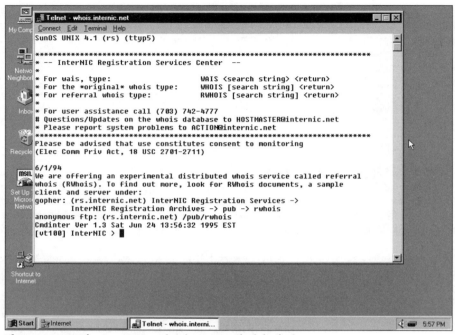

Figure 10-13: The InterNIC maintains a wonderful whois server.

Once connected, simply type **whois,** and then press Enter. This command connects you to the whois server, and you see the whois prompt:

```
Whois:
```

At this point, you can enter queries to determine the names of different hosts. Just enter a key word, and the whois server returns any entries that contain that word. For example, you may want to find a list of hosts having to do with milk. You type **milk**, and then press Enter. The server responds with information, as shown in Figure 10-14.

This search resulted in three matches, which are displayed. You can then search for other hosts, if you want. When you find one that looks interesting, simply jot down the address; you can then use it to attempt a telnet connection.

After you finish using the whois server, type **quit**, and you exit the whois server. You can then type **exit** to terminate the telnet session with the InterNIC.

Figure 10-14: Searching for hosts with key words is the purpose of a whois server.

Finding whois servers

Virtually anyone can start a whois server if the person has the resources, the inclination, and the time. Typically, whois servers are maintained by large organizations responsible for a large number of hosts or Internet connections. Because the Internet is such a dynamic place, the whois servers that are available change quite often.

You can find a current list of whois servers by using anonymous ftp to retrieve the file sipb.mit.edu/pub/whois/whois-servers.list. (Ftp is described in detail in Chapter 11.) This list, maintained by Matt Powers of MIT, currently contains over 175 entries. This file also includes some good background information on how whois servers work.

Netinfo

The University of California at Berkeley maintains a network service that is very helpful in finding addresses. This service, called netinfo, can by accessed by following these steps:

1. Open a telnet window.

2. Choose Remote System from the Connect menu. This option displays the Connect dialog box.

3. Use netinfo.berkeley.edu for the Host Name.

4. Use 117 as the Port.

5. Click on the Connect button. You see the first screen shortly, as shown in Figure 10-15.

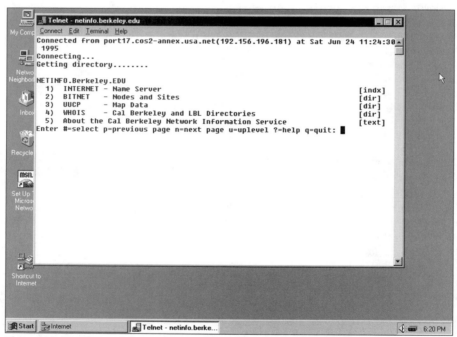

Figure 10-15: The netinfo service provides a variety of available options.

At this point, you have several options. You can access the UC Berkeley and LBL (Lawrence Berkeley Labs) whois server by choosing Option 4. This server functions similarly to the one described in the preceding section, except that it only maintains information on the addresses related to UCB and LBL.

The most interesting service at netinfo is accessed by choosing Option 1 — the Name Server. When you choose this option, you are asked to enter the arguments to use for a search. You can enter any key word, address, or host name that you desire. After you press Enter, you see a menu of searches that you can perform using the arguments (see Figure 10-16).

These seven choices indicate the various types of databases in which you can search for information. You should select the one that is most applicable to what you are searching for. For example, if you are looking for host names (names of remote systems), then you should choose Option 1, the HOST selection.

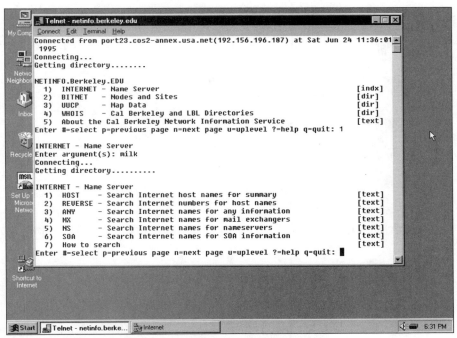

Figure 10-16: Netinfo allows you to do a number of searches.

Summary

The telnet program provided with Windows 95 is a Windows-based version of a UNIX program that has been around for decades. Telnet provides one of the original ways to connect to different systems on the Internet. In this chapter, you learn how you can use telnet to cruise the Internet and gather new information. Specifically, you learn the following items:

✦ You normally run the telnet program from the MS-DOS command line; when you do, a new telnet program window is opened.

✦ You can add the telnet program to your menu system to access it from within the Windows environment. Only a few steps are necessary to create the custom menus required.

✦ Connecting to a remote system using telnet is easy. All that you need are the address of the system and the port number. (You also learn that not all systems require an explicit port number.)

✦ Once you connect to a remote system using telnet, you in effect become a terminal on that system. Any commands that you enter are received and acted upon directly by the remote system.

✦ Log files are used to record the contents of a communication session. Telnet allows you to create log files using a simple menu command. These log files can be reviewed and edited later, when you are not connected to the Internet, using a normal text editor or word processor.

✦ There are literally thousands of telnet servers on the Internet. Finding them is largely a matter of perseverance and awareness, but you can find Internet addresses to help you track down telnet servers. Two useful tools for tracking down addresses are provided by whois servers and by the netinfo service at UC Berkeley.

In the next chapter, you learn about another basic Internet tool — the ftp program.

✦   ✦   ✦

Using Ftp

The Internet is an amazing conglomeration of systems, each of which has a multitude of resources to offer those tenacious enough to locate them. Once you locate information, you need some way of transferring it to your system. This is the point where the ftp program comes in. This chapter covers the use of ftp, including how to transfer files to your system. Here you learn the following items:

+ Exactly what ftp is
+ How to start the ftp client program on your system
+ What ftp commands are available
+ How to connect to an ftp server elsewhere on the Internet
+ How to navigate the directory structure on an ftp server
+ How to use index files to help you figure out what is on the ftp server
+ How to transfer a file to your system
+ How to break the ftp connection

Additionally, you learn how you can locate ftp servers around the Internet. By the time you are through with this chapter, you will be able to access files and transfer them to your system very easily.

What Is Ftp?

Ftp started out as a UNIX utility for transferring files. In fact, ftp is an acronym for *file transfer protocol*. Because so many UNIX systems were on the Internet, ftp was used extensively to transfer files across the Internet. In reality, ftp is more than a file transfer utility. As its name suggests, ftp is also a standard (a protocol) for how files are transferred.

Like many other Internet utilities, ftp relies of the concept of client/server relationships. On the Internet, many ftp servers are used as file archive sites. These sites can easily be accessed by anyone on the Internet, provided he or she has an ftp client program. Windows 95 includes an ftp client program that you can use to access any ftp server on the Net.

Starting the Ftp Client Program

Since the early days of the Internet, when most of the connected systems used UNIX, the ftp utility has migrated to machines that use different operating systems. Windows 95 provides a command-line version of ftp that you can use to transfer files from ftp servers. To use the ftp command, open an MS-DOS window. You do this by selecting Programs from the Start menu and then choosing MS-DOS Prompt. After the window is open and you are at the command line, the simplest way to start ftp is to type the following command:

```
ftp
```

After you press Enter, you see the ftp command line on the screen:

```
ftp>
```

This line means that ftp is running and awaiting your command. Later in this chapter, you learn the different commands that you can use at the ftp command line.

Although ftp is very easy to start, it does include some additional switches that you can use on the command line. Table 11-1 lists the various command-line switches for ftp.

Table 11-1
Command-Line Switches for the Ftp Command

Switch	Meaning
host	Specifies the host name or IP address of the ftp server to which you want to connect.
-d	Turns on debug mode, so that all ftp commands passed between the client and server are displayed.
-g	Turns off the ability to use wildcard characters in filename specifications.
-i	Turns off interactive prompting while transferring multiple files.
-n	Turns off autologon when initially connected to the server.
-s: filename	Specifies a script file named filename. This file contains ftp commands that run when the ftp command first starts.
-v	Turns off the display of ftp server responses.

To use the switches, all you need to do is include them after the ftp command. For example, if you want to start ftp and turn on the debug mode, you enter the command as follows:

```
ftp -d
```

Understanding Ftp Commands

When the ftp prompt is visible, you can no longer use MS-DOS commands. Instead, you must use commands that the ftp program understands. These commands allow you to perform tasks related to both your own system (the client) and the remote system (the server). Throughout the rest of this chapter, you learn how to use these commands to accomplish common ftp tasks. Table 11-2 lists the various ftp commands that you can use.

Table 11-2
Ftp Commands

Command	Purpose
! command	Runs the specified command on the local computer.
?	Displays descriptions for ftp commands. This is identical to help.
append	Appends a local file to a file on the remote computer, using the current file type setting.
ascii	Sets the file transfer type to ASCII (the default).
bell	Toggles the bell setting. If the bell is on, a bell rings after each file transfer is completed; if it is off (the default), no bell is used.
binary	Sets the file transfer type to binary.
bye	Breaks the connection with the ftp server and exits the ftp program. This is the same as the quit command.
cd directory	Changes to the specified directory on the remote computer.
close	Ends the ftp session with the remote server and returns to the command interpreter.
debug	Toggles the debug setting. If on, the messages between the client and server are displayed; if off (the default), these messages are suppressed. This command is the same as the -d command-line switch.
delete filename	Deletes the specified files on the ftp server.

(continued)

Table 11-2 *(continued)*

Command	Purpose
dir	Displays a directory on the ftp server.
disconnect	Breaks the connection with the ftp server but remains within the ftp program.
get *filename*	Copies *filename* from the ftp server to your system using the current file transfer type. This is the same as the recv command.
glob	Toggles the filename globbing setting. If on (the default), wildcard characters can be used in filenames; if off, wildcard characters cannot be used. This command is the same as the -g command-line switch.
hash	Toggles hash-mark setting. If on, a pound sign (#) prints for every 2048 bytes of data transferred with get or put; if off (the default), hash marks are not displayed.
help	Displays descriptions for ftp commands. This command is identical to the question-mark (?) command.
lcd *directory*	Changes to the specified directory on the local computer.
ls	Displays an abbreviated directory on the ftp server.
mdelete *filelist*	Deletes multiple files on the ftp server.
mdir *filelist*	This command is the same as the dir command but allows you to specify multiple files or directories.
mget *filelist*	Copies the files in *filelist* from the ftp server to your system using the current file transfer type.
mkdir *directory*	Creates a directory on the ftp server.
mls *filelist*	This command is the same as the ls command but allows you to specify multiple files or directories.
mput *filelist*	Copies the files in *filelist* from your system to the ftp server using the current file transfer type.
open *host*	Establishes a connection with the ftp server whose host name or IP address is specified by *host*.
prompt	Toggles the prompting setting. If on (the default), it prompts you during multiple file transfers before transferring each file; if off, then no prompting occurs. This is the same as the -I command-line switch.
put *filename*	Copies *filename* from your system to the ftp server using the current file transfer type. This command is the same as the send command.

Command	Purpose
pwd	Displays the name of the current directory on the ftp server.
quit	Breaks the connection with the ftp server and exits the ftp program. This command is the same as the bye command.
recv *filename*	Copies *filename* from the ftp server to your system using the current file transfer type. This command is the same as the get command.
rename *file1 file2*	On the ftp server, this command renames *file1* to *file2*.
rmdir *directory*	Deletes a directory on the ftp server.
send *filename*	Copies *filename* from your system to the ftp server using the current file transfer type. This is the same as the put command.
status	Displays the current status of the ftp connection and any toggles.
trace	Toggles the packet tracing setting. If on, it displays the route (between the client and server) of each data packet; if off (the default), then routing is not displayed.
type *xfertype*	Sets or displays the file transfer type. Type binary is the same as the binary command; type ascii is the same as the ascii command. Without the *xfertype* parameter, the current transfer type is displayed.
verbose	Toggles the verbose setting. If on (the default), it displays all ftp responses; if off, no responses are displayed. This is identical to the -v command-line switch.

Connecting to an Ftp Server

Before you can connect to an ftp server, you must know the address of the server you want to access. (Later in this chapter, you learn more about locating ftp addresses.) For the purposes of this chapter, assume that you want to connect to the ftp server at the University of North Carolina at Chapel Hill. The address for this server is sunsite.unc.edu.

After you have an address, exactly how you connect to an ftp server depends on where you start. If you start from the MS-DOS command line, you connect to a server using the following command:

```
ftp sunsite.unc.edu
```

This command starts the ftp client and establishes a connection to the specified host. If you have already started the ftp program (as discussed in the previous section), then you connect to an ftp server by typing the following at the ftp prompt:

```
open sunsite.unc.edu
```

Regardless of which method you use, you shortly see the greeting from the remote ftp server, as shown in Figure 11-1. If you are connecting to a system other than the ftp site at UNC, the information that displays after you connect is different.

At this point, the ftp server is waiting for you to log in to the system. If you are using ftp to connect to a system on which you have special rights, you provide your user ID and password at this point. Most ftp sessions are conducted using a guest status on the server. This status is called *anonymous ftp.* This means that you sign on the system as a guest and have the privilege level of a guest.

To start an anonymous ftp session, type **anonymous** as your user ID. After you press Enter, the server displays a message telling you what to do next and then prompts you for a password. This password is always your e-mail address. While access is not denied if you input someone else's e-mail address, common Internet courtesy dictates that you use your own address.

After you enter your password (e-mail address), you are fully connected with the remote ftp server. Your screen appears similar to Figure 11-2.

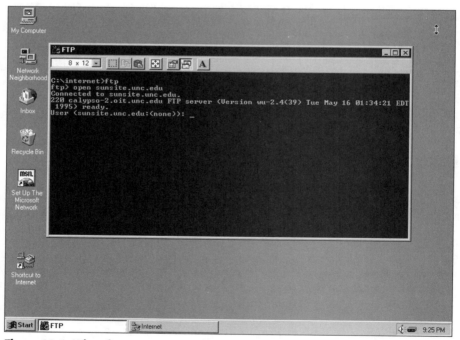

Figure 11-1: When ftp connects to a remote system, you see a message from that system.

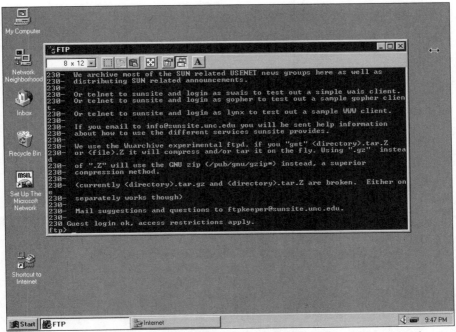

Figure 11-2: After logging in to the remote ftp server, you see the ftp command prompt.

Calling all anonymous guests

When using anonymous ftp, it is accepted behavior to use *anonymous* as the user ID and your full e-mail address as the password.

WHAT CAN GO WRONG

Connection problems

When trying to connect to an ftp server, you may not be able to get fully connected. The possible reasons for this problem are as follows:

✦ You may have misspelled the host name of the server while trying to connect. Use the open command to try connecting again.

✦ You may have forgotten to enter a password (which should be your e-mail address). Use the open command to try connecting again.

✦ The system that you are calling does not allow anonymous ftp 24 hours a day; you may need to try again later.

✦ The system has a limited number of anonymous ftp ports available; again, you may need to try later.

At this point, you can read any messages that the system administrator felt inspired to post. You may actually want to read through the information; you often find important information about where files are located or about new services.

During the Connection

After you connect to an ftp server and log in to the system, you are left at the ftp command prompt. You are now ready to use any of the ftp commands to accomplish the work that you need to do on the server. Typically, most people want to transfer files. This task involves moving around the directories on the remote server, finding the files you want, and then transferring them. (These tasks are covered in the following sections.)

If you ever forget the various ftp commands while you are connected, you can use either the ? or help commands (both produce the same results) to get a quick memory jogger. For example, if you type **help,** you see a list of the various commands available, as shown in Figure 11-3.

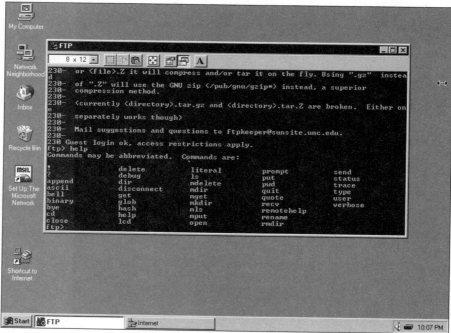

Figure 11-3: The help command displays a list of the ftp commands.

To see the specifics about an individual command, simply enter the help command followed by the command with which you need help. For example, if you forgot what the mget command was for, you can type the following to see a very short description:

```
help mget
```

Moving through directories

The first task in finding files on a remote ftp server is to learn how to navigate through the directories on that system. If you have worked with PCs for any length of time, you should be familiar with directories. A directory is a structure that allows a disk drive to have some semblance of order. In Windows 95, the term *folder* is used instead of directory, but the concept is the same.

To see what files and directories are available on the remote server, type **dir** at the ftp command line. Figure 11-4 shows an example of what such a directory looks like.

Figure 11-4: The dir command displays a directory of the remote server.

A second command that can provide directory information is the ls command. If you enter this command, you see only the names of the files and directories on the remote server. Figure 11-5 shows the results of the ls command. (Compare it to the results of the dir command in Figure 11-4.)

If, instead of looking at an entire directory, you want to view only part of a directory, you can use the MS-DOS wildcard characters; these characters also work on the remote system. The asterisk (*) represents any number of characters, while the question mark (?) represents a single character. Thus, you can use the following command to view all files that begin with the letters *abc*:

```
dir abc*
```

Take a look back at Figure 11-4. Notice that the dir command lists quite a bit of information about each file or directory. In fact, it lists more information than you can get with the MS-DOS dir command. This output is produced by a UNIX system, so the information provided follows the UNIX command protocol. If you are connected to a different system that runs an operating system other than UNIX, you see a differently formatted directory.

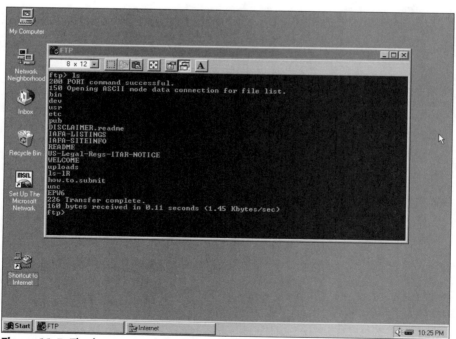

Figure 11-5: The ls command displays an abbreviated directory of the remote server.

At the right side of the directory list is the name of the file or directory. You probably noticed that filenames can be quite long in UNIX. While Windows 95 allows you to have long filenames, this feature is a relatively new development in the PC world. Notice, as well, that some files have more than one period. In UNIX, periods do not indicate the type of file; they are simply other characters that can be included in the filename.

At the left side of each directory entry, you see the attributes of the file or directory. The first character of the attributes is the key to understanding what you can do with the directory entry. The following are the common first-character attributes that you see:

Attribute	Meaning
-	Disk file
d	Directory
l	Linked reference

In short, you can use file management commands (such as those that download files) if the attributes of the file start with a dash. If the attributes start with d, then you can use the directory navigation commands to view the contents of those directories. If the attributes start with an l, then the name (at the right side of the entry) shows an alias — a link between one name and another. Thus, the ls-lR -> IAFA-LISTINGS entry is a linked reference. When a reference is linked, it means that if someone tried to download the ls-1R entry, he or she would instead receive the IAFA-LISTINGS file.

So how do you change from one directory to another? You use the same command that you use in the DOS environment. The cd command, followed by the name of the directory, sends you to that directory. Thus, if I want to change to the pub directory, I enter this command:

```
cd pub
```

If you forget which directory you are in, you can use the pwd command. (The command pwd is an acronym for *print working directory.*) Figure 11-6 shows the results of first using the cd command to change directories and then using the pwd command to show the name of the current directory.

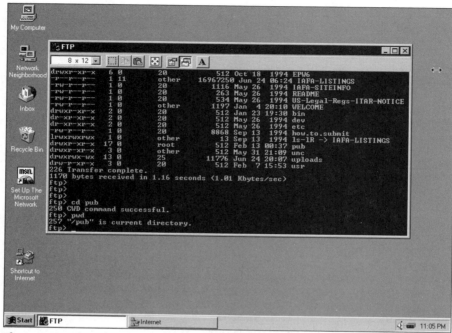

Figure 11-6: The cd and pwd commands are used to control the working directory on the ftp server.

Using index files

When you are connected to an ftp server, you are basically looking around in someone else's computer system. Because you are not familiar with the other system's structure, it is best to spend some time looking around to see what is available. (The navigation commands discussed in the preceding section allow you to do that.)

Ftp sites offer another type of help as well. These help files are called *index files*. These files are text files that explain what is in a certain directory. Most directories at most ftp sites have one of these types of files. The filename typically has the word "index" or "readme" in it; very often, the index file is near the top of the directory list.

To use an index file, you must transfer it to your computer system and then view it. (Transferring files is covered in the next section.) After you transfer the file, you can view it without even leaving ftp. For example, if you retrieve a file named Index.txt, you can enter the following at the ftp command prompt:

```
!more Index.txt
```

The exclamation point tells ftp to execute the command line using the local operating system. Thus, the MS-DOS window uses the more command to display the contents of Index.txt. The result is that you can review the index file for information about what is on the remote system. You can then use other ftp commands to transfer other files.

Transferring files

Transferring files is at the heart of ftp; this task is what most people love to do on the Internet. To transfer files, you need to do two things:

✦ Make sure that you are using the proper transfer type.

✦ Use a transfer command to copy the file to your system.

Transfer types can be ascii or binary. Ascii transfer types are appropriate if you are transferring a normal text file. If you are transferring anything else (including programs and multimedia files), you should switch to the binary transfer type. To change the transfer type, use either of the following commands at the ftp prompt:

Command	Result
ascii	Sets the file transfer type to ASCII
binary	Sets the file transfer type to binary

After you set the transfer type, it stays set until you explicitly change it again. You can see the current setting of the transfer type by using the type command. Figure 11-7 shows what happens when you use the type command after setting the file transfer type to binary.

Three commands are available that you can use to transfer files to your system. The get and recv commands are identical to each other; you use them to transfer a single file from the ftp server to your system. The mget command is used to transfer multiple files where a wildcard character cannot be used.

Before you transfer a file, particularly a large one, it is a good idea to turn on hash marks. This is a setting that, if enabled, displays a pound sign (#) every time 2,048 characters have been transferred to your system. When hash marks are not turned on, you see nothing while a file transfer is in progress. The only signal you have that tells you the transfer is progressing is the periodic accessing of your hard drive. To turn on hash marks, use the following command:

```
hash
```

If you use the command a second time, hash marks are turned off. The command is a toggle; every time you use it, the setting is reversed. Thus, the default value of off is changed to on the first time that you use the command.

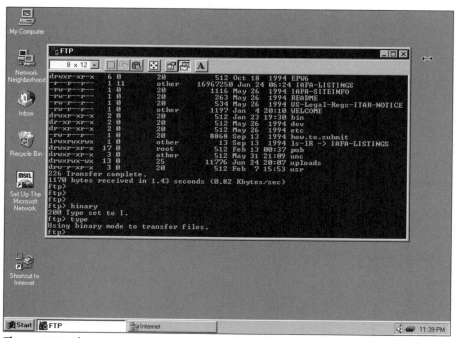

Figure 11-7: The type command is used to show the current transfer type setting.

WHAT CAN GO WRONG

Get won't get

If you use the get command to transfer a file and the ftp server indicates that it cannot find the file, there may be several causes for the problem. First, make sure that you are typing the filename correctly; misspelling a filename is quite easy. Second, make sure that you are not trying to download a directory. Remember that you can only download files that have a dash (-) in the first character of the left-most column or those that have an *l* and point to other files.

Finally, make sure that you used the same capitalization on your files as that on the ftp server. If the ftp server runs on a UNIX system, then capitalization is significant. In this case, the following two files are completely different from each other:

MyFile.txt

myfile.txt

If you are connected to an ftp server that runs on a Windows NT server, then the capitalization is not critical.

After you use the directory navigation commands (covered in an earlier section) to locate the file you want to transfer, you can use the get command. For example, Figure 11-8 shows the appearance of the screen after transferring a sound file (nosir.wav) from the UNC ftp server that I connected to earlier in the chapter.

Files that you transfer are placed in your current directory. If you want to change to a different directory on your own machine, you can use the lcd command. Use this command in the same manner that you use the cd command at the DOS prompt, but the leading *l* character indicates to the ftp client that this is a local command.

Another feature of the get command is that it allows you to rename a file as you copy it. For example, when nosir.wav was transferred in the previous example, it was copied to a file called nosir.wav in the current directory on the local machine. However, if you had wanted this file to be copied to a file called NewSound.wav on the local machine, you would have used the following command:

```
get nosir.wav NewSound.wav
```

The first file specification tells ftp the name of the file to retrieve, and the second filename indicates the name to be used on your system.

Figure 11-8: Transferring files with ftp is very easy.

Commands that affect the ftp server

Ftp provides a rich set of commands that deal with managing directories and files. This classification includes the following commands:

Command	Result
delete	Deletes a file
mdelete	Deletes multiple files
mkdir	Creates a directory
rename	Renames a file
rmdir	Deletes a directory

Most of these commands may look familiar to readers who know the DOS system. Ftp allows you to use these commands, but you may be stopped by the remote system. Typically, any commands that permanently affect files and directories on the ftp server require a higher security level than what you are given through an anonymous ftp session. If you feel that you need to use these commands on the server, you may need to contact the system administrator and get an ftp account and password.

In addition, ftp provides commands that are designed to transfer files to the ftp server. These commands, the opposite of the commands that transfer files to your system, are as follows:

Command	Result
append	Appends your file to a file on the server
mput	Copies multiple files to the server
put	Copies a single file to the server (same as send)
send	Copies a single file to the server (same as put)

Again, the applicability of any of these commands to a particular ftp server is up to the system administrator. Some systems allow you to upload files but possibly to a special area. Other systems are more strict, not allowing any file transfers to the server. If you have files that you need to upload, you again may need to contact the system administrator for an account that gives you the security clearance to use these commands.

Breaking the Connection

You can break your ftp session with the remote computer in two ways. If you are done with ftp completely, you can simply enter the following at the ftp prompt:

```
bye
```

This command logs you off the remote system and quits ftp. The bye command is identical to the quit command, so you can also use quit to achieve the same effect. If you want to remain within ftp (perhaps you want to contact a different ftp server), then you use the following command:

```
disconnect
```

The close command is the same as the disconnect command, so it can be used to achieve the same purpose. After you use either disconnect or close, you are left at the ftp prompt, where you can continue to issue ftp commands.

Finding Ftp Servers

As with finding telnet addresses, finding ftp servers can be a hit-and-miss proposition. If you find an address for a host on the Internet, you can always try to connect to it using ftp. No penalty exists if you make an error or a bad assumption about the server; you simply won't be able to connect.

Often, you see addresses in the following format:

ftp://ftp.celestin.com/xyz/abc/def.txt

This format is called *URL,* an acronym for universal resource locator. This format is used for the World Wide Web. You learn more about the Web in Chapter 15, but understanding how to read a URL is beneficial here.

The address in URL format simply means that the noted address (and file specification) is an ftp server. The portion of the address to the left of the two slashes (ftp:) indicates that this is an ftp server. The part up to the next slash (ftp.celestin.com) indicates the address that you use to connect with the ftp server. The balance of the information in the address indicates the path to the file on the remote server.

Summary

The ftp program is one of the core utilities that you use on the Internet. With ftp, you can locate and transfer files over the Internet. In this chapter, you learn all about the program. In particular, you learn the following items:

✦ Ftp is an acronym for file transfer protocol. It started as a UNIX utility but became a mainstay for transferring files over TCP/IP systems, including the Internet.

✦ Ftp works on the client/server model. Your system is the client, and you connect to servers around the Internet.

✦ Windows 95 includes an ftp client, which you can use to connect to remote ftp servers. You use the program in an MS-DOS window. To run the program, you enter the ftp command at the DOS prompt.

✦ The ftp client software is not a menu-oriented program. Instead, once you are running the ftp client software, a wide variety of commands are available. These commands are entered at the ftp command prompt. They allow you to perform common functions, such as navigate directories, transfer files, and break your connection.

✦ When you connect with an ftp server, you must have an account with the system or you use anonymous ftp, which allows you to sign on as a guest on the system.

✦ The directory structure of an ftp server is organized according to the dictates of the system administrator within the structure imposed by the host operating system. Most hosts on the network are UNIX-based, and therefore the UNIX structure is used.

✦ The ftp commands that you use to navigate directories are closely related to the directory commands that you use at an MS-DOS command prompt.

✦ Most ftp servers provide some sort of index files, which indicate what information is available on the server.

✦ To transfer a file to your computer system, you use either the get or the recv command.

✦ After you finish working on an ftp server, you use the bye (or quit) command to break the connection and leave ftp, or you use the disconnect (or close) command to break the connection and remain in the ftp program.

In the next chapter, you learn how to find Windows-related tools on the Internet.

✦   ✦   ✦

Other Internet Tools

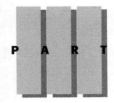

P A R T

III

◆ ◆ ◆ ◆

In This Part

Chapter 12
Finding Windows
Tools

Chapter 13
Using Gopher

Chapter 14
Understanding
WAIS

Chapter 15
Using the World
Wide Web

Chapter 16
Talking the
Night Away

Chapter 17
The Microsoft
Network

◆ ◆ ◆ ◆

Finding Windows Tools

Even though Windows 95 comes with a variety of tools that you can use to access the Internet, dozens of other tools are available on the Internet itself. Once you have mastered the ftp program, you can use it to copy other tools to your system. Once you download these other tools, you can use them to find additional tools, and so on. In this chapter, you learn what tools are available and how you can access them. Specifically, you learn the following items:

✦ What tools are available through the Internet

✦ Which types of tools you should select for your Windows 95 system (16-bit versus 32-bit programs)

✦ What cost is associated with Internet tools

✦ How you can use Archie to locate files on the Internet

✦ How to download tools to your system

✦ The steps that are necessary to install tools on your system

Some Tools That Are Available

Literally dozens of different programs are available on the Internet. These programs go by well-defined names, some of which you already know. For instance, different implementations of the ftp program are available that take advantage of the graphical interface of Windows, rather than relying on the command-line interface. Some of the more popular tools available on the Internet include the following:

✦ **Archie clients.** Archie is a tool that helps you find other programs at ftp sites around the Internet. Later in this chapter, you learn how to use an Archie client to find information.

✦ **Chatting tools.** The Internet is not used strictly for data files or electronic mail. There are quite a few alternative uses as well. Most of these other uses fall under the category of chatting tools. Programs in this category are designed to enable instant real-time communications through the Internet. The tools that are used to accomplish this go by many different names, with Internet Relay Chat (IRC) being one of the most popular. You learn about chatting tools (and IRC in particular) in Chapter 16.

✦ **E-mail.** You already know that electronic mail is one of the most popular Internet tools. Millions of people use electronic mail for all types of communication. A variety of electronic mail tools are available on the Internet; you learn about these in Chapter 8.

✦ **Finger.** The *finger* command is used to determine information about who is currently logged into a system as well as additional information about a specific user account.

✦ **Ftp clients.** You learn all about ftp in Chapter 11. The ftp program can be implemented in different ways, however. Many of the ftp clients available on the Internet are graphical in nature, meaning that they are easier to use than their command-line counterparts. Some ftp clients are reminiscent of File Manager in older versions of Windows.

✦ **Gopher clients.** Gopher is a tool that you use to locate and access information around the Internet. A Gopher client allows you to access the information stored in a Gopher server. You learn all about Gopher in Chapter 13.

✦ **Newsreaders.** A very popular method of distributing information on the Internet is through newsgroups. These are basically giant electronic bulletin board systems that use the Internet for access. To access information on newsgroups, you need to use a newsreader. You learn more about this Internet tool in Chapter 16.

✦ **NS-lookup.** NS is an acronym for name server. Thus, an *NS-lookup* program allows you to find information on a name server. With millions of DNS servers on the Internet, the NS-lookup command can be quite valuable in determining more information about hosts on the Internet.

✦ **Ping.** The ping command is one of the most basic ones that you can use on the Internet. It allows you to discover if distant hosts are available on the Net. As you learn in Chapter 7, Windows 95 includes a simple implementation of ping. On the Internet, you can find additional implementations of ping. Some have more (or fewer) switches, but they accomplish the same basic functions.

✦ **Telnet.** You first learn about telnet in Chapter 10. While Windows 95 provides a basic telnet tool that is quite handy, you may prefer one of the telnet programs that is available through the Internet. Each provides different capabilities and features.

✦ **Time synchronizers.** *Time synchronizers* may sound like a funny classification of a tool, but it can be very useful. There are Internet protocols that allow you to synchronize the time between two computers at remote sites. Time synchronizer programs allow you to connect to a remote time server, determine the time there, and set your own time to match it. This synchronization happens automatically; all you need to do is start the program.

✦ **Web browsers.** These tools are used to access the World Wide Web (WWW), the fastest-growing segment of the Internet. You learn more about the Web in Chapter 15.

✦ **Whois clients.** These are tools that help you discover more information about either hosts or users on the Internet. They access information from servers located throughout the Net and return the information to your screen. These tools are great when you are trying to discover where a host is located or who is in charge of a particular system.

Remember that this is not an all-inclusive list. In fact, it would be misleading to say that an all-inclusive list had been compiled. This is because the Internet is a very dynamic place. The millions of sites that are connected to the Internet add information daily. Every day, new tools are becoming available.

Windows 95–specific programs

Windows 95 is a brand new operating system, and so few programs have been written specifically for it. Instead, most programs have been written for Windows or Windows NT. The difference is this: Windows features 16-bit programs, while Windows NT uses 32-bit programs. Programmers for the Windows environment have adopted a form of shorthand for these programs. Sixteen-bit programs are known as Win16 software, and 32-bit programs are referred to as Win32 software.

Win16 programs are written to take advantage of the 16-bit addressing schemes that are used in older versions of Windows. Predominantly, these programs have been written for Windows 3.1 (or Windows for Workgroups), but they work fine under Windows 95. You install these programs as you would any other Windows 95 program.

So far, most Win32 programs have been written for the Windows NT environment. These programs are not as plentiful as the Win16 programs, but they are available. Even though they were originally intended for Windows NT systems, Win32 programs work just fine in the Windows 95 environment. You install these programs in the same way as any other Windows 95 program.

Many programs are available in both Win16 and Win32 versions. Given such a choice, you should select the 32-bit versions. These are more robust and take advantage of the internal improvements in Windows 95. It is not the purpose of this chapter (or this book) to list the numerous improvements implemented in Windows 95, but you will find that 32-bit programs are typically more responsive, faster running, and more stable than their 16-bit counterparts.

As more programs become available for Windows 95, Win16 programs will automatically become outdated. Until that point, however, you must be concerned with the type of programs that you download and make sure that you get the ones that will work best on your system.

The cost of tools

The cost of tools available through the Internet basically reflects the cost of tools that you can find through other sources. When looking at cost, there are three categories of software:

✦ Freeware

✦ Shareware

✦ Commercial

Freeware programs are those that you can use for free. The authors have either been subsidized in their efforts, or they enjoy programming so much that they decided to give away the software. Some very good programs fall in the freeware category, but so do some less-than-perfect programs as well. More often than not, if you get a freeware program that does not work, there is no recourse other than to find a different program. Freeware comes with no technical support, no printed manual, and no update schedule.

Shareware is, in some ways, similar to freeware. You can download and use the software for free. The difference is that the author requests that you only use the program for an evaluation period, after which you should register the program by sending money directly to the author. The registration fees are generally low ($5 to $30), and the software police won't come knocking on your door if you don't pay. However, the honorable thing to do is to make the payment. Most shareware programs are well written and documented, and some authors provide limited technical support (usually via e-mail) after you have registered the software.

Commercial software is making more of a presence on the Internet. You may be able to purchase these programs from your neighborhood computer store. The companies that publish these programs have established a presence on the Internet, and you can often get demo versions of their software for free. Some of these versions are limited in what they do, while others may be full-blown versions that are limited in the time frame during which they will work.

When you download a program from the Internet, you can generally find a text file in the download that includes information about what type of payment (if any) is expected for the software. Check this file to make sure that you understand the "rules of the game" before you start using the software.

Using Archie to Find Tools

Literally thousands of ftp sites exist around the world, each with hundreds of files available. Some files are the same, but others are unique; some files may only be found at one or two ftp sites. If you are searching for Internet tools, finding them at ftp sites can be like finding the proverbial needle in a haystack.

This is where *Archie* comes in. This tool, named after the comic book character, is used to find files at ftp sites. Actually, a number of Archie servers are around the Internet. These servers periodically poll known ftp sites to discover what they have available. The information that is gleaned is stored in databases by the Archie server. When you use an Archie client, you access these servers and perform searches on the databases. The information that is returned provides guidance on finding specific files. Archie can be invaluable in finding tools that you can use on the Internet.

Downloading an Archie client

The first step in using Archie is to download Archie client software to your system. Several different programs are available on the Internet, and you can access them using ftp. Perhaps the most popular of the Archie clients is the WS-Archie program. (The *WS* stands for WinSock, a TCP/IP implementation for older versions of Windows.) You can use anonymous ftp, as described in Chapter 11. Connect to the site at ftp.demon.co.uk. Once connected, issue the following commands at the ftp prompt:

```
cd pub/ibmpc/winsock/apps/wsarchie
binary
get wsarch08.zip
```

The file that you are transferring is a bit over 200K in size, and it may take a while to download it to your system. When the download finishes, you can break your Internet connection, because installing the software does not require an active connection.

Installing Archie

Once you have downloaded the WS-Archie software to your system, you are ready to install it. The first step is to "uncompress" the software. To minimize transmission times, the program was compressed before it was stored on the ftp server. Therefore, you need to use the PKUNZIP feature of the PKZIP program to convert the compressed file into the executable files that you can use. Many readers already have PKZIP; others may not. If you do not have it, you can generally find this utility on a local BBS, on any of the online systems, or at thousands of Internet sites.

Create a folder in which to uncompress the file that you downloaded, move the file to that folder, and then uncompress the file. For instance, assuming that you want to install the software in the Archie folder on your C drive, you would enter the following at the MS-DOS command prompt:

```
md c:\Archie
move wsarch08.zip c:\Archie
cd \Archie
pkunzip wsarch08
```

When these commands are completed, five new files appear in the Archie folder. At this point, you can delete the file that you downloaded, because it is no longer needed. In addition, you can add the Archie program to the Internet tools menu that you created in Chapter 10. To do this, follow these steps:

1. Right-click on the Start button. This displays the context menu for the Start button.

2. Choose Open from the context menu. This displays the Start Menu folder in a window.

3. Double-click on the Internet Tools icon. This displays a folder window for the Internet Tools folder.

4. Choose the New option from the File menu, and then choose Shortcut. You see the Create Shortcut dialog box, as shown in Figure 12-1.

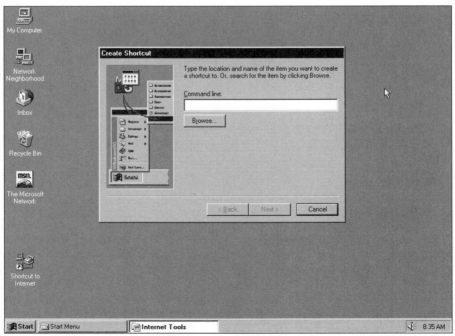

Figure 12-1: You can easily create a shortcut for the Archie client software that you downloaded.

5. In the Command Line box, type **c:\archie\wsarchie.exe**. (If you saved WS-Archie in a different directory, you should modify the path accordingly.)

6. Click on the Next button. You are asked for the name of this shortcut, as shown in Figure 12-2.

7. Modify the name as desired, and then click on the Finish button.

At this point, the new shortcut appears in the Internet Tools window. It also appears in the Internet Tools menu, which can be accessed from the Start menu. You are now ready to begin using WS-Archie.

Running WS-Archie

To run the WS-Archie program, make sure that you have established your PPP or SLIP connection to the Internet, and then select the Archie option from your Internet Tools menu. When you do, the program is loaded, and the program window appears, as shown in Figure 12-3.

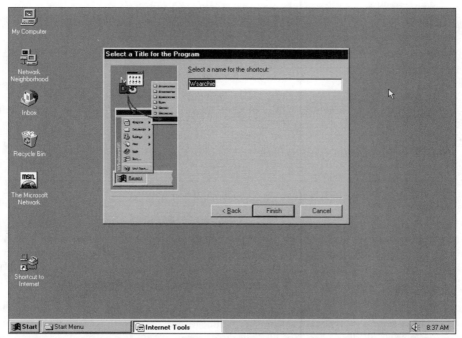

Figure 12-2: The final step in creating a shortcut is to supply a name for the new shortcut.

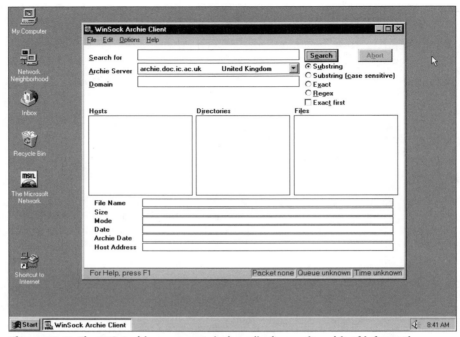

Figure 12-3: The WS-Archie program window displays quite a bit of information.

Although the program window may look formidable, it is not difficult to use. To use the program, follow these three steps:

1. Specify what you want to find.
2. Pick an Archie server.
3. Click on the Search button.

You accomplish the first step by filling in the Search for field. Here you should enter the characters that you want to use for the search. The names of files at ftp sites will be searched, and if they contain any of the characters that you entered here, then a match has been made. For instance, if you enter the characters *red,* then files such as dredful.zip, redress.txt, or astred.exe would all be considered matches.

The second step is to pick an Archie server. You do this by clicking on the arrow to the right of the Archie Server field. The available servers, along with their country, are shown in the pull-down list. Not all Archie servers contain the same information, so you may want to conduct a search on one server and then later conduct the same search on a different server. To begin, you should pick a server that is geographically located near you. Thus, if you live in Georgia, you may pick one along the East Coast of the United States.

In addition to these first two steps, you can also specify other guidelines for your search. For instance, you can indicate a domain in the Domain field that is used to limit the ftp servers considered in the search. This should be a high-level organizational or geographical domain such as com, edu, au, or uk. At the right side of the program window, you can also indicate the type of matching to be done during the search. In most cases, the Substring option is sufficient. You may want to choose one of the other options if you want the search to be more limited. (Detailed information about the matching methods can be found in the online documentation for WS-Archie.)

When you are ready to search, click on the Search button. WS-Archie makes contact with the specified server, and the search is conducted. The status bar at the bottom of the screen informs you of exactly what is happening, and shortly you should see information about your search. For instance, I was interested in finding Gopher client software. The assumption that I made was that the files would have the word *gopher* somewhere in the filename, so that is what I searched for. The results of the search are shown in Figure 12-4.

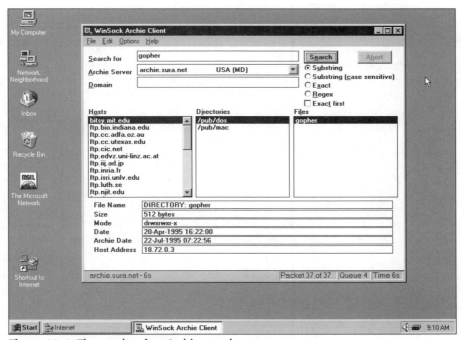

Figure 12-4: The results of an Archie search.

At this point, I can select different hosts in the Hosts list, and the contents of the Directories and Files lists change to show what is available on that host. If there is more than one directory at the host that contains information, I can select different directories, and the Files list will change. At the bottom of the screen, detailed information about individual files is provided.

When I locate a file that looks interesting, I can either jot down the location and filename for later use, or I can open a different window and use the ftp command to retrieve the desired file. While the file is being retrieved in an MS-DOS window, I can continue to use Archie to perform other searches.

Archie assumes that you have a general idea of what you are searching for. You should have some idea of the name of the program you are looking for. While this may seem to be a big assumption, it is better than starting from scratch. Many times, as you are reading a magazine or talking with a friend, you may hear about a program that is available through the Internet. Archie allows you to search for that program and find where it is located.

Downloading Tools

Once you have located a tool, you must download it to your system. You can download a file in a variety of ways; the most common method is ftp. You learn how to use ftp in Chapter 11, and you used the command earlier in this chapter to download the Archie tool.

Another method of downloading files gaining widespread use is the World Wide Web, which you learn about in Chapter 15. You can use most Web browsers to easily find tools and download ftp files. Only one problem exists with this approach — while your Web browser is busy downloading information, you cannot use it to do something else, like search for more information. To overcome this drawback, I like to use the browser to do my searching, but when I locate something I want, I open an MS-DOS window and use ftp to download the file. In this way, I can continue browsing the Web, using the Web browser, while the ftp download is occurring in a different window.

Installing New Tools

Installing Internet tools for use with Windows 95 involves only a few general steps. These steps vary little, regardless of the program that you are installing:

1. Move the downloaded software to its own folder. It is best to place the software that you get from the Internet into individual folders. This way, the software is not mixed with other programs you may have downloaded.

2. Uncompress the downloaded files, if necessary. For Windows 95, most programs are compressed with PKZIP, meaning they have a file extension of ZIP. Some files have an EXE extension, meaning they can be run directly. These programs may actually be compressed files that are self-extracting; when you run them, the files within the program are automatically uncompressed and stored on your hard drive.

3. Add the program to your Internet tools menu (created in Chapter 10). This is done by adding a shortcut to the Internet Tools folder, as you did with the Archie client software earlier in this chapter.

4. Run the program, and follow any necessary configuration steps. Running the program is simple; you select it from the Internet Tools menu. Configuring the program depends on the nature of the program, how complex it is, and what information is needed by the program to run. Instructions on how to configure any tools that you download should be provided in an instructions file that is supplied with the software.

These steps are fairly straightforward. They are the same steps discussed earlier in this chapter, and they are followed when discussing other tools later in this book.

Summary

A wide variety of tools have been developed to explore the Internet. In this chapter, you receive an overview of what those tools are and how you can find them. In particular, you learn the following items:

✦ A wide variety of tools are available through the Internet. These tools run the gamut from simple utilities to full-featured programs. Most share the common feature of being able to work across the Internet.

✦ You can use two types of Windows programs on your Windows 95 system. The first is Win16 programs, which are 16-bit programs written for older versions of Windows. The other type, Win32 programs, are 32-bit software written either for Windows 95 or Windows NT. All Win32 programs run on Windows 95 and offer the best performance.

✦ All types of software are available on the Internet, and there are three basic charges for the software. Freeware is software that is available for free. Shareware is software that you can try out for free, but you are requested to pay a registration fee if you decide that you want to continue using it. Commercial software is also making an appearance on the Internet, with prices and policies set by individual software vendors.

✦ A valuable tool to use when looking for programs on the Internet is Archie. This program allows you to discover the location of files within ftp servers around the Internet. You can search a wide variety of servers and quickly receive responses to your inquiries.

✦ Before you can use an Internet tool, you must download it to your system. This can be done in a variety of ways, with ftp being the most common transfer method. You can also use a Web browser to download files to your system.

✦ Installing most Internet tools is quick and easy. There are only a few general steps that you need to follow before using the software. Once installed, the software is available anytime you connect to the Internet.

For additional information on finding Internet tools, refer to Appendix B. In the next chapter, you learn how to take advantage of Internet tools. There you learn about using Gopher on your system.

✦   ✦   ✦

Using Gopher

One of the most common tools used on the Internet is *Gopher*, which was developed in early 1991 at the University of Minnesota's Minnesota Microcomputer, Workstation, and Networks Center. This tool allows you to quickly access vast amounts of information on the Internet. In this chapter, you learn about this powerful tool and how you can put it to work. Here you learn the following items:

✦ What Gopher is

✦ What you need to use Gopher on your Windows 95 system

✦ How to connect to a Gopher server

✦ How to search for information

✦ How to save information to your hard drive

✦ How to use bookmarks

What Is Gopher?

Gopher is a tool that lets you retrieve information stored at various servers around the Internet. It derives its name from the fact that you can use the software to "go for" a piece of information — it does the dirty work for you.

Gopher uses a client/server approach in which an Internet site that wants to make information available does so by setting up a Gopher server, and you access the server by using Gopher client software. Your software requests information from the server, which then fulfills the request. Information retrieved by Gopher is presented in a series of menus from which you can make additional choices.

Each menu choice presented by Gopher can be either a resource that leads you to an answer or a potential answer itself. If the menu choice is a resource, when you choose it, you are asked to supply search criteria that you want to use in selecting information from the resource. This resource can be on the local Gopher server or elsewhere on the Internet (a remote server). The collection of resources accessed through Gopher (whether local or remote) is referred to as *Gopherspace*. You can think of Gopherspace as the universe of potential answers (or resources that lead to answers) for your questions.

Some of the resources that Gopher can freely access are in reality other Internet tools. For instance, through Gopher you can access the following Internet tools:

✦ WAIS databases (see Chapter 14)

✦ ftp archives (see Chapter 11)

✦ telnet sites (see Chapter 10)

Even though these are Internet tools that can be used in their own right, Gopher allows you to use them transparently; that is, the Gopher interface and the program take care of converting information to and from the format expected by the other tool.

What You Need

To use Gopher, you need client software that you can run on your system. You can use several different Gopher clients with Windows 95. These clients can be downloaded from various sites around the Internet. The easiest way is to use ftp to transfer the files to your system and then install the software. The following is a list of the most popular Gopher clients and where you can find them.

Name	Ftp Site	Directory
BCGopher	bcinfo.bc.edu	ftp/pub/bcgopher
Hgopher	lister.cc.ic.ac.uk	pub/wingopher
WSGopher	dewey.tis.inel.gov	pub/wsgopher

Even though these Gopher clients perform the same basic functions, they each operate a bit differently. It doesn't matter which of the Gopher clients you use; you only need to download one and install it on your machine. You may want to download more than one, so that you can discover which is the best for your purposes. The examples used in this chapter focus on using the WSGopher software. This is not to imply that this tool is necessarily better than the other Gopher clients; I use it for illustration purposes.

Downloading a Gopher client

To download the WSGopher software, use the ftp command (covered in Chapter 11) to connect to the anonymous ftp site at dewey.tis.inel.gov. Once connected, issue the following command at the ftp prompt:

```
cd pub/wsgopher
binary
get wsg-12.exe
```

The file that you are transferring is over 360K in size, and it may take a while to download it to your system. When it is finished, you can break your Internet connection, because installing the software does not require an active connection.

Installing your Gopher client

Once you have downloaded the WSGopher software to your system, you are ready to install it. The first step is to "uncompress" the software. To reduce transmission times, the WSGopher software that you downloaded (wsg-12.exe) is a self-extracting ZIP file. This means that you just run the program (from the MS-DOS command line), and the WSGopher programs are uncompressed and saved on your hard disk. Because of this, you may want to run wsg-12.exe from a folder on your system that you have set aside for Gopher. For instance, on my system, I created a folder called Gopher in which I placed the wsg-12.exe program. When I ran the program, a number of files were created in the directory, as shown in Figure 13-1.

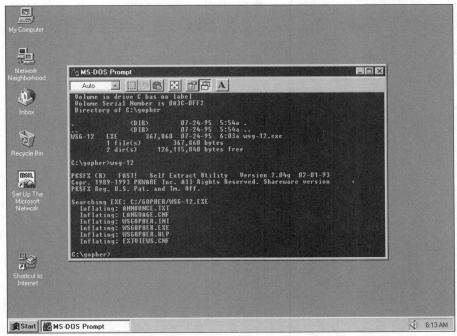

Figure 13-1: Running the WSGopher file that you transferred to your system results in additional files being created.

At this point, you can delete the wsg-12.exe file, because you have already run it. The ANNOUNCE.TXT file contains information about this release of WSGopher, and the rest of the files are used by the program itself. The WSGOPHER.EXE file is the program that you use. You may want to add the program to the Internet tools menu that you created in Chapter 10. To do this, follow these steps:

1. Right-click on the Start button. This displays the context menu for the Start button.

2. Choose Open from the context menu. This displays the Start Menu folder in a window.

3. Double-click on the Internet Tools icon. This displays a folder window for the Internet Tools folder.

4. Choose the New option from the File menu, and then choose Shortcut. You then see the Create Shortcut dialog box, as shown in Figure 13-2.

5. In the Command line box, type **c:\gopher\wsgopher.exe**. (If you saved WSGopher in a different directory, you should modify the path accordingly.)

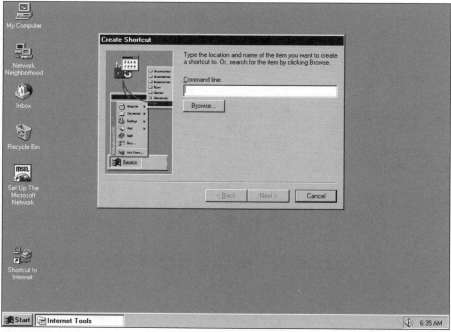

Figure 13-2: You can easily create a shortcut for the new WSGopher software that you have downloaded.

6. Click on the Next button. You are asked for the name of this shortcut, as shown in Figure 13-3.

7. Accept the shortcut name by clicking on the Finish button.

At this point, the new shortcut appears in the Internet Tools window, as shown in Figure 13-4. It also appears in the Internet Tools menu, which can be accessed from the Start menu. You are now ready to use Gopher.

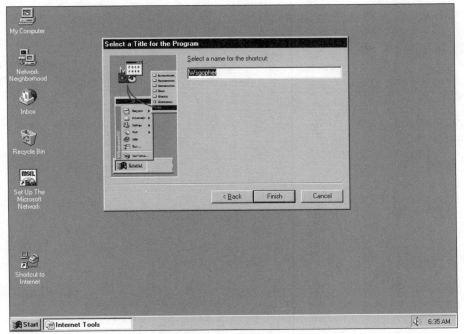

Figure 13-3: The final step in creating a shortcut is to supply its name.

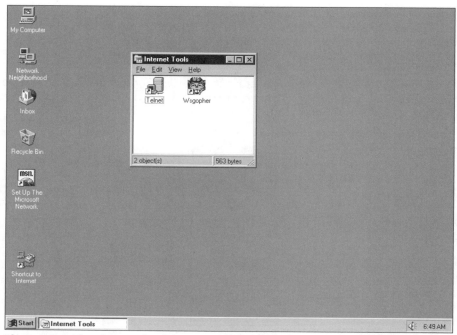

Figure 13-4: The shortcut for the WSGopher program appears in the Internet Tools window.

Connecting to a Gopher Server

To connect to a Gopher server, you must first establish your PPP or SLIP connection with your Internet provider. You can then start the WSGopher client software by choosing Wsgopher from the Internet Tools menu (as described in the previous section). Shortly, you see a screen similar to Figure 13-5.

At this point, you are connected to a Gopher server, this one at the University of Illinois at Urbana-Champaign. WSGopher refers to this location as a *Home Gopher*. This is simply the name by which your initial Gopher server contact is known. You can easily change the Home Gopher, as described shortly. First, however, you must learn the purpose of the WSGopher interface and the Gopher menu displayed on the screen.

WHAT CAN GO WRONG

I'm tired of waiting

If you start your Gopher client software and it hangs (meaning that the program does not respond), it could be because you have not established your PPP or SLIP connection through your provider. Make sure that you have established the modem connection, and then try to use the program again.

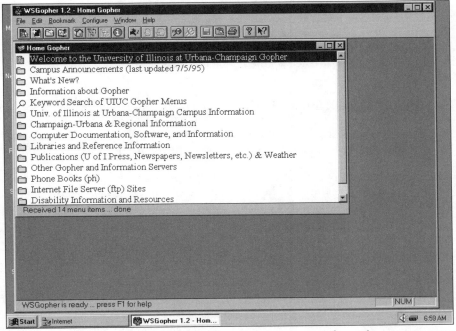

Figure 13-5: When you start the WSGopher program, you see the main program screen.

Understanding the Gopher interface

Different Gopher clients provide different interfaces for you to use. In the Windows 95 environment, all Gopher clients provide a similar interface. This interface consists of four areas, each of which is shown in Figure 13-5. These areas are the menus, icons, display area, and status bar.

At the top of the program window is a group of menus from which you can select program commands. For WSGopher, the menus are as follows:

✦ **File.** Commands related to retrieving, saving, or printing Gopher items

✦ **Edit.** Commands for copying or finding information in the current window

✦ **Bookmark.** Commands that are used to set, use, or manage bookmarks

✦ **Configure.** Commands that are related to the configuration of WSGopher

✦ **Window.** Commands used to arrange windows within the WSGopher program

✦ **Help.** Commands that provide help or display information about the program

Other programs may use a different menu structure, but the commands represented by these menus are fairly representative. Just below the menus is a group of icons, which comprise the second major component of the Gopher interface. These icons allow you to perform many of the same commands that you can perform with the menus, but they are more accessible. The icons available within a program depend on the program being used.

The third major area of the interface is also the largest area. This is the display area, which is where the program shows information retrieved from a Gopher server. The information within this area is shown using windows. For instance, in Figure 13-5, the Home Gopher window shows the information retrieved from the Gopher server.

Finally, a status bar appears at the bottom of the program window. This bar displays information about the status of the program itself or quick help about menu commands. Notice that each window in the display area also contains a status bar that indicates the status of the information within the window.

Understanding the Gopher menu

You know that a Gopher functions through a series of menus. In the WSGopher program window, the menu for your Home Gopher is shown within its own document window. At the bottom of the window, you see that 14 items appear in the menu. These menu items are made up of two parts: an icon and text. The text describes the menu item, and the icon indicates the type of menu item being displayed.

For example, in Figure 13-5, there are three different types of menu icons. The first menu item displays an icon that looks like a piece of paper. This indicates that the menu item represents a document. If you select the menu item, you see a document on your screen. The second menu item has an icon that looks like a folder. This means that when you select this menu item, you get an additional menu. For example, if you double-click on the What's New menu item (the third on the screen), you see another menu, as shown in Figure 13-6.

Finally, the third type of menu icon appears on the fifth menu item (Figure 13-5), Keyword Search of UIUC Gopher Menus. Searching is covered later in this chapter. Regardless of the type of resource shown on a menu, just double-click the mouse on the menu choice. This displays the information associated with that choice.

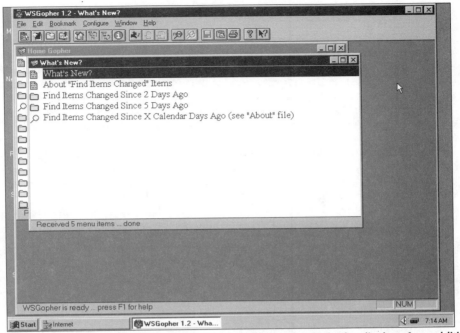

Figure 13-6: Selecting a menu item with a folder icon results in the display of an additional menu.

WHAT CAN GO WRONG

Where's my resource?

Just because something appears in a Gopher menu does not mean that you will be able to use it. Many Gopher resources don't reside on the same computer as the server. Instead, they represent links to remote systems that could be across the country or around the world. When you double-click on the menu choice, the remote server is accessed, and you start working with information on that system.

If the remote system is not available, then you are not be able to access the resource. You may see an error message indicating that the remote system is not available. In this case, you have a couple of choices: You can try the resource again later, or you can look for alternate resources that fit your needs.

Changing your Home Gopher

The Home Gopher is the first Gopher server to which you connect when you start WSGopher. You can easily change the Gopher server you use; for instance, you may want to have WSGopher default to a Gopher server that is maintained by your university or by your Internet provider. As an example, my Internet provider has a Gopher server located at usa.net, and I can direct WSGopher to use this server as my Home Gopher. To do this, I simply choose the Home Gopher Server command from the Configure menu. A dialog box appears, as shown in Figure 13-7.

The Home Gopher Server(s) dialog box allows you to specify two different servers, but you will probably only want to specify a single server. If you specify one server, then that is the one you are always connected to. If you specify two servers, then WSGopher randomly selects which of the two to access each time you direct it to connect to the Home Server. Thus, you can get very different Gopher menus (depending on which of the two servers is selected) unless the two servers are clones.

To specify a different Gopher server, simply provide the address of the server in the address field. For example, in Figure 13-7, the address for the Home Gopher is gopher.uiuc.edu. If I want to use my Internet provider's gopher server instead, I type the address **usa.net** in this field.

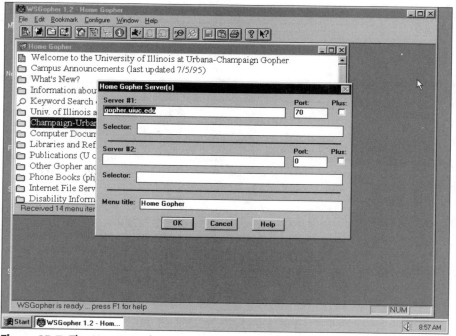

Figure 13-7: The Home Gopher Server(s) dialog box allows you to specify the location of your Home Gopher.

To the right of the address field, you can specify the port number to use. In most instances, Gopher servers use port 70, but your server may use something different. The only way to discover which port to use is to contact the server administrator.

At the right side of each server is a check box labeled Plus. This allows you to indicate whether the Gopher server supports the enhanced features of Gopher+. Many servers support Gopher+, but again, the only way to find out is to contact the server administrator.

After you finish specifying your Home Gopher, click on the OK button. The information is saved, and the next time you instruct WSGopher to access your Home Gopher (such as when you exit the program and restart it, or when you select the Home Gopher command from the File menu), the new Home Gopher is accessed and displayed. For example, my new Home Gopher (from my Internet provider) appears as shown in Figure 13-8.

Notice that the Home Gopher displayed in Figure 13-8 is different from the one displayed earlier in Figure 13-5. This is because the appearance of a Gopher server is left to the discretion of the system administrator at that site. The only consistency is that information is presented in a menu format; the content of that menu may change dramatically.

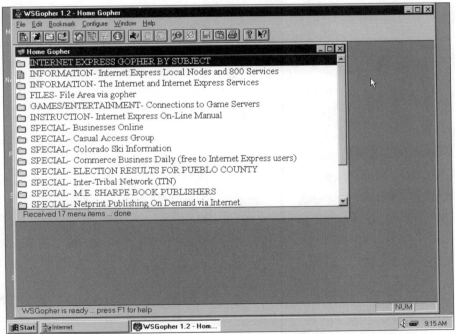

Figure 13-8: The Home Gopher window displayed for the usa.net Gopher.

It is best to choose a Home Gopher that is geographically close to your location or one that is intimately tied to the work that you do. For example, if your company or Internet provider sponsors a server, then you should use that one. Likewise, if you are a student or faculty member at a university, then you may want to use the server for that institution. If you are an individual interested in using Gopher, then you should choose a server close to your location. This improves access times and reduces the transfer of information over large areas.

Temporary Gopher servers

Your Home Gopher is the starting point for most of your adventures in Gopherspace. That is why WSGopher connects to the Home Gopher every time you start the program. You can also temporarily connect to specific Gopher servers. For example, you may need to connect to a server at a distant university to find information for which the university is renowned. When using WSGopher to connect to a specific server, choose the New Gopher Item option from the File menu. This displays the Fetch this Gopher Item dialog box, as shown in Figure 13-9.

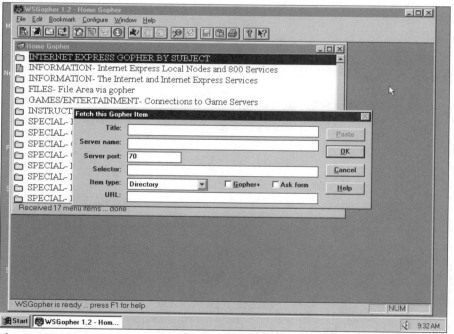

Figure 13-9: The Fetch this Gopher Item dialog box connects to a specific Gopher server.

The information requested in this dialog box is similar to the information you supplied when you changed your Home Gopher.

- ✦ **Title.** Used by WSGopher as the title bar of the window that is used for this Gopher. You can safely leave this field blank if the title bar contents don't matter to you.

- ✦ **Server name.** The Internet address of the Gopher server to which you want to connect.

- ✦ **Server port.** The port number used by the server. Typically, the default value of 70 is acceptable. If you know that the server expects a different port number, you can change it.

- ✦ **Selector.** A command used to retrieve a specific document at the Gopher server.

- ✦ **Item type.** The type of resource that is being retrieved. Typically, this is set to Directory, unless you have provided a command in the Selector field. In this case, the item type should match the type of information that you are retrieving.

- ✦ **Gopher+.** A check box that allows you to specify that the server uses Gopher+ commands.

- ✦ **Ask form.** A type of interactive form supported under Gopher+. An ask form is an on-screen form that you fill out and then "submit" to the server to retrieve information. This check box should be selected if you are retrieving an ask form.

- ✦ **URL.** The addressing method that was popularized by the World Wide Web. This address overrides anything that you enter in the Server name field.

In most instances, you only need to fill out the Server name field. The other fields are optional and should only be filled out if you have a specific need. Once you supply the appropriate information, click on the OK button to instruct WSGopher to connect to the server and open a new document window for the server, as shown in Figure 13-10. Your other windows are still visible in the display area, and you can still use them. The new server's window can be used to access information on the new Gopher server.

COOL PLACES

Gopher places

You can access thousands of Gopher servers on the Internet. The following addresses may be fun to try:

Server Address	Comments
ftp.worldbank.org	World Bank
gopher.acs.oakland.edu	Shareware archives
liberty.uc.wlu.edu	List of gopher servers in the world
marvel.loc.gov	Library of Congress
wuarchive.wustl.edu	Software archives

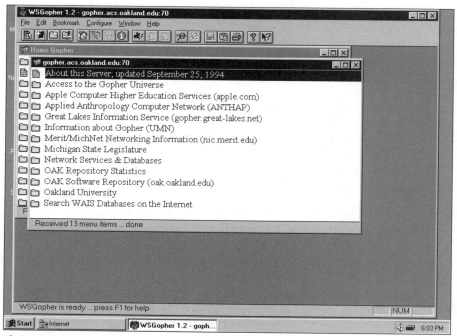

Figure 13-10: Connecting to a new Gopher server opens another window for interaction with that server.

Searching for Information

When you look through the information at a Gopher server, you periodically see icons that look like magnifying glasses. These icons indicate that choosing the menu item initiates a search. You supply the parameters for the search, and the Gopher server returns the results of the search; these results are then displayed on your screen. For example, if you click on a menu item that results in a search, you may see a dialog box like the one shown in Figure 13-11.

The exact dialog box that you see when you do a search depends on the type of information required by the Gopher. Typically, searches are conducted by using a variety of Internet tools, each of which may require different types of information. For example, if the resource being searched by Gopher is a WAIS database, then the information required is different from that needed when searching a different database.

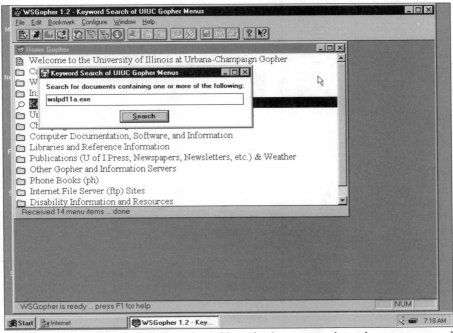

Figure 13-11: Searches can be conducted by selecting a menu item that uses a magnifying glass as an icon.

After you finish specifying the search parameters, click on the Search button. The request is sent to the remote resource server, and the returned information appears in a window on the screen. For example, one of the resources that I can access through my Gopher server is a list of travel advisories from the U.S. State Department. When I did a search of this resource using the keyword *Mexico,* there were 12 matches, as shown in Figure 13-12.

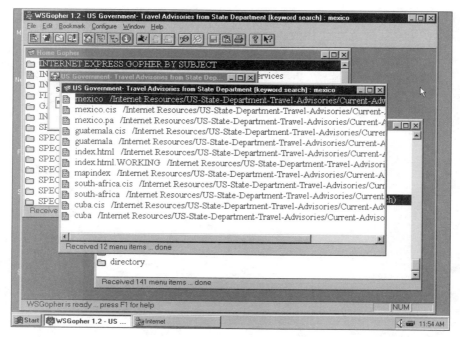

Figure 13-12: Performing a search returns results that you can continue to work with.

Saving Information

Once you locate information in Gopherspace, you may want to save it to your local hard drive. When you are viewing a document (not when you are viewing a directory), you can save the information to a file on your Windows 95 system. Select the Save Item command from the File menu. This displays the dialog box shown in Figure 13-13.

You are asked for the name of the file to be saved as well as the location in which the file should be saved. If you are familiar with Windows 95, this dialog box should look familiar. Supply a filename and then click on OK. The document is saved on disk, and you can work with it later on your system (when you aren't racking up online charges).

Using Bookmarks

The information that you want to access in Gopherspace can be far-flung. For instance, you may find wool-growing information from a Gopher server in Ireland and information about wine aging from a server in California. Rather than requiring you to write down the addresses of these resources, WSGopher (and virtually every other Gopher client) allows you to use bookmarks to remember a place in Gopherspace.

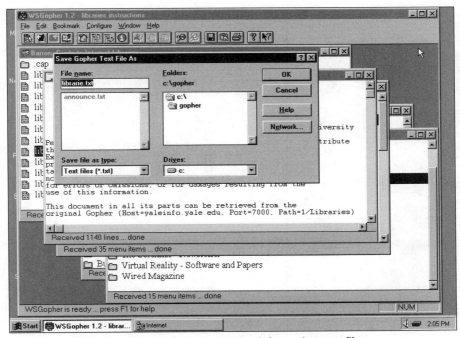

Figure 13-13: Gopher clients allow you to save information to a file.

Bookmarks are exactly what they sound like — a way to remember a location. You can add, delete, and retrieve (fetch) bookmarks. WSGopher also allows you to organize your bookmarks into categories.

Adding a bookmark

To add a bookmark, make sure that you have selected the window displaying the Gopher resource that you want noted, and then choose the Add Bookmark command from the Bookmark menu. (If you want to save only the information about the directory in the current window, you can choose the Add Directory Bookmark command.) You then see the dialog box shown in Figure 13-14.

You are asked for the organizational category in which you want this bookmark saved. The easiest way to use the dialog box is to select a category from the Categories list box, and then click on OK. If you want to save the bookmark in a new category, enter the new category in the Name field and then click on the Create button. The category is added, and the bookmark is saved.

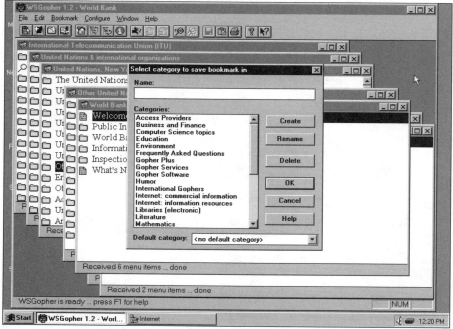

Figure 13-14: Adding a bookmark involves only a single dialog box.

When you add a bookmark, you instruct your client software to store the following information about the location:

✦ **Title.** The information that appears in the title bar of the window that is used for this Gopher item

✦ **Server name.** The Internet address of the Gopher server

✦ **Server port.** The port number that is used by the server

✦ **Selector.** The command that is used to retrieve the specific resource at the Gopher server

✦ **Item type.** The type of resource that is represented by the selector command

✦ **Gopher+.** A flag that indicates whether the server uses Gopher+ commands

✦ **Ask form.** An indication that shows whether the resource is an ask form

Retrieving a bookmark

A bookmark's purpose is to save the location of a Gopher resource. Without a way to recall the bookmark, the feature would be of little value. Using WSGopher, you can retrieve a bookmark by selecting the Fetch command from the Bookmark menu. This displays the dialog box shown in Figure 13-15.

At this point, you must pick the category in which the bookmark was saved. For example, if you saved a bookmark in the Music category, then click on the Music entry in the Categories list. The right side of the dialog box shows all bookmarks saved in that category, as shown in Figure 13-16.

When you find the bookmark that you want to retrieve, select it, and then click on the OK button. The client software connects to the remote server and issues the commands that recall a resource.

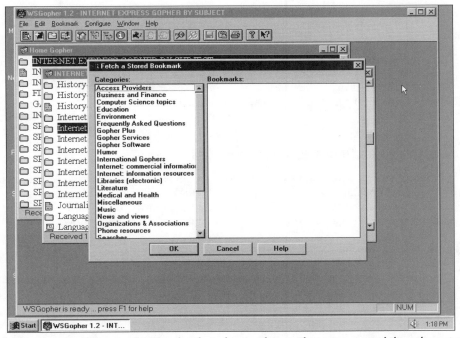

Figure 13-15: When retrieving a bookmark, you choose the category and then the actual bookmark.

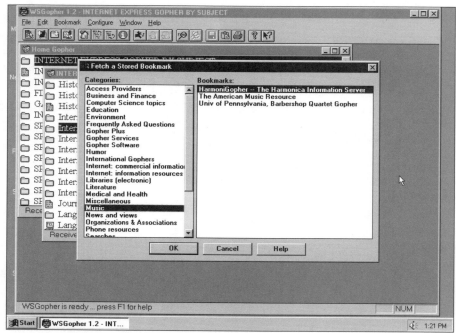

Figure 13-16: Picking a category displays different bookmark lists.

Modifying bookmark categories

WSGopher comes with quite a few categories (and bookmarks) already defined. You saw these predefined categories listed in Figure 13-14. You can also add, rename, or delete bookmark categories without actually saving a bookmark. You do so by choosing Categories from the Bookmark menu. This displays the dialog box shown in Figure 13-17.

At this point, you can perform three main tasks:

✦ **Create a bookmark.** Enter a new name in the Name field and then click on the Create button.

✦ **Rename a bookmark.** First, select an existing category from the Categories list, and then enter a new name in the Name field. Next, click on the Rename button. The category is renamed according to your specification.

✦ **Delete a bookmark.** First, select an existing category from the Categories list, and then click on the Delete button. You are asked to confirm your action, and the category is removed. Any bookmarks within the category are deleted as well.

When you finish working with categories, click on the OK button.

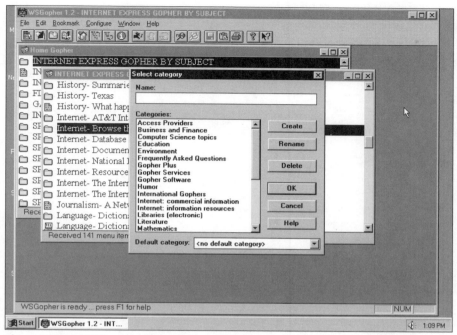

Figure 13-17: WSGopher allows you to easily change the bookmark categories that you have defined.

Modifying bookmarks

Once you define a bookmark, you can later modify it to a degree. For example, you can rename it, move it to a different category, or delete it. Each of these functions can be performed with the Edit Bookmarks command from the Bookmark menu. When you choose this command, you are asked to indicate the category of bookmarks that you want to edit. After you select a category and click on the OK button, you see the dialog box shown in Figure 13-18.

At the bottom of the dialog box is a list of the defined bookmarks in the selected category. If you select a bookmark by clicking on it, the information about that bookmark is displayed at the top of the dialog box. Once a bookmark is selected, you can perform any of the following actions:

✦ **Retrieve the bookmark.** Clicking on the Fetch button has the same effect as using the Fetch command from the Bookmark menu.

✦ **Delete the bookmark.** After clicking on the Delete button, you are asked to confirm that you want to remove the bookmark. Depending on your response, the bookmark is removed from the list of defined bookmarks.

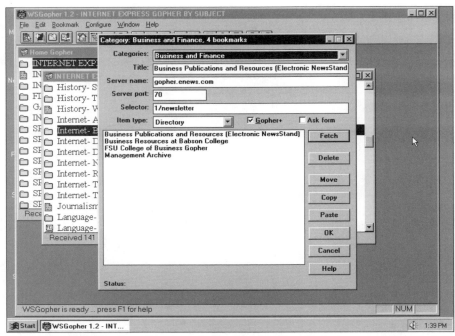

Figure 13-18: WSGopher allows you to manage bookmarks that were previously defined.

✦ **Move the bookmark.** Clicking on the Move button displays the list of categories. You can select a category from the list, and the bookmark is moved to that category.

✦ **Copy the bookmark.** If you click on the Copy button, the bookmark is copied to the Clipboard. You can later use the Paste button to paste the bookmark in another location.

Besides these actions, you can change the bookmark information shown at the top of the dialog box. The modified information is saved as soon as you select a different bookmark or leave the dialog box. Thus, you can change the title, server name, port, or any of the other items that were saved in the bookmark.

Summary

Gopher is a client/server-based tool that you use on the Internet to access large amounts of information. Many companies, universities, and other organizations sponsor Gopher servers that you access from your Windows 95 system. Well over 5,000 Gopher servers exist around the world.

In this chapter, you learn how you can use Gopher client software on your system to tap into different servers. Specifically, you learn the following items:

✦ Once you have a PPP or SLIP connection through an Internet provider, you can take advantage of Gopher by using readily available client software.

✦ A number of free Gopher clients are available on the Internet. You can transfer these programs to your system by using ftp, which is discussed in Chapter 11.

✦ After the Gopher client software is installed on your system and you establish a PPP or SLIP connection to the Internet, you can connect to a Gopher server. This is typically done by entering the address of the server into the client software.

✦ Information is presented by the Gopher client in a menu format. You select menu items to travel through Gopherspace, which is the universe of connected Gopher servers and related utilities.

✦ You search for information using tools that are connected to the Gopher server you are accessing. These tools appear in the Gopher menu structure as simple choices that you can make. For example, you can search regular databases and WAIS databases, or use telnet to access other Net sites.

✦ Most Gopher client software programs allow you to view documents and save them to your local hard drive. Once transferred to your system, you can then use them as you see fit.

✦ Bookmarks allow you to save the location of different Gopher resources. Bookmarks can be added, changed, organized, and deleted using your Gopher client.

In the next chapter, you learn how you can use the Wide Area Information Server (WAIS) to search specific databases.

✦   ✦   ✦

CHAPTER 14

Understanding WAIS

The amount of information available through the Internet is staggering. Making sense out of the avalanche of information can be a formidable task. A number of tools help with the sifting and searching that must occur before you can start using information. In previous chapters, you learn about some of those tools. For instance, in Chapter 13, you learn how you can use a gopher client to ferret out information. This chapter covers another similar tool — the *Wide Area Information Server* (WAIS). Here you learn the following items:

+ Exactly what WAIS is

+ How you conduct searches using relevance feedback

+ How you use telnet to connect with a WAIS client

+ How to retrieve documents located with WAIS

+ What commands are available as you use WAIS

+ How to quit the WAIS client

What Is WAIS?

WAIS is the brainchild of three companies that have a vested interest in both the Internet and in making information accessible to others. Apple Computer, Dow Jones, and Thinking Machines Corp. joined forces to come up with a distributed server system that allows textual information to be indexed and searched easily. For many people, WAIS has become a preferred method of searching the vast amount of information on the Internet.

Like so many other Internet tools, WAIS uses a client/server approach to finding information. A number of WAIS servers are located around the Internet and connected to each other. You use client software to send a query to the server. The client allows you to enter a query using a set of key words that describe what you are looking for. When you instruct the client to perform the search, it formats the query in a way that is understood by the server and then transmits the query to the server. The server does the actual search and then returns the information to the client, which in turn presents the information to you. As you can tell, the client is nothing more than the interface between you and the WAIS server.

Unfortunately, WAIS clients have not been developed yet for Windows 95 (or Windows NT). Instead, you must use telnet to connect to the public WAIS clients on the Internet. In a later section, you learn how to make the connection.

A WAIS server maintains nothing but an index of information. These indexes are compiled from databases, articles, journals, and other resources around the Internet. The indexes contain every word in the various sources, so you can search for virtually anything. For example, you can search for every occurrence of the word *diamond,* and the server would match your request to the sources that contain that word. If you search for *diamond mine,* then WAIS finds every source that contains both *diamond* and *mine*, but not necessarily together as a phrase or in that order.

Searching Through WAIS

You may be familiar with searching a database, particularly if you have been using computers for any length of time. Most computer databases can be searched using a technique that employs Boolean logic. This is a way of defining what you want by using key words and operators that limit the search criteria. In real life, we use Boolean logic every day. For example, you may say, "I want to invite John and Mary to dinner." This Boolean statement limits who will be coming to dinner; the Boolean operator here is the word *and,* which specifies the people who you are inviting. Had you used a different Boolean operator as in, "I want to invite John or Mary to dinner," the meaning is much different, and your dinner guests would have been more limited.

Boolean logic involves the use of operators such as AND, OR, and NOT. Although in regular conversation these terms are very understandable, in a computer implementation they can be rigid and limiting. For example, had your dinner party sentence been written in computer terms, it may appear as this:

dinner = (friend = "John") and (friend = "Mary")

Notice how much more structured this query is? The result (dinner) is derived by making sure that the friend field is equal to John and Mary. This is great if you come from a computer background; it is not so great if you do not. The drawbacks of using Boolean logic in a computer query can be summarized as follows:

✦ You must know the effect of Boolean operators.

✦ You must know what fields are used in the database.

✦ You must know what math symbols can be used for comparison.

As you can tell, a great deal of knowledge is required before you even start to do a search. Understanding these drawbacks, the developers of WAIS decided to use a different method of conducting searches. This method is referred to as *relevance feedback,* which simply means that you provide iterative feedback to the client regarding the relevance of the search results. In turn, the server provides more and more refined results based on your feedback. Later in this chapter, you discover how this search method allows you to quickly and easily home in on the information that you need.

Connecting to a WAIS Client

A number of different WAIS clients are available on the Internet; the one that you use is entirely up to you. The following are a few that you can telnet to:

✦ info.funet.fi

✦ kudzu.cnidr.org

✦ sunsite.unc.edu

✦ quake.think.com

To connect with one of these clients, all you need to do is use the telnet program, as described in Chapter 10. You can follow these steps to connect:

1. Establish a connection with your Internet provider.

2. Start the telnet program.

3. Choose Remote System from the Connect menu.

4. For the Host Name, use one of the WAIS client addresses that was previously provided (such as quake.think.com).

5. Click on the Connect button.

Shortly, you should connect to the remote system. At this point, your screen looks similar to what is shown in Figure 14-1.

At this point, you can use WAIS by typing **wais** as your login ID. (Some sites require a login ID of swais instead; try this if wais doesn't work.) You are then asked for your password, for which you should use your e-mail address. Depending on the system that you connect to, you may also be asked for a terminal type. The default terminal (usually VT100) is fine, so press Enter. At this point, your screen looks similar to Figure 14-2. This is the WAIS Source Selection screen; you are now fully logged in to the WAIS client software.

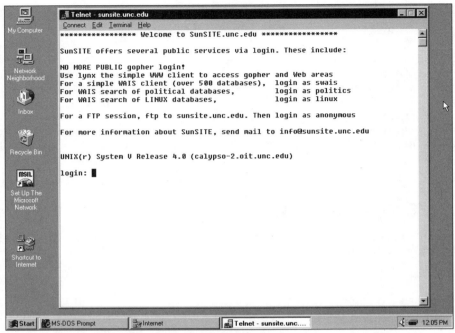

Figure 14-1: The first step in using a WAIS client is to log in to the system.

Understanding the WAIS interface

When you use the WAIS client software, you do all your work in one of two screens. The first screen, which you should see right now (Figure 14-2), is the Source Selection screen. This screen is used to select a source for your subsequent searching. The other screen is the Search Results screen, which you see in the following section. These two screens implement the relevance feedback used in WAIS. One screen is used to choose where you search, and the other is used to see the results. The relevant part of the results can then be copied to the Source Selection screen, and the cycle repeats.

Regardless of which screen you are using, you can use the same keys to navigate and control the screen. Table 14-1 lists the various keys that you can use at either screen.

Figure 14-2: The Source Selection screen is used to indicate where your search should begin.

Table 14-1
Screen Control Keys for WAIS

Keys	Meaning
h, ?	Display available commands
##	Jump to item number ##
/sss	Jump to item beginning with sss
down arrow, j, Ctrl+N	Down one item
up arrow, k, Ctrl+P	Up one item
J, Ctrl+V, Ctrl+D	Next page
K, Esc+V, Ctrl+U	Previous page

Conducting a search

Suppose that you want to search for documents related to population control. With the Source Selection screen in front of you, you are ready to start the search process. To find the information you want, you perform the following steps:

1. At the Source Selection screen, choose the sources you want to search.

2. Type **w** to specify key words for the search.

3. Instruct WAIS to conduct the search. The results of the search are shown in the Search Results screen.

4. Select the documents that you want to add to the source list.

5. Repeat Steps 1 through 4 until the documents that are returned match what you need.

To perform the first step, simply pick the sources that you want to search. You do this by highlighting the source and then pressing the spacebar. On this initial Source Selection screen, you can choose from 18 sources, but a total of 76 sources is listed on all the screens. Highlight the sources that you want to search, and then press the spacebar. An asterisk appears at the left side of the line to indicate that you have selected the source. If there are any sources that you absolutely don't want (and won't want at any time during this session), highlight them and type **X**.

When you finish specifying your sources, type **w** to signify that you are done selecting sources and that you are ready to specify key words for the search. At the bottom of the screen, you are prompted to enter the key words that you want. You can enter any key words desired, separated by spaces. For example, enter the words *population control.* When you finish, press Enter, and the search begins. The WAIS server is connected, and each source that you specified is searched for your key words. Shortly, you see the results of the search, shown in the Search Results screen (see Figure 14-3).

Each Search Results screen can display up to 18 found items. In the upper-right corner of the screen, you can see how many sources WAIS located (for this search, 27 sources were found). For each item that satisfied your search criteria, WAIS provides information to help you decide whether you want to use that item in subsequent searches. You should note three elements on each line.

Near the left side of the screen is a column labeled Score. This indicates how relevant WAIS judged the item to be, according to your key words. The score is determined based on the number of key words matched, how close they were to each other in the document, and whether their order matched the order in which you entered them. Simply because the item received a high score does not mean that it is your best bet for finding what you need. Instead, you should also make a judgment based on other elements for the item. For example, near the right side of each line is the column labeled Title. This indicates the title of the document or database, which can be very helpful in determining the relevance of the information.

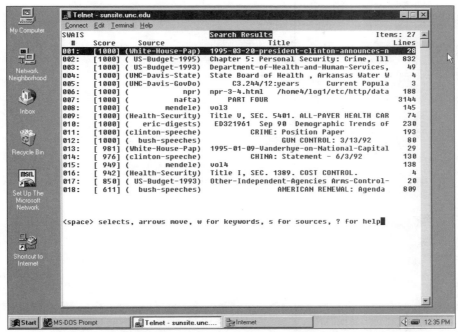

Figure 14-3: The Search Results screen displays what WAIS found based on your search criteria (sources and key words).

At the right side of each item, in the Lines column, you can see a number. This represents the number of lines of text that WAIS has available as a description of the document. You can see the description by highlighting the item and then pressing the spacebar or the Enter key. For example, Figure 14-4 shows the description for Item 13.

Notice that a description can contain information not only about the database itself, but about who created and maintains it and whether there is a charge to use the database. After reviewing the information, you can press a key to return to the Search Results screen.

Refining your search

Based on the information that was returned by your initial search, you will probably want to refine your search. You select the returned documents or databases that best meet your criteria and then search again. To indicate which sources you want to use, highlight the desired items in the Search Results screen, and then type **u** (this is short for *use source*). Every time you type **u**, an asterisk appears beside the item, and the item is added to the Source Selection screen. When you are done choosing items, type **s,** and you again see the Source Selection screen.

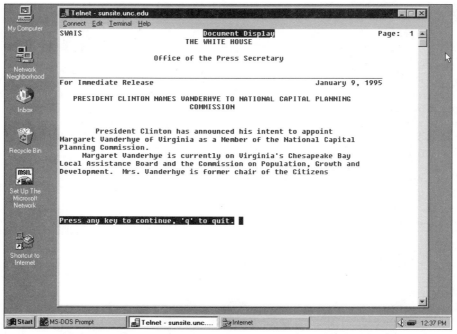

Figure 14-4: WAIS maintains a description for each document or database that it indexes.

If you scroll through the screen, notice that it now contains the sources that you added from the Search Results screen. You can further search through some of these sources by following the previous procedures:

1. Highlight the items that you want to search, pressing the spacebar to select each one.

2. Highlight the items marked with an asterisk that you no longer wish to search, pressing the spacebar to unselect each one.

3. Type **w** to enter key words and perform a search.

Again, WAIS conducts the search, and you see the Search Results screen, where you can continue to add documents to your source list and perform the search again. This iterative approach allows you to narrow and refine your search.

More on relevance feedback

Earlier in the chapter, you learn how relevance feedback works in WAIS, and you also learn how WAIS indicates the anticipated relevance of a source with a scoring mechanism. This score appears to the left of the source in the Search Results screen. As you know, WAIS bases this score on the number of matched key words, how close they were to each other in the document, and whether their order matched the order in which you entered them. There is one major item that WAIS does not take into account: context. There is really no way that WAIS can do this, because context is a purely human concept based on words and terms that have different meanings in different usages.

Although WAIS cannot read your mind, you can tune it more toward your way of thinking. For example, consider searching for information on gun control in the United States; you search using the key words *gun, control,* and *ammunition.* When you do the initial search, WAIS displays the information shown in Figure 14-5.

You can rest assured that each of the 30 documents retrieved by WAIS contains the specified key words. However, you can tell by looking at the Search Results screen that some of the documents clearly do not fit your intended search. Chances are good that the first document (the message to Congress on Haiti), which had the highest relevance score, does not fit your needs. Based on the information provided, Item 17 (the one from the eric digests) appears to be the closest fit. You can inform WAIS of your choice by selecting the item and then typing **r.** You won't see anything happen on the screen, but you have just let WAIS know which document is the most relevant to your needs.

Follow these steps to do the search again, using the same source documents:

1. Type **s** to return to the Source Selection screen.

2. Type **w** to specify key words.

3. Press Enter to indicate no change in key words.

The new Search Results screen is shown in Figure 14-6. Notice that this time the results have changed quite a bit. You can tell by the scores assigned to the documents that different relevance criteria have been used. This technique is very helpful in making fine adjustments to get exactly the search results you need.

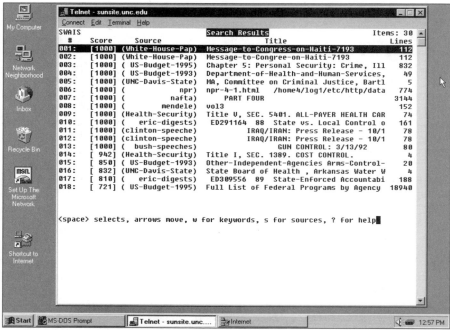

Figure 14-5: The Search Results screen.

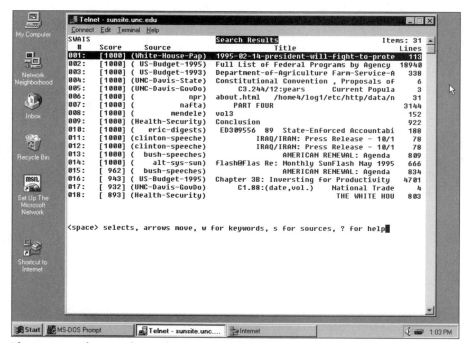

Figure 14-6: The Search Results screen after adjusting for relevance.

Retrieving Documents

Some people may consider WAIS as being complicated, but that perception is deceiving. WAIS is not particularly difficult; you simply require time and patience. This Internet tool provides an excellent way to zero in on documents that fulfill your needs. Once you go through the process and find the documents that you want, how can you get them to your computer?

One command provided by WAIS allows you to save a source document to a file. If you type **S,** you are prompted for a filename to use. The only problem here is that the command attempts to create the file on the disk drive at the computer running the WAIS client software. Thus, the command is not much help if you are connected to a WAIS client through telnet.

You have another option, however. If you highlight the document that you want, you can e-mail it to your account. This is done by typing **m.** When you do so, you are prompted for the e-mail address where you want the document sent. Enter your e-mail address, and the file is retrieved and sent to you. You can then use your e-mail program (as discussed in Chapter 8) to download the document.

Another way to retrieve short documents is to use the log file capabilities of telnet. Once you have found the document that you want and you are at the Search Results screen, follow these steps:

1. Highlight the document that you want to capture.

2. Choose Start Logging from the Terminal menu in telnet.

3. Provide a filename for the document that you are capturing, and then click on OK.

4. Press Enter to view the highlighted WAIS item.

5. When viewing is complete, choose Stop Logging from the Terminal menu in telnet.

At this point, you can use any text editor to modify the contents of your captured file. For instance, you may want to delete the lines that were added by WAIS when you were informed that you should press any key to continue. You can then use the captured file in any way.

The WAIS Command Set

So far in this chapter, you have learned how to use WAIS for day-to-day searching needs. Almost everything you may want to do with WAIS can be done by applying what you have learned. However, you can use many other commands with the client software. The commands that are available depend on the screen that you are viewing. Table 14-2 lists the different commands that you can use in WAIS. (Note the indication of which screen the commands are available from.)

Table 14-2
WAIS Commands

Keys	Source Selection	Search Results	Meaning
=	x		Unselect all previously selected sources
|		x	Pipe current item to a UNIX command
Enter	x		Perform search using previously defined key words
H	x	x	Display program history
h, ?	x	x	Display available commands
m		x	Mail highlighted item to an address
o	x	x	Set and display WAIS options
q	x	x	Exit WAIS
r		x	Make highlighted item a relevant document
S		x	Save highlighted item to a file
s	x		Select new sources
spacebar, Enter		x	View highlighted item
spacebar, period	x		Select current source
u		x	Add highlighted item to list of sources
v		x	View information on highlighted item
v, comma	x		View information on highlighted source
w	x	x	Specify new search key words
X, dash	x		Delete highlighted source from source list

If you look at the available commands, you notice that they are case sensitive. This means that an uppercase *H* performs a different function than a lowercase *h*. Make sure that the commands you use match these exactly.

Quitting WAIS

When you finish using WAIS, you can exit the program by typing **q** (lowercase) at any screen. This automatically disconnects your telnet connection, and you are informed by telnet (see Figure 14-7).

Figure 14-7: Quitting WAIS terminates your telnet connection.

Summary

A Wide Area Information Server (WAIS) provides a quick and easy way to locate information on a wide variety of topics. Hundreds of WAIS servers are available through the Internet, and each can provide a wealth of information. In this chapter, you learn how to use WAIS to locate information. Here you learn the following items:

✦ WAIS uses a search method known as relevance feedback. This is an iterative process that allows you to narrow your search scope based on the results of previous searches.

✦ You can connect to a WAIS client by using the telnet utility. (Telnet was covered in Chapter 10.)

✦ WAIS uses two different screens — Source Selection and Search Results — to define, view, and refine your searches.

✦ Once you have located a document (or documents) you want, you can use the log file capabilities of telnet to retrieve the document.

✦ A WAIS client provides a rich command set, but you only need to use a few of the commands to do normal searches with the program.

✦ When you are done using WAIS, typing **q** ends the program and terminates your telnet connection.

In the next chapter, you learn how you can use the World Wide Web — the hottest new tool on the Internet.

✦   ✦   ✦

CHAPTER 15

Using the World Wide Web

The *World Wide Web,* or Web for short, is the fastest-growing segment of the Internet. Literally thousands of resources are available through the Web. This is quite astonishing, because it was a small service on the Internet as recently as two years ago. This chapter introduces you to the Web. Here you learn the following information:

- ✦ What the World Wide Web is and how it works
- ✦ What you need to access the Web
- ✦ How to download and install a Web browser
- ✦ How to use a browser
- ✦ How the Web is organized
- ✦ The use of multimedia on the Web
- ✦ How you can speed your Web connections

In addition, you get hands-on experience on the Web with a free Web browser that you can download — Mosaic. Because the Web is so large and far-reaching, this chapter cannot provide you with more than a cursory examination of what is available. By the time you finish the chapter, however, you will know how to find your way around the Web and where you can start your exploration. If you need more detailed information, a number of books are dedicated to the Web.

What Is the World Wide Web?

As with other Internet tools, such as ftp and Gopher, the Web consists of clients and servers. When you are cruising the Web, you are the client. The servers provide information that consists of text, graphics, and sound. The multimedia nature of the Web has made it a popular medium for using the Internet.

Besides flashy graphics and sounds, the Web has another attribute that makes it very popular. The basis of the Web is a series of *hypertext links,* which make it easy to jump from one Web location to another with the click of a mouse. For example, you could be viewing a document from one Web site, but when you click on a key word, a link is activated that takes you to another Web site halfway around the world.

What You Need

You have learned that the World Wide Web is implemented by using a client/server approach. Therefore, to use the Web, you need client software. This software is referred to as a Web browser, which allows you to receive Web information and display it on your screen. The browser also manages the links from one system to another.

You can get a Web browser in several ways. First, many browsers are commercially available. You can find these in software stores or through mail-order outlets. If you purchase a commercial browser, make sure that it works with Windows 95 and with any Internet provider. Some browsers work only with a particular operating system, or they work only with a particular dial-up provider.

Another way to get a Web browser is by downloading a shareware copy. These are available on the Internet through a variety of sources. The most popular Web browsers are NetScape and Mosaic, which are quite similar to each other. This chapter uses examples from the Web using Mosaic, which is available via anonymous ftp from ftp.ncsa.uiuc.edu. This software works very well with Windows 95 and works with any Internet provider.

Downloading a Web browser

Mosaic can be easily downloaded using ftp. You learn how to use ftp in Chapter 11. To download Mosaic, follow these steps:

1. Connect to your Internet provider using Dial-Up Networking.

2. Open an MS-DOS window.

3. Change to the directory where you want the downloaded Mosaic to reside. Use a directory other than \Mosaic, because this is where the final program will be installed. Choose a temporary directory instead, such as \Temp.

4. At the DOS command prompt, enter the following command:

```
ftp ftp.ncsa.uiuc.edu
```

5. When prompted, your user ID should be *anonymous.*

6. When prompted, use your e-mail address as a password.

7. Use the following commands at the ftp prompt:

```
cd /Mosaic/Windows
binary
hash
```

8. Use the dir command to determine the latest version of the Mosaic software. As of this writing, the latest version is in the file mos20b4.exe.

9. Use the get command to copy the Mosaic software file to your system. For example, the following command transfers the mos20b4.exe file:

```
get mos20b4.exe
```

10. Use the bye command to end your ftp connection.

11. Disconnect from your Internet provider.

At this point, you have the Mosaic software on your system and are ready to install it. You disconnected from your Internet provider because it is not necessary to remain connected as you install the software.

Installing your Web browser

To install Mosaic, you first need to unzip the file. The Mosaic file that you downloaded is a self-extracting zip file. This means that it was compressed to minimize the time to transfer it to your machine. When you run the program by entering the filename, it uncompresses itself. For example, if the file that you downloaded is mos20b4.exe, you type the following at the DOS command prompt:

```
mos20b4
```

The files are uncompressed, and your screen appears as shown in Figure 15-1.

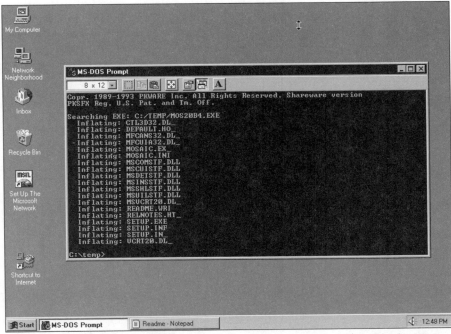

Figure 15-1: As the Mosaic files are uncompressed, you see them listed in the DOS window.

Next, choose Run from the Start menu. In the command line, run the Setup program that is in your temporary Mosaic directory. For example, if the Setup program were in the \Temp directory, you could type the command line **c:\Temp\setup.** When you click on OK, the Setup program is run, and you see the screen shown in Figure 15-2.

Mosaic is designed to run on a variety of Windows platforms, including older versions of Windows. Most information on this introductory screen does not apply to Windows 95 because you have a full 32-bit operating system. Click on the Continue button to proceed to the next step.

At this point, you see the screen shown in Figure 15-3. Here you are asked for the directory in which to install Mosaic. The default directory of C:\MOSAIC is a good choice. If you are running the Setup program from within the MOSAIC directory, you should choose a different directory at this point. If you install Mosaic into the same directory that you are installing it from, you get an error.

Click on the Continue button to proceed with the installation. Mosaic copies the necessary files from the installation directory into the program directory. When this is completed, you should see a window on your desktop that contains the Mosaic program (see Figure 15-4).

Once the installation is complete, you can delete the temporary directory that you used to install Mosaic.

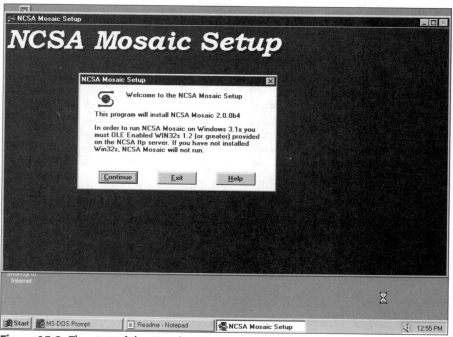

Figure 15-2: The start of the Mosaic Setup program.

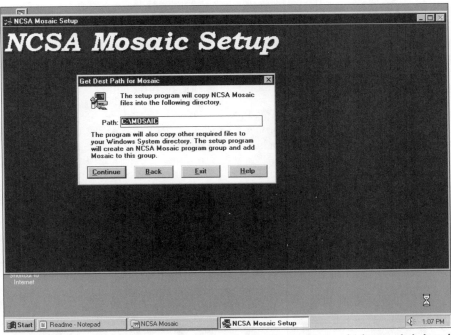

Figure 15-3: You have the opportunity to select a directory into which Mosaic is installed.

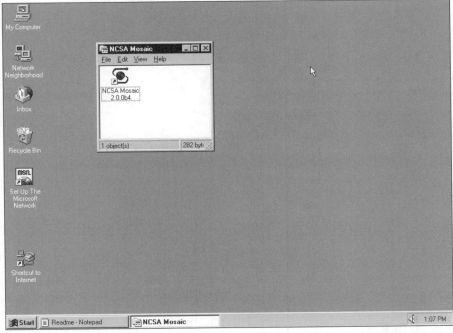

Figure 15-4: When the installation is complete, a Mosaic window appears on the desktop.

Using a Web Browser

After you install your Web browser, you are ready to use it. Before trying to use it, however, you must connect to your Internet provider using Dial-Up Networking. Then you can double-click on the Mosaic program icon (see Figure 15-4) to start the program. Shortly you see the welcome screen for the program, as shown in Figure 15-5.

Most Web browsers (including Mosaic) consist of several standard components. First, a menu bar is at the top of the browser window. This menu bar is similar to that in any other Windows program — you click on the menu that you want and then choose an option from the menu. Below the menu is a toolbar. This toolbar provides many of the same functions that you can access with the menus. The only difference is that you can often access them quicker using the toolbar.

Just beneath the toolbar is the address field. This is where you specify the Web document that you want to view. Web addressing is discussed fully in the next section. To the right of the toolbar and the address field is a picture of the world. This is a refresh icon that is animated while the browser is busy downloading information. For example, with Mosaic, the globe on the icon spins. If you click on the icon, the screen is automatically refreshed.

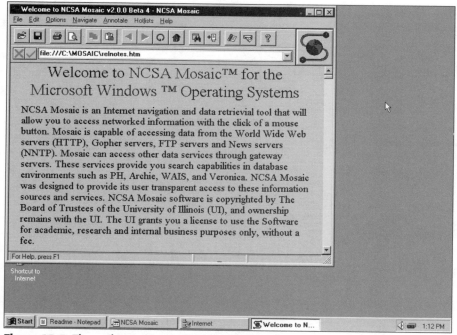

Figure 15-5: The welcome screen for Mosaic is simply the readme file provided with the program.

Finally, the bulk of the browser is taken up by the display area. This is where information downloaded from a Web server is displayed. Information in the display area can be graphics or text. Some text is displayed in a different color, such as blue. If you use the mouse to click on a word highlighted in this manner, you are activating a hyperlink that displays additional information about the topic. The information may be on the same server or on an entirely different server.

Understanding Web addressing

Web browsers, and in turn the entire World Wide Web, use a special form of addressing referred to as *URL*. This is an acronym for universal resource locator; it is simply an expanded address. You remember from earlier chapters in this book that addresses typically consist of a DNS specification that identifies the host on the Net. For example, the following is a host using the DNS naming conventions:

www.ncsa.uiuc.edu

A URL reference, however, contains quite a bit more information. The following is a URL reference:

http://www.ncsa.uiuc.edu/SDG/Software/WinMosaic/viewers.htm

Notice that the DNS address is still in there. The additional information lets the browser know that this is a Web page resource (http://) as well as the address of a particular file on the server (/SDG/Software/WinMosaic/viewers.htm). This final portion of the URL is the path to the resource on the server.

When you are working with the browser, you can take advantage of different resources on the Web by simply entering the URL in the address field on the screen. You will see many different URLs as you are working with the Net and with the Web in particular. Most Web browsers understand different types of resources and can adapt to them automatically. For example, the following is a URL that you learn about in Chapter 11:

ftp://ftp.celestin.com/xyz/abc/def.txt

This is a URL that the browser can recognize as an ftp resource. If you place it in the address field, the browser adjusts everything it does to accommodate the ftp file at this address.

COOL PLACES

Fun places on the Web	
If you have some time to kill or you need a break, try these locations for some fun:	
URL Address	**Comments**
http://eos.kub.nl:2080/calvin_hobbes	A guide to that wonderfully irreverent youngster, Calvin, and his stuffed sidekick, Hobbes
http://www.onsale.com	An online garage sale (yet a bit upscale)
http://www.match.com	A dating service for those on the information superhighway

Understanding viewers

A *viewer* is a program that allows you to display different Web resources. These viewers work with a Web browser to display information downloaded from different sites. For example, one viewer is necessary to display graphics in the GIF format, and another is required to display files stored as PostScript information. As you begin to use Mosaic, you will discover which viewers you need. Different people need different viewers, based on which Web sites they frequent.

When using Mosaic, a good place to download viewers is http://www.ncsa.uiuc.edu/SDG/Software/WinMosaic/viewers.htm. Here you find viewers for the file formats listed in Table 15-1.

Table 15-1		
File Formats for Mosaic Viewers		
Viewer	**File Format**	**Comments**
Adobe Acrobat Reader	pdf	Portable document format
GhostScript	ai	PostScript
GhostScript	eps	Encapsulated PostScript
GhostScript	ps	PostScript
LView Pro	gif	Graphics interchange format (GIF)
LView Pro	jpe	JPEG video
LView Pro	jpeg	Joint photographic experts group (JPEG) video format

Viewer	File Format	Comments
LView Pro	jpg	JPEG video
MPEGPlay	mpe	MPEG video
MPEGPlay	mpeg	Motion picture experts group (MPEG) video
MPEGPlay	mpg	MPEG video
Panorama	sgm	SGML files
Panorama	sgml	Standard generalized markup language (SGML) file
QuickTime	mov	QuickTime movie format
WordVu	doc	Microsoft Word documents
Wplany	au	Audio files

This list is current as of this writing, but additional viewers are added periodically. You should check this Web site and download the viewers that match your needs.

Organization of the Web

The Web has no overall guiding organization. Instead, a huge number of servers around the world offer information to browsers. Information on these servers is linked to information on other servers, so you can skip around the Web as you please.

The basis for presenting information on the Web is called a *home page*. This is a "table of contents" to related information. For example, if you are interested in products from Compaq Computer Co., you could visit its home page (html://www.compaq.com/homepage.graphic.html), as shown in Figure 15-6.

The home page offers links to other related information that can provide more detail on various topics. For example, if you want additional information on Compaq products, you would click on the Product Information area in the upper-right corner of the screen.

Figure 15-6: The home page for Compaq Computer Co.

Using hypertext links

As you are browsing through the Web, you see both text and graphics (or video) on your screen. If you see text in a different color, that color probably represents a hypertext link to another location on the Web. Just click on the text, and you are off to another location.

For example, you may be reading information about your favorite topic — coin collecting. After you have been browsing the Web for a while, you find yourself viewing information about the U.S. Mint, as shown in Figure 15-7.

You read about different programs and products of the mint. The colored text for American Eagle and Silver Bullion Coins grabs your attention, so you click on the button, and in a short time, you are whisked away to another Web site. This time, your screen looks like Figure 15-8.

In reality, the links on the Web are endless. You could continue to click on different hypertext links and visit different sites around the world indefinitely. The places where you go and the things that you see are entirely up to you.

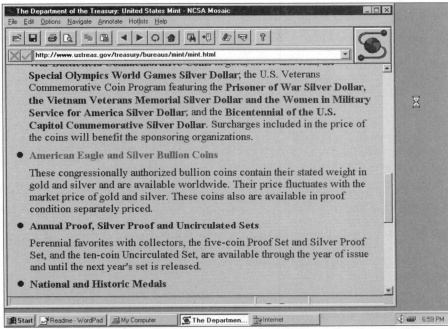

Figure 15-7: The Web even includes pages that describe various government bureaus.

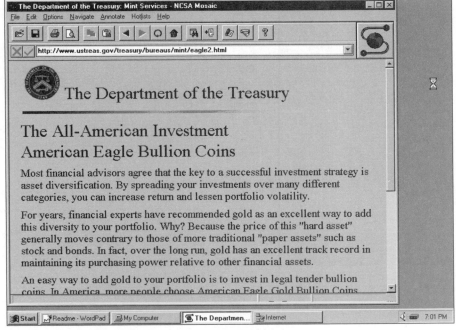

Figure 15-8: Information about U.S. Treasury gold coins.

Finding information on the Web

You know that you can use the various hypertext links to find related information on the Web. What if you want to find unrelated information? It would be pretty hard to make your way from "Fish Species of the Amazon" to "Man's First Space Flight" by simply clicking on hypertext links.

When you need to find information on the Web, a few places provide excellent links. One such place is the *Yahoo* search tool at http:/www.yahoo.com. This site provides a topical reference to information on the Web. There are no flashy graphics to slow you down, but the links available from this site can lead you to the graphics. Figure 15-9 shows the first screen that you see when you access this site.

The Yahoo site provides a series of topics from which you can choose. The numbers in parentheses after the topic indicate the number of additional topics available under that topic. For example, if you click on Education, you find 2,358 additional topics. You can continue to refine your search by selecting even more specific topics. If you have a good idea of what you are looking for, or if you simply like to browse for hours, the Yahoo site is a great place to start.

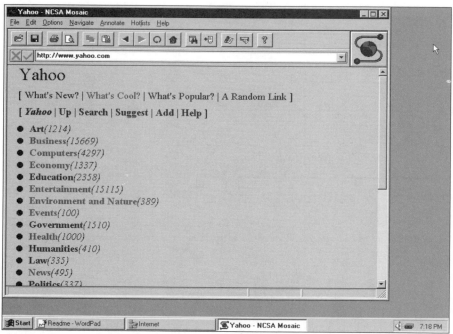

Figure 15-9: The Yahoo search tool is a great place to start looking for information.

Another starting place is the *Lycos* tool. This Web site, maintained by Carnegie Mellon University, provides an easy way to search millions of Web documents for key words. When you access the site at http://lycos.cs.cmu.edu, you see the screen shown in Figure 15-10.

If you were looking at this screen on your system, you would notice that one of the hypertext links on this home page is for the "big Lycos catalog." If you click on this phrase, you see a search page (Figure 15-11) that allows you to enter a key word or query at the bottom of the page.

Once you enter your search query and press Enter, the search is made, and you see the results. For example, I searched for the word *Wyoming,* and the results were displayed as shown in Figure 15-12.

Figure 15-10: The Lycos tool can help you search for Web documents by key word.

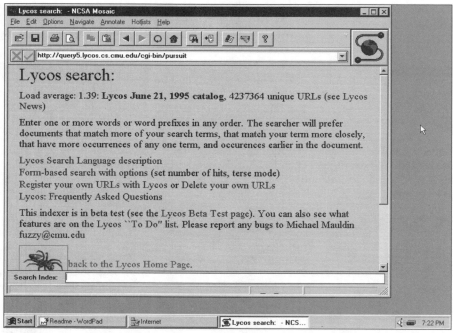

Figure 15-11: You need only to enter a key word or a complete query to conduct a Lycos search.

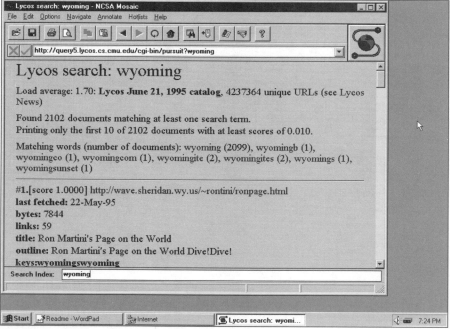

Figure 15-12: The results of a Lycos search.

Great Web sites for reference	
If you are looking for Web sites that can help you with your reference needs, check out these places:	
URL Address	**Comments**
http://www.yahoo.com	Subject-organized links to thousands of Web sites
http://lycos.cs.cmu.edu	Key word searches of millions of Web documents
http://www.ziff.com/~pccomp/webmap	A great graphical index to thousands of Web sites
http://www.sbaonline.sba.gov	Quick access to a variety of governmental resources

Multimedia on the Internet

The lure of the Web for many people is the flashy graphics, cool videos, and great sounds that you can find. The Web allows you to access virtually the entire world at the click of a button, and you need to do little to take advantage of it. The only requirement is that you have a browser (such as Mosaic) and the proper viewers. After that, the browser takes care of the rest. When you visit a Web site, the information is downloaded and converted into something you can view or hear automatically.

As an example, Figure 15-13 shows the image that you see when you access http://www.disney.com and browse through the *Lion King* portion of the theater. These types of graphics are available at many different points on the Web.

To take advantage of all the multimedia benefits of the Web, make sure that you have the appropriate viewers installed on your system. Earlier in this chapter, you learned about the different viewers that are available. Although you don't need every viewer that you run across, you do need the ones that convert the files that you want to see on your system.

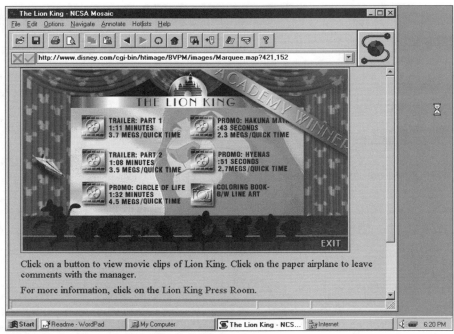

Figure 15-13: An example of multimedia on the Web.

Speeding Up Your Display

Although the graphics on the Web are quite awesome, they can be time consuming. It takes time to download information and display it on your screen — even with a fast modem. To overcome this, the Mosaic browser includes a feature that allows you to limit the graphics that are displayed on your system.

If you click on the Options menu and then choose Preferences, you see the dialog box shown in Figure 15-14.

You can change many options in this dialog box. This chapter is not intended to provide detailed documentation on how to use Mosaic; you should refer to the online program documentation for that. At the top-center of the dialog box, however, there is a choice titled Display Inline Images. If you clear this check box, then images are not downloaded and displayed on the screen.

Once you turn off the display of inline graphics, you only see placeholders on the screen (see Figure 15-15). To display the graphics for a certain page, simply turn the inline graphics back on. When you leave the page and return, the graphics are downloaded and appear on the screen.

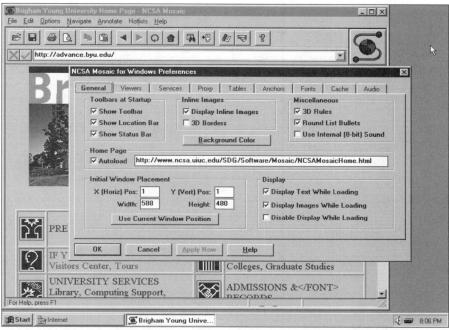

Figure 15-14: Mosaic allows you to change your program preferences.

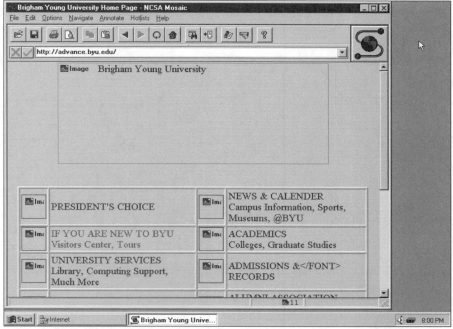

Figure 15-15: With inline graphics turned off, you are shown picture placeholders instead of the actual images.

Summary

The World Wide Web is a fast-growing segment of the Internet that allows easy access to information and resources. Using a Web browser is the best way to take advantage of the Web; such browsers are readily available either commercially or through the Internet itself. In this chapter, you receive a quick tour of what is available on the Web. Here you learn the following items:

✦ Web browsers, such as Mosaic or NetScape, can be used to navigate the Web and retrieve information.

✦ The Web is organized as a series of interrelated documents. These documents are called home pages, and they contain links to other documents.

✦ The use of hypertext links in Web documents allows you to freely move around the Web and view information that is of interest. The links do not need to connect to resources on the same server but can be connected to servers located all over the world.

✦ Multimedia, including graphics, video, and sound, is a big part of the Web's appeal. Information in these (as well as text) formats can be automatically downloaded and displayed on your system by your Web browser.

✦ Downloading multimedia elements can take a great deal of time. If you desire, you can configure your browser so that inline graphics are not displayed. This text-only approach greatly speeds navigation through the Web.

In the next chapter, you learn how to take advantage of newsgroups and online chatting.

✦   ✦   ✦

Talking the Night Away

The Internet offers different ways to communicate with people. In earlier chapters, you learn about some of these communications methods, such as e-mail and mailing lists. This chapter discusses two other popular methods of communicating: Usenet newsgroups and IRC. By the end of this chapter, you learn the following items:

- ✦ What Usenet and newsgroups are
- ✦ How you can understand newsgroups by their names
- ✦ How to download and install your own newsreader
- ✦ How to configure your newsreader
- ✦ What it means to subscribe to a newsgroup
- ✦ How to read and post messages
- ✦ What IRC is and how you can chat on the Internet
- ✦ Where you can find IRC software on the Internet
- ✦ How to use an IRC client program

Using Usenet

One of the most popular parts of the Internet is *Usenet*. In most respects, you can compare Usenet to electronic bulletin board systems (BBSs). The difference between a BBS and Usenet is one of scale. Several million people are accessing over 7,000 Usenet topic categories (called *newsgroups*) every day. These people read messages and post responses for others to read — just like with a BBS. With so many topics available, the possibilities for discussion cover the spectrum from the mundane to the obscure and even the bizarre.

Because so many people access Usenet on a daily basis, it has become a primary source of news and information for the public. In most cases, this information is from other people, just like you, who are also using the newsgroups. As you post messages, people around the world read them. These people can then respond to your messages, and the cycle continues.

With the ability to read and post information to newsgroups, you may be tempted to compare newsgroups to mailing lists (as discussed in Chapter 9). This is where the similarities end, however. Newsgroups and mailing lists are fundamentally different in how information is accessed.

Whereas mailing lists are disseminated through regular e-mail services, newsgroups are disseminated only through the use of a *newsreader*. This is a special program that allows you to tap into the newsgroups of your choice and manage the messages posted there. Whereas mailing list information is visible every time you open your e-mailbox, you need the special newsreader to access Usenet newsgroups.

When you post messages to a newsgroup, the message does not appear instantly around the world. The Usenet is not like e-mail, where delivery can be almost instantaneous. Instead, it takes time for the message to make its way through a myriad of computer systems and be posted in all the appropriate places. Postings can take up to a couple of hours to appear, thus the conversations conducted through Usenet tend to be more public and long term.

When you use a newsreader, you connect to a news server somewhere on the Internet. The newsgroups that you can access are determined by the system administrator for that news server. Many newsgroups are available on a number of news servers; the parallel nature of these servers represents the reason it can take several hours for newsgroup postings to be widely available. Some newsgroups are available only on a single news server or for a particular region. Collectively, the newsgroups that are available through a server are referred to as a *newsfeed*. It is the system administrator, balancing the needs of local and regional users against the availability of resources, who determines what the newsfeed consists of.

In most instances, the Usenet newsgroups are considered to be recreational. This does not mean that serious conversations do not go on — on the contrary, they can be very serious in nature. It simply means that the conversations, because they are so public, often mirror the quality of conversation that you hear at a cocktail party or some other informal gathering. In such an environment, you can become educated and glean important tidbits of information, but not as you would at a formal lecture or in a classroom situation.

This means that, in some ways, the term newsgroup is a misnomer — after all, we are not dealing with "real" news in newsgroups. However, there are ways to receive real news over the Internet. Whereas newsgroups deal with people talking to people, *netnews* refers to the dissemination of traditional news through the Internet. One service that distributes netnews in the Usenet format is called Clarinet. This service electronically publishes prime-time, quality news, including Associated Press (AP) and United Press International (UPI) news feeds. Such netnews services are not interactive; that is, you cannot post responses to articles as you can with other Usenet newsgroups. It is also important to understand that netnews services (such as Clarinet) are not free. Someone must pay the cost of such a service, and thus they are not available on all news servers.

Newsgroup categories

Each newsgroup that is accessible with a newsreader has a name. These names consist of words separated by periods, such as rec.arts.movies or comp.os.ms-windows.misc. The position of these words defines a hierarchy of newsgroups, and if you understand the different categories, you can more readily take advantage of the available newsgroups.

Newsgroups are organized into hierarchies, which make it easier to find a particular newsgroup that may meet your interests. The main newsgroup categories are shown in Table 16-1. These are the highest-level hierarchical organizations, and they appear as the first word in any newsgroup name. Thus, the newsgroup sci.math.symbolic belongs to the sci, or scientific, category.

Table 16-1
Primary Newsgroup Categories

Category	Meaning
comp	Computer-related newsgroups
misc	Miscellaneous newsgroups
news	News
rec	Recreational and arts-oriented newsgroups
sci	Science technology and scientific newsgroups
soc	Social issues and socializing newsgroups
talk	Current issues newsgroups

Newsgroups that belong to the primary classifications are generally available on all news servers around the Net. Other categories, however, may not be as available. Table 16-2 lists other newsgroup categories that may be available through some (but not all) news servers.

Table 16-2
Common Newsgroup Categories

Category	Meaning
alt	Alternative newsgroups
bionet	Newsgroups of interest to biologists
bit	Newsgroups that provide mailing list digests
biz	Newsgroups that are related to business or business products
ieee	Newsgroups for the Institute of Electrical and Electronics Engineers (IEEE)
info	Newsgroups that originate through the University of Illinois
k12	Newsgroups that are related to elementary and secondary education
relcom	Russian-language newsgroups
vmsnet	Discussions that are related to VAX/VMS systems

In addition to the categories listed in Tables 16-1 and 16-2, you may see newsgroup categories that are regional or local in nature. For example, newsgroups beginning with the letters *sf* may be for San Francisco, California, while those beginning with *cns* are for users of the Internet provider CNS.

Newsgroup names are formed by combining category names in a more specific direction, from left to right. For example, the newsgroup talk.politics.mideast deals with current issues (the talk portion) of a political nature (the politics portion) about the Mideast (the mideast portion). Another topic is rec.pets, which is recreational and about pets. As interest in this group grew, additional classifications were developed within rec.pets that further defined the interests of the newsgroup subscribers. For example, rec.pets.birds is related to birds as pets, while rec.pets.dogs is about dogs. As interest in other pets develops, additional newsgroups can be formed.

Downloading a newsreader

To access newsgroups, you need a newsreader. Several different newsreaders are available on the Internet, and you can download them to your system using ftp (see Chapter 11). The following is a list of the most popular newsreaders and where you can find them.

Name	Ftp Site	Directory
Free Agent	ftp.forteinc.com	pub/forte/free_agent
Trumpet Newsreader	ftp.trumpet.com.au	wintrump
WinVN	ftp.ksc.nasa.gov	pub/winvn/nt

In addition, you can find some newsreaders on the World Wide Web. The following is a list of several popular newsreaders and where you can find them on the Web.

Name	URL
News	http://gfecnet.gmi.edu/Software/files/news.zip
News Xpress	http://gfecnet.gmi.edu/Software/files/nx10b4-p.zip
Qnews	http://www.magi.com/~rdavies/qn09a5.zip

Although these newsreaders perform the same basic functions, each operates a bit differently. It doesn't matter which of the newsreaders you use; you simply need to download one and install it on your machine. You may want to download more than one so that you can find the one that you feel most comfortable with. The examples in this chapter focus on using the WinVN 32-bit newsreader. This does not imply that this tool is necessarily better than the other newsreaders; it is simply used for illustration purposes.

To download the WinVN software, use the ftp command to connect to the anonymous ftp site at ftp.ksc.nasa.gov. Once connected, issue the following commands at the ftp prompt:

```
cd pub/winvn/nt
binary
get winvn_99_05_intel.zip
```

The file that you are transferring is over 300K in size, and it may take a while to download it to your system. After it finishes transferring, you can break your Internet connection, because installing the software does not require an active connection.

Installing your newsreader

Once you have downloaded the WinVN software to your system, you are ready to install it. The first step is to "uncompress" the software. To reduce transmission times, the software that you downloaded (winvn_99_05_intel.zip) is compressed. This means that you need the PKUNZIP portion of the PKZIP program to convert the compressed file into the executable files that you can use. Many readers already have PKZIP; others may not. If you do not have it, you can generally find this utility on a BBS, on any of the online systems, or at thousands of Internet sites.

You may actually want to uncompress the ZIP file in a directory that you have set aside for your newsreader. (For example, on my system, I created a folder called Reader in which I placed the winvn_99_05_intel.zip file.) When you are ready to uncompress the file, enter the following command from the MS-DOS command line:

```
pkunzip winvn_~1
```

This uncompresses the file that you downloaded, saving a total of seven files on your hard drive. At this point, you can delete the file that you downloaded, and you must move the DLL file needed by the newsreader to the proper directory on your system. You do this by entering the following commands:

```
del winvn_99_05_intel.zip
move ctl3d32.dll \windows\system
```

You can now add the program to the Internet tools menu that you created in Chapter 10. To do this, follow these steps:

1. Right-click on the Start button. This displays the context menu for the Start button.

2. Choose Open from the context menu. This displays the Start Menu folder in a window.

3. Double-click on the Internet Tools icon. This displays a folder window for the Internet Tools folder.

4. Choose the New option from the File menu, and then choose Shortcut. You will see the Create Shortcut dialog box, as shown in Figure 16-1.

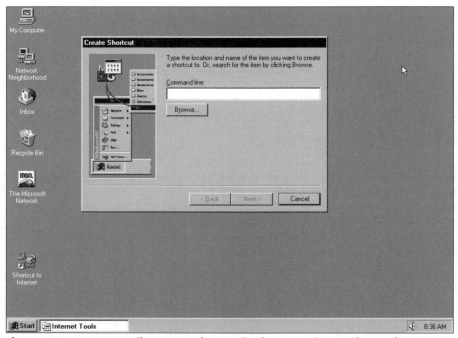

Figure 16-1: You can easily create a shortcut for the new WinVN software that you downloaded.

5. In the Command Line box, type **c:\reader\winvn.exe**. (If you saved WinVN in a different directory, you should modify the path accordingly.)

6. Click on the Next button. You are asked for the name to use for this shortcut, as shown in Figure 16-2.

7. Accept the shortcut name by clicking on the Finish button.

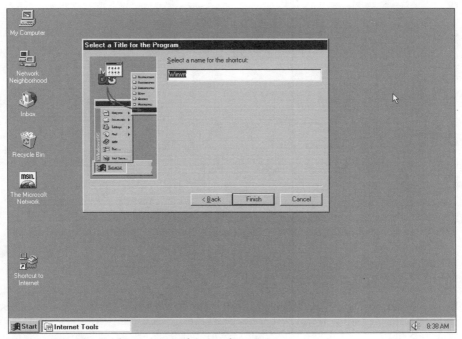

Figure 16-2: The final step is supplying a shortcut's name.

At this point, the new shortcut appears in the Internet Tools window, as shown in Figure 16-3. It also appears in the Internet Tools menu, which can be accessed from the Start menu. You are now ready to begin using WinVN.

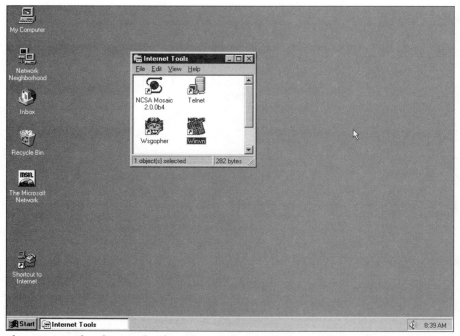

Figure 16-3: The shortcut for the WinVN program appears in the Internet Tools window.

Your first time on the newsreader

Before you use your newsreader for the first time, you must determine the address of the news server that you will be connecting with. The best way to do this is to contact your MIS department or your Internet provider and ask them for the proper address. This way, you can access the newsgroups that are most appropriate to your location. For example, when I contacted my Internet provider, I was given the address news.usa.net.

To connect to the news server, you must first establish your PPP or SLIP connection with your Internet provider. You can then start the WinVN program by choosing Winvn from the Internet Tools menu (as described in the preceding section). Shortly, you see a dialog box that is similar to Figure 16-4.

Here you are asked for the name of the INI file that will be used by WinVN. This file keeps track of configuration information for the program. Because this is the first time that you have run the program, simply click on the Open button. You are asked to confirm that you really want to create the INI file; click on the Yes button, and a new INI file is created in the same directory in which you installed WinVN. Then you see a dialog box similar to the one shown in Figure 16-5.

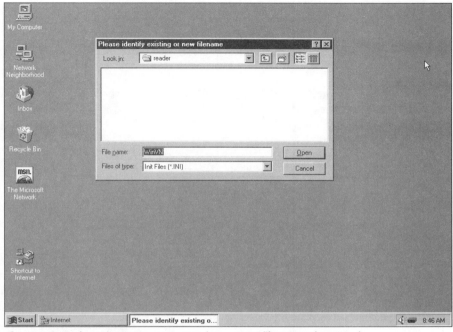

Figure 16-4: The WinVN program requires an INI file to work properly.

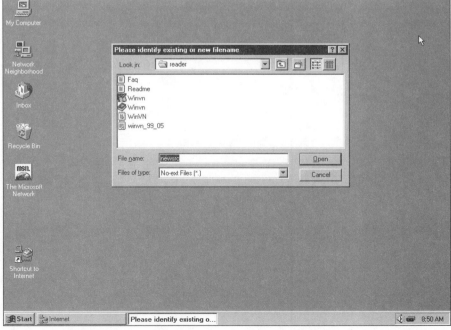

Figure 16-5: The WinVN program also requires a file called NEWSRC to work properly.

This dialog box is asking where the NEWSRC file is located. This file keeps track of the newsgroups to which you subscribe. Again, this is the first time that you have used the program, so click on Open. You are asked to confirm that you want to create the file; click on Yes. After the NEWSRC file is created, your screen appears similar to that shown in Figure 16-6.

In the top of the Communications Options dialog box, enter the name of your news server. For example, the server name I received from my Internet provider was news.usa.net. I entered this in the NNTP Server field, and I clicked on the Connect at startup check box (because I want to check the news server every time I start the program). When you click on the OK button, the information is saved, and you are asked for some personal information, as shown in Figure 16-7.

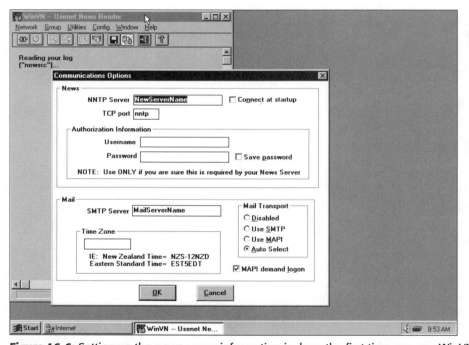

Figure 16-6: Setting up the news server information is done the first time you use WinVN.

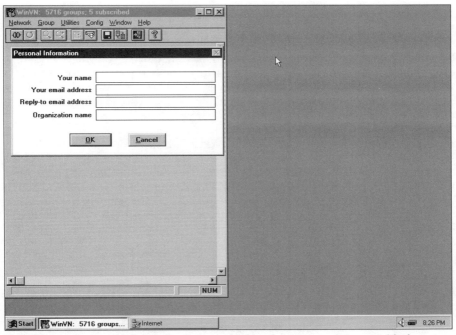

Figure 16-7: Personal information is requested so that you can interact with the newsgroups properly.

Here you should enter the following information about yourself:

✦ **Your name.** This name is used to sign your newsgroup postings; enter it exactly as you want it to appear.

✦ **Your email address.** This is your regular e-mail address, which people use to send you personal postings.

✦ **Reply-to email address.** Here you can indicate a special e-mail address that people can use. In most instances, you can leave this field blank.

✦ **Organization name.** This can be your school name, your company name, or some other identifier that shows the organization that you are affiliated with.

When you finish, click on the OK button. Your configuration is now complete, and you won't see these preliminary screens again. If you indicated that you wanted to connect with the news server at startup, the link is established right away.

Subscribing and unsubscribing to newsgroups

Whenever you start the WinVN program, it can check the news server to determine if any new newsgroups are available. You are then asked if you want to download the latest list of newsgroups from the server. In most instances, you will want to do this, even though it takes a while. Without the list, you have no way of knowing which newsgroups are available through the server. When I requested the list, 5,700 groups were downloaded, and it took just under a minute. If you are using a slower modem than mine (28,800 bps), then your download time will be longer.

When the download process is complete, WinVN displays a window that allows you to select which newsgroups you want to track, as shown in Figure 16-8. The process of tracking a newsgroup is known as *subscribing*. This means nothing as far as the news server is concerned; subscribing is purely a local interaction between you and the WinVN program. When you subscribe to a newsgroup, the name of the newsgroup is stored in the NEWSRC file, and messages from the newsgroup are constantly tracked for you. When you later unsubscribe, the newsgroup name is removed from NEWSRC, and tracking of the newsgroup is suspended.

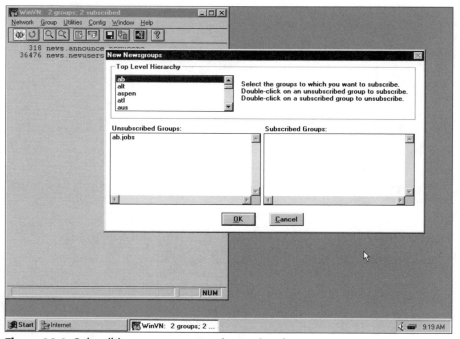

Figure 16-8: Subscribing to a newsgroup is easy in WinVN.

To subscribe to a particular newsgroup, simply pick a category at the top of the dialog box. You are then shown the newsgroups within that category to which you subscribe and those to which you don't. When you double-click on a newsgroup to which you don't subscribe, it moves to the list of those you do subscribe to, and vice versa. When you finish, click on the <u>O</u>K button.

Understanding the WinVN interface

When you finish adding or removing newsgroups, the WinVN program window appears similar to what is shown in Figure 16-9.

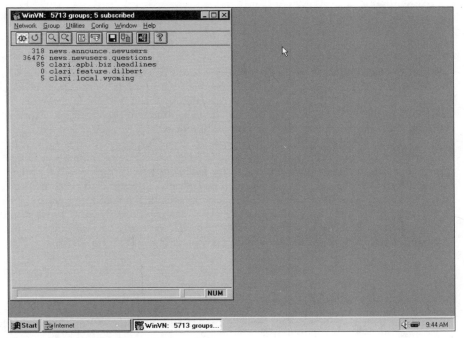

Figure 16-9: The WinVN program window.

At the top of the screen are the menus that allow you to perform various actions on your newsgroups. Six menus are available, and they perform the following general functions:

- ✦ **Network.** Commands related to connecting to and disconnecting from a news server, as well as exiting the program

- ✦ **Group.** Commands for finding newsgroup information, subscribing and unsubscribing to newsgroups, and saving your newsgroup information

✦ **Utilities.** Commands that allow you to post messages to newsgroups, and encode and later decode files

✦ **Config.** Commands related to the configuration of WinVN and how it operates by default

✦ **Window.** Commands used to arrange or control windows within the WinVN program

✦ **Help.** Commands designed to provide help or to display information about the program

Below the menus is a toolbar that allows you to perform many of the same functions that you can perform with the menus. The only difference is that the toolbar icons are more accessible than the menu commands.

Below the toolbar is the display area of the newsreader. This area contains a list of all newsgroups to which you subscribe. At the left of each newsgroup name is the number of messages available for that newsgroup. (In the next section, you learn how you can read the messages in a newsgroup.) Finally, at the bottom of the WinVN program window is a status bar. This bar displays information about the status of the program itself or quick help about menu commands.

The WinVN program is rich in features and follows the Windows interface. The same cannot be said for all newsreader programs. Different programs have different capabilities and features. Every newsreader program allows you to read messages and post responses, however. Because this chapter discusses newsreaders and newsgroups in general, those basic functions are covered. However, I suggest that you spend some time learning about the more advanced features of your newsreader, because these features can greatly enhance the value that you receive from newsgroups.

Reading the news

When using WinVN, you can read the messages in a newsgroup by double-clicking on the newsgroup name in the program window. For example, if you look back at Figure 16-9, you can see that there are 85 messages available in the newsgroup clari.apbl.biz.headlines. If you want to read these messages, double-click on the newsgroup name. WinVN queries the news server and downloads the available messages.

WHAT CAN GO WRONG

I didn't get all my messages

Just because the main newsreader screen indicates that a certain number of messages are available, this is not necessarily true. For reasons known only to the powers that be, the actual number of messages available often differs from the number indicated in the newsreader. The actual number can be higher or lower.

Remember that the newsgroups are very dynamic. This means that the number of available messages constantly changes. For example, the number of messages available when you start the newsreader is typically different from the number available when you read a newsgroup. Do not be concerned if you retrieve a newsgroup and you find that it doesn't contain all the messages that you anticipated.

After downloading the messages, you see a synopsis of each one in a window, as shown in Figure 16-10. This list contains a message number, date, source (if applicable), and title. If the message does not have a title, then none is shown; the only way to see what the message is about is to read it.

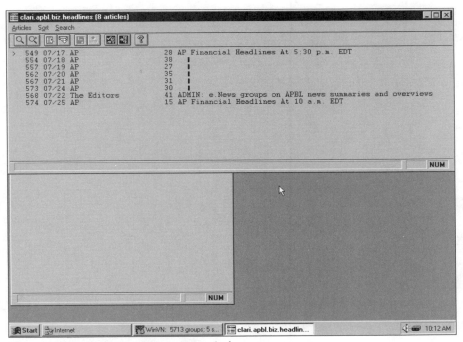

Figure 16-10: A newsgroup message window.

Messages are listed in chronological order, from the oldest (at the top of the list) to the newest (at the bottom). You can change the order in which messages are listed by choosing a command from the Sort menu. This is particularly helpful if you belong to a newsgroup that is quite active and has a large number of postings. Using the commands on the Sort menu, you can sort by any of the following:

✦ Date

✦ Subject

✦ Lines (length of posting)

✦ Thread (original postings and replies grouped together)

✦ Article (message) number

✦ Author

If you want to read a message, double-click on the message in the list. WinVN then opens another window that contains the contents of the message. For example, if you want to read the financial headlines from July 17, double-click on that message, and the contents of the message appear as shown in Figure 16-11.

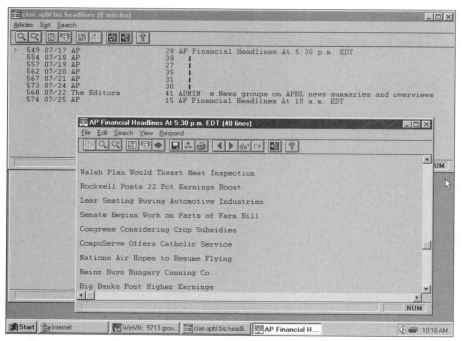

Figure 16-11: The contents of a newsgroup message are shown in its own window.

While you are reading a message, WinVN allows you to perform numerous commands. For example, you can forward the message to someone via e-mail, send it to your printer, or save it to your hard drive. Different newsreader programs provide different features for working with newsgroup messages, and you should spend time familiarizing yourself with the available bells and whistles.

A message and the messages posted as responses to that message are referred to as a *thread*. Threads can be very short (for instance, a single message that no one responds to) or very long. Because reading message threads can be much more enlightening than reading a group of disjointed messages, most newsreaders include some feature that allows you to work with entire message threads. WinVN is no exception. You can sort the messages within a newsgroup by thread, which can be very helpful.

Posting messages

A good portion of the popularity of newsgroups is that they are interactive. You can post two types of messages with a newsreader. The first is a message that is a response to an existing message, and the other is an original message that is not a response. If you are responding to an existing message, you generally do so by using a menu command as you are reading the message. Posting an original message may be done from some other menu or window.

In WinVN, messages are referred to as *articles*. Every type of window used by the system includes a command to create a new article, which is then posted to a newsgroup. Here you initiate the command indicating the type of posting that you are performing. For example, if you initiate the command while reading a message (by using the Respond menu), then the program automatically assumes that you are responding to the message that you are currently reading. Regardless of where you initiate the command, the composition window shown on your desktop is the same, as shown in Figure 16-12.

In many respects, composing a message for a newsgroup is very similar to composing an e-mail message. The only difference is the header information that is used to track the thread in which your message belongs. You should check the newsgroup designation for the message and make sure that the rest of the header fields (such as topic) are correct. Then you can type your message in the text box at the bottom of the Followup Article dialog box.

When you finish entering your message, choose the Send command from the Post menu. This sends your message to the news server and from there to other news servers around the world.

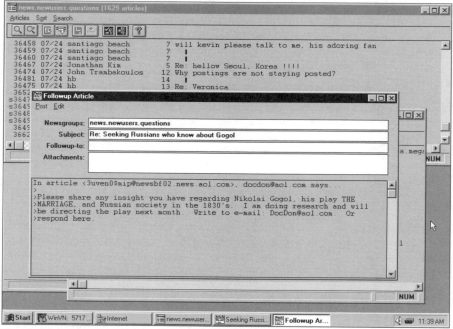

Figure 16-12: Composing a message is easy in WinVN.

Using IRC

IRC is an acronym for Internet Relay Chat, which is a tool that you can use to communicate with other Internet users in real time. Thus, what you type on your system appears on another person's system as you type it and vice versa. Although such communications are not as fast or efficient as a telephone conversation, they can often be cheaper. For example, if you must communicate with someone in Tibet, the Internet connection charges through a local provider will most likely be less than the cost of a telephone call halfway around the world. When you combine this with the fact that most IRC sessions involve more than two people, the cost can be significantly lower than wide-area conference calls.

To use IRC, all the people who want to communicate simultaneously must be connected to the Internet at the same time. If you want to communicate with "just anyone" about a given topic, this is no problem; you can probably find someone to discuss your topic with. If you want to communicate with a specific person, however, then you must make sure that this person is available. This means that you must schedule a time with the other person, typically through e-mail.

Downloading IRC software

To use IRC, you need special software that allows you to make the connection. IRC software can be found at several places on the Net, and you can typically download it using ftp, as discussed in Chapter 11. Exactly how IRC software has been implemented can vary, and unlike other Internet tools, there is no "standard" around which chatting has developed. Thus, if you use a particular type of chatting software that works on the WWW, then you can only engage in real-time communications with others that are using the same software at the same time. Likewise, if you are using a chat program that allows real-time voice transmittal over the Internet, you can only communicate with others that are using the same software.

Table 16-3 lists some of the IRC programs that you can download from the Internet, along with their general capabilities:

Table 16-3			
Ftp Sites for Downloading IRC Programs			
Name	*Ftp Site*	*Directory*	*Type of Chatting*
Internet Phone	ftp.vocaltec.com	pub/iphone09.exe	Demo version of full-duplex voice chatting
PowWow	simtel.coast.net	SimTel/win3/winsock	Text chatting, file transfer
mIRC	ftp.demon.co.uk	pub/ibmpc/winsock/apps/mirc	IRC client for Windows
Sesame	ftp.ubique.com	pub/outgoing/pc	Chatting via the WWW
WinTalk	ftp.elf.com	pub/wintalk	Voice chatting over the Internet
WS Chat	oak.oakland.edu	simtel/win3/winsock	Simple text chatting

In addition, you can find some chatting software on the World Wide Web. Table 16-4 lists several popular IRC programs and where you can find them on the Web.

Name	URL	Type of Chatting
Global Chat	http://www.prospero.com/globalchat.download.html	Chatting via the WWW
Internet VoiceChat	http://gfecnet.gmi.edu/Software/files/ivc11.zip	Real-time audio communications
IRC 4 Client	http://gfecnet.gmi.edu/Software/files/irc4win.zip	IRC client for Windows
Worlds Chat	http://www.worlds.net	3-D chatting
XTalk	http://www.ugrad.cs.ubc.ca/spider/q7f192/bin /xtalk/xtalk04.zip	Chatting client for use with UNIX servers

Table 16-4
World Wide Web Sites for Downloading IRC Programs

Although these IRC programs allow you to chat with others, each functions in different ways. You may want to download some or all so that you can try them out and determine which you like the best. The examples used in this chapter rely on mIRC.

To download the mIRC software, use the ftp command to connect to the anonymous ftp site at ftp.demon.co.uk. Once connected, issue the following commands at the ftp prompt:

```
cd pub/ibmpc/winsock/apps/mirc
binary
get mirc342.zip
```

The file that you are transferring is just over 200K in size, and it may take a while to download it to your system. After it finishes transferring, you can break your Internet connection, because installing the software does not require an active connection.

Installing your software

Once you download mIRC to your system, you are ready to install it. The first step is to "uncompress" the software. This is done using PKUNZIP, as described earlier in the chapter. Uncompress the ZIP file in a folder that you have set aside for your chatting software. (On my system, I created a folder called Chat in which I placed the mirc342.zip file.) When you are ready to uncompress the file, enter the following command from the MS-DOS command line:

```
pkunzip mirc342
```

This uncompresses the file that you downloaded, in the process saving five files on your hard drive. At this point, you can delete the file that you downloaded (mirc342.zip), because it is no longer needed. You should also copy the MIRC.INI file to your Windows directory, because that is where the program expects to find the initialization file. To accomplish these two steps, enter these commands at the command prompt:

```
del mirc342.zip
move mirc.ini \windows
```

Next, you can add the program to the Internet tools menu that you created in Chapter 10 by following these steps:

1. Right-click on the Start button. This displays the context menu for the Start button.

2. Choose Open from the context menu. This displays the Start Menu folder in a window.

3. Double-click on the Internet Tools icon. This displays a folder window for the Internet Tools folder.

4. Choose the New option from the File menu, and then choose Shortcut. You see the Create Shortcut dialog box, as shown earlier in Figure 16-1.

5. In the Command Line box, type **c:\chat\mirc.exe**. (If you saved mIRC in a different directory, you should modify the path accordingly.)

6. Click on the Next button. You are asked for the name of this shortcut, as shown earlier in Figure 16-2.

7. Accept the shortcut name by clicking on the Finish button.

At this point, the new shortcut appears in the Internet Tools window as well as in the Internet Tools menu, which can be accessed from the Start menu. You are now ready to configure the program.

Configuring mIRC

Before you can use mIRC, you must provide some configuration information for the program. You don't need to be connected to the Internet when you run the program to configure it. When you start the program, select the Setup option from the File menu. You then see the dialog box shown in Figure 16-13.

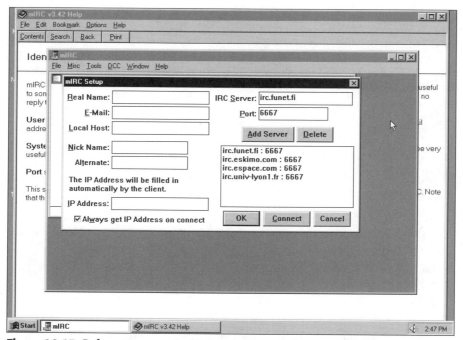

Figure 16-13: Before you can use mIRC, you must configure the program.

If you normally connect to your Internet provider through a PPP or SLIP account, you must provide only a few items in this dialog box:

✦ **Real Name.** Enter your full name. This is used for e-mail purposes and for logging into IRC sessions.

✦ **E-Mail.** Supply your e-mail address. This is so someone can send you an e-mail message outside of the normal chat sessions.

✦ **Nick Name.** The name that you want to use as your "handle" when chatting with other people. Many times, handles are easier to use than real names.

✦ **Alternate.** The alternate nickname to use, in case someone else is already using your primary nickname.

After you have filled in these four fields, click on the OK button; your information is then saved on disk. Next, choose the Ident Server command from the File menu. This displays the dialog box shown in Figure 16-14.

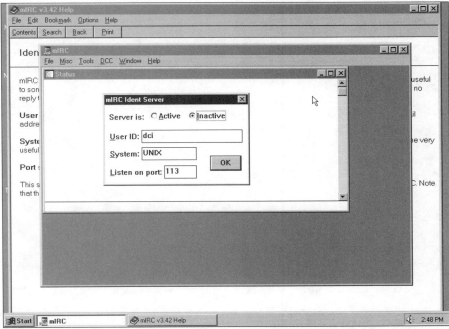

Figure 16-14: The Ident Server identifies you to the remote IRC server.

The Ident Server establishes connections with some IRC servers. If it is not set to <u>A</u>ctive, you must change the setting. Choose the <u>A</u>ctive radio button, and then click on the OK button. You are now ready to use mIRC.

Connecting to an IRC server

To use mIRC, you must establish your connection to the Internet. Once this is done, start the program by selecting Mirc from your Internet Tools menu (as described earlier in this chapter). When you start the program, it appears as shown in Figure 16-15. At this point, you are not connected to an IRC server; you have simply started the mIRC program.

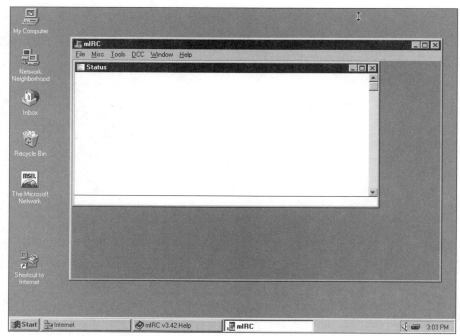

Figure 16-15: When you start mIRC, you can see the program window and the channel window.

There are two main parts to the mIRC interface. The first is the menu at the top of the program menu. The menu options allow you to perform commands that affect your IRC session. Within the program window is a channel window (titled Status), which shows communication over an IRC channel. To connect with a server, you have two choices:

✦ Connect to your default server by selecting Connect from the File menu.

✦ Connect to a specific server by choosing Setup from the File menu, clicking on a server name from the list of servers, and clicking on the Connect button. (The first server in the file list is the default server.)

Regardless of how you attempt to make a connection, mIRC attempts to establish a link with the remote server. When you are connected, you see a welcome message that may scroll out of the channel window (see Figure 16-16).

At this point, you can use IRC commands, which are entered in the command line at the bottom of the channel window, to control your IRC session.

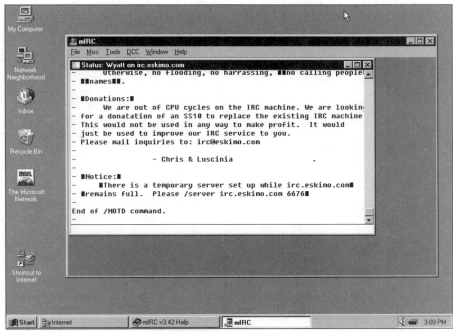

Figure 16-16: When you are connected to an IRC server, you usually see a welcome message.

IRC commands

IRC uses an entire set of commands to manage your session. When using mIRC, these commands are entered in the command line at the bottom of a channel window. The commands that you enter affect only the communications that are occurring in the selected channel window (you can have up to four channel windows open at a time). Table 16-5 lists the different IRC commands that you can use within mIRC.

Table 16-5
Common IRC Commands

Command	Meaning
/LIST [#*text*] [-MIN *value*] [-MAX *value*]	Lists the currently active channels (discussion groups) on the IRC server. If you use the option *text specifier,* then only those channels containing text within the channel title will be listed. If you include the -MIN or -MAX values, then only those channels with the specified minimum or maximum of participants are listed.

(continued)

Table 16-5 (continued)	
Command	**Meaning**
/JOIN #*channel*	Joins the specified *channel,* showing the communication in the current channel window. The channel should be the same spelling as the channels that are returned by the /LIST command; if you enter a different channel, then you create your own channel (discussion group) on the IRC server.
/PART #*channel*	Disconnects the current channel window from the specified *channel.*
/QUIT [*reason*]	Disconnects you from the IRC server and broadcasts the optional *reason* to the participants in the channels that you had joined.
/AWAY [*message*]	Indicates that you are away from the discussion that is currently taking place. Other participants who use the /WHOIS command to see more about you will see the *message* that you specified. Using /AWAY without the optional message indicates that you are again an active participant.
/QUERY *nickname message*	Opens a query window and sends a private *message* to the participant using the specified *nickname.*
/MSG *nickname message*	Same as the /QUERY command, except a query window is not opened.
/NICK *nickname*	Changes your nickname from the default (set up in the mIRC configuration) to *nickname.*
/ME *message*	Broadcasts to the current channel or query window what you are doing.
/WHOIS *nickname*	Displays information about the participant who is designated as *nickname.*
/TOPIC #*channel topicname*	Changes the topic for the specified *channel* to the indicated *topicname.*
/INVITE *nickname* #*channel*	Issues an invitation to the participant who is identified as *nickname* to join the specified *channel.*

Notice that a slash (/) precedes each IRC command. This indicates to mIRC that you are entering a command. If you start a line with any other character, then what you type is broadcast on the channel, and all other channel users see the message.

The commands in Table 16-5 are the most common ones. However, you can use many other commands, but they are more esoteric or have special purposes not normally needed in routine chatting. For more information on IRC commands, refer to the online help manual provided with mIRC.

Chatting with others

The theme of IRC is that you can intersperse commands (beginning with the slash) with actual text. Others can see your text, and you can thereby communicate with them. In practice, you need to accomplish several things:

1. Use the /LIST command to list the available discussion channels.

2. Use the /JOIN command to join a discussion channel of interest.

3. Participate as you see fit.

4. Use the /PART or /QUIT command to leave a discussion group.

Chatting with others is an online activity. During your entire session, you must be connected to the Internet. Thus, make sure that whatever you are discussing is worth the money (and time) that you are spending to be connected to the Net.

As an example of chatting, the four chatting steps are done as follows. The first step (once you are connected to the IRC server) is to use the /LIST command to find out what discussion channels are available. This command is entered in the command line at the bottom of the channel window within mIRC. On most IRC servers, the channel list can be quite long. Most channels have only a single participant, waiting for others to join the fray. (One recent list netted over 2,100 IRC channels on a single server.) If you want active conversation, it is best to limit the channel list to those that already have three or perhaps four participants; you do this using the -MIN command. When I entered my /LIST -MIN 4 command, I received the results shown in Figure 16-17.

Exactly what you see when you use the same command varies depending on who is using the IRC server, the time of day you are calling, and how well the IRC server is known. You can scroll through the listing of channels and choose one that interests you. When you have found one, use the /JOIN command to participate in the channel. For example, if you want to participate in the jokes channel, enter the following command at the channel window control line:

```
/JOIN #jokes
```

If you typed the name of the discussion channel properly, you should start seeing communication from other people right away. Remember that the messages you see are occurring in real time.

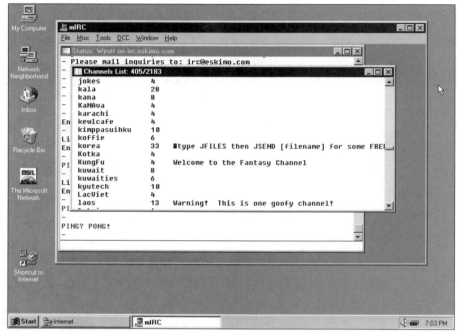

Figure 16-17: Some discussion channel lists can be quite long.

Ending your session

You can break your session with the IRC server in two ways. The first is to use the /QUIT command, which signs you off of all the different channels that you have joined. The other method is to simply close the mIRC program. Although both methods have the same end result, neither method logs you out of your Internet provider. You remain connected and can use other Internet commands.

Netiquette

Politely leaving the party

Just as it is impolite to slam the door in someone's face, it is also impolite to leave a discussion group without announcing that you are leaving. The /QUIT command allows you to give an optional reason that is broadcast on the discussion channels. In this way, others will not continue to direct comments to you, thinking that you are still available to provide a response.

Summary

You can use the Internet to learn and relax. Two of the most popular ways to do this are through Usenet newsgroups and chatting. In this chapter, you learn about both of these communications methods. Millions of people use these methods on a daily basis. Here you learn the following items:

✦ Usenet is a network of people who are trading messages through newsgroups. Newsgroups are similar to giant electronic bulletin board systems.

✦ Newsgroups are organized according to a hierarchy. The organization of the group (and its focus) is evidenced in its name.

✦ To access a newsgroup, you need a special Internet tool called a newsreader. You can download a newsreader from the Internet and configure it to work with Windows 95.

✦ When you set up your newsreader, you need to know the address of the news server that you want to access. These servers are typically sponsored by large companies or Internet providers; you can get the address from them.

✦ Subscribing to a newsgroup is the process of informing your newsreader which newsgroups you want to monitor. The newsreader then takes care of download-ing messages, displaying them, and allowing you to respond to them.

✦ You can post your own messages on a newsgroup. These messages can be original, or they can be in response to an existing message. An original message, along with its responses, is referred to as a message thread.

✦ IRC is an acronym for Internet Relay Chat. This is a program that allows you to communicate with other people around the world in real time.

✦ Many chatting software programs are available. Some conform to the original IRC specifications, whereas others follow their own guidelines. In general, you can only use a particular chatting tool to communicate with others that are using the same or a compatible tool.

✦ Using a chatting tool is a relatively simple process of installing the software, connecting to a server, joining a discussion group (sometimes called a channel), and typing away. What you enter is immediately viewed by everyone else tuned into the same group.

In the next chapter, you learn how to use an exciting new tool provided with Windows 95 — The Microsoft Network.

✦   ✦   ✦

The Microsoft Network

S o far in this book, you have learned how you can access the Internet through dial-up services. These services are supplied by Internet providers, who function as your gateway into the Internet. Another easy way to access the Internet is through online services. Virtually every major online service is providing some form of Internet access. If you are a member of CompuServe, America Online, Prodigy, or Delphi, you can gain access to the Internet through your membership there. The features that you can access vary depending on the online service that you use, and the access typically carries a surcharge.

For Windows 95 users, there is another way that you can gain access to the Internet — through The Microsoft Network. This network is an online service started by Microsoft and rolled out with the introduction of Windows 95. In this chapter, you learn a bit about this service and how you can take advantage of the Internet through it. Here you learn the following items:

- ✦ How to join The Microsoft Network
- ✦ How to connect to The Microsoft Network
- ✦ The organization of The Microsoft Network
- ✦ How to navigate through The Microsoft Network
- ✦ How forums are organized
- ✦ How to access the Internet through The Microsoft Network
- ✦ How to end your Microsoft Network session

Joining The Microsoft Network

To join The Microsoft Network, click on your desktop icon that represents the service. To access the Network, you must have a modem connected to your system, as well as a major credit card. Once you have the modem properly connected (as described in Chapter 4), double-click on the Set Up The Microsoft Network icon on your desktop. You see the dialog box shown in Figure 17-1.

In setting up The Microsoft Network, you have started a sequence of operations that involves the following steps:

✦ Installing The Microsoft Network software and drivers (if necessary)

✦ Filling out the sign-up forms

✦ Establishing your account on The Microsoft Network

Each of these steps occurs in sequence and is covered in the following sections.

Figure 17-1: When you double-click on The Microsoft Network desktop icon, you are asked if you want to install the service on your system.

Installing the software

With the opening setup dialog box on your screen, make sure that the Yes option is selected (as it is in Figure 17-1), and then click on the OK button. You may be asked to insert your Windows 95 diskettes or CD-ROM as the necessary programs and drivers are transferred to your system. After the necessary files are copied, the icon on your desktop is modified, and you see the dialog box shown in Figure 17-2.

This screen contains information about what you can find on The Microsoft Network. A check box in the lower left corner lets you indicate that you are already a member of The Microsoft Network. This check box allows you to simply set up The Microsoft Network software on your system without going through another sign-up procedure. You would use this option if you had signed up for The Microsoft Network on a different computer (you already have an account), and you need access from this computer as well.

When you are done reading the screen, click on the OK button, and you see another dialog box, as shown in Figure 17-3.

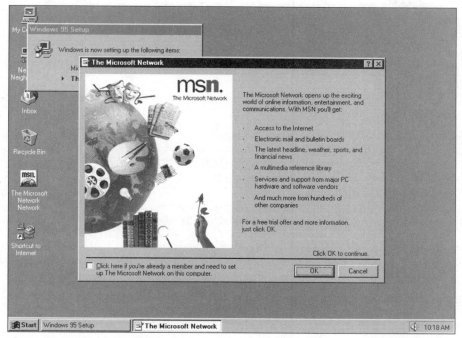

Figure 17-2: After the software is copied to your system, you are ready to join The Microsoft Network.

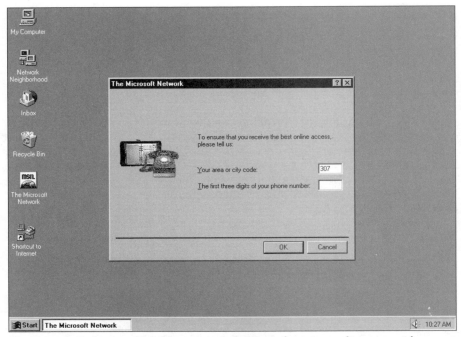

Figure 17-3: To know which phone number to use, the setup software must know your phone exchange.

Here you are asked for the phone exchange from which you are accessing The Microsoft Network. This information allows the setup program to determine the access number to be dialed. In many areas of the world, Microsoft has set up local access numbers. This means that The Microsoft Network can often be accessed through a local phone call, which is much cheaper for you. If you live in a small rural area, then your initial access (to sign up) is through a toll-free number. After your initial access, all subsequent access requires a long distance call to one of the access numbers set up for The Microsoft Network. Unfortunately, no toll-free access is available.

To supply the requested information, enter your area code and the first three digits of your local phone number (which identifies the phone exchange that you use). When you finish, click on the OK button. The access number is determined, and shortly you see a dialog box informing you of that number. (See Figure 17-4.)

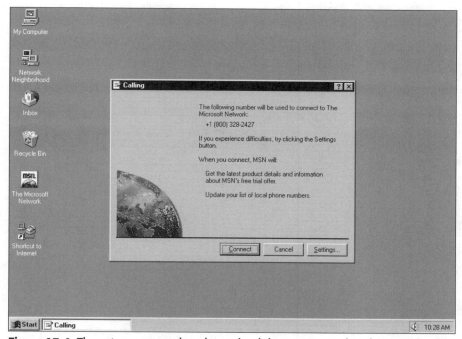

Figure 17-4: The setup program has determined the access number that you should use for setting up The Microsoft Network.

Filling out the sign-up forms

At this point, you are ready to connect to The Microsoft Network. This connection is for a limited time to retrieve information that is critical to the initial setup. You start the connection by clicking on the Connect button. Your settings are saved to disk, and your modem is used to call The Microsoft Network computers. At the bottom of the dialog box, you see information that indicates what is happening during the connection attempt. Once a connection is made, information transfers to your computer, and you are ready to sign up for the service. At this point, you are disconnected from The Microsoft Network. The first dialog box that you see is shown in Figure 17-5.

This dialog box indicates three steps that you need to follow to complete your registration:

✦ Provide some personal information (name, address, and so on)

✦ Indicate how you want to pay for your access to The Microsoft Network

✦ Read the rules by which your access is governed

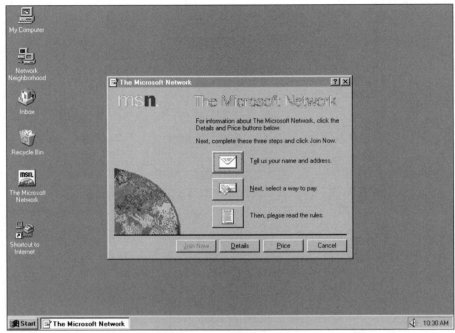

Figure 17-5: Signing up for The Microsoft Network involves filling in a few forms.

To accomplish the first step, click on the first button — the one with the envelope on it. You see a dialog box requesting the information that you must supply, as shown in Figure 17-6.

The requested information is not unlike what you supply when you register for any other online service. Your name and address are needed so that you can receive your billing information and correspondence. Quite honestly, it is also probably necessary for receiving marketing information. This will increase your junk mail quotient but also helps Microsoft determine the areas in which improved services are required. If enough customers sign up for the service from my phone exchange, Microsoft may add a local dial-up number, which will save Microsoft money in the long run.

Take your time to fill in all information. You should at least fill in your address, but including your phone number is not mandatory. If you don't want to receive junk mail (sometimes referred to as "special offers"), then make sure that you check the box at the bottom-left corner of the dialog box. When you finish, click on the OK button. Your information is saved, and you are returned to the sign-up dialog box shown in Figure 17-5.

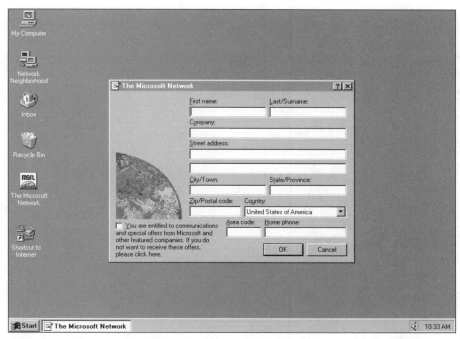

Figure 17-6: You must supply your name and address to register for The Microsoft Network.

You are now ready for the second sign-up step. You must indicate how you want to pay for your access to The Microsoft Network. Click on the second button, the one that incorporates a picture of a check and a credit card. You then see the dialog box shown in Figure 17-7.

Notice that you can pay for your service with any number of credit cards. One interesting note is that the sign-up screen (the last one you saw) also used a picture of a check on the button for this dialog box, but you are not given the opportunity to pay by direct billing. To complete this dialog box, first select the credit card that you wish to use. Once you have done this, the dialog box will change to request additional information. Supply your credit card number and expiration date, and then click on the OK button. This information is also saved, and you are returned to the sign-up dialog box shown in Figure 17-5.

You are now ready to complete the third and final registration step. This involves reading and agreeing to the rules by which The Microsoft Network is governed. To see these rules, click on the third button in the dialog box, the one with the sheet of paper on it. You then see the dialog box shown in Figure 17-8.

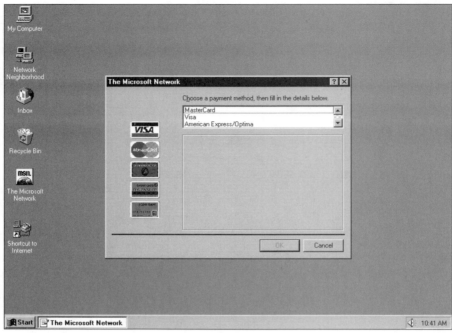

Figure 17-7: Microsoft allows you to pay for your access through a variety of methods.

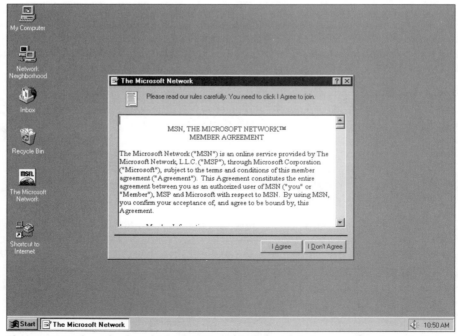

Figure 17-8: The rules by which The Microsoft Network is governed are long and complex.

The rules are legal in nature, because they affect the relationship between you, Microsoft, and vendors on The Microsoft Network. Microsoft wants you to read through them all and then click on the I Agree button. If you don't agree to the rules, you cannot use The Microsoft Network. There is no chance for dickering or negotiation; after all, it is their service. The rules and regulations for The Microsoft Network are in stark contrast to the free and unfettered access to the Internet as a whole.

After you have read the agreement, click on the I Agree button. This returns you to the sign-up dialog box. You are now ready to transfer the information on your forms to The Microsoft Network.

Establishing your account

Once you complete the sign-up forms, you are ready to establish your account on The Microsoft Network. You initiate this process by clicking on the Join Now button from the sign-up dialog box. The setup software then checks to find a local access number in your community. If it cannot find one that matches both your area code and telephone exchange, you see the dialog box shown in Figure 17-9.

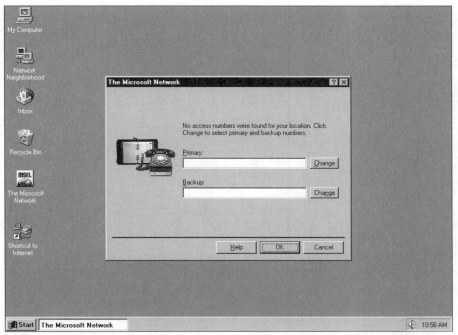

Figure 17-9: If no local numbers exist for your access to The Microsoft Network, then you see this dialog box.

Remember that this dialog box appears only if you live in an area where there is no local access to The Microsoft Network. Click on the Change button to the right of the Primary phone number option. You then see the dialog box shown in Figure 17-10.

Choose the state in which you live, followed by the locality within that state. You should pick the access point that is closest to you, and then click on the OK button. You can also choose a secondary (backup) access number to use in case the primary number is busy. When you finish, click on the OK button. You then see a dialog box that is similar to Figure 17-4. When you are ready to make the connection, click on the Connect button.

At this point, a connection is established with The Microsoft Network using the phone number that is appropriate for your locality. When you first connect to The Microsoft Network, you see the dialog box shown in Figure 17-11.

Here you supply a user ID and a password. As the dialog box indicates, there are certain limitations on what you can use. You must use a Member ID (same as a user ID) that contains no spaces and a password that is between 8 and 16 characters long. Once you supply these, click on the OK button. Your account is set up, and shortly you should see the final setup screen (Figure 17-12), which indicates that you are ready to use The Microsoft Network. Click on the Finish button when you want to close the dialog box.

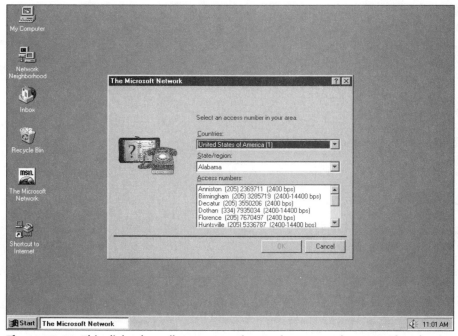

Figure 17-10: This dialog box allows you to choose the access phone number that is right for you.

Figure 17-11: When you log in to The Microsoft Network, you must supply a name and password.

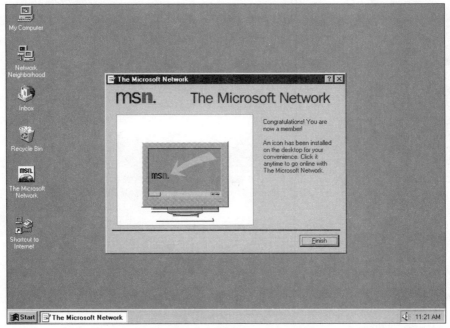

Figure 17-12: When you have successfully set up your account on The Microsoft Network, you will see this dialog box.

Connecting to The Microsoft Network

After your Microsoft Network account is established, you must log in every time that you want to use the service. This is done by double-clicking on The Microsoft Network icon on your desktop. You then see the Sign In dialog box, as shown in Figure 17-13.

Here you are asked for your Member ID and password; these are the same ones that you chose when you first joined The Microsoft Network. Enter them in the appropriate fields on the dialog box, and then click on the Connect button. A connection is then established with The Microsoft Network computers, and your account is verified. Once you are connected, you see The Microsoft Network window, as shown in Figure 17-14. This is known as MSN Central, as discussed in the following section.

Figure 17-13: To connect to The Microsoft Network, you must sign in.

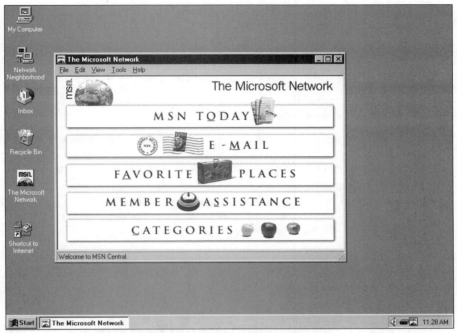

Figure 17-14: MSN Central is the beginning point for the network.

A Quick Tour Around the Block

Once you connect to The Microsoft Network, you are faced with the challenge of learning your way around. Like any new place (The Microsoft Network *can* be thought of as a place), getting a feel for what is possible can take some time. The purpose of this section is to give you a quick tour of the landscape. Understand that this is not be an in-depth tour; an in-depth look at The Microsoft Network could fill an entire book.

After you first connected to The Microsoft Network, you filled out some sign-up information. This information appears only one time — when you sign up. After that, you always see the screen referred to as MSN Central. This is the highest-level of access that you have to The Microsoft Network. From here, you can select which areas of The Microsoft Network you want to use:

✦ **MSN Today.** This area updates you on the latest happenings in The Microsoft Network. Here you learn about new services or features that you can take advantage of.

✦ **E-Mail.** Selecting this tool starts Microsoft Exchange, which you learn about in Chapter 8. MS Exchange is the default tool that you use to send and receive mail from The Microsoft Network, including Internet mail that you may transmit through The Microsoft Network.

✦ **Favorite Places.** This is an area that you can customize to reflect your personal preferences. For example, you can move icons from your favorite bulletin boards or chat rooms to this area. This area is similar to a desktop folder in which you place your favorite items.

✦ **Member Assistance.** This area contains information that you may find helpful when using The Microsoft Network. Here you find online help, membership agreement information, maps for The Microsoft Network, and other helpful information.

✦ **Categories.** This is the area that contains the "heart" of The Microsoft Network. Here you gain access to the myriad of forums available through the service. Forums are discussed fully later in this chapter.

To use one of these selections, click on your choice. The support files for the requested service are downloaded to your system, and you shortly see a window containing the information that you need.

Navigating through The Microsoft Network

If you are familiar with navigating through Windows 95 (which you should be by now), then you will have no problem navigating through The Microsoft Network. The service uses the same navigational concepts that are inherent in Windows 95. For example, if you want to open a feature, tool, or service, you double-click on it.

To illustrate how closely The Microsoft Network follows the Windows 95 interface, start at MSN Central, and then click on the Categories selection. Shortly your Microsoft Network window appears, as shown in Figure 17-15. Notice the familiar use of windows, folders, and icons. You navigate through the network by using the same steps that you would in browsing through your computer or through your local area network.

You can also create shortcuts for services and tools that are on The Microsoft Network. For example, if you have a favorite bulletin board, then you can create a desktop shortcut for that bulletin board. Later, after you have disconnected from The Microsoft Network, you can double-click on the shortcut. A link is automatically established with The Microsoft Network, and you are taken directly to the bulletin board. These shortcuts are created in the same way that you create any other shortcut in Windows 95.

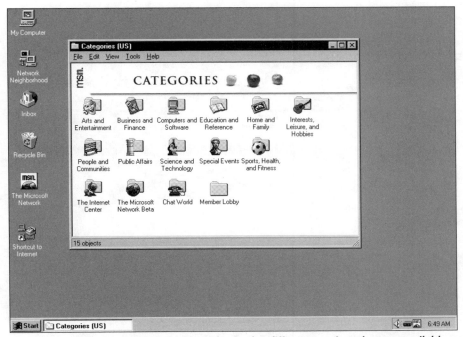

Figure 17-15: The Categories window shows the different services that are available on The Microsoft Network.

The Microsoft Network makes one addition to the Windows 95 interface that will be familiar to CompuServe users. Each forum, and many components of forums (such as bulletin boards or chat rooms), have a Go word associated with them. By entering the Go word, you can directly access the services that you desire without traversing the tree structure of The Microsoft Network. Go words can be found in the information kiosks in each forum. To enter a Go word, choose Go to from the Edit menu of any service of The Microsoft Network, and then click on the Other location option. You then see the Go To Service dialog box, as shown in Figure 17-16.

Enter the Go word for the service that you want to access, and then click on the OK button. You are immediately taken to the service that you specified.

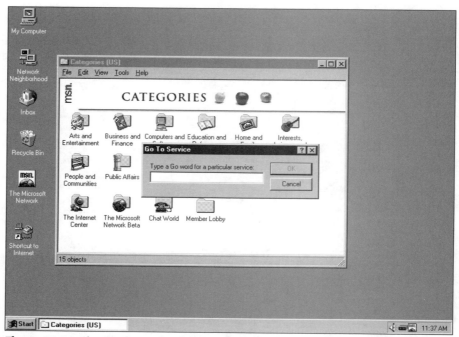

Figure 17-16: The Go To Service dialog box directly accesses different services on The Microsoft Network.

The Microsoft Network forums

In the previous sections, you learn that the heart of The Microsoft Network is forums. If you are a user of other online services such as CompuServe, you may be familiar with the concept of forums. These are nothing more than collections of related services. For example, one forum may relate to sports, whereas another is organized around computer topics.

On The Microsoft Network, forums can contain bulletin boards, chat rooms, kiosks, and file libraries. Bulletin boards are places where you can send and receive messages with others about various topics of interest. They are great places to get help, learn from others, and provide your own voice of experience. In many ways, bulletin boards are similar to the Usenet newsgroups discussed in Chapter 16. Messages that are within bulletin boards are posted by users and can be read by other users. Responses to messages, when combined with the original message, form threads, which are essentially chains of messages that form a discussion about a topic. Figure 17-17 shows an example of the message index in a bulletin board dedicated to product support for Dell computer systems.

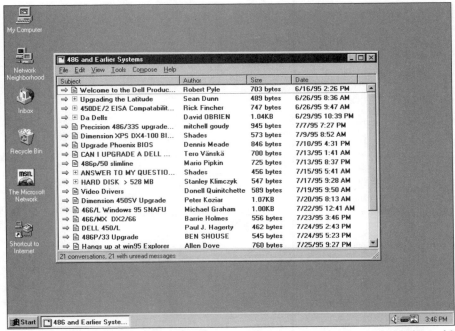

Figure 17-17: Each bulletin board includes a message index that is used to select which message to read.

Chat rooms are similar to bulletin boards (in that they allow communication), but they are much less organized. Here, users of The Microsoft Network congregate to discuss matters in real time. This is similar to the IRC features of the Internet, as discussed in Chapter 16. Figure 17-18 shows an example of a chat screen on The Microsoft Network.

Kiosks are information areas where you can discover more about a forum. They are similar to the directory for a large building — you know, the ones that you see posted on the wall when you enter the building. In a forum, a kiosk contains information about the following items:

✦ The subjects that are discussed in the forum's bulletin boards

✦ Who the forum manager is and how you can contact him or her

✦ The proper "Go" word that is necessary to access the forum

✦ A calendar describing upcoming events

✦ Any other information that is deemed appropriate by the forum manager

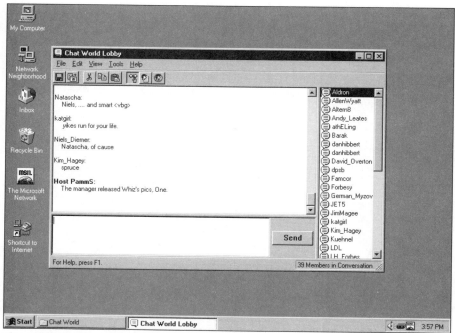

Figure 17-18: Chat screens in The Microsoft Network are similar to chat screens that are used with IRC in the Internet.

When you access a kiosk, a file is downloaded to your system and then displayed in WordPad. The information that is in this file is completely up to the forum managers. Figure 17-19 shows an example of the kiosk file downloaded from the Education and Reference forum.

Finally, forums often contain file libraries. These are repositories of programs, data, and other filed information that you can download to your system. The file interface is similar to that for the bulletin board areas of a forum, as you can see from Figure 17-20.

Files in the libraries can be free, or the person providing the file can charge a price for the download. For example, in a forum sponsored by a hardware vendor, there may be a charge for downloading device drivers. Likewise, in a forum sponsored by a software vendor, there is often a charge for downloading the full version of a software product. Before you download the file, you are informed of any charges associated with it, and you are informed how long the download will take. If you choose to proceed, then the file transfers over the modem link to your hard drive.

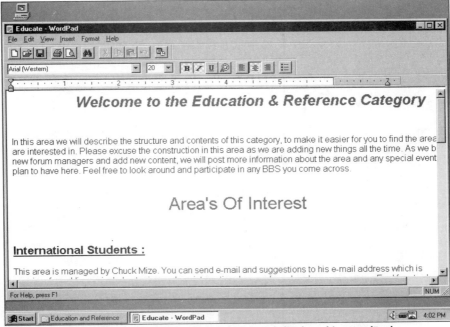

Figure 17-19: Kiosk information is downloaded and displayed in WordPad.

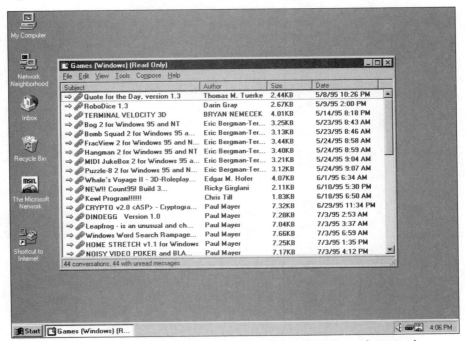

Figure 17-20: You can download files from libraries on The Microsoft Network.

Accessing the Internet

Currently, The Microsoft Network allows only limited access to the Internet. You can access two types of Internet resources through the Network:

✦ Electronic mail

✦ Usenet newsgroups

Beyond this, no other Internet access is available. Although this may initially seem to be a drawback, consider two important factors. First, for many people, e-mail is the only type of access that they need to the Internet. As long as they can conduct routine communications with the rest of the world, their Internet needs have been fulfilled. Second, Microsoft has promised to expand The Microsoft Network to access the Internet. The latest word is that by early 1996, complete Internet access (including the use of all the tools that were mentioned) will be available to users of The Microsoft Network.

Internet electronic mail

It stands to reason that you would use the electronic mail features of The Microsoft Network to take advantage of Internet e-mail. As you learn earlier in this chapter, Microsoft Exchange is the mail service used by The Microsoft Network. Thus, you would use Microsoft Exchange, as described in Chapter 8, to compose, send, and receive e-mail through The Microsoft Network.

To address mail so that it is properly routed to the Internet, you must understand how addressing is handled in The Microsoft Network. When you signed up for The Microsoft Network, you chose a Member ID. This ID could be any group of characters that you wanted, but it could contain no spaces. For example, my Member ID is AllenWyatt (no spaces), and someone else may have a Member ID of Jim456. The Member ID is how e-mail messages are addressed to people on The Microsoft Network. If you connect to the network and want to send a message to another person who is also on the network, you use the person's Member ID as an address.

As an example, to send a message to my friend Carl whose Member ID is Wilson27, I would use the following as the entire e-mail address:

Wilson27

Likewise, if he wanted to send a message to me, then he would use the following address:

AllenWyatt

The message is routed to The Microsoft Network, and the e-mail is sent to the user with the specified Member ID. This works great for users of The Microsoft Network. As you learn in Chapter 2, Internet addresses are different. The Microsoft Network understands this, and if you enter a standard Internet address as the recipient's address, it is routed correctly to the Internet through The Microsoft Network. Thus, I may have another friend whose Internet address is the following:

gdavis@usa.net

I would use this as the e-mail address in my message, and it will be routed correctly by The Microsoft Network.

If you decide that you want to do all of your Internet access through The Microsoft Network, then you also must know how others should address messages to you. This is just as easy. The only change to your Member ID is that you add a suffix to it to indicate where on the Internet the mail should be routed. If someone on the Internet wants to send me an e-mail message through The Microsoft Network, the person uses the following address:

AllenWyatt@msn.com

Notice the use of my Member ID and msn.com as the host and domain. This is the domain address for the Internet mail gateway for The Microsoft Network. You can make the same conversion with any address on The Microsoft Network so that your mail arrives at the proper destination.

Usenet newsgroups

You know that Usenet newsgroups provide a great way to discuss virtually any issue that you can think of. In Chapter 16, you learn how you can use these newsgroups for recreation, education, and information. Besides electronic mail, The Microsoft Network provides you access to a variety of newsgroups on the Internet.

You can access newsgroups at many points within The Microsoft Network. Perhaps the easiest access method is to start at MSN Central and then click on Categories. From the displayed categories, click on The Internet Center. Finally, click on the icon titled The Most Popular Newsgroups. This displays the different newsgroups that have been assigned to this area. Figure 17-21 shows what you see if you choose this icon.

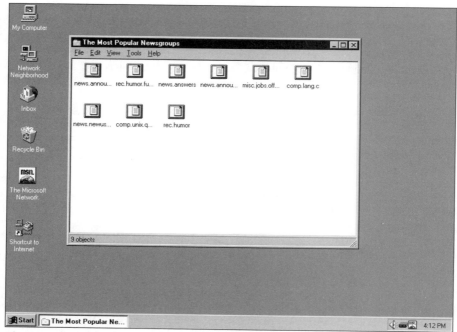

Figure 17-21: Usenet newsgroups have been integrated into The Microsoft Network bulletin board concept.

Obviously this is not all of the newsgroups that you can access from The Microsoft Network. Other icons available at the Internet Center level allow you to view other newsgroups. As you can tell from Figure 17-21, newsgroups are displayed in the same manner as any other bulletin board. You can access newsgroups just as you would regular bulletin boards anywhere else in The Microsoft Network.

Disconnecting from The Microsoft Network

Because of the tight integration between Windows 95 and the appearance of The Microsoft Network, it is often easy to forget that you are online. Fortunately, at the right side of the taskbar, you see a small icon indicating that your modem is active and that you are connected to The Microsoft Network.

When you finish with your session, you should disconnect. This is particularly true if you are using long-distance phone numbers to access the service. You can disconnect in either of two ways:

   ✦ Select Sign Out from the File menu in any Microsoft Network window.

✦ Double-click on The Microsoft Network icon at the right side of the taskbar.

Regardless of which method you choose, you see a dialog box asking if you really want to break your connection. (See Figure 17-22.) If you click on the No button, the termination cancels, and you remain connected to the network. If you click on the Yes button, you are signed off of the network, and the modem connection is terminated. If you later want to use The Microsoft Network, you must again establish your connection.

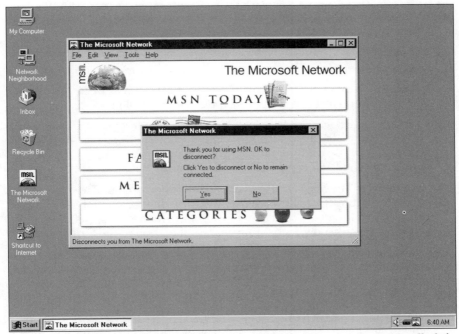

Figure 17-22: You are always asked to verify your actions if you want to sign off of The Microsoft Network.

Summary

The Microsoft Network is the new online service introduced with Windows 95. It features many of the same services available through other online services but is presented in a manner that is tightly integrated with the Windows 95 interface. In this chapter, you learn how you can start putting this new service to work for you as well as how to access the Internet through The Microsoft Network. Specifically, you learn the following items:

✦ You join The Microsoft Network by using software provided with Windows 95. Simply click on the appropriate icon and fill out a few forms, and you connect to The Microsoft Network.

✦ After you have signed up, you can subsequently connect to The Microsoft Network by double-clicking on The Microsoft Network icon on your desktop.

✦ The starting point of The Microsoft Network is known as MSN Central. From here you can select five major categories for your online work.

✦ Navigating through The Microsoft Network is simple if you are familiar with using Windows 95. It uses the same interface of windows, folders, and icons. You can also navigate using Go words, which allow you to jump directly to the portion of The Microsoft Network that you want.

✦ The heart of The Microsoft Network is a series of forums. These are organizational structures that allow the network to be divided into interest categories. Within each forum are bulletin boards, information kiosks, chat rooms, and file libraries. Exactly how each forum is presented is up to the forum manager.

✦ Once connected to The Microsoft Network, you have limited access to the Internet. You can send and receive e-mail messages, and you can access a collection of Usenet newsgroups. Microsoft has promised fuller access to the Internet in the future.

✦ When you are ready to disconnect from The Microsoft Network, you do so by choosing Sign Out from any File menu or by double-clicking on The Microsoft Network icon at the right side of the taskbar.

✦   ✦   ✦

Appendixes

P A R T

IV

◆ ◆ ◆ ◆

In This Part

Appendix A
Internet Providers

Appendix B
Windows Tools
on the Net

Appendix C
Glossary

◆ ◆ ◆ ◆

Internet Providers

The information in this appendix was provided courtesy of the Celestin Co. of Port Townsend, WA. This group maintains the POCIA (providers of commercial Internet access) Directory, which is available either through a Web site on the Net or through an anonymous ftp site. You may contact the company as follows:

> Celestin Co.
> 1152 Hastings Ave.
> Port Townsend, WA 98368
> 360-385-3767 (voice)
> 360-385-3586 (fax)
> Internet address: pocia@celestin.com

To access the most up-to-date list on the Net, connect to the following locations:

> Web: http://www.celestin.com/pocia
> ftp: ftp://ftp.celestin.com/biz/celestin/pocia/pocia.txt

The online versions list numerous ways that you can contact each provider, including e-mail addresses. In the Web version, you see short descriptions of what each provider charges.

Nationwide Providers

Table A-1 includes Internet providers that have a nationwide service. You must contact them directly to determine what services they offer.

Table A-1
Nationwide Providers

Company	Phone Number	E-Mail Information
AGIS (Apex Global Information Services)	313 730 1130	info@agis.net
ANS	703 758 7700	info@ans.net
Concentric Research Corporation	800 745 2747	info@cris.com
CRL Network Services	415 837 5300	sales@crl.com
Delphi Internet Services Corporation	800 695 4005	info@delphi.com
Global Connect, Inc.	804 229 4484	info@gc.net
Information Access Technologies (Holonet)	510 704 0160	info@holonet.net
Institute for Global Communications	415 442 0220	igc-info@igc.apc.org
Liberty Information Network	800 218 5157	info@liberty.com
MIDnet	800 682 5550	info@mid.net
Moran Communications	716 639 1254	info@moran.com
NETCOM On-Line Communications Services	408 554 8649	info@netcom.com
Netrex, Inc	800 3 NETREX	info@netrex.com
Network 99, Inc.	800 NET 99IP	net99@cluster.mcs.net
Performance Systems International	800 827 7482	all-info@psi.com
Portal Information Network	408 973 9111	info@portal.com
SprintLink—Nationwide 56K-45M access	800 817 7755	info@sprint.net
The ThoughtPort Authority Inc.	800 ISP 6870	info@thoughtport.com
WareNet	714 348 3295	info@ware.net
Zocalo Engineering	510 540 8000	info@zocalo.net

U.S. and Canadian Providers

Table A-2 contains a listing of providers, by area code. To use this list, look up your area code, and then start contacting providers that serve that area code. If your area code is not listed, check under area code 800, which represents providers that have toll-free access.

Table A-2
U.S. and Canadian Providers

Area Code	Company	Phone Number	E-Mail Information
201	Carroll-Net	201 488 1332	info@carroll.com
201	Digital Express Group	301 847 5000	info@digex.net
201	Eclipse Internet Access	800 483 1223	info@eclipse.net
201	Galaxy Networks	201 825 2310	info@galaxy.net
201	GBN InternetAccess	201 343 6427	gbninfo@gbn.net
201	I-2000 Inc.	800 464 3820	info@i-2000.com
201	INTAC Access Corporation	800 504 6822	info@intac.com
201	Interactive Networks, Inc.	201 881 1878	info@interactive.net
201	InterCom Online	212 714 7183	info@intercom.com
201	Internet Online Services	201 928 1000 x226	help@ios.com
201	Mordor International BBS	201 433 4222	ritz@mordor.com
201	NETCOM On-Line Communications Services	408 554 8649	info@netcom.com
201	New York Net	718 776 6811	sales@new-york.net
201	NIC — Neighborhood Internet Connection	201 934 1445	info@nic.com
201	Openix — Open Internet Exchange	201 443 0400	info@openix.com
201	The Internet Connection Corp.	201 435 4414	info@cnct.com
202	American Information Network	410 855 2353	info@ai.net
202	CAPCON Library Network	202 331 5771	info@capcon.net
202	Charm.Net	410 558 3900	info@charm.net
202	Digital Express Group	301 847 5000	info@digex.net
202	Genuine Computing Resources	703 878 4680	info@gcr.com
202	I-Link Ltd	800 ILINK 99	info@i-link.net
202	Internet Online, Inc.	301 652 4468	info@intr.net
202	Interpath	800 849 6305	info@interpath.net
202	LaserNet	703 591 4232	info@laser.net

(continued)

Table A-2 *(continued)*

Area Code	Company	Phone Number	E-Mail Information
202	Quantum Networking Solutions, Inc.	805 538 2028	info@qnet.com
202	RadixNet Internet Services	301 567 9831	info@radix.net
202	US Net, Incorporated	301 572 5926	info@us.net
202	World Web Limited	703 838 2000	info@worldweb.net
203	Computerized Horizons	203 335 7431	sysop@fcc.com
203	Connix: Connecticut Internet Exchange	203 349 7059	info@connix.com
203	Futuris Networks, Inc.	203 359 8868	info@futuris.net
203	I-2000 Inc.	800 464 3820	info@i-2000.com
203	NETPLEX	203 233 1111	info@ntplx.net
203	North American Internet Company	800 952 INET	info@nai.net
203	Paradigm Communications, Inc.	203 250 7397	info@pcnet.com
204	Cycor Communications Incorporated	902 892 7354	signup@cycor.ca
205	AIRnet Internet Services, Inc.	800 247 6388	efelton@AIRnet.net
205	Community Internet Connect, Inc.	205 722 0199	info@cici.com
205	HiWAAY Information Services	205 533 3131	info@HiWAAY.net
205	interQuest, Inc.	205 464 8280	info@iquest.com
205	MindSpring Enterprises, Inc.	800 719 4332	info@mindspring.com
205	Scott Network Services, Inc.	205 987 5889	info@scott.net
206	Blarg! Online Services	206 782 6578	info@blarg.com
206	Eskimo North	206 367 7457	nanook@eskimo.com
206	I-Link Ltd	800 ILINK 99	info@i-link.net
206	InEx Net	206 670 1131	info@inex.com
206	Interconnected Associates Inc. (IXA)	206 622 7337	mike@ixa.com
206	Internet Express	719 592 1240	info@usa.net
206	ISOMEDIA.COM	206 881 8769	info@isomedia.com
206	NETCOM On-Line Communications Services	408 554 8649	info@netcom.com
206	Northwest Nexus, Inc.	206 455 3505	info@nwnexus.wa.com

Area Code	Company	Phone Number	E-Mail Information
206	Olympic Computing Solutions	206 989 6698	ocs@oz.net
206	Pacific Rim Network, Inc.	360 650 0442	info@pacificrim.net
206	Seanet Online Services	206 343 7828	info@seanet.com
206	SenseMedia	408 335 9400	sm@picosof.com
206	Structured Network Systems, Inc.	503 656 3530	info@structured.net
206	Teleport, Inc.	503 223 4245	info@teleport.com
206	Transport Logic	503 243 1940	sales@transport.com
206	WLN	800 342 5956	info@wln.com
207	Agate Internet Services	207 947 8248	ais@agate.net
207	MV Communications, Inc.	603 429 2223	info@mv.mv.com
208	Micron Internet Services	208 368 5400	sales@micron.net
208	Minnesota Regional Network	612 342 2570	info@mr.net
208	NICOH Net	208 233 5802	info@nicoh.com
208	Primenet	602 870 1010	info@primenet.com
208	SRVnet	208 524 6237	nlp@srv.net
208	Transport Logic	503 243 1940	sales@transport.com
209	Cybergate Information Services	209 486 4283	cis@cybergate.com
209	InterNex Tiara	408 496 5466	info@internex.net
209	Primenet	602 870 1010	info@primenet.com
209	ValleyNet Communications	209 486 8638	info@valleynet.com
209	West Coast Online	707 586 3060	info@calon.com
210	I-Link Ltd	800 ILINK 99	info@i-link.net
210	The Eden Matrix	512 478 9900	info@eden.com
212	Alternet (UUNET Technologies, Inc.)	703 204 8000	info@alter.net
212	Blythe Systems	212 226 7171	infodesk@blythe.org
212	BrainLINK	718 805 6559	info@beast.brainlink.com
212	Calyx Internet Access	212 475 5051	info@calyx.net
212	Creative Data Consultants (SILLY.COM)	718 229 0489	info@silly.com
212	Digital Express Group	301 847 5000	info@digex.net

(continued)

Table A-2 (continued)

Area Code	Company	Phone Number	E-Mail Information
212	Echo Communications Group	212 255 3839	info@echonyc.com
212	escape.com — Kazan Corp	212 888 8780	info@escape.com
212	I-2000 Inc.	800 464 3820	info@i-2000.com
212	I-Link Ltd	800 ILINK 99	info@i-link.net
212	Ingress Communications Inc.	212 679 2838	info@ingress.com
212	INTAC Access Corporation	800 504 6822	info@intac.com
212	Intellitech Walrus	212 406 5000	info@walrus.com
212	Interactive Networks, Inc.	201 881 1878	info@interactive.net
212	InterCom Online	212 714 7183	info@intercom.com
212	Internet Online Services	201 928 1000 x226	help@ios.com
212	Internet QuickLink Corp.	212 307 1669	info@quicklink.com
212	Interport Communications Corp.	212 989 1128	info@interport.net
212	Mnematics, Incorporated	914 359 4546	service@mne.com
212	Mordor International BBS	201 433 4222	ritz@mordor.com
212	NETCOM On-Line Communications Services	408 554 8649	info@netcom.com
212	New York Net	718 776 6811	sales@new-york.net
212	NY WEBB, Inc.	800 458 4660	wayne@webb.com
212	Panix (Public Access uNIX)	212 741 4545	info@panix.com
212	Phantom Access Technologies, Inc.	212 989 2418	bruce@phantom.com
212	Pipeline New York	212 267 3636	info@pipeline.com
212	The Internet Connection Corp.	201 435 4414	info@cnct.com
212	The ThoughtPort Authority Inc.	800 ISP 6870	info@thoughtport.com
212	ThoughtPort of New York City	212 645 7970	info@precipice.com
213	Abode Computer Service	818 287 5115	eric@abode.ttank.com
213	Cogent Software, Inc.	818 585 2788	info@cogsoft.com
213	Delta Internet Services	714 778 0370	info@deltanet.com
213	DigiLink Network Services	310 542 7421	info@digilink.net

Area Code	Company	Phone Number	E-Mail Information
213	DirectNet	213 383 3144	info@directnet.com
213	EarthLink Network, Inc.	213 644 9500	sales@earthlink.net
213	Electriciti	619 338 9000	info@powergrid.electriciti.com
213	Exodus Communications, Inc.	408 522 8450	info@exodus.net
213	Flamingo Communications Inc.	310 532 3533	sales@fcom.com
213	I-Link Ltd	800 ILINK 99	info@i-link.net
213	KAIWAN Internet	714 638 2139	info@kaiwan.com
213	Leonardo Internet	310 395 5500	jimp@leonardo.net
213	Liberty Information Network	800 218 5157	info@liberty.com
213	Network Intensive	714 450 8400	info@ni.net
213	OutWest Network Services	818 545 1996	OWInfo@outwest.com
213	Primenet	602 870 1010	info@primenet.com
213	The Loop Internet Switch Co.	213 465 1311	info@loop.com
213	ViaNet Communications	415 903 2242	info@via.net
214	Alternet (UUNET Technologies, Inc.)	703 204 8000	info@alter.net
214	CompuTek	214 994 0190	info@computek.net
214	DFW Internet Services, Inc.	817 332 5116	info@dfw.net
214	I-Link Ltd	800 ILINK 99	info@i-link.net
214	NETCOM On-Line Communications Services	408 554 8649	info@netcom.com
214	OnRamp Technologies, Inc.	214 746 4710	info@onramp.net
214	Texas Metronet, Inc.	214 705 2900	info@metronet.com
215	Digital Express Group	301 847 5000	info@digex.net
215	FishNet	610 337 9994	info@pond.com
215	GlobalQUEST, Inc.	610 696 8111	info@globalquest.net
215	I-2000 Inc.	800 464 3820	info@i-2000.com
215	Microserve Information Systems	717 779 4430	info@microserve.com
215	Net Access	215 576 8669	support@netaxs.com

(continued)

Table A-2 *(continued)*

Area Code	Company	Phone Number	E-Mail Information
215	Network Analysis Group	800 624 9240	nag@good.freedom.net
215	OpNet	610 520 2880	info@op.net
215	You Tools Corporation / FASTNET	610 954 5910	info@fast.net
216	APK Public Access UNI* Site	216 481 9436	info@wariat.org
216	Branch Information Services	313 741 4442	branch-info@branch.com
216	ExchangeNet	216 261 4593	info@en.com
216	Multiverse, Inc.	216 344 3080	multiverse.com
216	New Age Consulting Service	216 524 3162	damin@nacs.net
216	OARnet (corporate clients only)	614 728 8100	info@oar.net
217	Allied Access Inc.	618 684 2255	sales@intrnet.net
217	Sol Tec, Inc.	317 920 1SOL	info@soltec.com
218	Minnesota OnLine	612 225 1110	info@mn.state.net
218	Protocol Communications, Inc.	612 541 9900	info@protocom.com
218	Red River Net	701 232 2227	info@rrnet.com
301	American Information Network	410 855 2353	info@ai.net
301	Charm.Net	410 558 3900	info@charm.net
301	Clark Internet Services, Inc. ClarkNet	410 995 0691	info@clark.net
301	Digital Express Group	301 847 5000	info@digex.net
301	FredNet	301 631 5300	info@fred.net
301	Genuine Computing Resources	703 878 4680	info@gcr.com
301	Internet Online, Inc.	301 652 4468	info@intr.net
301	LaserNet	703 591 4232	info@laser.net
301	Quantum Networking Solutions, Inc.	805 538 2028	info@qnet.com
301	RadixNet Internet Services	301 567 9831	info@radix.net
301	SURAnet	301 982 4600	marketing@sura.net
301	US Net, Incorporated	301 572 5926	info@us.net
301	World Web Limited	703 838 2000	info@worldweb.net
302	Delaware Common Access Network	302 654 1019	info@dca.net
302	SSNet, Inc.	302 378 1386	info@ssnet.com

Area Code	Company	Phone Number	E-Mail Information
302	The Magnetic Page (tmp) O N L I N E	302 651 9753	info@magpage.com
303	ABWAM, Inc.	303 730 6050	info@entertain.com
303	Colorado SuperNet, Inc.	303 296 8202	info@csn.org
303	CSDC, Inc.	303 665 8053	support@ares.csd.net
303	ENVISIONET, Inc.	303 770 2408	info@envisionet.net
303	EZLink Internet Access	970 482 0807	ezadmin@ezlink.com
303	I-Link Ltd	800 ILINK 99	info@i-link.net
303	Indra's Net, Inc.	303 546 9151	info@indra.com
303	Internet Express	719 592 1240	info@usa.net
303	NETCOM On-Line Communications Services	408 554 8649	info@netcom.com
303	NetWay 2001, Inc.	303 794 1000	info@netway.net
303	New Mexico Technet, Inc.	505 345 6555	granoff@technet.nm.org
303	Rocky Mountain Internet	800 900 7644	info@rmii.com
303	Shaman Exchange, Inc.	303 674 9784	info@dash.com
303	Stonehenge Internet Communications	800 RUN INET	info@henge.com
303	The Denver Exchange, Inc.	303 455 4252	info@tde.com
304	RAM Technologies Inc.	800 950 1726	info@ramlink.net
305	Acquired Knowledge Systems, Inc.	305 525 2574	info@aksi.net
305	CyberGate, Inc.	305 428 4283	sales@gate.net
305	InteleCom Data Systems, Inc.	401 885 6855	info@ids.net
305	Internet Providers of Florida, Inc.	305 273 7978	office@ipof.fla.net
305	Magg Information Services, Inc.	407 642 9841	help@magg.net
305	NetMiami Internet Corporation	305 554 4463	picard@netmiami.com
305	Netpoint Communications, Inc.	305 891 1955	info@netpoint.net
305	NetRunner Inc.	305 255 5800	info@netrunner.net
305	PSS InterNet Services	800 463 8499	support@america.com
305	SatelNET Communications, Inc.	305 434 8738	admin@satelnet.org
306	Cycor Communications Incorporated	902 892 7354	signup@cycor.ca
307	wyoming.com	307 332 3030	info@wyoming.com

(continued)

Table A-2 *(continued)*

Area Code	Company	Phone Number	E-Mail Information
308	Synergy Communications, Inc.	800 345 9669	info@synergy.net
310	Abode Computer Service	818 287 5115	eric@abode.ttank.com
310	Cloverleaf Communications	714 895 3075	sales@cloverleaf.com
310	Cogent Software, Inc.	818 585 2788	info@cogsoft.com
310	Delta Internet Services	714 778 0370	info@deltanet.com
310	DigiLink Network Services	310 542 7421	info@digilink.net
310	EarthLink Network, Inc.	213 644 9500	sales@earthlink.net
310	Exodus Communications, Inc.	408 522 8450	info@exodus.net
310	Flamingo Communications Inc.	310 532 3533	sales@fcom.com
310	KAIWAN Internet	714 638 2139	info@kaiwan.com
310	Leonardo Internet	310 395 5500	jimp@leonardo.net
310	Liberty Information Network	800 218 5157	info@liberty.com
310	Lightside, Inc.	818 858 9261	Lightside@Lightside.Com
310	NETCOM On-Line Communications Services	408 554 8649	info@netcom.com
310	Network Intensive	714 450 8400	info@ni.net
310	OutWest Network Services	818 545 1996	OWInfo@outwest.com
310	SoftAware	310 305 0275	info@softaware.com
310	The Loop Internet Switch Co.	213 465 1311	info@loop.com
310	ViaNet Communications	415 903 2242	info@via.net
312	American Information Systems, Inc.	708 413 8400	info@ais.net
312	CICNet, Inc.	313 998 6103	info@cic.net
312	InterAccess Co.	800 967 1580	info@interaccess.com
312	Interactive Network Systems, Inc.	312 881 3039	info@insnet.com
312	MCSNet	312 248 8649	info@mcs.net
312	NETCOM On-Line Communications Services	408 554 8649	info@netcom.com
312	Open Business Systems, Inc.	708 250 0260	info@obs.net
312	Ripco Communications, Inc.	312 477 6210	info@ripco.com

Area Code	Company	Phone Number	E-Mail Information
312	Tezcatlipoca, Inc.	312 850 0181	info@tezcat.com
312	The ThoughtPort Authority Inc.	800 ISP 6870	info@thoughtport.com
312	WorldWide Access	708 367 1870	info@wwa.com
312	XNet Information Systems	708 983 6064	info@xnet.com
313	Branch Information Services	313 741 4442	branch-info@branch.com
313	CICNet, Inc.	313 998 6103	info@cic.net
313	ICNET/Innovative Concepts	313 998 0090	info@ic.net
313	Isthmus Corporation	313 973 2100	info@izzy.net
313	Mich.com, Inc.	810 478 4300	info@mich.com
313	Michigan Internet Cooperative Association	810 355 1438	info@coop.mica.net
313	Msen, Inc.	313 998 4562	info@msen.com
313	RustNet, Inc.	810 650 6812	info@rust.net
314	Allied Access Inc.	618 684 2255	sales@intrnet.net
314	Inlink	314 432 0935	support@inlink.com
314	NeoSoft, Inc.	713 684 5969	info@neosoft.com
314	Online Information Access Network	618 692 9813	info@oia.net
314	P-Net, Inc.	314 731 2252	info@MO.NET
314	The ThoughtPort Authority Inc.	800 ISP 6870	info@thoughtport.com
315	ServiceTech, Inc.	716 263 3360	info@servtech.com
315	Spectra.net	607 798 7300	info@spectra.net
315	Syracuse Internet	315 233 1948	info@vcomm.net
316	Elysian Fields, Inc.	316 267 2636	info@elysian.net
316	SouthWind Internet Access, Inc.	316 263 7963	info@southwind.net
317	HolliCom Internet Services	317 883 4500	cale@holli.com
317	IQuest Network Services	317 259 5050	info@iquest.net
317	Metropolitan Data Networks Limited	317 449 0539	info@mdn.com
317	Net Direct	317 251 5252	kat@inetdirect.net
317	Sol Tec, Inc.	317 920 1SOL	info@soltec.com
318	Linknet Internet Services	318 442 5465	rdalton@linknet.net

(continued)

Table A-2 *(continued)*

Area Code	Company	Phone Number	E-Mail Information
318	Net-Connect, Ltd.	318 234 4396	services@net-connect.net
319	Gryffin Information Services	319 399 3690	Info@gryffin.com
334	MindSpring Enterprises, Inc.	800 719 4332	info@mindspring.com
334	OnLine Montgomery	334 271 9576	rverble@bbs.olm.com
334	Scott Network Services, Inc.	205 987 5889	info@scott.net
334	WSNetwork Communications Services, Inc.	334 263 5505	custserv@wsnet.com
360	Interconnected Associates Inc. (IXA)	206 622 7337	mike@ixa.com
360	NorthWest CommLink	360 336 0103	info@nwcl.net
360	Pacific Rim Network, Inc.	360 650 0442	info@pacificrim.net
360	Pacifier Computers	360 693 2116	info@pacifier.com
360	Premier1 Internet Services	360 793 3658	info@premier1.net
360	Skagit On-Line Services	360 755 0190	info@sos.net
360	Townsend Communications, Inc.	360 385 0464	info@olympus.net
360	Transport Logic	503 243 1940	sales@transport.com
360	Whidbey Connections, Inc.	360 678 1070	info@whidbey.net
360	WLN	800 342 5956	info@wln.com
401	brainiac services inc.	401 539 9050	info@brainiac.com
401	InteleCom Data Systems, Inc.	401 885 6855	info@ids.net
401	Plymouth Commercial Internet Exchange	617 741 5900	info@pcix.com
401	The Internet Connection, Inc.	508 261 0383	info@ici.net
402	Greater Omaha Public Access Unix Corp	402 558 5030	info@gonix.com
402	Internet Nebraska	402 434 8680	info@inetnebr.com
402	Synergy Communications, Inc.	800 345 9669	info@synergy.net
403	Alberta SuperNet Inc.	403 441 3663	info@supernet.ab.ca
403	CCI Networks	403 450 6787	info@ccinet.ab.ca
403	Cycor Communications Incorporated	902 892 7354	signup@cycor.ca
403	Debug Computer Services	403 248 5798	root@debug.cuc.ab.ca

Area Code	Company	Phone Number	E-Mail Information
403	UUNET Canada, Inc.	416 368 6621	info@uunet.ca
404	CyberNet Communications Corporation	404 518 5711	sfeingold@atlwin.com
404	I-Link Ltd	800 ILINK 99	info@i-link.net
404	Internet Atlanta	404 410 9000	info@atlanta.com
404	MindSpring Enterprises, Inc.	800 719 4332	info@mindspring.com
404	NETCOM On-Line Communications Services	408 554 8649	info@netcom.com
404	Random Access, Inc.	404 804 1190	sales@randomc.com
404	vividnet	770 933 0999	webadmin@vivid.net
405	Internet Oklahoma	405 721 1580	info@ionet.net
405	Questar Network Services	405 848 3228	info@qns.net
406	CyberPort Montana	406 863 3221	skippy@cyberport.net
406	Internet Montana	406 255 9699	support@comp-unltd.com
406	Montana Online	406 721 4952	info@montana.com
407	Acquired Knowledge Systems, Inc.	305 525 2574	info@aksi.net
407	CyberGate, Inc.	305 428 4283	sales@gate.net
407	Florida Online	407 635 8888	info@digital.net
407	I-Link Ltd	800 ILINK 99	info@i-link.net
407	InteleCom Data Systems, Inc.	401 885 6855	info@ids.net
407	Internet Providers of Florida, Inc	305 273 7978	office@ipof.fla.net
407	InternetU	407 952 8487	info@iu.net
407	Magg Information Services, Inc.	407 642 9841	help@magg.net
407	MagicNet, Inc.	407 657 2202	info@magicnet.net
407	MetroLink Internet Services	407 726 6707	jtaylor@metrolink.net
407	PSS InterNet Services	800 463 8499	support@america.com
407	The EmiNet Domain	407 731 0222	info@emi.net
408	Aimnet Information Services	408 257 0900	info@aimnet.com
408	Alternet (UUNET Technologies, Inc.)	703 204 8000	info@alter.net

(continued)

Table A-2 *(continued)*

Area Code	Company	Phone Number	E-Mail Information
408	Brainstorm's Internet Power Connection	415 473 6411	info@brainstorm.net
408	BTR Communications Company	415 966 1429	support@btr.com
408	Direct Net Access Incorporated	510 649 6110	support@dnai.com
408	Electriciti	619 338 9000	info@powergrid.electriciti.com
408	Exodus Communications, Inc.	408 522 8450	info@exodus.net
408	Infoserv Connections	408 335 5600	root@infoserv.com
408	InterNex Tiara	408 496 5466	info@internex.net
408	ISP Networks	408 653 0100	info@isp.net
408	Liberty Information Network	800 218 5157	info@liberty.com
408	MediaCity World	415 321 6800	info@MediaCity.com
408	NETCOM On-Line Communications Services	408 554 8649	info@netcom.com
408	NetGate Communications	408 565 9601	sales@netgate.net
408	Scruz-Net	408 457 5050	info@scruz.net
408	SenseMedia	408 335 9400	sm@picosof.com
408	South Valley Internet	408 683 4533	info@garlic.com
408	The Duck Pond Public Unix	modem: 408 249 9630	postmaster@kfu.com
408	West Coast Online	707 586 3060	info@calon.com
408	zNET	619 755 7772	info@znet.com
408	Zocalo Engineering	510 540 8000	info@zocalo.net
409	Brazos Information Highway Services	409 693 9336	info@bihs.net
409	Cybercom Corporation	409 268 0771	www@cy-net.net
409	Internet Connect Services, Inc.	512 572 9987	info@icsi.net
409	PERnet Communications, Inc.	409 729 4638	info@mail.pernet.net
410	American Information Network	410 855 2353	info@ai.net
410	CAPCON Library Network	202 331 5771	info@capcon.net

Area Code	Company	Phone Number	E-Mail Information
410	Charm.Net	410 558 3900	info@charm.net
410	Clark Internet Services, Inc. ClarkNet	410 995 0691	info@clark.net
410	Digital Express Group	301 847 5000	info@digex.net
410	jaguNET Access Services	410 931 3157	info@jagunet.com
410	Softaid Internet Services Inc.	410 290 7763	sales@softaid.net
410	US Net, Incorporated	301 572 5926	info@us.net
412	CityNet, Inc.	412 481 5406	info@city-net.com
412	FYI Networks	412 898 2323	info@fyi.net
412	Pittsburgh OnLine Inc.	412 681 6130	sales@pgh.net
412	Stargate Industries, Inc.	412 942 4218	info@sgi.net
412	Telerama Public Access Internet	412 481 3505	info@telerama.lm.com
412	The ThoughtPort Authority Inc.	800 ISP 6870	info@thoughtport.com
413	Mallard Electronics, Inc.	413 732 0214	gheacock@map.com
413	MediaCity World	415 321 6800	info@MediaCity.com
413	ShaysNet.COM	413 772 3774	staff@shaysnet.com
413	the spa!, inc.	413 539 9818	info@the-spa.com
414	Excel.Net, Inc.	414 452 0455	manager@excel.net
414	Exec-PC, Inc.	414 789 4200	info@execpc.com
414	FullFeed Communications	608 246 4239	info@fullfeed.com
414	MIX Communications	414 351 1868	info@mixcom.com
414	NetNet, Inc.	414 499 1339	info@netnet.net
415	Aimnet Information Services	408 257 0900	info@aimnet.com
415	Alternet (UUNET Technologies, Inc.)	703 204 8000	info@alter.net
415	Brainstorm's Internet Power Connection	415 473 6411	info@brainstorm.net
415	BTR Communications Company	415 966 1429	support@btr.com
415	Community ConneXion — NEXUS-Berkeley	510 549 1383	info@c2.org
415	Datatamers	415 367 7919	info@datatamers.com

(continued)

Table A-2 *(continued)*

Area Code	Company	Phone Number	E-Mail Information
415	Direct Net Access Incorporated	510 649 6110	support@dnai.com
415	Exodus Communications, Inc.	408 522 8450	info@exodus.net
415	I-Link Ltd	800 ILINK 99	info@i-link.net
415	Idiom Consulting	510 644 0441	info@idiom.com
415	InterNex Tiara	408 496 5466	info@internex.net
415	LanMinds, Inc.	510 843 6389	info@lanminds.com
415	Liberty Information Network	800 218 5157	info@liberty.com
415	LineX Communications	415 455 1650	info@linex.com
415	MediaCity World	415 321 6800	info@MediaCity.com
415	MobiusNet	415 821 0600	info@mobius.net
415	NETCOM On-Line Communications Services	408 554 8649	info@netcom.com
415	NetGate Communications	408 565 9601	sales@netgate.net
415	QuakeNet	415 655 6607	info@quake.net
415	Sirius	415 284 4700	info@sirius.com
415	SLIPNET	415 281 3132	info@slip.net
415	The WELL	415 332 4335	info@well.com
415	ViaNet Communications	415 903 2242	info@via.net
415	West Coast Online	707 586 3060	info@calon.com
415	zNET	619 755 7772	info@znet.com
415	Zocalo Engineering	510 540 8000	info@zocalo.net
416	Cycor Communications Incorporated	902 892 7354	signup@cycor.ca
416	HookUp Communications	905 847 8000	info@hookup.net
416	InterLog Internet Services	416 975 2655	internet@interlog.com
416	Internet Light and Power	416 502 1512	staff@ilap.com
416	Internex Online, Inc.	416 363 8676	support@io.org
416	Magic Online Services International Inc.	416 591 6490	info@magic.ca
416	UUNET Canada, Inc.	416 368 6621	info@uunet.ca

Area Code	Company	Phone Number	E-Mail Information
417	Woodtech Information Systems, Inc.	417 886 0234	info@woodtech.com
418	UUNET Canada, Inc.	416 368 6621	info@uunet.ca
419	Branch Information Services	313 741 4442	branch-info@branch.com
419	OARnet (corporate clients only)	614 728 8100	info@oar.net
419	Primenet	602 870 1010	info@primenet.com
501	Cloverleaf Technologies	903 832 1367	helpdesk@clover.cleaf.com
501	IntelliNet ISP	501 376 7676	info@intellinet.com
502	IgLou Internet Services	800 436 4456	info@iglou.com
502	Mikrotec Internet Services, Inc.	606 225 1488	info@mis.net
503	Alternet (UUNET Technologies, Inc.)	703 204 8000	info@alter.net
503	aracnet.com	503 626 8696	info@aracnet.com
503	Cenornet	503 557 9047	info@cenornet.com
503	Colossus Inc.	312 528 1000 x19	colossus@romney.mtjeff.com
503	Data Research Group, Inc.	503 465 3282	info@ordata.com
503	DTR Communications Services	503 252 5059	info@dtr.com
503	Europa	503 222 9508	info@europa.com
503	Gorge Networks	503 386 8300	postmaster@gorge.net
503	Hevanet Communications	503 228 3520	info@hevanet.com
503	I-Link Ltd	800 ILINK 99	info@i-link.net
503	Interconnected Associates Inc. (IXA)	206 622 7337	mike@ixa.com
503	NETCOM On-Line Communications Services	408 554 8649	info@netcom.com
503	Open Door Networks, Inc.	503 488 4127	info@opendoor.com
503	Pacifier Computers	360 693 2116	info@pacifier.com
503	RainDrop Laboratories/Agora	503 293 1772	info@agora.rdrop.com
503	Structured Network Systems, Inc.	503 656 3530	info@structured.net
503	Teleport, Inc.	503 223 4245	info@teleport.com
503	Transport Logic	503 243 1940	sales@transport.com
503	WLN	800 342 5956	info@wln.com
504	AccessCom Internet Services	504 887 0022	info@accesscom.net

(continued)

Table A-2 *(continued)*

Area Code	Company	Phone Number	E-Mail Information
504	Communique Inc.	504 527 6200	info@communique.net
504	Cyberlink	504 277 4186	cladmin@eayor.cyberlink-no.com
504	I-Link Ltd	800 ILINK 99	info@i-link.net
504	NeoSoft, Inc.	713 684 5969	info@neosoft.com
505	Computer Systems Consulting	505 984 0085	info@spy.org
505	Internet Direct, Inc.	800 879 3624	info@direct.net
505	Internet Express	719 592 1240	info@usa.net
505	Network Intensive	714 450 8400	info@ni.net
505	New Mexico Internet Access	505 877 0617	info@nmia.com
505	New Mexico Technet, Inc.	505 345 6555	granoff@technet.nm.org
505	Southwest Cyberport	505 271 0009	info@swcp.com
505	WhiteHorse Communications, Inc.	915 584 6630	whc.net.html
505	ZyNet SouthWest	505 343 8846	zycor@zynet.com
506	Agate Internet Services	207 947 8248	ais@agate.net
506	Cycor Communications Incorporated	902 892 7354	signup@cycor.ca
507	Desktop Media	507 373 2155	isp@dm.deskmedia.com
507	Internet Connections, Inc.	507 625 7320	info@ic.mankato.mn.us
507	Millennium Communications, Inc.	612 338 5509	info@millcomm.com
507	Minnesota OnLine	612 225 1110	info@mn.state.net
507	Minnesota Regional Network	612 342 2570	info@mr.net
507	Protocol Communications, Inc.	612 541 9900	info@protocom.com
508	Argo Communications	508 261 6121	info@argo.net
508	Channel 1	617 864 0100	support@channel1.com
508	Empire.Net, Inc.	603 889 1220	info@empire.net
508	FOURnet Information Network	508 291 2900	info@four.net
508	intuitive information, inc.	508 342 1100	info@iii.net
508	MV Communications, Inc.	603 429 2223	info@mv.mv.com
508	North Shore Access	617 593 3110	info@shore.net
508	Pioneer Global Telecommunications, Inc.	617 375 0200	info@pn.com

Area Code	Company	Phone Number	E-Mail Information
508	Plymouth Commercial Internet Exchange	617 741 5900	info@pcix.com
508	StarNet	508 922 8238	info@venus.star.net
508	TerraNet, Inc.	617 450 9000	info@terra.net
508	The Destek Group, Inc.	603 635 3857	inquire@destek.net
508	The Internet Access Company (TIAC)	617 276 7200	info@tiac.net
508	The Internet Connection, Inc.	508 261 0383	info@ici.net
508	The World	617 739 0202	info@world.std.com
508	UltraNet Communications, Inc.	508 229 8400	info@ultra.net.com
508	Wilder Systems, Inc.	617 933 8810	info@id.wing.net
508	Wrentham Internet Services	508 384 1404	info@riva.com
509	Cascade Connections, Inc.	509 663 4259	carrie@cascade.net
509	Interconnected Associates Inc. (IXA)	206 622 7337	mike@ixa.com
509	Internet On-Ramp, Inc.	509 624 RAMP	info@on-ramp.ior.com
509	Transport Logic	503 243 1940	sales@transport.com
509	WLN	800 342 5956	info@wln.com
510	Aimnet Information Services	408 257 0900	info@aimnet.com
510	Alternet (UUNET Technologies, Inc.)	703 204 8000	info@alter.net
510	BTR Communications Company	415 966 1429	support@btr.com
510	Community ConneXion — NEXUS-Berkeley	510 549 1383	info@c2.org
510	Direct Net Access Incorporated	510 649 6110	support@dnai.com
510	Exodus Communications, Inc.	408 522 8450	info@exodus.net
510	Idiom Consulting	510 644 0441	info@idiom.com
510	InterNex Tiara	408 496 5466	info@internex.net
510	LanMinds, Inc.	510 843 6389	info@lanminds.com
510	Liberty Information Network	800 218 5157	info@liberty.com
510	LineX Communications	415 455 1650	info@linex.com
510	MediaCity World	415 321 6800	info@MediaCity.com

(continued)

Table A-2 *(continued)*

Area Code	Company	Phone Number	E-Mail Information
510	MobiusNet	415 821 0600	info@mobius.net
510	NETCOM On-Line Communications Services	408 554 8649	info@netcom.com
510	Sirius	415 284 4700	info@sirius.com
510	SLIPNET	415 281 3132	info@slip.net
510	West Coast Online	707 586 3060	info@calon.com
510	Zocalo Engineering	510 540 8000	info@zocalo.net
512	@sig.net	512 306 0700	sales@aus.sig.net
512	I-Link Ltd	800 ILINK 99	info@i-link.net
512	Illuminati Online	512 462 0999	info@io.com
512	Internet Connect Services, Inc.	512 572 9987	info@icsi.net
512	NETCOM On-Line Communications Services	408 554 8649	info@netcom.com
512	OuterNet Connection Strategies	512 345 3573	question@outer.net
512	Real/Time Communications	512 451 0046	info@realtime.net
512	The Eden Matrix	512 478 9900	info@eden.com
512	Turning Point Information Services, Inc.	512 499 8400	info@tpoint.net
512	Zilker Internet Park, Inc.	512 206 3850	info@zilker.net
513	IgLou Internet Services	800 436 4456	info@iglou.com
513	Internet Access Cincinnati	513 887 8877	info@iac.net
513	Local Internet Gateway Co.	510 503 9227	sdw@lig.net
513	OARnet (corporate clients only)	614 728 8100	info@oar.net
513	Premier Internet Cincinnati, Inc.	513 561 6245	pic@cinti.net
513	The Dayton Network Access Company	513 237 6868	info@dnaco.net
514	Accent Internet	514 737 6077	admin@accent.net
514	CiteNet Telecom Inc.	514 721 1351	info@citenet.net
514	Communication Accessibles Montreal	514 288 2581	info@cam.org

Area Code	Company	Phone Number	E-Mail Information
514	Communications Inter-Acces	514 367 0002	info@interax.net
514	Cycor Communications Incorporated	902 892 7354	signup@cycor.ca
514	Odyssee Internet	514 861 3432	info@odyssee.net
514	UUNET Canada, Inc.	416 368 6621	info@uunet.ca
515	JTM MultiMedia, Inc.	515 277 1990	jtm@ecity.net
515	Minnesota OnLine	612 225 1110	info@mn.state.net
515	Synergy Communications, Inc.	800 345 9669	info@synergy.net
516	ASB Internet Services	516 981 1953	info@asb.com
516	Creative Data Consultants (SILLY.COM)	718 229 0489	info@silly.com
516	Echo Communications Group	212 255 3839	info@echonyc.com
516	I-2000 Inc.	800 464 3820	info@i-2000.com
516	INTAC Access Corporation	800 504 6822	info@intac.com
516	LI Net, Inc.	516 476 1168	info@li.net
516	Long Island Information, Inc.	516 294 0124	info@liii.com
516	Network Internet Services	516 543 0234	info@netusa.net
516	Panix (Public Access uNIX)	212 741 4545	info@panix.com
516	Pipeline New York	212 267 3636	info@pipeline.com
517	Branch Information Services	313 741 4442	branch-info@branch.com
517	Mich.com, Inc.	810 478 4300	info@mich.com
517	Msen, Inc.	313 998 4562	info@msen.com
518	Global One, Inc.	518 452 1465	lorin@global1.net
518	Wizvax Communications	518 273 4325	info@wizvax.com
519	HookUp Communications	905 847 8000	info@hookup.net
519	Inter*Com Information Services	519 679 1620	info@icis.on.ca
519	Magic Online Services International Inc.	416 591 6490	info@magic.ca
519	MGL Systems Computer Technologies Inc.	519 836 1295	info@mgl.ca
519	UUNET Canada, Inc.	416 368 6621	info@uunet.ca

(continued)

Table A-2 *(continued)*

Area Code	Company	Phone Number	E-Mail Information
519	Windsor Information Network Company	519 945 9462	kim@wincom.net
520	InfoMagic, Inc.	520 526 9565	info@infomagic.com
520	Internet Direct, Inc.	800 879 3624	info@direct.net
520	Opus One	602 324 0494	sales@opus1.com
520	Primenet	602 870 1010	info@primenet.com
520	RTD Systems & Networking, Inc.	602 318 0696	info@rtd.com
520	Sedona Internet Services, Inc.	520 204 2247	info@sedona.net
601	Datasync Internet Services	601 872 0001	info@datasync.com
602	Crossroads Communications	602 813 9040	crossroads@xroads.com
602	I-Link Ltd	800 ILINK 99	info@i-link.net
602	InfoMagic, Inc.	520 526 9565	info@infomagic.com
602	Internet Direct, Inc.	800 879 3624	info@direct.net
602	Internet Express	719 592 1240	info@usa.net
602	NETCOM On-Line Communications Services	408 554 8649	info@netcom.com
602	New Mexico Technet, Inc.	505 345 6555	granoff@technet.nm.org
602	Opus One	602 324 0494	sales@opus1.com
602	Primenet	602 870 1010	info@primenet.com
602	RTD Systems & Networking, Inc.	602 318 0696	info@rtd.com
602	Systems Solutions Inc.	602 955 5566	support@syspac.com
603	Agate Internet Services	207 947 8248	ais@agate.net
603	Empire.Net, Inc.	603 889 1220	info@empire.net
603	MV Communications, Inc.	603 429 2223	info@mv.mv.com
603	NETIS Public Access Internet	603 437 1811	epoole@leotech.mv.com
603	StarNet	508 922 8238	info@venus.star.net
603	The Destek Group, Inc.	603 635 3857	inquire@destek.net
604	AMT Solutions Group, Inc. Island Net	604 727 6030	info@islandnet.com
604	auroraNET Inc.	604 294 4357	sales@aurora.net

Area Code	Company	Phone Number	E-Mail Information
604	Cycor Communications Incorporated	902 892 7354	signup@cycor.ca
604	Mind Link!	604 534 5663	info@mindlink.bc.ca
604	Okanagan Internet Junction	604 549 1036	info@junction.net
604	Sunshine Net, Inc.	604 886 4120	admin@sunshine.net
604	The InterNet Shop Inc.	604 376 3710	info@netshop.net
604	UUNET Canada, Inc.	416 368 6621	info@uunet.ca
606	IgLou Internet Services	800 436 4456	info@iglou.com
606	Internet Access Cincinnati	513 887 8877	info@iac.net
606	Mikrotec Internet Services, Inc.	606 225 1488	info@mis.net
606	RAM Technologies Inc.	800 950 1726	info@ramlink.net
607	ServiceTech, Inc.	716 263 3360	info@servtech.com
607	Spectra.net	607 798 7300	info@spectra.net
608	BOSSNet Internet Services	608 362 1340	mbusam@bossnt.com
608	FullFeed Communications	608 246 4239	info@fullfeed.com
609	Digital Express Group	301 847 5000	info@digex.net
609	Eclipse Internet Access	800 483 1223	info@eclipse.net
609	K2NE Software	609 893 0673	vince-q@k2nesoft.com
609	Net Access	215 576 8669	support@netaxs.com
609	New Jersey Computer Connection	609 896 2799	info@pluto.njcc.com
609	Texel International	908 297 0290	info@texel.com
610	Digital Express Group	301 847 5000	info@digex.net
610	ENTER.Net	610 366 1300	info@enter.net
610	FishNet	610 337 9994	info@pond.com
610	GlobalQUEST, Inc.	610 696 8111	info@globalquest.net
610	Microserve Information Systems	717 779 4430	info@microserve.com
610	Net Access	215 576 8669	support@netaxs.com
610	Network Analysis Group	800 624 9240	nag@good.freedom.net
610	Oasis Telecommunications, Inc.	610 439 8560	staff@oasis.ot.com
610	OpNet	610 520 2880	info@op.net

(continued)

Area Code	Company	Phone Number	E-Mail Information
610	SSNet, Inc.	302 378 1386	info@ssnet.com
610	You Tools Corporation / FASTNET	610 954 5910	info@fast.net
612	DCC Inc.	612 378 4000	kgastony@dcc.com
612	GlobalCom	612 920 9920	info@globalc.com
612	James River Group Inc.	612 339 2521	jriver@jriver.jriver.COM
612	Millennium Communications, Inc.	612 338 5509	info@millcomm.com
612	Minnesota OnLine	612 225 1110	info@mn.state.net
612	Minnesota Regional Network	612 342 2570	info@mr.net
612	Orbis Internet Services, Inc.	612 645 9663	info@orbis.net
612	pclink.com	612 541 5656	infomatic@pclink.com
612	Primenet	602 870 1010	info@primenet.com
612	Protocol Communications, Inc.	612 541 9900	info@protocom.com
612	StarNet Communications, Inc.	612 941 9177	info@winternet.com
612	Synergy Communications, Inc.	800 345 9669	info@synergy.net
613	Cyberius Online Inc.	613 233 1215	info@cyberus.ca
613	Cycor Communications Incorporated	902 892 7354	signup@cycor.ca
613	HookUp Communications	905 847 8000	info@hookup.net
613	Information Gateway Services (Ottawa)	613 592 5619	info@igs.net
613	Interactive Telecom Inc.	613 727 5258	info@intertel.net
613	o://info.web	613 225 3354	kevin@magi.com
613	UUNET Canada, Inc.	416 368 6621	info@uunet.ca
614	ASCInet (Columbus)	614 798 5321	info@ascinet.com
614	Branch Information Services	313 741 4442	branch-info@branch.com
614	Internet Access Cincinnati	513 887 8877	info@iac.net
614	OARnet (corporate clients only)	614 728 8100	info@oar.net
614	RAM Technologies Inc.	800 950 1726	info@ramlink.net
615	ERC, Inc./The Edge	615 455 9915	staff@edge.ercnet.com

Table A-2 (continued)

Area Code	Company	Phone Number	E-Mail Information
615	GoldSword Systems	615 691 6498	info@goldsword.com
615	ISDN-Net Inc	615 377 7672	jdunlap@rex.isdn.net
615	MindSpring Enterprises, Inc.	800 719 4332	info@mindspring.com
615	The Telalink Corporation	615 321 9100	sales@telalink.net
615	The Tri-Cities Connection	615 378 5355	info@tricon.net
615	U.S. Internet	615 522 6788	info@usit.net
616	Branch Information Services	313 741 4442	branch-info@branch.com
616	Mich.com, Inc.	810 478 4300	info@mich.com
616	Msen, Inc.	313 998 4562	info@msen.com
616	The iserv Co.	616 281 5254	info@iserv.net
616	Traverse Communication Company	616 935 1705	info@traverse.com
617	Alternet (UUNET Technologies, Inc.)	703 204 8000	info@alter.net
617	Argo Communications	508 261 6121	info@argo.net
617	Channel 1	617 864 0100	support@channel1.com
617	COWZ Technologies	617 497 0058	system@cow.net
617	Cyber Access Internet Communications, Inc	617 396 0491	info@cybercom.net
617	FOURnet Information Network	508 291 2900	info@four.net
617	intuitive information, inc.	508 342 1100	info@iii.net
617	NETCOM On-Line Communications Services	408 554 8649	info@netcom.com
617	North Shore Access	617 593 3110	info@shore.net
617	Pioneer Global Telecommunications, Inc.	617 375 0200	info@pn.com
617	Plymouth Commercial Internet Exchange	617 741 5900	info@pcix.com
617	TerraNet, Inc.	617 450 9000	info@terra.net
617	The Internet Access Company (TIAC)	617 276 7200	info@tiac.net
617	The World	617 739 0202	info@world.std.com
617	UltraNet Communications, Inc.	508 229 8400	info@ultra.net.com
617	Wilder Systems, Inc.	617 933 8810	info@id.wing.net

(continued)

Table A-2 *(continued)*

Area Code	Company	Phone Number	E-Mail Information
618	Allied Access Inc.	618 684 2255	sales@intrnet.net
618	Online Information Access Network	618 692 9813	info@oia.net
618	P-Net, Inc.	314 731 2252	info@MO.NET
619	CONNECTnet Internet Network Services	619 450 0254	info@connectnet.com
619	CTS Network Services	619 637 3637	info@cts.com
619	Electriciti	619 338 9000	info@powergrid.electriciti.com
619	I-Link Ltd	800 ILINK 99	info@i-link.net
619	Liberty Information Network	800 218 5157	info@liberty.com
619	NETCOM On-Line Communications Services	408 554 8649	info@netcom.com
619	Primenet	602 870 1010	info@primenet.com
619	RidgeNET	619 371 3501	saic@owens.ridgecrest.ca.us
619	Sierra-Net	702 831 3353	giles@sierra.net
619	The Cyberspace Station	619 634 2894	info@cyber.net
701	Red River Net	701 232 2227	info@rrnet.com
702	@wizard.com	702 871 4461	info@wizard.com
702	Connectus, Inc.	702 323 2008	info@connectus.com
702	Great Basin Internet Services	702 829 2244	info@greatbasin.com
702	InterMind	702 878 6111	support@terminus.intermind.net
702	NETCOM On-Line Communications Services	408 554 8649	info@netcom.com
702	Sierra-Net	702 831 3353	giles@sierra.net
703	Alternet (UUNET Technologies, Inc.)	703 204 8000	info@alter.net
703	CAPCON Library Network	202 331 5771	info@capcon.net
703	Charm.Net	410 558 3900	info@charm.net
703	Clark Internet Services, Inc. ClarkNet	410 995 0691	info@clark.net
703	DataBank, Inc.	913 842 6699	info@databank.com
703	Digital Express Group	301 847 5000	info@digex.net
703	Genuine Computing Resources	703 878 4680	info@gcr.com

Area Code	Company	Phone Number	E-Mail Information
703	Internet Online, Inc.	301 652 4468	info@intr.net
703	Interpath	800 849 6305	info@interpath.net
703	LaserNet	703 591 4232	info@laser.net
703	NETCOM On-Line Communications Services	408 554 8649	info@netcom.com
703	Quantum Networking Solutions, Inc.	805 538 2028	info@qnet.com
703	RadixNet Internet Services	301 567 9831	info@radix.net
703	US Net, Incorporated	301 572 5926	info@us.net
703	World Web Limited	703 838 2000	info@worldweb.net
704	Interpath	800 849 6305	info@interpath.net
704	SunBelt.Net	803 328 1500	info@sunbelt.net
704	Vnet Internet Access	704 334 3282	info@vnet.net
705	Barrie Connex Inc.	705 725 0819	info@bconnex.net
705	Magic Online Services International Inc.	416 591 6490	info@magic.ca
705	Mindemoya Computing	705 523 0243	info@mcd.on.ca
705	SooNet Corporation	705 253 4700	service@soonet.ca
706	InteliNet	803 279 9775	administrator@intelinet.net
706	Internet Atlanta	404 410 9000	info@atlanta.com
706	MindSpring Enterprises, Inc.	800 719 4332	info@mindspring.com
707	Datatamers	415 367 7919	info@datatamers.com
707	Liberty Information Network	800 218 5157	info@liberty.com
707	West Coast Online	707 586 3060	info@calon.com
707	Zocalo Engineering	510 540 8000	info@zocalo.net
708	American Information Systems, Inc.	708 413 8400	info@ais.net
708	CICNet, Inc.	313 998 6103	info@cic.net
708	I Connection, Inc.	708 662 0877	info@iconnect.net
708	InterAccess Co.	800 967 1580	info@interaccess.com
708	Interactive Network Systems, Inc.	312 881 3039	info@insnet.com
708	MCSNet	312 248 8649	info@mcs.net
708	Open Business Systems, Inc.	708 250 0260	info@obs.net

(continued)

Table A-2 *(continued)*

Area Code	Company	Phone Number	E-Mail Information
708	Ripco Communications, Inc.	312 477 6210	info@ripco.com
708	Tezcatlipoca, Inc.	312 850 0181	info@tezcat.com
708	WorldWide Access	708 367 1870	info@wwa.com
708	XNet Information Systems	708 983 6064	info@xnet.com
709	InterActions Limited	709 745 4638	connect@nfld.com
712	Greater Omaha Public Access Unix Corp	402 558 5030	info@gonix.com
712	Synergy Communications, Inc.	800 345 9669	info@synergy.net
713	Alternet (UUNET Technologies, Inc.)	703 204 8000	info@alter.net
713	ELECTROTEX, Inc.	713 526 3456	info@electrotex.com
713	I-Link Ltd	800 ILINK 99	info@i-link.net
713	Internet Connect Services, Inc.	512 572 9987	info@icsi.net
713	NeoSoft, Inc.	713 684 5969	info@neosoft.com
713	OnRamp Technologies, Inc.	214 746 4710	info@onramp.net
713	The Black Box	713 480 2684	info@blkbox.com
713	USiS	713 682 1666	admin@usis.com
714	Cloverleaf Communications	714 895 3075	sales@cloverleaf.com
714	Cogent Software, Inc.	818 585 2788	info@cogsoft.com
714	Dana Point Communications	714 443 4172	connect@beach.net
714	Delta Internet Services	714 778 0370	info@deltanet.com
714	DigiLink Network Services	310 542 7421	info@digilink.net
714	EarthLink Network, Inc.	213 644 9500	sales@earthlink.net
714	Electriciti	619 338 9000	info@powergrid.electriciti.com
714	Exodus Communications, Inc.	408 522 8450	info@exodus.net
714	InterNex Tiara	408 496 5466	info@internex.net
714	KAIWAN Internet	714 638 2139	info@kaiwan.com
714	Liberty Information Network	800 218 5157	info@liberty.com
714	Lightside, Inc.	818 858 9261	Lightside@Lightside.Com

Area Code	Company	Phone Number	E-Mail Information
714	NETCOM On-Line Communications Services	408 554 8649	info@netcom.com
714	Network Intensive	714 450 8400	info@ni.net
714	Primenet	602 870 1010	info@primenet.com
715	FullFeed Communications	608 246 4239	info@fullfeed.com
715	Minnesota OnLine	612 225 1110	info@mn.state.net
716	BuffNET	800 463 6499	info@buffnet.net
716	E-Znet, Inc.	716 262 2485	
716	ServiceTech, Inc.	716 263 3360	info@servtech.com
717	Keystone Information Access Systems	717 741 2626	office@yrkpa.kias.com
717	Microserve Information Systems	717 779 4430	info@microserve.com
717	Oasis Telecommunications, Inc.	610 439 8560	staff@oasis.ot.com
717	PenNet	717 368 1577	safrye@pennet.net
717	Spectra.net	607 798 7300	info@spectra.net
717	The Internet Cafe	717 344 1969	info@lydian.scranton.com
717	You Tools Corporation / FASTNET	610 954 5910	info@fast.net
718	Blythe Systems	212 226 7171	infodesk@blythe.org
718	BrainLINK	718 805 6559	info@beast.brainlink.com
718	Creative Data Consultants (SILLY.COM)	718 229 0489	info@silly.com
718	escape.com — Kazan Corp	212 888 8780	info@escape.com
718	Ingress Communications Inc.	212 679 2838	info@ingress.com
718	INTAC Access Corporation	800 504 6822	info@intac.com
718	Intellitech Walrus	212 406 5000	info@walrus.com
718	InterCom Online	212 714 7183	info@intercom.com
718	Internet QuickLink Corp.	212 307 1669	info@quicklink.com
718	Interport Communications Corp.	212 989 1128	info@interport.net
718	Long Island Information, Inc.	516 294 0124	info@liii.com
718	Mnematics, Incorporated	914 359 4546	service@mne.com

(continued)

	Table A-2 *(continued)*		
Area Code	**Company**	**Phone Number**	**E-Mail Information**
718	Mordor International BBS	201 433 4222	ritz@mordor.com
718	Panix (Public Access uNIX)	212 741 4545	info@panix.com
718	Phantom Access Technologies, Inc.	212 989 2418	bruce@phantom.com
718	Pipeline New York	212 267 3636	info@pipeline.com
718	ThoughtPort of New York City	212 645 7970	info@precipice.com
719	Colorado SuperNet, Inc.	303 296 8202	info@csn.org
719	Internet Express	719 592 1240	info@usa.net
719	Old Colorado City Communications	719 528 5849	thefox@oldcolo.com
719	Rocky Mountain Internet	800 900 7644	info@rmii.com
770	MindSpring Enterprises, Inc.	800 719 4332	info@mindspring.com
770	vividnet	770 933 0999	webadmin@vivid.net
800	Allied Access Inc.	618 684 2255	sales@intrnet.net
800	American Information Systems, Inc.	708 413 8400	info@ais.net
800	Association for Computing Machinery	817 776 6876	account-info@acm.org
800	CICNet, Inc.	313 998 6103	info@cic.net
800	Cogent Software, Inc.	818 585 2788	info@cogsoft.com
800	Colorado SuperNet, Inc.	303 296 8202	info@csn.org
800	Cyberius Online Inc.	613 233 1215	info@cyberus.ca
800	DataBank, Inc.	913 842 6699	info@databank.com
800	EarthLink Network, Inc.	213 644 9500	sales@earthlink.net
800	Global Connect, Inc.	804 229 4484	info@gc.net
800	Internet Express	719 592 1240	info@usa.net
800	Mnematics, Incorporated	914 359 4546	service@mne.com
800	Msen, Inc.	313 998 4562	info@msen.com
800	NeoSoft, Inc.	713 684 5969	info@neosoft.com
800	New Mexico Technet, Inc.	505 345 6555	granoff@technet.nm.org
800	Pacific Rim Network, Inc.	360 650 0442	info@pacificrim.net

Area Code	Company	Phone Number	E-Mail Information
800	Rocky Mountain Internet	800 900 7644	info@rmii.com
800	Synergy Communications, Inc.	800 345 9669	info@synergy.net
800	WLN	800 342 5956	info@wln.com
801	DataBank, Inc.	913 842 6699	info@databank.com
801	I-Link Ltd	800 ILINK 99	info@i-link.net
801	Infonaut Communication Services	801 370 3068	info@infonaut.com
801	Internet Technology Systems (ITS)	801 375 0538	admin@itsnet.com
801	The ThoughtPort Authority Inc.	800 ISP 6870	info@thoughtport.com
801	XMission	801 539 0852	support@xmission.com
803	A World of Difference, Inc.	803 769 4488	info@awod.com
803	Global Vision Inc.	803 241 0901	info@globalvision.net
803	Hargray Telephone Company	803 686 5000	info@hargray.com
803	InteliNet	803 279 9775	administrator@intelinet.net
803	Interpath	800 849 6305	info@interpath.net
803	SIMS, Inc.	803 762 4956	info@sims.net
803	SunBelt.Net	803 328 1500	info@sunbelt.net
804	Widomaker Communication Service	804 253 7621	bloyall@widowmaker.com
805	Cogent Software, Inc.	818 585 2788	info@cogsoft.com
805	EarthLink Network, Inc.	213 644 9500	sales@earthlink.net
805	Internet Access of Ventura County	805 383 3500	info@vcnet.com
805	KAIWAN Internet	714 638 2139	info@kaiwan.com
805	Lancaster Internet (California)	805 943 2112	dennis@gargamel.ptw.com
805	Liberty Information Network	800 218 5157	info@liberty.com
805	Netport Internet Access	805 538 2860	info@netport.com
805	Network Intensive	714 450 8400	info@ni.net
805	OutWest Network Services	818 545 1996	OWInfo@outwest.com
805	Quantum Networking Solutions, Inc.	805 538 2028	info@qnet.com
805	Regional Alliance for Info Networking	805 967 7246	info@rain.org
805	The Catalina BBS InterNet Services	fax: 805 687 1185	help@catalina.org

(continued)

	Table A-2 *(continued)*		
Area Code	**Company**	**Phone Number**	**E-Mail Information**
805	The Central Connection	818 735 3000	info@centcon.com
805	ValleyNet Communications	209 486 8638	info@valleynet.com
805	WestNet Communications, Inc.	805 892 2133	info@west.net
806	OnRamp Technologies, Inc.	214 746 4710	info@onramp.net
808	FlexNet Inc.	808 732 8849	info@aloha.com
808	Hawaii OnLine	808 533 6981	support@aloha.net
808	Inter-Pacific Network Services	808 935 5550	sales@interpac.net
808	LavaNet, Inc.	808 545 5282	info@lava.net
808	Pacific Information Exchange, Inc.	808 596 7494	info@pixi.com
810	Branch Information Services	313 741 4442	branch-info@branch.com
810	ICNET/Innovative Concepts	313 998 0090	info@ic.net
810	Local Internet Service Provider	810 687 4221	hostmaster@lisp.com
810	Mich.com, Inc.	810 478 4300	info@mich.com
810	Michigan Internet Cooperative Association	810 355 1438	info@coop.mica.net
810	Msen, Inc.	313 998 4562	info@msen.com
810	RustNet, Inc.	810 650 6812	info@rust.net
812	HolliCom Internet Services	317 883 4500	cale@holli.com
812	IgLou Internet Services	800 436 4456	info@iglou.com
812	World Connection Services	812 479 1700	info@evansville.net
813	Bay-A-Net	813 988 7772	info@bayanet.com
813	Centurion Technology, Inc.	813 538 1919	info@tpa.cent.com
813	CFTnet	813 980 1317	sales@cftnet.com
813	CocoNet Corporation	813 945 0055	info@coconet.com
813	CyberGate, Inc.	305 428 4283	sales@gate.net
813	Florida Online	407 635 8888	info@digital.net
813	Intelligence Network Online, Inc.	813 442 0114 x22	info@intnet.net
813	PacketWorks, Inc.	813 446 8826	info@packet.net

Area Code	Company	Phone Number	E-Mail Information
813	The ThoughtPort Authority Inc.	800 ISP 6870	info@thoughtport.com
814	PenNet	717 368 1577	safrye@pennet.net
815	American Information Systems, Inc.	708 413 8400	info@ais.net
815	BOSSNet Internet Services	608 362 1340	mbusam@bossnt.com
815	InterAccess Co.	800 967 1580	info@interaccess.com
815	T.B.C. Online Data-Net	815 758 5040	info@tbcnet.com
816	Interstate Networking Corporation	816 472 4949	staff@interstate.net
816	Primenet	602 870 1010	info@primenet.com
817	Association for Computing Machinery	817 776 6876	account-info@acm.org
817	CompuTek	214 994 0190	info@computek.net
817	DFW Internet Services, Inc.	817 332 5116	info@dfw.net
817	OnRamp Technologies, Inc.	214 746 4710	info@onramp.net
817	Texas Metronet, Inc.	214 705 2900	info@metronet.com
818	Cogent Software, Inc.	818 585 2788	info@cogsoft.com
818	Delta Internet Services	714 778 0370	info@deltanet.com
818	DigiLink Network Services	310 542 7421	info@digilink.net
818	EarthLink Network, Inc.	213 644 9500	sales@earthlink.net
818	Exodus Communications, Inc.	408 522 8450	info@exodus.net
818	Flamingo Communications Inc.	310 532 3533	sales@fcom.com
818	InterNex Tiara	408 496 5466	info@internex.net
818	KAIWAN Internet	714 638 2139	info@kaiwan.com
818	Leonardo Internet	310 395 5500	jimp@leonardo.net
818	Liberty Information Network	800 218 5157	info@liberty.com
818	Lightside, Inc.	818 858 9261	Lightside@Lightside.Com
818	NETCOM On-Line Communications Services	408 554 8649	info@netcom.com
818	Network Intensive	714 450 8400	info@ni.net
818	OutWest Network Services	818 545 1996	OWInfo@outwest.com

(continued)

	Table A-2 *(continued)*		
Area Code	**Company**	**Phone Number**	**E-Mail Information**
818	Primenet	602 870 1010	info@primenet.com
818	Regional Alliance for Info Networking	805 967 7246	info@rain.org
818	The Central Connection	818 735 3000	info@centcon.com
818	The Loop Internet Switch Co.	213 465 1311	info@loop.com
818	ViaNet Communications	415 903 2242	info@via.net
819	Information Gateway Services (Ottawa)	613 592 5619	info@igs.net
819	Interactive Telecom Inc.	613 727 5258	info@intertel.net
819	o://info.web	613 225 3354	kevin@magi.com
901	ISDN-Net Inc.	615 377 7672	jdunlap@rex.isdn.net
901	Magibox Incorporated	901 757 7835	info@magibox.net
902	Cycor Communications Incorporated	902 892 7354	signup@cycor.ca
903	Cloverleaf Technologies	903 832 1367	helpdesk@clover.cleaf.com
904	CyberGate, Inc.	305 428 4283	sales@gate.net
904	Florida Online	407 635 8888	info@digital.net
904	Internet Connect Company	904 375 2912	info@atlantic.net
904	Jax Gateway to the World	904 730 7692	sales@gttw.com
904	MagicNet, Inc.	407 657 2202	info@magicnet.net
904	Polaris Network, Inc.	904 878 9745	staff@polaris.net
904	PSS InterNet Services	800 463 8499	support@america.com
904	SymNet	904 385 1061	info@symnet.net
905	Cycor Communications Incorporated	902 892 7354	signup@cycor.ca
905	HookUp Communications	905 847 8000	info@hookup.net
905	iCOM Internet Services	905 522 1220	sales@icom.ca
905	InterLog Internet Services	416 975 2655	internet@interlog.com
905	Internet Access Worldwide	905 714 1400	info@iaw.on.ca
905	Internet Connect Niagara Inc.	905 988 9909	info@niagara.com
905	Internex Online, Inc.	416 363 8676	support@io.org

Area Code	Company	Phone Number	E-Mail Information
905	Magic Online Services International Inc.	416 591 6490	info@magic.ca
905	Times.net	905 775 4471	rfonger@times.net
905	Vaxxine Computer Systems Inc.	905 562 3500	admin@vaxxine.com
906	Branch Information Services	313 741 4442	branch-info@branch.com
906	Mich.com, Inc.	810 478 4300	info@mich.com
906	Msen, Inc.	313 998 4562	info@msen.com
906	The Portage at Micro + Computers	906 487 9832	admin@mail.portup.com
907	Internet Alaska	907 562 4638	info@alaska.net
908	Castle Network, Inc.	908 548 8881	request@castle.net
908	Digital Express Group	301 847 5000	info@digex.net
908	Eclipse Internet Access	800 483 1223	info@eclipse.net
908	I-2000 Inc.	800 464 3820	info@i-2000.com
908	INTAC Access Corporation	800 504 6822	info@intac.com
908	Internet For `U'	800 NET WAY1	info@ifu.net
908	Internet Online Services	201 928 1000 x226	help@ios.com
908	Openix — Open Internet Exchange	201 443 0400	info@openix.com
908	Texel International	908 297 0290	info@texel.com
908	You Tools Corporation / FASTNET	610 954 5910	info@fast.net
909	Cogent Software, Inc.	818 585 2788	info@cogsoft.com
909	CONNECTnet Internet Network Services	619 450 0254	info@connectnet.com
909	Dana Point Communications	714 443 4172	connect@beach.net
909	Delta Internet Services	714 778 0370	info@deltanet.com
909	EmpireNet	909 787 4969	support@empirenet.com
909	KAIWAN Internet	714 638 2139	info@kaiwan.com
909	Liberty Information Network	800 218 5157	info@liberty.com
909	Lightside, Inc.	818 858 9261	Lightside@Lightside.Com
909	Network Intensive	714 450 8400	info@ni.net
909	Primenet	602 870 1010	info@primenet.com
910	Interpath	800 849 6305	info@interpath.net

(continued)

Table A-2 *(continued)*

Area Code	Company	Phone Number	E-Mail Information
910	Red Barn Data Center	910 750 9809	tom@rbdc.rbdc.com
910	Vnet Internet Access	704 334 3282	info@vnet.net
912	Hargray Telephone Company	803 686 5000	info@hargray.com
912	Homenet Communications, Inc.	912 329 8638	info@hom.net
912	Internet Atlanta	404 410 9000	info@atlanta.com
912	MindSpring Enterprises, Inc.	800 719 4332	info@mindspring.com
913	DataBank, Inc.	913 842 6699	info@databank.com
913	Flint Hills Computers, Inc.	913 776 4333	gil@flinthills.com
913	Interstate Networking Corporation	816 472 4949	staff@interstate.net
914	Cloud 9 Internet	914 682 0626	info@cloud9.net
914	Computer Solutions by Hawkinson	914 229 9853	info@mhv.net
914	Creative Data Consultants (SILLY.COM)	718 229 0489	info@silly.com
914	DataBank, Inc.	913 842 6699	info@databank.com
914	GBN InternetAccess	201 343 6427	gbninfo@gbn.net
914	I-2000 Inc.	800 464 3820	info@i-2000.com
914	ICU On-Line	914 627 3800	info@icu.com
914	INTAC Access Corporation	800 504 6822	info@intac.com
914	InteleCom Data Systems, Inc.	401 885 6855	info@ids.net
914	Mnematics, Incorporated	914 359 4546	service@mne.com
914	Panix (Public Access uNIX)	212 741 4545	info@panix.com
914	Pipeline New York	212 267 3636	info@pipeline.com
914	TZ-Link Internet	914 353 5443	info@j51.com
914	WestNet Internet Services	914 967 7816	info@westnet.com
915	New Mexico Technet, Inc.	505 345 6555	granoff@technet.nm.org
915	Primenet	602 870 1010	info@primenet.com
915	WhiteHorse Communications, Inc.	915 584 6630	whc.net.html
916	Connectus, Inc.	702 323 2008	info@connectus.com

Area Code	Company	Phone Number	E-Mail Information
916	Great Basin Internet Services	702 829 2244	info@greatbasin.com
916	InterStar Network Services	916 224 6866	gfrank@shasta.com
916	mother.com	916 757 8070	info@mail.mother.com
916	NETCOM On-Line Communications Services	408 554 8649	info@netcom.com
916	Psyberware Internet Access	916 645 9451	info@psyber.com
916	Sacramento Network Access	916 565 4500	info@sna.com
916	Sierra-Net	702 831 3353	giles@sierra.net
916	Sutter Yuba Internet Exchange	916 755 1751	dave@syix.com
916	VFR, Inc.	916 652 7237	vfr@vfr.net
916	West Coast Online	707 586 3060	info@calon.com
916	Zocalo Engineering	510 540 8000	info@zocalo.net
918	Galaxy Star Systems	918 835 3655	info@galstar.com
918	Internet Oklahoma	918 583 1161	info@ionet.net
919	Atlantic Internet Corporation	919 833 1252	info@ainet.net
919	Interpath	800 849 6305	info@interpath.net
919	NETCOM On-Line Communications Services	408 554 8649	info@netcom.com
919	Vnet Internet Access	704 334 3282	info@vnet.net
941	Centurion Technology, Inc.	813 538 1919	info@tpa.cent.com
941	Net Sarasota	941 371 1966	info@netsrq.com
941	PacketWorks, Inc.	813 446 8826	info@packet.net
970	EZLink Internet Access	970 482 0807	ezadmin@ezlink.com
970	Frontier Internet, Inc.	970 385 4177	info@frontier.net

International Providers

Table A-3 lists international service providers. You should first look up the country in which you want service, and then see which providers operate there.

Table A-3
International Providers

Country	Company	Phone Number	E-Mail Information
Australia	AusNet Services Pty Ltd	+61 2 241 5888	sales@world.net
Australia	Byron Public Access	+61 18 823 541	admin@byron.apana.org.au
Australia	DIALix Services	+61 2 948 6995	justin@sydney.dialix.oz.au
Australia	Global Data Access	+61 9 421 1222	info@ednet.com.au
Australia	Highway 1	+61 9 370 4584	info@highway1.com.au
Australia	Hunter Network Association	+61 49 621783	mbrown@hna.com.au
Australia	iiNet Technologies	+61 9 3071183	iinet@iinet.com.au
Australia	Kralizec Dialup Unix System	+61 2 837 1397	nick@kralizec.zeta.org.au
Australia	Informed Technology	+61 9 245 2279	info@it.com.au
Australia	The Message eXchange Pty Ltd	+61 2 550 5014	info@tmx.com.au
Australia	Microplex Pty. Ltd.	+61 2 888 3685	info@mpx.com.au
Australia	Pegasus Networks Pty Ltd	+61 7 257 1111	fwhitmee@peg.apc.org
Australia	PPIT Pty. Ltd. (059 051 320)	+61 3 747 9823	info@ppit.com.au
Australia	Stour System Services	+61 9 571 1949	stour@stour.net.au
Australia	Winthrop Technology	+61 9 380 3564	wthelp@yarrow.wt.uwa.edu.au
Australia	Zip Australia Pty. Ltd.	+61 2 482 7015	info@zip.com.au
Austria	ARGE DATEN	+43 1 4897893	info@email.ad.or.at
Austria	EUnet EDV	+43 1 3174969	info@austria.eu.net
Austria	Hochschuelerschaft...	+43 1 586 1868	sysop@link-atu.comlink.apc.org
Austria	Net4You	+43 4242 257367	office@net4you.co.at
Austria	netwing	+43 5337 65315	info@netwing.at
Austria	PING EDV	+43 1 3194336	info@ping.at
Austria	Vianet Austria Ltd.	+43 1 5892920	info@via.at
Bashkiria	UD JV `DiasPro'	+7 3472 387454	iskander@diaspro.bashkiria.su
Belarus	Open Contact, Ltd.	+7 017 2206134	admin@brc.minsk.by
Belgium	EUnet Belgium NV	+32 16 236099	info@belgium.eu.net
Belgium	Infoboard Telematics	+32 2 475 22 99	info@infoboard.be

Country	Company	Phone Number	E-Mail Information
Belgium	INnet NV/SA	+32 14 319937	info@inbe.net
Belgium	KnoopPunt VZW	+32 9 2333 686	support@knooppunt.be
Bulgaria	EUnet Bulgaria	+359 52 259135	info@bulgaria.eu.net
Denmark	DKnet / EUnet Denmark	+45 3917 9900	info@dknet.dk
Finland	Clinet Ltd	+358 0 437 5209	clinet@clinet.fi
Finland	EUnet Finland Ltd.	+358 0 400 2060	helpdesk@eunet.fi
France	French Data Network	+33 1 4797 5873	info@fdn.org
France	Internet Way	+33 1 4143 2110	info@iway.fr
France	OLEANE	+33 1 4328 3232	info-internet@oleane.net
France	REMCOMP SARL	+33 1 4479 0642	info@liber.net
France	STI	+33 1 3463 1919	fb101@calvacom.fr
Georgia	Mimosi Hard	+7 8832 232857	kisho@sanet.ge
Germany	bbTT Electronic Networks	+49 30 817 42 06	willem@b-2.de.contrib.net
Germany	EUnet Germany GmbH	+49 231 972 2222	info@germany.eu.net
Germany	Individual Network e.V.	+49 441 980 8556	in-info@individual.net
Germany	INS Inter Networking Systems	+49 2305 356505	info@ins.net
Germany	Internet PoP Frankfurt	+49 69 94439192	joerg@pop-frankfurt.com
Germany	MUC.DE e.V.	+49 89 324 683 0	postmaster@muc.de
Germany	Onlineservice Nuernberg	+49 911 9933882	info@osn.de
Germany	PFM News & Mail Xlink POP	+49 171 331 0862	info@pfm.pfm-mainz.de
Germany	Point of Presence GmbH	+49 40 2519 2025	info@pop.de
Germany	POP Contrib.Net Netzdienste	+49 521 9683011	info@teuto.de
Germany	SpaceNet GmbH	+49 89 324 683 0	info@space.net
Germany	TouchNET GmbH	+49 89 5447 1111	info@touch.net
Germany	Westend GbR	+49 241 911879	info@westend.com
Ghana	Chonia Informatica	+233 21 66 94 20	info@ghana.net
Greece	Ariadne	+30 1 651 3392	dialup@leon.nrcps.ariadne-t.gr
Greece	Foundation of Research	+30 81 221171	forthnet-pr@forthnet.gr
Greece	Hellenic Informatics	+30 1 620 3040	info@hol.gr

(continued)

Table A-3 *(continued)*

Country	Company	Phone Number	E-Mail Information
Hong Kong	Asia On-Line Limited	+852 2866 6018	info@asiaonline.net
Hong Kong	Hong Kong SuperNet	+852 358 7924	trouble@hk.super.net
Iceland	SURIS / ISnet	+354 1 694747	isnet-info@isnet.is
Ireland	Cork Internet Services	+353 21 277124	info@cis.ie
Ireland	Ieunet Limited	+353 1 679 0832	info@ieunet.ie
Ireland	Ireland On-Line	+353 91 592727	info@iol.ie
Israel	ACTCOM	+972 4 676115	office@actcom.co.il
Israel	Elronet	+972 313534	info@elron.net
Israel	NetVision LTD.	+972 550330	info@netvision.net.il
Italy	Abacom s.a.s.	+39 434 660911	info@system.abacom.it
Italy	ITnet S.p.A.	+39 10 6563324	info@it.net
Japan	Asahi Net	+81 3 3666 2811	info@asahi-net.or.jp
Japan	Global OnLine	+81 3 5330 9380	info@gol.org
Japan	HA Telecom Corporation	+81 58 253 7641	info@hatelecom.or.jp
Japan	Internet Initiative Japan	+81 3 3580 3781	info@iij.ad.jp
Japan	M.R.T., Inc.	+81 3 3255 8880	sysop@janis-tok.com
Japan	TWICS	+81 3 3351 5977	info@twics.com
Japan	Typhoon Inc.	+81 3 3757 2118	info@typhoon.co.jp
Kazakhstan	Bogas Soft Laboratory Co.	+7 322 262 4990	pasha@sl.semsk.su
Kuwait	Gulfnet Kuwait	+965 242 6728	info@kw.us.com
Latvia	LvNet-Teleport	+371 2 551133	vit@riga.lv
Latvia	Versia Ltd.	+371 2 417000	postmaster@vernet.lv
Lisboa	Esoterica	716 2395	info@esoterica.com
Luxemburg	EUnet Luxemburg	+352 47 02 61 361	info@luxemburg.eu.net
Mexico	Datanet S.A. de C.V.	+52 5 1075400	info@data.net.mx
Mexico	Internet de Mexico S.A.	+52 5 3602931	info@mail.internet.com.mx
Netherlands	The Delft Connection	+31 15560079	info@void.tdcnet.nl

Country	Company	Phone Number	E-Mail Information
Netherlands	Hobbynet	+31 365361683	henk@hgatenl.hobby.nl
Netherlands	Internet Access Foundation	+31 5982 2720	mail-server@iafnl.iaf.nl
Netherlands	NEST	+31 206265566	info@nest.nl
Netherlands	NetLand	+31 206943664	info@netland.nl
Netherlands	NLnet (EUnet)	+31 206639366	info@nl.net
Netherlands	Psyline	+31 80445801	postmaster@psyline.nl
Netherlands	Simplex Networking	+31 206932433	skelmir@simplex.nl
Netherlands	Stichting XS4ALL	+31 206225222	helpdesk@xs4all.nl
New Zealand	Actrix Networks Limited	+64 4 389 6356	john@actrix.gen.nz
New Zealand	Efficient Software Limited	+64 3 4738274	bart@dunedin.es.co.nz
Norway	Oslonett A/S	+47 22 46 10 99	oslonett@oslonett.no
Poland	PDi Ltd. — Public Internet	+48 42 30 21 94	info@pdi.lodz.pl
Romania	EUnet Romania SRL	+40 1 312 6886	info@romania.eu.net
Russia	ELCOM	+7 092 223 2208	root@centre.elcom.ru
Russia	GlasNet	+7 95 262 7079	support@glas.apc.org
Russia	InterCommunications Ltd.	+7 8632 620562	postmaster@icomm.rnd.su
Russia	NEVAlink Ltd.	+7 812 592 3737	serg@arcom.spb.su
Russia	Relcom CO	+7 95 194 25 40	postmaster@ussr.eu.net
Russia	SvjazInform	+7 351 265 3600	pol@rich.chel.su
Singapore	Singapore Telecom Limited	+65 7308079	admin@singnet.com.sg
Slovakia	EUnet Slovakia	+42 7 725 306	info@slovakia.eu.net
Slovenia	NIL, System Integration	+386 61 1405 183	info@slovenia.eu.net
South Africa	Aztec	+27 21 419 2690	info@aztec.co.za
South Africa	Internet Africa	+27 0800 020003	info@iaccess.za
South Africa	The Internet Solution	+27 11 447 5566	info@is.co.za
Spain	OFFCAMPUS SL	+34 1 577 3026	infonet@offcampus.es
Sweden	NetGuide	+46 31 28 03 73	info@netg.se
Switzerland	EUnet AG, Zurich	+41 1 291 45 80	info@eunet.ch
Switzerland	EUnet SA, Geneva	+41 22 348 80 45	deffer@eunet.ch

(continued)

Table A-3 *(continued)*

Country	Company	Phone Number	E-Mail Information
Switzerland	SWITCH	+41 1 268 1515	postmaster@switch.ch
Tataretan	KAMAZ Incorporated	+7 8439 53 03 34	postmaster@kamaz.kazan.su
Ukraine	ConCom, Ltd.	+7 0572 27 69 13	igor@ktts.kharkov.ua
Ukraine	Crimea Communication Centre	+380 0652 257214	sem@snail.crimea.ua
Ukraine	Electronni Visti	+7 44 2713457	info%elvisti.kiev.ua@kiae.su
Ukraine	PACO Links Int'l Ltd.	+7 48 2200057	info@vista.odessa.ua
Ukraine	UkrCom-Kherson Ltd	+7 5522 64098	postmaster@ukrcom.kherson.ua
United Kingdom	Compulink (CIX Ltd)	+44 181 390 8446	cixadmin@cix.compulink.co.uk
United Kingdom	CONNECT — PC User Group	+44 181 863 1191	info@ibmpcug.co.uk
United Kingdom	Demon Internet Limited	+44 181 371 1000	internet@demon.net
United Kingdom	The Direct Connection	+44 81 313 0100	helpdesk@dircon.co.uk
United Kingdom	EUnet GB	+44 1227 266466	sales@britain.eu.net
United Kingdom	ExNet Systems Ltd.	+44 81 244 0077	info@exnet.com
United Kingdom	Frontier Internet Services	+44 171 242 3383	info@ftech.net
United Kingdom	GreenNet	+44 71 713 1941	support@gn.apc.org
United Kingdom	Lunatech Research	+44 1734 791900	info@luna.co.uk
United Kingdom	Pavilion Internet plc	+44 1273 606072	info@pavilion.co.uk
United Kingdom	Sound & Visions BBS	+44 1932 253131	info@span.com
United Kingdom	Specialix	+44 932 3522251	keith@specialix.co.uk
United Kingdom	WinNET (UK)	+44 181 863 1191	info@win-uk.ne
Venezuela	Internet Comunicaciones c.a.	+58 959 9550	admin@ccs.internet.ve

Windows Tools on the Net

As you learn throughout this book, you can find a wide variety of tools on the Internet. You can use these tools to widen your use of the Net and to enrich your learning and recreational experiences. This appendix provides a concise guide of where you can find different tools on the Internet. These tools have been developed to work exclusively with Windows.

Ftp Sources

Table B-1 lists some of the most popular Internet tools and where they can be found through anonymous ftp. Whenever possible, the 32-bit versions of the programs are cited in this table.

Remember that the filenames provided are as of this writing; you may want to search the directory at any time to determine if a later version is available. In addition, these sites are not the only locations from which you can get these files. To find other ftp occurrences of these program names, use the Archie tool, which is discussed in Chapter 12.

Table B-1
Internet Tools Available Through Ftp Servers

Type of Tool	Program Name	Ftp Address	Directory	Filename
Archie	WS-Archie	oak.oakland.edu	simtel/win3/winsock	wsarch08.zip
Chatting	Internet Phone	ftp.vocaltec.com	pub	iphone09.exe
Chatting	mIRC	ftp.demon.co.uk	pub/ibmpc/winsock/apps/mirc	mirc342.zip
Chatting	PowWow	ftp.coast.net	simtel/win3/winsock	powwow15.zip
Chatting	Sesame	ftp.ubique.com	pub/outgoing/pc	install.exe
Chatting	WinTalk	ftp.elf.com	pub/wintalk	wtalk124.zip
Chatting	WS Chat	oak.oakland.edu	simtel/win3/winsock	ws_cha30.zip
Chatting	WS IRC	oak.oakland.edu	simtel/win3/winsock	wsirc20.zip
E-mail	E-Mail Connection	emc.connectsoft.com	pub/emc25	emcsetup.exe
E-mail	Eudora	ftp.qualcomm.com	windows/eudora/1.4	eudor144.exe
E-mail	Ladybird	tpts1.seed.net.tw	UPLOAD/jenwen	lbird12x.exe
E-mail	Pegasus Mail	risc.ua.edu	pub/network/pegasus	winpm201.zip
Finger	IE Finger	ftp.cadvision.com	pub/win	iefng098_complete.zip
Finger	WsFinger	sparky.umd.edu	pub/winsock	wsfngr15.zip
Ftp	IIFTP	aquila.com	pub/ksi	iiftp110.zip
Ftp	WS-FTP32	winftp.cica.indiana.edu	pub/pc/win3/winsock	ws_ftp32.zip
Gopher	BCGopher	bcinfo.bc.edu	ftp/pub/bcgopher	
Gopher	Hgopher	lister.cc.ic.ac.uk	pub/wingopher	hgopher2.3.zip
Gopher	WSGopher	dewey.tis.inel.gov	pub/wsgopher	wsg-12.exe

Type of Tool	Program Name	Ftp Address	Directory	Filename
Newsreader	Free Agent	ftp.forteinc.com	pub/forte/free_agent	fagent10.zip
Newsreader	WinVN	ftp.ksc.nasa.gov	pub/winvn/nt	winvn_99_05_intel.zip
NS Lookup	NSLOOKUP	ftp.demon.co.uk	pub/trumphurst/nslookup	
Ping	WS Ping	oak.oakland.edu	simtel/win3/winsock	ws_ping.zip
Time Synchronizers	TimeSync	ftphost.cac.washington.edu	pub/winsock	tsync1_8.zip
Time Synchronizers	Windows Time Client	sunsite.unc.edu	pub/micro/pc-stuff/ms-windows/winsock/apps	wstim101.zip
WAIS	winWAIS	ftp.einet.net	einet/pc	ewais204.exe
Web Browser	Emissary	www.twg.com	pub	emis_b4.exe
Web Browser	I-Comm	ftp.best.com	pub/icomm/icomm-shell	
Web Browser	Mosaic	ftp.ncsa.uiuc.edu	Mosaic/Windows	mos20b4.exe
Web Browser	Netscape	nyu.edu	nyu-net/apps/windows/netscape	n32e11n.exe
Web Browser	SlipKnot	oak.oakland.edu	SimTel/win3/internet	slnot110.zip
Web Browser	WinWeb	ftp.einet.net	einet/pc/winweb	winweb.zip

Web Sources

Table B-2 lists some Internet tools that are accessible through the World Wide Web. Because the Web is currently the most dynamic area of the Internet, some addresses provided here may have changed since this information was compiled. If that is the case, do not despair. Simply drop the last part of the URL (the part that specifies the filename) and try connecting again. You will often get a message indicating the location of the tool that you are looking for.

Table B-2
Internet Tools Available Through the World Wide Web

Type of Tool	Program Name	URL
Archie	Trumpet Archie	http://www.trumpet.com.au
Chatting	Global Chat	http://www.prospero.com/globalchat.download.html
Chatting	Internet VoiceChat	http://gfecnet.gmi.edu/Software/files/ivc11.zip
Chatting	IRC 4 Client	http://gfecnet.gmi.edu/Software/files/irc4win.zip
Chatting	Worlds Chat	http://www.worlds.net
Chatting	XTalk	http://www.ugrad.cs.ubc.ca/spider/q7f192/bin/xtalk/xtalk04.zip
E-mail	dMail	http://gfecnet.gmi.edu/Software/files/dmailwin.zip
E-mail	E-Mail Connection	http://www.connectsoft.com
E-mail	Eudora	http://www.qualcomm.com/quest
E-mail	Ladybird	http://www.seed.net.tw/~jenwen/ladybird.htm
E-mail	P.O. (Post Office)	http://www.cis.ksu.edu/~novak/po.html
E-mail	Pegasus Mail	http://www.cuslm.ca/pegasus
Finger	C-Finger	http://gfecnet.gmi.edu/Software/files/cfing11.zip
Finger	Xfinger	http://www.ugrad.cs.ubc.ca/spider/q7f192/bin/xfinger/xfing06.zip
Ftp	CuteFTP	http://gfecnet.gmi.edu/Software/files/cftp14b3.zip
Ftp	Trumpet FTP	http://www.trumpet.com.au
Newsreader	News	http://gfecnet.gmi.edu/Software/files/news.zip
Newsreader	News Xpress	http://gfecnet.gmi.edu/Software/files/nx10b4-p.zip
Newsreader	Qnews	http://www.magi.com/~rdavies/qn09a5.zip
Ping	Trumpet Ping	http://www.trumpet.com.au
Web Browser	Air Mosaic Express	http://www.spry.com

Type of Tool	Program Name	URL
Web Browser	Emissary	http://www.twg.com
Web Browser	Mathbrowser	http://www.mathsoft.com/browser/index.html
Whois	WinWhois	http://gfecnet.gmi.edu/Software/files/whois32.zip

Glossary

Administrator. A person or computer program responsible for managing a mailing list. In some mailing lists, the human administrator may also act as a moderator.

Anonymous ftp. A method of using ftp in which you don't need to have an account on the ftp server. During an anonymous ftp session, you use the word *anonymous* as the user ID and your e-mail address as the password.

ARPA. An acronym for the Department of Defense's Advanced Research Projects Agency.

ARPANet. A network developed and sponsored by ARPA and widely viewed as the chief forerunner of the Internet.

Asynchronous communication. A method of data communication in which information is sent over the communication channel as it is ready, without regard to the timing between characters. Each character of data being transferred is enclosed within framing bits, which indicate the start and stop of the data. This overhead means that data throughput is slower than with synchronous modems, but it is less expensive to implement. See also *synchronous communication.*

AUP. An acronym for *acceptable use policy.* A set of guidelines that controls what type of communications can occur through a provider's facilities.

Bang path. An Internet address in which elements of the address are separated by an exclamation point (a bang). These addresses are primarily for use with gateways to other addressing systems, such as Bitnet.

Binding. In a network environment, an association between a protocol and an adapter. Bindings are used to specify which protocols are used with which network adapters.

Bit. A binary digit, the smallest representation of data within a computer. The value of a bit can be 0 or 1, which is equivalent to off or on, respectively.

Bitnet. An older electronic network that has been absorbed into the Internet. Bitnet uses a mailing-list based organization that allows members to receive timely information on a variety of subjects.

Boolean. A branch of mathematics and related fields based on the works of George Boole, an English mathematician. This branch deals with logical expressions, using operators such as AND, OR, NOT, and others, in accordance with set theory and rules.

bps. An acronym meaning *bits per second.* This is a unit of measurement indicating the speed at which information can flow through a communications channel.

Browser. A program that allows you to view information on the World Wide Web. The browser takes care of automatically connecting to resources (as specified by a URL), downloading information, displaying information in the requisite format, and maintaining hypertext links.

Byte. A collection of eight bits. A byte can contain a value between 0 and 255 and is used to represent a single character, such as a letter or number.

Client. A computer or computer program that interacts with a server to procure or use resources that are managed by the server. A client is half of a client/server relationship, in which the client requests resources and the server provides them.

COM. A name assigned to serial ports within a PC. COM is short for communications, and there are up to four COM ports (COM1 through COM4) in a typical PC.

CPU. An acronym for *central processing unit,* which contains the circuitry that is necessary to interpret and execute program instructions.

DHCP. An acronym for *dynamic host configuration protocol.* This is a set of standards by which an IP address can be automatically assigned to a workstation as needed.

DHCP server. A computer that administers DHCP policies within a particular network. It is the responsibility of the DHCP server to assign IP addresses to workstations as they log in and to make sure that the same address is not assigned to more than one workstation. A DHCP server greatly simplifies some network management tasks that had previously been done manually.

Dial-up adapter. A logical network adapter that is used for dial-up network connections.

Dial-Up Networking. A communications service that allows a Windows 95 system to establish a link with a remote computer. Dial-Up Networking can use a variety of communication protocols (such as SLIP or PPP) to manage the communications channel.

DNS. An acronym for *domain naming system.* DNS is used within the Internet to convert human-readable addresses into machine-readable IP addresses.

DNS server. A computer or computer program that is responsible for resolving domain names. The program converts the domain name into an IP address so that the message can be routed across the network.

Domain. An organizational structure that is used in Internet addressing; it is the portion of the address that appears to the right of the @ sign. In the address *jdavis@cwc.com,* the domain is *cwc.com.*

Dotted decimal. A notational format for IP addresses in which each byte of the 32-bit address is written in decimal form, separated by periods. For example, 102.43.8.101 is dotted-decimal notation for an IP address. Dotted-decimal notation may also be referred to as *dotted-quad* notation.

Dotted quad. See *dotted decimal.*

DS1. See *T1.*

DS3. See *T3.*

Electronic mail. See *e-mail.*

e-mail. A contraction of the term *electronic mail.* E-mail is composed of messages and possibly files that are transmitted over a computer network. E-mail is one of the most popular features of the Internet.

Framing bits. The start and stop bits that are attached to every byte transferred over an asynchronous communications channel.

ftp. An acronym for *file transfer protocol,* a program that facilitates file transfers.

Home page. A World Wide Web location that offers a "table of contents" for a group, individual, or organization. The address to a home page is specified by a universal resource locator (URL).

IAB. An acronym for *Internet Architecture Board.* This is a committee within the ISOC that sets technical standards by which the Internet is operated. The IAB relies heavily on the IETF for standards recommendations.

IETF. An acronym for *Internet Engineering Task Force.* The IETF is a committee that functions within the broader umbrella of the ISOC. The IETF is responsible for solving technical issues concerning the Internet. Once issues are solved, the IETF can issue its decisions in the form of suggestions or pass them on to the IAB for formal standardization.

Internet. A contraction of the term *internetwork system* or *interconnected networks.* The term identifies the widely used worldwide connection of computer systems.

Internet provider. An organization that provides a way for you to connect to the Internet. Internet providers can be local, regional, or national in scope, and generally offer a range of services. Different providers charge different fees, and shopping around is a good way to save money.

IP address. The unique 32-bit address that is assigned to a host system attached to the Internet. For humans, IP addresses are typically shown as a series of four numbers separated by periods. Each number represents the value of one byte within the 32-bit address and thus must be between 0 and 255. If a message is routed using a domain name instead of an IP address, the domain name is converted to an IP address by the DNS server.

IRC. An acronym for *Internet Relay Chat,* a method of conducting real-time conversations over the Internet.

IRQ. A contraction for *interrupt request.* This refers to the internal electrical signals in your PC that are used to indicate when a device needs the attention of the CPU.

ISOC. A contraction of *Internet Society,* the group that is responsible for governing how the Internet functions. The ISOC does not exercise any constraint or control except in the technical areas of connecting to and communicating with the Internet.

ITU-T. The *International Telecommunications Union – Telecommunication* sector. This is the international organization that sets standards for the telegraphic and telephone industries; these standards also apply to modems and fax machines.

Listserv. A program that is used to administer a mailing list. Listserv programs are used predominantly on Bitnet, which is accessible through the Internet.

LPT. A name that is assigned to a parallel port in a PC. LPT is short for *line printer,* and a typical PC contains one or two such ports. The first parallel port is designated LPT1, and the second is LPT2.

Lurking. The practice of joining a discussion group (mailing list) or newsgroup and simply reading the information that is available without actively participating.

Mailing list. A list of people who want to receive information about a particular topic on a regular basis. Mailing lists provide an electronic method of forwarding messages to a large number of people on the Internet.

Majordomo. A program that is used to administer a mailing list on the Internet. The program is written in Perl and runs on UNIX-based machines. The name of the program is taken from the name that is given to a servant or person who acts in the stead of another.

MILNet. A network developed by the Department of Defense for military installations. In 1982, MILNet joined ARPANet and other networks to form the Internet.

Moderated. A condition of a mailing list in which the mail that is intended for group recipients is first filtered by a mailing list administrator. The purpose of moderation is to remove any mail that is repetitive, off-topic, or objectionable.

Name resolution. See *resolve.*

Network. A connection between two or more computers that allows information to be shared between them. Networks come in many different types, configurations, and capabilities. Windows 95 includes networking capability as a part of the operating system.

Network adapter. An interface card that is used to communicate with other systems over a network. Without an adapter, you cannot physically connect to the network.

Newsgroup. A BBS-style discussion forum that is accessible through the Internet. To read a newsgroup, you must use a newsreader program.

Newsreader. A program that allows you to read messages that are posted in various newsgroups on the Internet.

NIC. An acronym for *network interface card.* See *network adapter.*

Octet. A single number in an IP address. For example, in the IP address 102.43.8.101, any single number (102, 43, 8, or 101) is an octet.

Organizational domain. A suffix that is attached to a domain name that indicates the category to which the domain name belongs. Common organizational domains are edu (educational institutions), gov (nonmilitary government organizations), com (commercial concerns), mil (U.S. military institutions), int (international organizations), net (network resources), and org (nonprofit organizations).

Packet. A self-contained piece of information. Many networks, including the Internet, rely on information packets to communicate effectively. Packets generally contain a header that indicates the nature of the packet and who it is intended for, as well as the information itself.

Packet-switched network. A networking protocol that uses packets of information as a means of communication. A larger file or message is broken down into smaller packets that are routed over the network toward a destination. At the destination, they are reassembled into the final message.

PC. An acronym for *personal computer.*

Ping. A TCP/IP utility program that allows you to see whether a remote system is actively connected to the Net.

POCIA Directory. A comprehensive list of commercial Internet providers that is maintained by the Celestin Co. POCIA is an acronym for *providers of commercial Internet access.*

PPP. An acronym for *point-to-point protocol,* which is used in Windows 95 for implementing TCP/IP over a dial-up connection.

Protocol. A series of rules, agreements, and conventions that define how communication between two entities (such as computers, people, or organizations) is to effectively take place.

Provider. See *Internet provider.*

RAS. An acronym for *Remote Access Service,* which was used in earlier versions of Windows and in Windows NT. RAS provides a way for physically remote computers to establish a network connection over an ordinary modem link. In Windows 95, RAS has been replaced with Dial-Up Networking, which is available in the Accessories menu.

Relevance feedback. A method of searching that is implemented in WAIS. Relevance feedback relies on progressive refinement of what you are searching for.

Resolve. The process of converting a domain name into an IP address. See also *DNS server.*

Server. A computer or computer program that provides resources to other computers on a network. A server is half of a client/server relationship, in which the client requests resources and the server provides them.

SLIP. An acronym for *serial line Internet protocol,* a protocol for using TCP/IP over a dial-up connection.

Start bits. The bits that are added at the beginning of a character sent over an asynchronous communications channel. Start bits are used to give the receiving modem a warning that a character is arriving.

Stop bits. The bits that are added at the end of a character sent over an asynchronous communications channel. These bits are used to mark the end of the data packet that contains the byte of data.

Supercomputer. A large, high-capacity computer system. Supercomputers are most often used for complex or very lengthy computations. For example, they are often used in atmospheric or space studies.

Synchronous communication. A method of data communication in which the timing of information that is sent to the channel is very tightly controlled. Synchronous communication requires special modems with circuitry to generate the timing signals that are overlaid on the carrier frequency used by the modems. Synchronous modems can transfer data faster than asynchronous modems because they don't need to send framing bits with each character. The downside to synchronous communication is that synchronous modems are more expensive and therefore less widely used. See also *asynchronous communication.*

T1. A wiring specification that, in common use, denotes the type of phone-line connection that is used for data communications. A T1 line is capable of handling approximately 1.544 Mbps of data, which is known as a DS1 level of service. T1 lines are used for high-volume connections to the Internet.

T3. A phone system wiring specification that is used for extremely high-volume data communications needs. A T3 line is capable of handling data at approximately 45 Mbps, which is known as a DS3 level of service. T3 lines, typically made of fiber-optic wire, make up the backbone of the Internet.

TCP/IP. A set of network protocols that defines how communication on the network occurs. The TCP/IP protocols are used on the Internet.

telnet. A TCP/IP protocol program that allows you to connect to other computer systems through the network. Once active, you appear as a terminal to the other computer, and you can interact with the system as if you were sitting at one of its local terminals.

Tracert. A TCP/IP utility program that allows you to determine the approximate electronic route between your system and a remote system.

UART. An acronym for *universal asynchronous receiver/transmitter.* This is the heart of your modem; it performs the task of converting data from digital to analog format and back again.

UNIX. A command-line-oriented operating system that is used on a variety of computers throughout the world. There are several different variations of UNIX, each with its own command set and idiosyncrasies.

URL. An acronym for *universal resource locator.* This is the addressing scheme that is used in the World Wide Web. The URL is composed of a resource type (followed by two slashes), the DNS host name, and a path on that server to the resource itself. For example, http://www.ncsa.uiuc.edu/SDG/Software/WinMosaic/viewers.htm is a URL.

Usenet. A network connected to the Internet that features newsgroups, which allow subscribers to exchange information and views. It is similar to electronic BBSs that flourish in many communities.

User ID. In the Internet addressing scheme, the portion of the address to the left of the @ sign. In the address *jdavis@cwc.com,* the user ID is *jdavis.*

WAIS. An acronym for *Wide Area Information Server.* WAIS is an Internet tool that allows you to access widely distributed information from a relatively centralized source. It was a predecessor to the WWW but never caught on well.

Web. A nickname for the World Wide Web. See *WWW.*

Web browser. See *browser.*

WINS. An acronym for *Windows Internet name service.* This protocol is used to translate between an IP address and the name by which the workstation is known to the Windows network. WINS works hand in hand with DHCP to ensure that information is routed to the proper workstation.

WWW. An acronym for *World Wide Web,* an Internet protocol that allows information to be searched, accessed, and downloaded to the user in an easy-to-use manner. The Web consists of a series of servers, where information is dynamically interlinked. You access a Web server by using a Web browser; one of the most popular browsers is Mosaic, which is available as freeware.

Index

Note: Page numbers in refer to charts, illustrations, and listings.

✦ Symbols & Numbers ✦

32-bit vs. 16-bit programs, 231–232
56-kilobit channels, phone lines and Internet service providers, 43
* (asterisk), as wildcard character in ftp, 218
/ (slash), in IRC commands, 323
! (bang)
  bang paths, 175–176, 401
  in ftp, 221
  mailing list gateways, 175–176
? (question mark), as wildcard character in ftp, 218
@ (at symbol), domain names, 21, 82

✦ A ✦

acceptable use policies (AUPs)
  defined, 401
  Internet service providers, 37, 38
access numbers, Microsoft Network, 330, 335–336
accounts, Microsoft Network, 335–336
Add/Remove Programs Properties dialog box, 83, 89
addresses
  assigning, 25–26
  converting Bitnet, 175
  DNS (domain naming system), 21–24
  domain naming, 20–21
  e-mail, 135–136
  Gopher, 253
  IP structure, 26–30
  mailing list, 171, 172, 175–176
  Microsoft Network, 346–347
  news servers, 304
  online system conversions, 136
  ping command, 115, 116
  resolving, 27
administrators, defined, 401
algorithms, error correction, 52–53
America Online, address conversions, 136
analog/digital conversions, modems and phone lines, 50
anonymous ftp, 214, 215, 401
Archie, 233–238
  adding to Internet Tools menu, 234–235
  directory navigation, 238
  Domain field, 237
  downloading client, 233
  installing, 233–235
  as Internet tool, 229
  running WS-Archie, 235–238
  servers, 236
  uncompressing files, 233–234
  WS-Archie program window, 236
ARPA, defined, 401
ARPANet
  defined, 401
  history of Internet, 8–9
ascii file transfers, ftp, 221
asterisk (*), as wildcard character in ftp, 218
asynchronous communication, defined, 401
attachments
See also e-mail; messages; Microsoft Exchange
  e-mail, 137–138, 145–146, 147
  extracted files, 146, 147
  Message Attachments dialog box, 146
  Microsoft Exchange, 162–164
attributes, ftp, 219
AUPs (acceptable use policies)
  defined, 401
  Internet service providers, 37, 38

✦ B ✦

bangs (!)
  bang paths, 175–176, 401
  in ftp, 221
  mailing list gateways, 175–176
binary file transfers, ftp, 221
bindings
  defined, 401
  TCP/IP properties, 80–81
  TCP/IP protocols, 76
bis, defined, 51
Bitnet, defined, 402
Bitnet addresses, converting for mailing
  lists, 175
bits, defined, 402
bookmarks, Gopher, 256–262
Boolean logic
  defined, 402
  WAIS and, 266–267
bps (bits per second)
  defined, 402
  modems and, 51
browsers. *See* Web browsers
Buffer Size setting, telnet, 190
bytes, defined, 402

✦ C ✦

call waiting disablement
  Dial-Up Networking, *113*
  modems, 66
calling cards, Change Calling Card dialog
  box, *67*
Canadian and U.S. Internet service providers,
  354–389
Categories area, Microsoft Network, 340
CC: field, e-mail, 136
Celestin Co., POCIA directory, 35, 353
channels, phone lines, and Internet service
  providers, 43
Chat screens, Microsoft Network, *344*
chat. *See* IRC (Internet Relay Chat)
classes, IP address structure, 26–27
clients
See also servers
  Archie, 229
  defined, 402
  e-mail, 126
  ftp, 230
  Gopher, 230
  Microsoft Exchange, 148–149

Microsoft Plus! Companion for Windows 95,
  126, 154–159
  network, 72
  WAIS, 267–273
  whois, 231
COM
  defined, 402
  port conflicts, 58
command-line switches
  ftp command, *210*
  ping command, *116*
  tracert command, *118*
commercial software, tools, 232
communications
See also e-mail; Microsoft Exchange; modems
  asynchronous, 401
  Internet, 14
  serial, 49–54
  synchronous, 407
  telnet, 185–208
Communications Options dialog box,
  newsreaders, 306
Communications Port Properties dialog box,
  modem installation, *56*
compressing files. *See* PKZIP
CompuServe, address conversions, *136*
configuration profiles, Microsoft Exchange,
  160–161
configuring
  e-mail software, 129–132
  Internet clients, 157–159
  mIRC software, 317–319
  Windows 95 for Internet, 71–85
Connect dialog box, telnet, *195*
Connect To dialog box, Dial-Up
  Networking, *103*
Connected To Internet dialog box, Dial-Up
  Networking, 110–112
connecting to
  ftp servers, 213–216
  Gopher servers, 246–253, *254*
  IRC servers, 319–320, *321*
  Microsoft Network, 338
  remote sites, telnet, 194–203
  WAIS clients, 267–273
connection technology basics, 17–32
  connection protocols, 30–31
  connection requirements, 15
  DHCP (Dynamic Host Configuration
    Protocol), 28–29
  DNS (domain naming system), 21–24
  domain naming, 20–21
  how addresses are assigned, 25–26

IP address structure, 26–30
packet-switched networking, 17–19
summary, 32
TCP/IP, 19–26
TCP/IP workstation requirements, 28
WINS (Windows Internet Name Service),
    29–30
connection types, Internet service providers,
    39–44
connections
  Dial-Up Networking, 101–113
  mail server, 164
  telnet, 197–198
CPU, defined, 402
credit card payments, Microsoft Network,
    333, *334*

✦ D ✦

data compression, modems, 53
database services, how addresses are
    assigned, 25
dedicated service, 41–44
  dial-up comparison, 45
  phone lines, 42–43
  routers, 42
  servers, 43–44
default gateway address, IP address
    structure, 28
deleting e-mail messages, 144
Details button, Dial-Up Networking, 111–112
DHCP (Dynamic Host Configuration Protocol),
    28–29, 402
DHCP servers, defined, 402
diagnostics, modem, 68–70
dial-up adapter
  adding to Windows 95, 72–74
  defined, 402
Dial-Up Networking, 87–100, 101–121
  call waiting disablement, 66, *113*
  configuring definitions, 94–98
  Connect To dialog box, *103*
  Connected To Internet dialog box, 110–112
  connecting to service providers, 104–105
  defined, 403
  defining dial-up connections, 91–93
  described, 87–88
  Details button, 111–112
  dialing-related properties, 95–96
  disconnection troubleshooting, *113*
  ending sessions, 118, *119*
  establishing connections, 101–113

first calls, 101–121
installing, 88–89
Internet utilities, 113–118
login problems, *106*
Make New Connection dialog box, *92, 93, 94*
passwords, 103–104
paying for, 119–120
renaming and deleting definitions, 99–100
server-related properties, 96–98
setting up, 90–98
shortcuts for, 120–121
SLIP and, 98, 109–110
status box, 111–112
summary, 100, 121
terminal windows, 102–103, 106–108
dial-up service, 40–41, 45
dialing properties, modem, 65–67
directory navigation
  Archie, 238
  ftp, 217–219, *220*
Directory Services, how addresses are
    assigned, 25
disconnecting from sessions, Internet service
    providers, 118, *119*
disconnection troubleshooting, Dial-Up
    Networking, *113*
discussion groups, mailing lists, 170, 171–172,
    177–178
DNS (domain naming system), 21–24
  defined, 403
  geographic domains, 23–24
  how addresses are assigned, 25–26
  organizational domains, 22
  TCP/IP properties, 81–82
DNS servers, defined, 403
Domain field, Archie, 237
domain names
  @ symbol, 21, 82
  TCP/IP, 20–21
domains, defined, 403
dotted decimals
See also IP address structure
  defined, 403
downloading
  Archie clients, 233
  e-mail software, 127
  files while browsing, 238
  Gopher clients, 242–243
  IRC software, 315–316
  newsreaders, 300–301
  tools, 238
  Web browsers, 280–281
DS1 & DS3. *See* T1 & T3 channels

✦ E ✦

e-mail, 125–167
See also messages; Microsoft Exchange
  accumulating in Inbox folder, 145
  addressing, 135–136
  attachments, 137–138, 145–146, *147*
  CC: field, 136
  clients, 126
  composing messages, 134–138
  configuring software, 129–132
  defined, 403
  deleting messages, 144
  described, 125–126
  downloading software, 127
  E-Mail Connection, 127–132
  E-Mail Connection interface, 133–134
  extracted files, 146, *147*
  forwarding messages, 140–141, *142*
  headers, 147–148
  Inbox folder, 140–145
  incoming, 140–145
  installing software, 127–129
  Internet connections, 138–139
  Internet Mail Setup dialog box, *132*
  Internet tools, 230
  mailing lists, 169–183
  Message Attachments dialog box, *146*
  message parts, 147–148
  message templates, *142, 143*
  Microsoft Exchange, 148–166
  Microsoft Network, 340, 346–347
  New User Information dialog box, *131*
  printing messages, 144
  reading, 139–148
  replying to messages, 141–143
  software, 126–134
  Subject: field, 136
  summary, 167
  To: field, 136
  typing messages, 137
Echo option, telnet, *198*
Emulation section, telnet, 189
error correction, modem, 52–53
external modems
  bottleneck caveat, 52
  installing, 58–59
extracted files, e-mail attachments, 146, *147*

✦ F ✦

Favorite Places, Microsoft Network, 340
Fetch this Gopher Item dialog box, *252*, 253
56-kilobit channels, phone lines and Internet
    service providers, 43
file libraries, Microsoft Network, 344, *345*
filenames, ftp and, 219
files
  downloading while browsing, 238
  extracted, 146, *147*
  transferring via ftp, 221–223
  uncompressing, 233–234, 239
finding
See also searching
  ftp servers, 225
  information on World Wide Web, 290–291,
    292
  mailing lists, 172
  telnet servers, 203–207
  tools, 229–240
finger command, Internet tools, 230
folder navigation
  Archie, 238
  ftp, 217–219, *220*
folders, Microsoft Exchange and, 164
Font dialog box, telnet, 190–191
forums, Microsoft Network, 342–344
forwarding e-mail messages, 140–141, *142*
framing bits, defined, 403
freeware tools, 232
ftp (file transfer protocol), 209–226
  ! (bang), 221
  anonymous status, 214, 215
  ascii file transfers, 221
  attributes, 219
  binary file transfers, 221
  case sensitivity, *222*
  cd command, 219, *220*
  clients, 230
  command-line switches, *210*
  commands, *211–213*, 216–217
  commands that affect ftp servers, 224
  connecting to servers, 213–216
  connection problems, *215*
  defined, 403
  described, 209–210
  dir command, 217
  directory navigation, 217–219, *220*

disconnecting from, 225
downloading files while browsing, 238
filenames and, 219
finding servers, 225
get command, 221, *222*, 223
hash marks, 221
help command, 216–217
help files, 220–221
index files, 220–221
IRC software sites, *315*
lcd command, 223
ls command, 218
mget command, 221
pwd command, 219, *220*
rcv command, 221
renaming files while transferring, 223
sources for Windows 95 tools, 395, *396–397*
starting client, 210–211
summary, 226
transferring files, 221–223
type command, *222*
wildcard characters, 218
full access accounts, Internet service
    providers, 39

✦ G ✦

gateways
  IP address structure, 28
  TCP/IP properties, 78–79
geographic domains, DNS, 23–24
get command, ftp, 221, *222*, 223
Go words, Microsoft Network, 341, *342*
Gopher, 241–263
  addresses, *253*
  bookmarks, 256–262
  clients, 230, 242–245
  connecting to Gopher servers, 246–253, *254*
  described, 241–242
  downloading clients, 242–243
  Fetch this Gopher Item dialog box, *252*, 253
  Home Gophers, 246, 250–252
  icons, 248
  installing clients, 243–245
  interface, 247–248
  main screen, *247*
  menus, 247–248, *249*
  requirements, 242–245
  resources, *249*

saving information, 255–256
searching for information via, 254–255
shortcut to, 244–245, *246*
status bar, 248
summary, 263
temporary Gopher servers, 252–253, *254*

✦ H ✦

hash marks, ftp, 221
headers, e-mail, 147–148
Home Gophers, 246, 250–252
home pages
  defined, 403
  World Wide Web, 287
host names, telnet, 195
http:// (URLs), Web browsers, 285
hypertext links, World Wide Web, 287–288

✦ I ✦

IAB (Internet Architecture Board), 10–11
  defined, 403
  future of IP addressing, 30
icons
  Gopher, 248
  this book's, 4
Ident Server command, IRC, 318–319
IETF, defined, 404
Inbox folders
  e-mail, 140–145
  Microsoft Exchange, 165–166
Inbox Setup Wizard, Microsoft Exchange,
    150–153
index files, ftp, 220–221
indexes, WAIS, 266
information, Internet, 14
INI files, newsreader, 304, *305*
Install New Modem dialog box, *61*
installing
  Archie, 233–235
  Dial-Up Networking, 88–89
  e-mail software, 127–129
  Gopher clients, 243–245
  Internet client for Microsoft Exchange,
      154–157
  IRC software, 316–317
  Microsoft Exchange, 149–153

(continued)

Installing (continued)
  Microsoft Network, 329–330
  modems, 54–59
  newsreaders, 301–303
  TCP/IP protocols, 74–76
  tools, 238–239
  Web browsers, 281–282, 283
internal modems, installing, 54–58
international service providers, 389–394
Internet
See also networks
  chatting on. See IRC (Internet Relay Chat)
  client, 154–159
  communication, 14
  configuring Windows 95 for, 71–85
  Connected To Internet dialog box, 110–112
  connection requirements, 15
  defined, 404
  e-mail connections, 138–139
  finding tools on, 229–240
  history of, 8–10
  IAB (Internet Architecture Board), 10–11
  information, 14
  Internet Mail Setup dialog box, 132
  ISOC (Internet Society), 10–11
  Microsoft Exchange and, 160–166
  Microsoft Network and, 346–348
  multimedia on, 293
  overview, 7–16
  POCIA (providers of Commercial Internet access), 35
  reasons to connect to, 12–14
  Relay Chat. See IRC (Internet Relay Chat)
  resources, 13–14
  service providers, 33–47
  summary, 16
  UNIX and, 11–12
  utilities, 113–118
  who pays for, 11
  who runs, 10–11
  Windows 95 tools on, 395–399
InterNIC
  how addresses are assigned, 25–26
  whois servers, 203–205
IP address structure, 26–30
  classes of, 26–27
  defined, 404
  DHCP, 28–29
  future of, 30
  gateways, 28
  octets, 26
  resolution, 27
  subnet mask, 28

  TCP/IP properties, 78
  WINS, 29–30
IRC (Internet Relay Chat), 314–324
  / (slash) in commands, 323
  chatting with others, 323
  chatting tools, 230
  commands, 321–323
  configuring mIRC software, 317–319
  connecting to IRC servers, 319–320, 321
  defined, 404
  downloading software, 315–316
  ftp software sites, 315
  Ident Server command, 318–319
  installing IRC software, 316–317
  JOIN command, 322, 323
  LIST command, 321, 323
  PKZIP, 316–317
  QUIT command, 322, 324
  Setup dialog box, 317–318
  Summary, 325
  World Wide Web software sites, 316
IRQs
  COM port conflicts, 58
  defined, 404
ISOC (Internet Society), 10–11, 404
ITU-T, defined, 404

✦ J ✦

JOIN command, IRC, 322, 323
joining mailing lists, 173–177

✦ K ✦

key words, whois servers, 204, 205
kiosks, Microsoft Network, 343–344, 345

✦ L ✦

LANs, Microsoft Exchange and, 151
LAP-M error correction, modems, 53
LawNet, telnet and, 199
libraries, Microsoft Network, 344, 345
limited access accounts, Internet service providers, 39
LIST command, IRC, 321, 323
Listserv
  defined, 404
  mailing lists, 170–171, 174–176, 178–179, 181

Local Echo option, telnet, *198*
log files, telnet, 201–202
login problems, Dial-Up Networking, *106*
LPT, defined, 404
lurking
  defined, 404
  in mailing lists, 178
Lycos search tool, World Wide Web, 291, *292*

✦ M ✦

mail. *See* e-mail; Microsoft Exchange
mail server connections, Microsoft
    Exchange, 164
mailing lists, 169–183
  ! (bang), 175–176
  addresses, *171*, 172, 175–176
  administration of, 170–172
  automatic management of, 170–171
  canceling subscriptions to, 180–182
  defined, 404
  described, 169–170
  discussion groups, 170, 171–172, 177–178
  finding, 172
  human management of, 171, 177, 180, 182
  joining, 173–177
  Listserv, 170–171, 174–176, 178–179, 181
  lurking in, 178
  Majordomo, 170–171, 176–177, 179–180, 181
  managing subscriptions to, 178–180
  moderated vs. unmoderated, 171–172
  signature files, *176*
  subscribing to, 173–177
  summary, 183
Majordomo
  defined, 405
  mailing lists, 170–171, 176–177, 179–180, 181
Make New Connection dialog box, Dial-Up
    Networking, *92*, *93*, *94*
Member Assistance, Microsoft Network, 340
Member IDs, Microsoft Network, 336, *337*, 338
menus. *See Under specific application*
Message Attachments dialog box, e-mail, *146*
message templates
  e-mail, *142*, *143*
  Microsoft Exchange, 162, *163*
messages
See also attachments; e-mail; Microsoft
    Exchange
  e-mail, 134–138, 140–145
  Microsoft Exchange, 162–166
  newsreader, 310–313

Microsoft Exchange
See also attachments; e-mail; messages
  attachments, 162–164
  clients, 148–149
  configuration profiles, 160–161
  configuring Internet client, 157–159
  e-mail and, 148–159
  folders and, 164
  Inbox folder, 165–166
  Inbox Setup Wizard, 150–153
  installing, 149–153
  installing Internet client, 154–157
  Internet and, 160–166
  LANs and, 151
  mail server connections, 164
  message templates, 162, *163*
  messages, 162–164
  post offices, 148, 151–152
  reading messages, 165–166
Microsoft Network, 327–350
  access numbers, 330, 335–336
  addresses, 346–347
  Categories area, 340
  Chat screens, *344*
  connecting to, 338
  credit card payments, 333, *334*
  disconnecting from, 348–349
  e-mail, 340, 346–347
  establishing accounts, 335–336
  Favorite Places, 340
  file libraries, 344, *345*
  forums, 342–344
  Go words, 341, *342*
  installing software, 329–330
  Internet access, 346–348
  Internet e-mail, 346–347
  joining, 328
  kiosks, 343–344, *345*
  libraries, 344, *345*
  Member Assistance, 340
  Member IDs, 336, *337*, 338
  MSN Central, 339–340
  MSN Today, 339
  navigating through, 340–341
  newsgroups, 347–348
  passwords, 336, *337*, 338
  phone numbers, 330, 335–336
  rules of use, 333–335
  shortcuts, 340
  sign-up forms, 331–335
  summary, 350
Microsoft Plus! Companion for Windows 95,
    client software, 126, 154–159

MILNet, defined, 405
mIRC software. *See* IRC (Internet Relay Chat)
MNP-*x* error correction algorithms, 52–53
modems, 49–70
  adding to Windows 95, 59–67
  analog/digital conversions, 50
  bis standards, 51
  bps (bits per second), 51
  call waiting disablement, 66, *113*
  Change Calling Card dialog box, *67*
  COM port conflicts, 58
  data compression, 53
  defined and described, 50
  determining need for, 53–54
  diagnostics, 68–70
  dialing properties, 65–67
  error correction, 52–53
  external bottlenecks, 52
  installing external, 58–59
  installing internal, 54–58
  LAP-M error correction, 53
  MNP-*x* error correction, 52–53
  ping command, 115
  properties, *60*, 62–65
  protocols, 51
  serial communications, 49–54
  speeds of, 50–52
  summary, 70
  tone vs. pulse dialing, 66
  UART chips, 50, 52
  Verify Modem dialog box, *62*
  V.*x* modulation standards, 51, 53
Modems Properties dialog box, *60*
moderated, defined, 405
Mosaic. *See* Web browsers
MSN Central, Microsoft Network, 339–340
MSN Today, Microsoft Network, 339
multimedia on Internet, World Wide Web, 293

✦ N ✦

netinfo service, finding telnet servers, 206–207
netnews, 299
networking
  Dial-Up Networking, 87–100, 101–121
  packet-switched, 17–19
networks
See also Internet
  adapters, 72, 405
  clients, 72
  defined, 405
  DHCP, 28–29
  Microsoft Network, 327–350

Network dialog box, *73*
  protocols, 72
New User Information dialog box, e-mail, *131*
newsgroups, 297–313
  articles, 313
  categories, 299–300
  defined, 405
  Microsoft Network, 347–348
  netnews, 299
  newsfeeds, 298
  newsreaders. *See* newsreaders
  overview, 297–299
  posting messages, 313
  subscribing to and unsubscribing from,
    308–309
  summary, 325
  threads, 313
NEWSRC file, newsreaders, *305*, 306
newsreaders, 298, 300–313
  addresses, 304
  articles, 313
  Communications Options dialog box, 306
  defined, 405
  downloading, 300–301
  first time use, 304–307
  INI file, 304, *305*
  installing, 301–303
  interface, 309–310
  Internet tools, 230
  menus, 309–310
  messages, 310–313
  NEWSRC file, *305*, 306
  Personal Information dialog box, 307
  PKZIP, 301–302
  reading news, 310–313
  shortcuts, 302–303, *304*
  threads, 313
  toolbar, 310
NIC, defined, 405
NorthWestNet, acceptable use policy, *38*
NS-lookup, Internet tools, 230

✦ O ✦

octets
  defined, 405
  IP address structure, 26
online systems, address conversions, *136*
organizational domains
  defined, 405
  DNS, 22

✦ P ✦

packet-switched networks, 17–19, 405
packets
  defined, 405
  parts of, 18
passwords
  Dial-Up Networking, 103–104
  Microsoft Network, 336, *337*, 338
PCs, defined, 406
phone lines, dedicated service, 42–43
phone numbers, Microsoft Network, 330,
  335–336
ping command, 113–116
  addresses, *116*
  bad addresses, *115*
  command-line switches, *116*
  defined, 406
  as Internet tool, 230
  modem speeds, 115
PKZIP
  uncompressing Archie software, 233–234, 239
  uncompressing IRC software, 316–317
  uncompressing newsreaders, 301–302
POCIA directory
  Celestin Co., 35, 353
  defined, 406
port types, telnet, 195–196
post offices, Microsoft Exchange, 148, 151–152
posting messages, newsgroups, 313
PPP (Point-to-Point Protocol)
  connection protocols, 31
  defined, 406
  Internet service providers and, 41
printing e-mail messages, 144
Prodigy, address conversions, *136*
protocols
  connection, 30–31
  defined, 406
  dial-up adapters, 72
  file transfer. *See* ftp
  modem, 51
  network, 72
  Point-to-Point. *See* PPP
  TCP/IP, 19–26, 74–76
providers. *See* service providers (Internet)
pulse dialing vs. tone dialing, 66

✦ Q ✦

question mark (?), as wildcard character in
  ftp, 218

✦ R ✦

RAS, defined, 406
reading
  e-mail messages, 139–148
  Microsoft Exchange messages, 165–166
  news via newsreaders, 310–313
reference sites, World Wide Web, *293*
Registration Services, how addresses are
  assigned, 25
relevence feedback
  defined, 406
  WAIS, 267, 273
Remote System option, telnet, 194–195
resolving
  defined, 406
  IP address structures, 27
resources
  Gopher and, *249*
  Internet, 13–14
routers, dedicated service and, 42

✦ S ✦

searching
See also finding
  via Archie, 236–238
  via Gopher, 254–255
  via WAIS, 265–278
Select Network Adapter dialog box, *74*
Select Network Component Type dialog box,
  75, 76
serial communications, 49–54
servers
See also clients
  Archie, 236
  dedicated service, 43–44
  defined, 406
  finding ftp, 225
  ftp, 213–216
  Gopher, 246–253, *254*
  IRC, 319–320, *321*
  mail, 164
  news, 304
  properties, 96–98
  telnet, 203–207
  temporary Gopher, 252–253, *254*
  Wide Area Information. *See* WAIS
service providers (Internet), 33–47, 353–394
  acceptable use policies, 37, *38*
  connection types, 39–44
  cost of, 44

(continued)

service providers *(continued)*
dedicated service, 41–44, 45
defined, 33–34
Dial-Up Networking, 104–105
dial-up service, 40–41, 45
full access accounts, 39
importance of, 34
international, 389–394
limited access accounts, 39
nationwide, 353–354
overview, 11
phone lines, 42–43
PPP service, 41
requirements from, 46
routers, 42
selecting, 45–46
servers and, 43–44
service types, 37–39
shell accounts, 40–41
SLIP service, 41
summary, 47
toll-free access, *36*
U.S. and Canadian, 354–389
where to find, 34–36
sessions, ending, 118, *119*
shareware tools, 232
shell accounts, Internet service providers,
40–41
shortcuts
Dial-Up Networking, 120–121
Gopher, 244–245, *246*
Microsoft Network, 340
newsreader, 302–303, *304*
telnet, 192–193, *194*
signature files, mailing lists, *176*
SLIP (Serial Line Internet Protocol)
adding support to Windows 95, 83–84
connection protocols, 31
defined, 406
Dial-Up Networking and, 98, 109–110
Internet service providers and, 41
software. *See specific applications*
start bits, defined, 406
status box, Dial-Up Networking, 111–112
stop bits, defined, 406
Subject: field, e-mail, 136
subnet masks, IP address structure, 28
subscribing to
mailing lists, 173–180
newsgroups, 308–309
supercomputers, defined, 406
synchronous communication, defined, 407
System Properties dialog box, modem
installation, *55*

✦ T ✦

T1 & T3 channels
defined, 407
phone lines and Internet service
providers, 43
TCP/IP, 19–26
bindings, 76, 80–81
defined, 407
domain naming, 20–21
overview, 19–20
protocol installation, 74–76
Select Network Component Type dialog box,
75, 76
workstation requirements, 28
TCP/IP properties, 77–82
bindings, 76, 80–81
DNS configuration, 81–82
gateways, 78–79
IP addresses, 78
WINS configuration, 79–80
telnet, 185–208
adding to Windows 95 menu system,
191–193, *194*
Buffer Size setting, 190
commands, 187–188
Connect dialog box, *195*
connecting to remote sites, 194–203
Create Shortcut Wizard, 192–193, *194*
defined, 407
described, 185–186
disconnecting from, 202–203
Echo option, *198*
Emulation section, 189
finding servers, 203–207
Font dialog box, 190–191
gibberish on screen, *200*
host names, 195
interface, *187*
interface color, 191
Internet tools, 230
LawNet, *199*
Local Echo option, *198*
log files, 201–202
making connections, 197–198
menus, 187–188
netinfo service, 206–207
port types, 195–196
preferences, 188–191
Remote System option, 194–195
servers, 203–207

summary, 208
Terminal Options section, 190
Terminal Preferences dialog box, *189*
terminal types, 196–197
UNIX and, *200*
WAIS and, 267
whois servers, 203–205
Terminal Options section, telnet, 190
Terminal Preferences dialog box, telnet, *189*
terminal types, telnet, 196–197
terminal windows, Dial-Up Networking,
    102–103, 106–108
time synchronizers, Internet tools, 231
To: field, e-mail, 136
toll-free access, Internet service providers, *36*
tone dialing vs. pulse dialing, 66
tools, 229–240
  availability listing, 229–231
  commercial software, 232
  cost of, 232–233
  downloading, 238
  finding with Archie, 233–238
  freeware, 232
  ftp sources, 395, *396–397*
  installing, 238–239
  shareware, 232
  summary, 240
  Windows 95, 231–232, 395–399
tracert command, 117–118
  command-line switches, *118*
  defined, 407
transferring files via ftp, 221–223
typing e-mail messages, 137

UART chips
  defined, 407
  modems and, 50, 52
uncompressing files. *See* PKZIP
UNIX
  defined, 407
  Internet and, 11–12
  SLIP and, 31
  telnet and, *200*
URLs (Universal Resource Locators)
  defined, 407
  Web browsers and, 285
U.S. and Canadian service providers (Internet),
    354–389

Usenet
See also newsgroups
  defined, 407
User ID, defined, 408
utilities, Internet, 113–118

Verify Modem dialog box, *62*
viewers, Web browsers and, 286–287
V.*x* modulation standards, modems, 51, 53

✦ **W** ✦

WAIS (Wide Area Information Servers),
    265–278
  Boolean logic, 266–267
  commands, 275–276
  connecting to clients, 267–273
  defined, 408
  described, 265–266
  interface, 268, *269*
  Lines column, 271
  quitting, 277
  refining searches, 271–272
  relevence feedback, 267, 273
  retrieving documents, 275
  Score column, 270, *271*
  screen control keys, *269*
  Search Results screen, 270–271, *274*
  searching via, 266–267, 270–272
  Source Selection screen, 268, *269*
  summary, 278
  telnet and, 267
Web browsers, 280–286
  See also World Wide Web
  address fields, 284
  addresses, 285
  defined, 402
  display area, 285
  downloading, 280–281
  downloading files while browsing, 238
  http:// (URLs), 285
  installing, 281–282, *283*
  as Internet tool, 231
  menu bar, 284
  toolbar, 284
  URLs, 285
  using, 284–287
  viewers, 286–287

whois clients, Internet tools, 231
whois servers, finding telnet servers, 203–205
wildcard characters, ftp, 218
Windows 95
  32-bit vs. 16-bit programs, 231–232
  Add/Remove Programs Properties dialog
    box, *83, 89*
  dial-up adapters, 72–74
  ftp and, 209–226
  ftp sources for tools, 395, *396–397*
  Internet configuration, 71–85
  Microsoft Exchange, 148–166
  Microsoft Network, 327–350
  Microsoft Plus! Companion, 126
  modem installation, 59–67
  SLIP support, 83–84
  telnet and, 185–208
  tools, 231–232, 395–399
WINS (Windows Internet Name Service), 29–30
  configuring, 79–80
  defined, 408
WinVN 32-bit newsreader. *See* newsreaders
workstation requirements, TCP/IP, 28
World Wide Web, 279–296
  described, 279–280
  display speed, 293–294, *296*
  downloading Web browsers, 280–281
  file formats for Mosaic viewers, *286–287*
  finding information on, 290–291, *292*
  home pages, 287
  hypertext links, 287–288
  images toggle, 294
  IRC software sites, *316*
  Lycos search tool, 291, *292*
  multimedia on Internet, 293
  organization of, 287–291
  reference sites, *293*
  requirements, 280–283
  summary, 296
  viewers, 286–287
  Web browsers, 280–286
  Windows 95 tools available through, *398–399*
  Yahoo search tool, 290
WS-Archie. *See* Archie
WSGopher. *See* Gopher
WWW. *See* World Wide Web

✦ Y ✦

Yahoo search tool, World Wide Web, 290

DUMMIES PRESS

12/20/94

Title	Author	ISBN	Price
INTERNET / COMMUNICATIONS / NETWORKING			
CompuServe For Dummies™	by Wallace Wang	1-56884-181-7	$19.95 USA/$26.95 Canada
Modems For Dummies™, 2nd Edition	by Tina Rathbone	1-56884-223-6	$19.99 USA/$26.99 Canada
Modems For Dummies™	by Tina Rathbone	1-56884-001-2	$19.95 USA/$26.95 Canada
MORE Internet For Dummies™	by John R. Levine & Margaret Levine Young	1-56884-164-7	$19.95 USA/$26.95 Canada
NetWare For Dummies™	by Ed Tittel & Deni Connor	1-56884-003-9	$19.95 USA/$26.95 Canada
Networking For Dummies™	by Doug Lowe	1-56884-079-9	$19.95 USA/$26.95 Canada
ProComm Plus 2 For Windows For Dummies™	by Wallace Wang	1-56884-219-8	$19.99 USA/$26.99 Canada
The Internet For Dummies™, 2nd Edition	by John R. Levine & Carol Baroudi	1-56884-222-8	$19.99 USA/$26.99 Canada
The Internet For Macs For Dummies™	by Charles Seiter	1-56884-184-1	$19.95 USA/$26.95 Canada
MACINTOSH			
Macs For Dummies®	by David Pogue	1-56884-173-6	$19.95 USA/$26.95 Canada
Macintosh System 7.5 For Dummies™	by Bob LeVitus	1-56884-197-3	$19.95 USA/$26.95 Canada
MORE Macs For Dummies™	by David Pogue	1-56884-087-X	$19.95 USA/$26.95 Canada
PageMaker 5 For Macs For Dummies™	by Galen Gruman	1-56884-178-7	$19.95 USA/$26.95 Canada
QuarkXPress 3.3 For Dummies™	by Galen Gruman & Barbara Assadi	1-56884-217-1	$19.99 USA/$26.99 Canada
Upgrading and Fixing Macs For Dummies™	by Kearney Rietmann & Frank Higgins	1-56884-189-2	$19.95 USA/$26.95 Canada
MULTIMEDIA			
Multimedia & CD-ROMs For Dummies™, Interactive Multimedia Value Pack	by Andy Rathbone	1-56884-225-2	$29.95 USA/$39.95 Canada
Multimedia & CD-ROMs For Dummies™	by Andy Rathbone	1-56884-089-6	$19.95 USA/$26.95 Canada
OPERATING SYSTEMS / DOS			
MORE DOS For Dummies™	by Dan Gookin	1-56884-046-2	$19.95 USA/$26.95 Canada
S.O.S. For DOS™	by Katherine Murray	1-56884-043-8	$12.95 USA/$16.95 Canada
OS/2 For Dummies™	by Andy Rathbone	1-878058-76-2	$19.95 USA/$26.95 Canada
UNIX			
UNIX For Dummies™	by John R. Levine & Margaret Levine Young	1-878058-58-4	$19.95 USA/$26.95 Canada
WINDOWS			
S.O.S. For Windows™	by Katherine Murray	1-56884-045-4	$12.95 USA/$16.95 Canada
MORE Windows 3.1 For Dummies™, 3rd Edition	by Andy Rathbone	1-56884-240-6	$19.99 USA/$26.99 Canada
PCs / HARDWARE			
Illustrated Computer Dictionary For Dummies™	by Dan Gookin, Wally Wang, & Chris Van Buren	1-56884-004-7	$12.95 USA/$16.95 Canada
Upgrading and Fixing PCs For Dummies™	by Andy Rathbone	1-56884-002-0	$19.95 USA/$26.95 Canada
PRESENTATION / AUTOCAD			
AutoCAD For Dummies™	by Bud Smith	1-56884-191-4	$19.95 USA/$26.95 Canada
PowerPoint 4 For Windows For Dummies™	by Doug Lowe	1-56884-161-2	$16.95 USA/$22.95 Canada
PROGRAMMING			
Borland C++ For Dummies™	by Michael Hyman	1-56884-162-0	$19.95 USA/$26.95 Canada
"Borland's New Language Product" For Dummies™	by Neil Rubenking	1-56884-200-7	$19.95 USA/$26.95 Canada
C For Dummies™	by Dan Gookin	1-878058-78-9	$19.95 USA/$26.95 Canada
C++ For Dummies™	by Stephen R. Davis	1-56884-163-9	$19.95 USA/$26.95 Canada
Mac Programming For Dummies™	by Dan Parks Sydow	1-56884-173-6	$19.95 USA/$26.95 Canada
QBasic Programming For Dummies™	by Douglas Hergert	1-56884-093-4	$19.95 USA/$26.95 Canada
Visual Basic "X" For Dummies™, 2nd Edition	by Wallace Wang	1-56884-230-9	$19.99 USA/$26.99 Canada
Visual Basic 3 For Dummies™	by Wallace Wang	1-56884-076-4	$19.95 USA/$26.95 Canada
SPREADSHEET			
1-2-3 For Dummies™	by Greg Harvey	1-878058-60-6	$16.95 USA/$21.95 Canada
1-2-3 For Windows 5 For Dummies™, 2nd Edition	by John Walkenbach	1-56884-216-3	$16.95 USA/$21.95 Canada
1-2-3 For Windows For Dummies™	by John Walkenbach	1-56884-052-7	$16.95 USA/$21.95 Canada
Excel 5 For Macs For Dummies™	by Greg Harvey	1-56884-186-8	$19.95 USA/$26.95 Canada
Excel For Dummies™, 2nd Edition	by Greg Harvey	1-56884-050-0	$16.95 USA/$21.95 Canada
MORE Excel 5 For Windows For Dummies™	by Greg Harvey	1-56884-207-4	$19.95 USA/$26.95 Canada
Quattro Pro 6 For Windows For Dummies™	by John Walkenbach	1-56884-174-4	$19.95 USA/$26.95 Canada
Quattro Pro For DOS For Dummies™	by John Walkenbach	1-56884-023-3	$16.95 USA/$21.95 Canada
UTILITIES / VCRs & CAMCORDERS			
Norton Utilities 8 For Dummies™	by Beth Slick	1-56884-166-3	$19.95 USA/$26.95 Canada
VCRs & Camcorders For Dummies™	by Andy Rathbone & Gordon McComb	1-56884-229-5	$14.99 USA/$20.99 Canada
WORD PROCESSING			
Ami Pro For Dummies™	by Jim Meade	1-56884-049-7	$19.95 USA/$26.95 Canada
MORE Word For Windows 6 For Dummies™	by Doug Lowe	1-56884-165-5	$19.95 USA/$26.95 Canada
MORE WordPerfect 6 For Windows For Dummies™	by Margaret Levine Young & David C. Kay	1-56884-206-6	$19.95 USA/$26.95 Canada
MORE WordPerfect 6 For DOS For Dummies™	by Wallace Wang, edited by Dan Gookin	1-56884-047-0	$19.95 USA/$26.95 Canada
S.O.S. For WordPerfect™	by Katherine Murray	1-56884-053-5	$12.95 USA/$16.95 Canada
Word 6 For Macs For Dummies™	by Dan Gookin	1-56884-190-6	$19.95 USA/$26.95 Canada
Word For Windows 6 For Dummies™	by Dan Gookin	1-56884-075-6	$16.95 USA/$21.95 Canada
Word For Windows For Dummies™	by Dan Gookin	1-878058-86-X	$16.95 USA/$21.95 Canada
WordPerfect 6 For Dummies™	by Dan Gookin	1-878058-77-0	$16.95 USA/$21.95 Canada
WordPerfect For Dummies™	by Dan Gookin	1-878058-52-5	$16.95 USA/$21.95 Canada
WordPerfect For Windows For Dummies™	by Margaret Levine Young & David C. Kay	1-56884-032-2	$16.95 USA/$21.95 Canada

FOR MORE INFORMATION OR TO ORDER, PLEASE CALL ▶ 800 762 2974

For volume discounts & special orders please call
Tony Real, Special Sales, at 415. 655. 3048

Fun, Fast, & Cheap!

1/26/95

NEW!

CorelDRAW! 5 For Dummies™ Quick Reference
by Raymond E. Werner

ISBN: 1-56884-952-4
$9.99 USA/$12.99 Canada

NEW!

Windows "X" For Dummies™ Quick Reference, 3rd Edition
by Greg Harvey

ISBN: 1-56884-964-8
$9.99 USA/$12.99 Canada

SUPER STAR

Word For Windows 6 For Dummies™ Quick Reference
by George Lynch

ISBN: 1-56884-095-0
$8.95 USA/$12.95 Canada

SUPER STAR

WordPerfect For DOS For Dummies™ Quick Reference
by Greg Harvey

ISBN: 1-56884-009-8
$8.95 USA/$11.95 Canada

Title	Author	ISBN	Price
DATABASE			
Access 2 For Dummies™ Quick Reference	by Stuart A. Stuple	1-56884-167-1	$8.95 USA/$11.95 Canada
dBASE 5 For DOS For Dummies™ Quick Reference	by Barry Sosinsky	1-56884-954-0	$9.99 USA/$12.99 Canada
dBASE 5 For Windows For Dummies™ Quick Reference	by Stuart J. Stuple	1-56884-953-2	$9.99 USA/$12.99 Canada
Paradox 5 For Windows For Dummies™ Quick Reference	by Scott Palmer	1-56884-960-5	$9.99 USA/$12.99 Canada
DESKTOP PUBLISHING / ILLUSTRATION/GRAPHICS			
Harvard Graphics 3 For Windows For Dummies™ Quick Reference	by Raymond E. Werner	1-56884-962-1	$9.99 USA/$12.99 Canada
FINANCE / PERSONAL FINANCE			
Quicken 4 For Windows For Dummies™ Quick Reference	by Stephen L. Nelson	1-56884-950-8	$9.95 USA/$12.95 Canada
GROUPWARE / INTEGRATED			
Microsoft Office 4 For Windows For Dummies™ Quick Reference	by Doug Lowe	1-56884-958-3	$9.99 USA/$12.99 Canada
Microsoft Works For Windows 3 For Dummies™ Quick Reference	by Michael Partington	1-56884-959-1	$9.99 USA/$12.99 Canada
INTERNET / COMMUNICATIONS / NETWORKING			
The Internet For Dummies™ Quick Reference	by John R. Levine	1-56884-168-X	$8.95 USA/$11.95 Canada
MACINTOSH			
Macintosh System 7.5 For Dummies™ Quick Reference	by Stuart J. Stuple	1-56884-956-7	$9.99 USA/$12.99 Canada
OPERATING SYSTEMS / DOS			
DOS For Dummies® Quick Reference	by Greg Harvey	1-56884-007-1	$8.95 USA/$11.95 Canada
UNIX			
UNIX For Dummies™ Quick Reference	by Margaret Levine Young & John R. Levine	1-56884-094-2	$8.95 USA/$11.95 Canada
WINDOWS			
Windows 3.1 For Dummies™ Quick Reference, 2nd Edition	by Greg Harvey	1-56884-951-6	$8.95 USA/$11.95 Canada
PRESENTATION / AUTOCAD			
AutoCAD For Dummies™ Quick Reference	by Ellen Finkelstein	1-56884-198-1	$9.95 USA/$12.95 Canada
SPREADSHEET			
1-2-3 For Dummies™ Quick Reference	by John Walkenbach	1-56884-027-6	$8.95 USA/$11.95 Canada
1-2-3 For Windows 5 For Dummies™ Quick Reference	by John Walkenbach	1-56884-957-5	$9.95 USA/$12.95 Canada
Excel For Windows For Dummies™ Quick Reference, 2nd Edition	by John Walkenbach	1-56884-096-9	$8.95 USA/$11.95 Canada
Quattro Pro 6 For Windows For Dummies™ Quick Reference	by Stuart A. Stuple	1-56884-172-8	$9.95 USA/$12.95 Canada
WORD PROCESSING			
Word For Windows 6 For Dummies™ Quick Reference	by George Lynch	1-56884-095-0	$8.95 USA/$11.95 Canada
WordPerfect For Windows For Dummies™ Quick Reference	by Greg Harvey	1-56884-039-X	$8.95 USA/$11.95 Canada

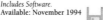

"A lot easier to use than the book Excel gives you!"

Lisa Schmeckpeper, New Berlin, WI, on PC World Excel 5 For Windows Handbook

Official Hayes Modem Communications Companion
by Caroline M. Halliday

ISBN: 1-56884-072-1
$29.95 USA/$39.95 Canada
Includes software.

PC World Excel 5 For Windows Handbook, 2nd Edition
by John Walkenbach & Dave Maguiness

ISBN: 1-56884-056-X
$34.95 USA/$44.95 Canada
Includes software.

PC World DOS 6 Handbook, 2nd Edition
by John Socha, Clint Hicks, & Devra Hall

ISBN: 1-878058-79-7
$34.95 USA/$44.95 Canada
Includes software.

PC World Word For Windows 6 Handbook
by Brent Heslop & David Angell

ISBN: 1-56884-054-3
$34.95 USA/$44.95 Canada
Includes software.

PC World Microsoft Access 2 Bible, 2nd Edition
by Cary N. Prague & Michael R. Irwin

ISBN: 1-56884-086-1
$39.95 USA/$52.95 Canada
Includes software.

"Easy and enjoyable to read, well structured and so detailed you cannot fail to learn! It's the best computer book I have ever used."

John Wildsmith, Gateshead, England, on PC World Microsoft Access 2 Bible, 2nd Edition

PC World WordPerfect 6 Handbook
by Greg Harvey

ISBN: 1-878058-80-0
$34.95 USA/$44.95 Canada
Includes software.

QuarkXPress For Windows Designer Handbook
by Barbara Assadi & Galen Gruman

ISBN: 1-878058-45-2
$29.95 USA/$39.95 Canada

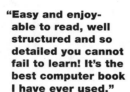

Official XTree Companion, 3rd Edition
by Beth Slick

ISBN: 1-878058-57-6
$19.95 USA/$26.95 Canada

PC World DOS 6 Command Reference and Problem Solver
by John Socha & Devra Hall

ISBN: 1-56884-055-1
$24.95 USA/$32.95 Canada

Client/Server Strategies: A Survival Guide for Corporate Reengineers
by David Vaskevitch

ISBN: 1-56884-064-0
$29.95 USA/$39.95 Canada

"PC World Word For Windows 6 Handbook is very easy to follow with lots of 'hands on' examples. The 'Task at a Glance' is very helpful!"

Jacqueline Martens, Tacoma, WA

"Thanks for publishing this book! It's the best money I've spent this year!"

Robert D. Templeton, Ft. Worth, TX, on MORE Windows 3.1 SECRETS

FOR MORE INFORMATION OR TO ORDER, PLEASE CALL ▶ 800 762 2974   For volume discounts & special orders please call Tony Real, Special Sales, at 415. 655. 3048

Macworld QuarkXPress 3.2/3.3 Bible
by Barbara Assadi & Galen Gruman

ISBN: 1-878058-85-1
$39.95 USA/$52.95 Canada

Includes disk with QuarkXPress XTensions and scripts.

Macworld PageMaker 5 Bible
by Craig Danuloff

ISBN: 1-878058-84-3
$39.95 USA/$52.95 Canada

Includes 2 disks with Pagemaker utilities, clip art, and more.

Macworld FileMaker Pro 2.0/2.1 Bible
by Steven A. Schwartz

ISBN: 1-56884-201-5
$34.95 USA/$46.95 Canada

Includes disk with ready-to-run databases.

Macworld Word 6 Companion, 2nd Edition
by Jim Heid

ISBN: 1-56884-082-9
$24.95 USA/$34.95 Canada

Macworld Guide To Microsoft Word 5/5.1
by Jim Heid

ISBN: 1-878058-39-8
$22.95 USA/$29.95 Canada

Macworld ClarisWorks 2.0/2.1 Companion, 2nd Edition
by Steven A. Schwartz

ISBN: 1-56884-180-9
$24.95 USA/$34.95 Canada

Macworld Guide To Microsoft Works 3
by Barrie Sosinsky

ISBN: 1-878058-42-8
$22.95 USA/$29.95 Canada

Macworld Excel 5 Companion, 2nd Edition
by Chris Van Buren & David Maguiness

ISBN: 1-56884-081-0
$24.95 USA/$34.95 Canada

Macworld Guide To Microsoft Excel 4
by David Maguiness

ISBN: 1-878058-40-1
$22.95 USA/$29.95 Canada

FOR MORE INFORMATION OR TO ORDER, PLEASE CALL ▶ 800 762 2974

For volume discounts & special orders please call Tony Real, Special Sales, at 415. 655. 3048

IDG BOOKS

Order Center: **(800) 762-2974** *(8 a.m.–6 p.m., EST, weekdays)*

Quantity	ISBN	Title	Price	Total

Shipping & Handling Charges

	Description	First book	Each additional book	Total
Domestic	Normal	$4.50	$1.50	$
	Two Day Air	$8.50	$2.50	$
	Overnight	$18.00	$3.00	$
International	Surface	$8.00	$8.00	$
	Airmail	$16.00	$16.00	$
	DHL Air	$17.00	$17.00	$

*For large quantities call for shipping & handling charges.
**Prices are subject to change without notice.

Ship to:

Name _____

Company _____

Address _____

City/State/Zip _____

Daytime Phone _____

Payment: ☐ Check to IDG Books (US Funds Only)

☐ VISA   ☐ MasterCard   ☐ American Express

Card # _____ Expires _____

Signature _____

Subtotal _____

CA residents add
applicable sales tax _____

IN, MA, and MD
residents add
5% sales tax _____

IL residents add
6.25% sales tax _____

RI residents add
7% sales tax _____

TX residents add
8.25% sales tax _____

Shipping _____

Total _____

Please send this order form to:
IDG Books Worldwide
7260 Shadeland Station, Suite 100
Indianapolis, IN 46256

Allow up to 3 weeks for delivery.
Thank you!